A Circle of Five

Harris Joshua

Faylisha & Lennox

JACARANDA

TWENTY in 2020

Black Writers, British Voices

This edition first published in Great Britain 2020
Jacaranda Books Art Music Ltd
27 Old Gloucester Street,
London WC1N 3AX
www.jacarandabooksartmusic.co.uk

A CIP catalogue record for this book is available from the British
Library

ISBN: 9781913090289
eISBN: 9781913090487

Cover image copyright © Jim Grover 2018
'Stockwell Good Neighbours' from *Windrush: A Portrait of a
Generation* by Jim Grover used with permission of the artist
www.jimgroverphotography.com

Cover Design: Rodney Dive
Typeset by: Kamillah Brandes
Printed and bound by CPI Group (UK) Ltd, Croydon, CR0 4YY

Foreword

On a misty Monday—21ˢᵗ June 1948—the MV Empire Windrush sailed up the Thames and anchored at Tilbury Dock, London. There were a total of 1027 passengers on board with 802 passengers from British Colonies in the West Indies. Of these individuals, 539 or 67% were from Jamaica.

Passengers were not allowed to disembark until the following morning—Tuesday, 22ⁿᵈ June. By then the media had got wind of the story and the focus of newsreels and press coverage was on the large number of Black men, women and some children walking down the gangplank of the Empire Windrush and leaving Tilbury Dock. This was the moment the Windrush Generation came to be. The term 'Windrush Generation' refers to West Indian Commonwealth citizens migrating to England and Wales between June 1948 and the 1971 Immigration Act, after which immigration was severely restricted. The geographer Ceri Peach estimated the overall number of West Indians arriving between these dates at 304,000.

This was the beginning of significant postwar immigration to Great Britain and the establishment of African Caribbean communities in the UK. It involved a substantial number of people arriving from all over the Caribbean—mostly by air—and settling mainly in London and Birmingham. Yet until recently, triggered by the eruption of the Windrush scandal, it is remarkable how little was known about who they are. The history of this generation was, for the most part encapsulated and summarised by a single image—'Black men and women walking down the gangplank of the Empire Windrush and leaving Tilbury Dock'. Other than the historical preservation of the that fact these migrants arrived to help the 'Mother Country' rebuild after the Second World War, there was no historical context provided about this community of people.

The contribution of New Commonwealth immigration to the UK in this period was huge. The Windrush Generation remains an important part of British history. However, from the very beginning, much of the media coverage focused on a limited number of issues. Within days of the MV Empire Windrush arriving, eleven Labour MP's wrote to the Prime Minister— Clement Attlee—complaining about excessive 'coloured' immigration. This narrative along with the increase in racial tensions came to dominate the news and politics cycle.

The approach to the Windrush Generation taken in this book may be regarded by some as disarmingly simple. It is neither another thesis based on questionnaires and statistics, nor is it a book that seeks to rehash the findings of previous sociological studies. It is also not an analytical account from an 'outsider' looking in. *A Circle of Five* is a historical account of the Windrush Generation by the Windrush Generation.

This book follows the community of Caribbean migrants on the MV Empire Windrush gangplank at its point of departure. From there it goes back in time by asking: 'Where did these new arrivals come from?' 'What was the nature of their lives in British West Indian Colonies?' 'What influenced their decision to immigrate to England?' The story then moves forward in time by asking: 'What happened to them after they arrived?' This story is not solely about the eight hundred or so arriving aboard the Windrush. It is also about representing the experience of the three hundred thousand that followed in their footsteps between 1948 and 1971.

Rather than snapshot interviews and quotes from a great many, *A Circle of Five* is based on the detailed life histories of just five people. All five are Jamaican. All five are women. All five live in either London and Birmingham—the two cities that account for the majority of African Caribbean settlement in England and Wales.

None of 'The Five' had any reason to believe that anyone would ever want to tell their story. They were chosen because they were part of a much larger community, a few faces amongst many thousands.

I did not know any of 'The Five' and they did not know each other. They were contacted by a member of my family who approached delegates attending African Caribbean Conferences and Conventions. A good few of those who agreed to partici-pate initially, declined when I contacted them. Eventually five women accepted my offer to write their stories. The life histo-ries of 'The Five' were gathered from recorded and transcribed interviews. It was agreed that the book would not reveal their identities or the identities of their families. Each of 'The Five' received an audio recording of our conversation and a bound copy of interviews.

My role as narrator was to provide continuity and histor-ical context where necessary. It was also about highlighting and sustaining the intricate drama of each story. I have done my very best not to be judgmental. Over the course of my conversations with 'The Five', I let them decide what they wanted to speak about and it was insightful and at times surprising to hear the issues they chose to dwell on.

With a view to make *A Circle of Five* accessible to a wide audience, the format of the book is episodic. Each of 'The Five' tell their part of the journey stage by stage, chapter by chapter. Though they did now know each other, it reads as though they were sitting together, sharing their stories side by side. As the enthralling and compelling drama of their lives unfolded, it became clear to me that the 'The Five' were not simply, faces in the crowd. They represented something far bigger—the extraordinary within the ordinary.

There are times when the events and memories of 'The Five' are introduced through narration and other times through the exact and unchanged words of one of 'The Five'—this was done to ensure the continued authenticity of the stories shared.

The opening chapter provides an account of their different journeys across the Atlantic along with their first impressions and emotions upon arriving in Great Britain.

Each account then looks at the circumstances of their birth, family and upbringing in Jamaica. This spans Chapters 2, 3 and 4, bringing to life a graphic portrayal of Jamaican society in 1930's, 40's and 50's.

The story then recounts how 'The Five' find their footing in the new land that is England.

In Chapters 5, 6 and 7 virtually nothing is predictable. The final chapter gathers their thoughts on how their lives turned out, where they are now and their reflections on family and community looking back.

Chapter One

Boats and Planes

EVELYN

It is early morning on Monday, 3rd October, 1955 and Evelyn is making her way to the wharf in Kingston, Jamaica. She is about to board a ship that will take her to England. Being that she lives in the city at the time, it is a short trip to the wharf.

Evelyn is twenty-three years old. There is no way she could have known it at the time but she is amongst the first of many who will be making this journey over the next decade. In 1955 the overwhelming majority of those making this trip are men. Women and children are to follow later.

She is not travelling alone though. Against the explicit advice of her mother Winifred, Evelyn is eloping with the man who she hopes to marry.

> I did not have a lot of discussion with my mother about my plan to come to England. She had made a decision that if I am not going to do what she wanted, then I won't get her approval. My mom knew I was coming to England with Reggie. She wasn't very happy with that either because he used to drink a lot. She always says to me: 'Don't marry a man who drinks.' But I wanted to do what I want.

On the face of it, Winifred's 'objections' are not unreasonable. Her daughter is unmarried and about to leave their island to a foreign land with a man she does not like. She has no idea if or when she will see her daughter again. What remains clear, however, is that Evelyn is determined to get her way. Her decision to leave Jamaica and create a new future in England is based on precious little. She doesn't know much about England. None of her immediate family had gone before. Reggie, Evelyn's fiancé, agrees with Winifred—he too is far from certain about Evelyn's plan to immigrate.

> I started talking to him about it because his brother came. So we decided to come. It was a joint decision because he didn't want me to leave him. He didn't want to lose me, so we came together. He said: "If you want to go—I'm coming." So both of us decided to leave.

Evelyn presents Reggie with an ultimatum—he either joins her on her journey to England or they end their relationship. Evelyn did, however, admit to having some doubts at the time.

> Looking back, it was taking a big chance and I was told not to. It was not long when the war had ended and England was on its knees.

Though she is in her early twenties and living in Kingston, Jamaica, Evelyn is not in paid employment. No doubt this is a factor in her decision, made all the easier by what she was then reading in local newspapers.

They were advertising for people to come to England and help build the country. So immigrants started coming. A lot of people was coming and we decided that we would come.

It has to be said that anybody reading the newspapers in Jamaica in the early 1950's and 1960's could not avoid the message that 'Going to England' was the correct thing to do.

The advertisement section of the Daily Gleaner—Jamaica's national newspaper—was full of promotions and adverts enticing Jamaicans to leave their home country for England. At the time these commercials were put in place by local travel agents and shipping lines advertising their wares. Airlines—in particular the British Overseas Airways Corporation (BOAC)—would come into the mix later. In short, if you were Jamaican and thinking of immigrating to England at the time, you would be spoiled for choice.

IF YOU PLAN TO TRAVEL
TO ENGLAND—GO SITMAR

TRAVEL THE EASY WAY!
BOOK THROUGH CHIN YEE'S TRAVEL
SERVICE TO GO TO ENGLAND

SAILING FOR ENGLAND
THE COXE BROS TRAVEL AGENTS

TO ENGLAND?
SEE MR. TRAVEL ADVISER
PHILIP SEAGA

PICK YOUR DATE
PICK YOUR PRICE TO ENGLAND
CARIBBEAN TOURS

Travel agents and shipping lines were not competing on price. Whichever ship you chose; the standard fare was £75. Today, that would equate to around £1160. One way!

This was the immediate postwar period where there was excess shipping capacity and shipping lines were trying to fill their ships. One of the ways they did this was by combining European tourist cruises to South America and the Caribbean with West Indian passengers travelling to southern European ports. The final part of this journey would be to England and would be completed by train and ferry.

By 1959 travel agents in Jamaica had a thorough knowledge of the market and knew what factors could influence customer choice. They are aware that Jamaicans wanting to get to England were not interested in tourist routes. They, simply, wanted to go direct. An advert in the Daily Gleaner sets out the latest offer.

Your Opportunity Year—1959
TRAVEL TO ENGLAND—ASCANIA
DIRECT TO SOUTHAMPTON
Here are some of the reasons
why you should go ASCANIA
WELFARE OFFICER

To ensure that you enjoy your "ASCANIA"
Trip in every detail, we have arranged
for an experienced Jamaican Welfare Officer
and a Jamaican Cook to travel with
you on your Opportunity Trip to England.

Other travel agents continue to make similar offers but with the addition of perks such us an onboard 'Jamaican Nurse'. Whilst this is happening, the airlines do more to attract customers and begin to offer transport to people from Jamaica to England the 'next day' with a stopover in New York. The standard fare is £85, not significantly more than travelling by sea. Like the shipping lines, the airlines are also competing. In October 1958, the British Overseas Airways Corporation (BOAC)—the main carrier—which would later become British Airways, cut their fares in order to attract more customers.

Your Family Flies For Less When
Flying Together By BOAC.

By then a great many men—who were the first to migrate—are sending for their wives and children. Travel by air is now the preferred option. Travel agents, who were previously focused on selling travel to England by sea, are quick to catch on to the changing market and soon find ways of outcompeting BOAC. Chin Yee's Travel Service—for example—begins offering a new service.

Chartered Immigrant Fights to London.
Full assistance given with travel documents.

Competition for customers between travel agents, shipping lines and airlines grows fierce. As early as 1955, corrupt travel agents have already penetrated the market in Jamaica. Non-existing trips to England are being advertised in local newspapers and trips are getting cancelled with customers never receiving refunds. The extent of these illegal activities are enough to prompt the Jamaican government to launch an official inquiry in 1956. Following the report, travel agents are at pains to stress their legal accreditation in their marketing.

YOUR MONEY IS SAFE
YOUR PASSAGE IS CERTAIN
CHIN YEE'S

TO ENGLAND
BOOK WHERE YOUR MONEY IS SAFE
PHILIP SEAGA

APPROVED SALES AGENT
CARIBBEAN TOURS

BOOK WITH A RECOGNISED
TRAVEL AGENT
SAIL SAFELY! SAIL SURELY! SAIL SITMAR!

Evelyn, in 1955, would have seen the many adverts that were plastered across the newspapers. She would have, almost certainly, come across this one:

BOOK NOW
on the
T.V. SANTA MARIA
MORE Travel Agents are sending More
People to England on this fine ship.
IT COSTS NO MORE to travel on the
Luxurious SANTA MARIA but you get MORE
luxurious Accommodation... MORE
excellent service and food on this Ship of the Line
that is famous the world over.

SAILING From KINGSTON OCT. 3rd
To VIGO, SPAIN via
Havana, Tenerife, Funchal.

This is the ship that Evelyn and Reggie board. Typical of the period, it offers those travelling from Jamaica a luxury voyage of discovery to England. This trip involves visiting other islands in the Caribbean, ports in the Canaries, Portugal and Spain before taking a train across Europe to Calais and then a ferry to Dover.

The Santa Maria is one of those ships taking European tourists on an outward-bound cruise to South America and the Caribbean. This ship picks up West Indian passengers bound for England on the way back. Typical of the class and racial attitudes of the period, tourists and passengers were likely to be on separate decks in different dining rooms or made to dine at different times to each other.

When Evelyn made her decision to go to England, apart from what she remembered being taught in school—she had little or no knowledge of her destination.

> I didn't know anything about England then. It
> was just what I read about England. History tells
> you about the Mother Country. You read about
> Sir Walter Raleigh and you read about Captain
> Morgan and the whole thing. You realise so
> many things were sent and exported there. Your
> school books came from there. Everything, it was
> England.

Nor did she know how they were going to earn a living once
they arrived. There were many reasons behind her decision to
leave Jamacia but in the end it all came back to Winifred—her
mother.

> I didn't know what I was going to do in England.
> I got on the boat not knowing. You do not know
> what you're going to do or see. But you think to
> yourself: 'At least, if I work, I can better myself
> and do what I want.'
>   I was determined to do what I wanted to do
> and not what I have to do to please my mom.

As the day of Evelyn's departure came, Winifred made her position absolutely clear.

> She didn't say a lot. She said: "I won't even come
> to see you off."

To Evelyn, this declaration was tantamount to being disowned.
She is greatly relieved when Winifred changes her mind and

chooses to see her daughter off. In hindsight Evelyn thinks she knows the reason why.

> She did come—she did come. There's a thing between a mother and a child. You can be as hard as anything but there's that little tug in your stomach that's telling you: 'You'll give in, you'll give in.' You sort of stretch it to see whether or not you'll win. But she did come and see me off.

Despite her desire to go to England, as she goes on board the liner that will take Reggie and her part of the way, her emotions are in turmoil.

> The Santa Maria was new. It was a Spanish ship— an absolutely beautiful ship.
>
> Going on board I was a bit excited and a bit sad. My mom came with me. We went down to the harbour to get on the boat.
>
> I remember standing on deck and I could see her waving—just a tear. In my heart I wondered: 'Will I see her again?'
>
> It so happened that I did not. When I saw her again, she was dead.
>
> So I carry a guilt for a long time—for a very long time. It affected me which at first I never thought it would. But it did affect me—it did affect me.

In their journey across the Atlantic, their first port of call is

Havana, Cuba and then on to Tenerife in the Canary Islands.
They go ashore on both islands, but Evelyn is not enjoying the
trip.

> We spent eleven days on the ship and I was sick
> for ten. I couldn't go to the dining room. I was
> in the hospital; I couldn't do anything. It was
> terrible. Don't care what the doctors did, they
> couldn't get me to settle. Everything, I just heave
> up. If the ship docks—I'm fine. The minute it
> moves—I'm ill.

Unlike his fiancé, Reggie is fine on the journey across the
Atlantic. He tells her about the dolphins and the flying fish
he has seen. They get off the ship in Spain and it takes another
day travelling by train to get to Calais. Given her experience on
board the Santa Maria, Evelyn is not looking forward to the trip
by ferry across the English Channel to Dover.

> I did not go down. I stayed on the deck and sat
> with my head between my knees. It so happened I
> wasn't sick, but others who wasn't sick on the ship
> were sick on the ferry.

Evelyn vows never to travel by ship again. From Dover they
travel to Birmingham by train where they expect to be met by
Reggie's brother. He's not there.

> We were at New Street station and I didn't know
> where to turn. Everybody's gone off the station

and the two of us just stood there. A guard came
to see what was wrong and ask if he could help.
We told him where we wanted to go. He actually
got us a taxi.

They end up in a room at a house in Langley owned by one of
Reggie's cousins.

The first morning when I got up and looked around,
I thought: 'Where the hell was everything?' All I
could see was brick. The only thing I knew made
of bricks in Jamaica was Wray Town Prison. That
was the only thing I saw bricks was made of. So I
thought: 'Where the hell is this?'

There was smoke coming through the chimneys because it was October. It was cold as well—
it was cold. The situation—when you saw how
many people was in the house—was awful. It was
not nice. I cried for days. I thought I'd made the
biggest mistake.

EMMA

It is Saturday 13th June 1959, and Emma is being taken to Palisadoes Airport just outside Kingston, Jamaica where she is to board a plane that will take her to England. She is eight years old and travelling with her younger sister Emily who is seven years old.

They are going to join their parents, Millie and John Robinson.

> Dad came towards the end of 1952 and Mum came in 1953. My earliest recollection of them was really from the age of eight and a half because I was quite young when they immigrated to England.

Emma was only two years old when her mother left Jamaica and her baby sister Emily was just over a year old.

> We were both pretty young. I was left in the care of my mum's parents—Clarence and Emma Bernard. My sister was left in the care of my dad's younger sister and her husband.

Her mother's parents' home is in Port Antonio—Portland. Her father's younger sister—Aunt Isobel—lives in Kingston, some thirty miles away. Having been separated at a very early age, the two sisters would not come together until 1956.

At the time of their departure, Emma is settled in a school not far from her grandparents' home. She has been a pupil there for just over a year.

> The first time I knew I was coming to England was when my grandma told me: "Your mother and father are sending for you."
>
> That news saddened me because I'm thinking: 'Mother and Father? To me they're strangers.' I felt what I now know to be like you're going through a bereavement. It was a shock to my system. I didn't want to come. I didn't want to leave my grandmother because my grandmother was me mum. I did not want to come. I was sick at the time and my grandmother said: "You'll get better, you'll get better. You know you have to go."

Her grandmother tries to reassure her by passing on what little she knows about the *Mother Country*. Both sisters are told not to worry and they will know their mum and dad when they see them.

> My grandma did tell us things about England before we came. She told us it was a really cold country and the people was of a different complexion.

25

> Mum had got photographs of us and we'd got
> some photographs of Mum and Dad so we could
> see what they looked like before we came up.

In the late 1950's many Jamaican parents were sending for their children. John and Millie's decison to send for their daughters therefore, seemed a normal thing to do at the time. However, a few weeks before Emma and her sister are about to leave, things take a strange turn.

> I'd had fallen ill, seriously ill. Whatever it was, it
> was quite a mystery. I can only say unknown. All
> kind of stories was behind it including Witchcraft
> and Obeah.
>
> My sister wasn't sick. I was the one who was
> sick. From what I recalled, I wasn't in school for
> a while. People had to be with me continuously.
> The nightmares I use to have!
>
> Part of the story was something, whatever it
> was, had hit me and I fell ill. That's the story I
> heard. Apparently my grandmother had said to
> me mum: 'If you don't want your child to die, you
> have to get her away from here.' I heard different
> stories after that from my mum. She said that it
> might have been some sort of love triangle.
>
> Anyway I came to England and had a good
> recovery.

Later on, Emma finds out that her mysterious illness may somehow have been linked to one of her relatives.

I had heard that this cousin of mine was supposed to come to England after me and my sister. My mum didn't want it to happen and apparently my cousin also started being sick in Jamaica.

Money had been sent to Jamaica for her and to prevent her from coming she was always falling ill. Who was behind that I don't know but maybe mum didn't want her to come to England and her mother didn't want her to come either.

The dialogue, which I later realise that was going on behind the scene, was that if I didn't leave, I would have died. That was the seriousness of it. The life was draining out of me, yet Emily was fine.

More has been able to come out since my parents passed away by talking to other members of the family, but my parents took their secrets to the grave.

Emma's illness is serious enough to prevent her from going to school and, whatever the cause, her parents take the view that she would be better off leaving Jamaica.

I remember the day that we packed to come to England. Oh my goodness! By this time I was starting to get excited and still sad because I was going to be leaving Grandma behind.

I was like hoping that as we were leaving that day, she'd be coming with us. Then it dawned on me that I wouldn't be seeing her again.

Their grandmother did not accompany the two girls to the airport.

That day on leaving, I kicked and I screamed.

I told her I would not lose her. It was a very bitter and emotional time for me. I don't know whether she had the same feelings because I can't remember seeing her cry.

The next time I saw of my grandma was a picture of her coffin going down into the grave.

We were collected by Uncle George who took us to Kingston. This was the first time I went to Kingston. Before that I cannot recall going anywhere apart from to Buff Bay. We were privileged. We went on outings as regular as anything—picnics—and it was almost always around the church. All that was a part of my life that I was suddenly going to lose.

This was going to be the first real change in my life. As hard as that was, I had to go and Emily had to go.

Looking back, Emma did not think leaving her grandmother behind affected her younger sister Emily in the same way.

My sister had already been uprooted from Kingston where she was already living a freer lifestyle.

Even though she was a child, she was made to feel equal to her aunty who she was living with.

She found it difficult to come from that, when she came to Grandma. Leaving from Grandma which was a strict household and moving on, she could deal with the change of coming to England more than me.

Emma and Emily are both minors and can only travel in the care of a responsible adult—an escort.

She was a fair skin lady. I can't remember her name. She was somebody my parents knew, maybe a relative. As people from the Caribbean, you know we're very close knit in those days. She was a relative of someone that my parents knew. It had to be somebody that they could trust.

Mum and Dad sent some clothes down that were identical so we dressed alike—blue and white. The only difference was I think Emily who had an additional color but the clothes were identical. That was the way our parents would know us.

They had photos of us taken at a studio. Oh gosh, my sister must still have those photographs.

Emma recalls with clear memory when she and her little sister saw their parents.

We left Kingston on the Saturday and we stopped in New York on the journey. I think it was to refuel; we didn't change planes. We arrived at me mum and dad's house, I think it was late the Sunday evening. By the time they got us home I think it was late the Sunday evening. That would tell you it was a long journey.

My mum and dad came to meet us. It must have been at Digbeth bus station in Birmingham. I recognised them because of the pictures.

We saw smoke coming out of the roofs of houses. I thought the houses were on fire with the smoke coming out of the chimneys. My parents had their own house. When we got home they had a three-quarters bed as we called them in those days in their bedroom in readiness for us. It had a screen around it, so it was like they didn't want to let us out of their sight—to get us settled. That was only a temporary thing for us to get familiar with them. Then they got a small bedroom for us to move into—the smallest bedroom in the house.

Before long I was loving it but I still had this hankering. I wanted to see me grandmother.

Seeing my parents for the first time because I didn't remember them, it was a bit of a shock to my system. I later realised that I dealt with that change pretty well.

The following Monday morning both sisters are enrolled in school.

IRENE

Irene grew up in Spanish Town, St. Catherine—around ten miles from Kingston. She is seven years old when she is taken to Palisadoes Airport. It is the year 1960 and she is going to England.

Irene's mother, Lucy, came to England a year before and Irene was left with one of her aunties. Understandably, she cannot remember that much about this early period in her life.

My aunt was a teacher and had other children.
I was one of five and was not treated the best.
I wasn't mistreated by my aunt but I wasn't the favourite.

Unlike Emma who made the same journey when she was eight, Irene was not bothered about leaving Jamaica. She had not been with her aunt long enough to form a lasting bond.

Irene remembers the day she got the news that she would be leaving Jamaica.

When I knew I was going to England I was excited. I was going to see my mum again.
My aunt said: "You're going with a lady and

when you get there you will meet your mum." It was a white lady. I think my aunt must have taken me to the airport in Jamaica and I must have met the chaperone there. I remember going on a plane for the first time.

The lady had already warned me that when I got to England: "Your mum will not be meeting you. I'll be taking you to my house."

I remember when I came off the plane I had to stay at her house until my mum came to pick me up. That was quite strange because I'd never been in a white lady's house before. I vaguely remember all this. Then my mum came and she hugged me.

My mum was living in Finsbury Park and took me to her house. I think she was really glad to see me.

IVY

It is 1962 and Ivy is on her way to the wharf in Kingston. She is about to board a ship that will take her to Southampton, England.

She is twenty-seven years old, single and travelling alone. For the last few years she has been living on her own in a rented room in Kingston, not that far from her parents and her two siblings.

No one came to see me off. I just got my bag, got on a bus and went to the wharf.

I didn't ask anyone in my family for help with the fare. I didn't ask for their views on coming to England either. I told my mum I was going and she said: "Are you sure?" I just said: "Yeah!" I told my dad and he said: "People say in England the streets are paved with gold. But when you go there don't look for gold on the streets. It's just a saying."

I didn't tell my aunt Mabel. I didn't tell my brother or my sister. I just disappeared. I left my mother and father to give answers to anyone who wanted to find out where I was.

In part, it is what she is told by her close friend, Jay, that persuades her to go to England. She grew up with Jay and trusts her.

> My friend came here a couple of years before. She wrote to me—she and I kept in touch. She told me about England in her letters. She told me that England was a nice place and I could make a lot of money.
>
> The idea of me coming to England had not come up before this. It was my friend's idea. I came on her recommendation.

But that is not all. Ivy has a deeper motivation that causes her to leave her home in Jamaica.

> I think what made me finally decide to come to England was the idea of getting away. Getting away from having my mother in one place, my dad up there in another and I'm in the middle.
>
> I don't know. Maybe it was something I couldn't deal with at that time. My mother couldn't do anything to help herself, so I just decided it was nice to be on my own—to come to England and be on my own.

Despite what Jay is says in her letters, Ivy is unsure about how she is going to make her way in England.

> I didn't really form anything in my mind about

where I was going to. It's just that I'm getting away and it's going to be far, far away from everybody else. I didn't really actually sit and think about it. Maybe if I did, I wouldn't have come for fear of how I am going to survive on my own and all that. I didn't think about it.

It turns out that Jay, who told Ivy she could make a good living in England, has not been employed since first arriving in the UK. She is, in fact, a housewife with children and knows little of what it is like find a job and survive on her own.

I was coming to live with my friend Jay and her husband. They lived in Peckham at the time. I knew they were coming to meet me in Southampton. They met me as I came down the gangplank. I knew her husband from Jamaica.

We go on trains and buses. It was a long journey. They paid half fare for me on the buses because even as a twenty-seven-year-old woman, I didn't look that big.

Ivy cannot recall her passage across the Atlantic in any detail. She does not remember the exact date of her departure or the name of the ship. However, what little she can recall is rather insightful.

I know we were at sea for a while but I don't remember how long. It was like a lifetime. I can't remember if food was given to us or we had to buy food. I can't remember who was on the ship, it was just people. People who you don't want to get besides because you weren't up to their standard.

I was in my little corner on a big ship, that's all it was to me. Four of us was in a cabin, all girls, all Jamaicans coming to England to find their fortune. I don't think any of the others knew where they were going to in England. No one kept in contact after the journey.

All indications point to her travelling on a tourist ship picking up West Indian passengers on a return trip to Europe. On arrival, she immediately questions her decision to come to England in the first place.

My first impression was I could turn back, go on the boat and go back to Jamaica.

It wasn't the nice England I'm coming to. There was no impression of anything nice and Peckham was just the same. I was too big and too old to cry, and there wasn't anyone to go back to. So I had to make the most of it. The strangest thing about it was that it was black and dark and you don't see anybody on the streets in the evenings.

I thought England was going to be a nice place only to be disappointed when I got here.

MELISSA

Melissa is sixteen years old when she boards a BOAC flight that will take her to England on the 20th October, 1964. She is travelling alone to join her mother, Pengal, and her stepfather, Martin Macdonald.

Her stepfather was the first out of the family to leave Jamaica. He immigrated in 1959, when Melissa was eleven years old.

> I remember when Mr Macdonald was going to
> England. In those days people don't talk a lot
> about their intention to travel. I knew—so did
> the family—but nobody else in the district knew.
> He kissed me, said goodbye. That was it.
>
> He went out on the main road and got the bus
> to Montego Bay. The bus took him to the harbour
> in Kingston. I think Mama went with him to say
> goodbye at the ship.

Melissa recalls how a great many people in her area booked their passage to England around that time.

> We had a travel agent—a Chinese man. His

agency is called Chin Yee's Travel Service. Most of the people who came to England from Jamaica in the 50's and in the 60's went through Chin Yee's. He had one office in Kingston—which is the capital of Jamaica—and the second is in Montego Bay. £89 you had to pay to buy a ticket.

In 1962, three years after he had left Jamaica, Melissa's stepfather sends for her mother, Pengal. Melissa is fourteen years old and Pengal leaves her in the care of her grandmother Doule.

It was the same thing again when Mama was leaving. She told me she was going. She just said: "My husband is there and I have to go. I'll send for you. We're going to look for a better life." She came by boat.

It didn't bother me because my grandmother was there. I miss my mother but I didn't feel any lost. I didn't mind because my grandmother was there for me.

I didn't go to see her off and Doule didn't go either. I think her younger sister Aunty Pearl—God rest her soul—went to see Mama off at the harbour.

She just caught the bus with her grip. Again it was £89 for the fare.

Melissa's grandparents are living in Hampton—St. James Parish—a few miles from Montego Bay, which is just over a hundred miles from Kingston. Though she asserts that Pengal's departure did not bother her at the time, Melissa could not understand why her mother was leaving for England without her. Pengal promises her daughter that she will send for her but Melissa later finds out whose decision it actually was.

> It wasn't my mother who sent for me. It's me step-
> father Mr Macdonald who send for me. It's Mr
> Macdonald who save the money and say to my
> mother: "Pengal, now I have the money, send for
> Melissa."
> I got on very well with Mr Macdonald. Never
> one day has he raised a voice to me. His name is
> Martin and I just call him Mas Martie.

Even though Melissa is only sixteen, she has already decided what she wants to do when she arrives in England.

> Once I went into the hospital in Montego Bay
> and I saw the nurses in their uniform and their
> cap—so well starch and they were looking so nice.
> I thought: 'I'm going to be a nurse.'
> I never thought of staying in Jamaica with
> my grandmother and doing my nursing training
> there. I was coming to England so I would train
> in England.

Melissa feels hopeful and excited by the opportunity to travel abroad and join her parents.

> I didn't know a thing about England before I

came.

My mum and stepfather wrote to me in Jamaica but they didn't give me any description about England. They just say you have to work every day. I knew the street wasn't paved with gold because my mother said you have to work too hard. Nobody in the district knew anything about England.

All I know is that England is England. The Queen is our mother and I was going to go to the motherland. I know that they have red telephone boxes, red post boxes and black taxis.

Melissa is already quite independent and though she would not have noticed it at the time, she is following in her mother's footsteps.

My mother worked in Mayday Hospital in Croydon from the day she came to England till the day she went back to Jamaica in 1973.

On the day of her departure, Melissa's grandmother Doule and her aunt Pearl take her to the airport.

I came on BOAC. It was lovely—it was wonderful. I had never been on a plane before and you know when you're having turbulence—I thought I was going to die. I cried because I miss my grandmother.

Melissa's stepfather Mas Martie was working on the day of Melissa's arrival, so it was her mother, Pengal who met her at Heathrow Airport. Melissa remembers her first impression of England.

> It was a bleaky day. The sun was out but it was cold and it was very grey and dull. Although the sun was shining, the sun wasn't hot. I never knew you could see the sun and not feel it being hot.

Pengal takes Melissa to the family home in Croydon, London. When in London, Melissa has difficulty adjusting to what she sees around her.

> I look at the houses and they were bricks, bricks, bricks. I thought: 'Oh my God, all bricks!' I thought England was supposed to be beautiful, it wasn't.
>
> When you look on the roof, there's smoke coming out of chimneys. Is all this England? Is this the place?

Melissa recalls a one positive memory about London upon her arrival.

> I could hear the birds singing. That is what I remember of England, the birds chirping.

It is two years since she last saw her mother and there's is a pressing issue she would like Pengal to explain.

We talked. She ask me how life was in Jamaica.

I kept saying to her: 'Why didn't you take me when you were coming up the same time.' Obviously, I couldn't think why she didn't take me then.

A great many of the 'left behind' children likely experienced a similar sense of loss and abandonment. Melissa is perhaps one of the few to confront her parents and press for an explanation. Within Jamaican and wider West Indian culture at the time, challenging your parents—especially your mother—was almost unthinkable. She did not say exactly how her mother responded but in hindsight she is understanding, even forgiving, of her mother's decision.

There is uncertainty coming here. You don't know where you're going. You don't know what you're going to do. Financially, they came with maybe £5 in their pocket which wasn't much.

You don't know where you're going to live. You don't know how the child will be looked after when you go to work—school and all those things—until you get use to the system. When you get use to the system, then you know that you're more solid and you can take care of the child. That was when they sent for me.

Chapter Two

Grandma, Grandpa, Mum and Dad

EVELYN

Evelyn is living in Kingston when she and Reggie board the Santa Maria that will take them to England in October 1955. She is not a Kingstonian and grew up in Mandeville, capital of the Parish of Manchester in the County of Middlesex, some sixty miles west of Kingston.

Most place names in Jamaica reflect the island's turbulent colonial history. Mandeville was originally a British Army Hill Station and later became a town founded in 1816 by the Duke of Manchester, then Governor of Jamaica. He named the settlement after his eldest son, Viscount Mandeville. Over two thousand feet above sea level and enjoying a more temperate climate, this is where wealthy English settlers built their mansions and country houses. With its picturesque countryside, the area probably reminded them of home. By 1868 the town already had its own golf club, thought to be the first in the Caribbean. A major hotel opened a few years later, also thought to be one of the oldest in the Caribbean. It soon became known as a 'mountain resort' and widely regarded as 'the most English town' in Jamaica.

Evelyn remembers the area with a great deal of affection.

Mandeville is mostly a tourist area. It's one of the

best parts of Jamaica. It's in the middle.

It's very cold, you've got to wear cardigans. I can knit things before I come here because it was cold. You go out and you're shaking like that. You got to hug each other.

There was dew in the mornings. You could shake a leaf and catch a cup of water. So quite naturally my memory of my youth is beautiful.

Her mother, Winifred Sparks, and father, Bolas Spence, live in the Mayday District just outside Mandeville where she was born on the 9th October, 1932. They are not married and live across the road from each other.

I am one of three children by my mother. Me, Louise and Eloise.

I'll be honest with you, my dad had so many children. I don't know how many. I still have sisters and brothers I do not know. I knew a few of them, the older ones. He had five children by his wife: Gloria, Joseph, Clarence, Lenard and Bolan. My dad's wife, I only know her as Pun. I don't know her other name. Then he had another son named Roy. His mother was Madelyn.

Her mother Winifred is, in fact, not Jamaican.

She was born in Panama. When her mother died she was sent along with Mavis, Lillian, Alan and George—her brothers and sisters—to Jamaica to learn English and finish school.

I don't know exactly when they came to Jamaica but I think she was ten years old when she came.

Her dad used to work for an American shipping company in the Canal Zone and because he didn't have a wife to care for them, he sent them to his wife's mother Catherine in Jamaica.

He sent back for the boys, Alan and George. He never sent back for my mother because she got pregnant and he was very upset. He never sent back for her. It's funny but he did not send back for any of the girls. So you had my Aunty Mavis, Lillian and my mum left in Jamaica.

It was not unusual that Winifred along with her siblings were Panamanian. There was a time when the Panama Canal was being built. Construction began in 1881 under French control with a large proportion of the labour recruited from Caribbean islands. When France abandoned the project in 1894, most of the workers were stranded in Panama and had to be repatriated at the expense of British West Indian Colonial governments.

Construction later resumed in 1904 when the project was financed and controlled by the United States. Recruiting agents were again dispatched to different Caribbean islands. Given their previous experience with the French, colonial governments were unwilling to sanction any large scale recruitment and refused to co-operate. Barbados was the first to concede and this was where American recruiting agents focused. Some twenty thousand construction workers—estimated at around forty percent of the island's adult male working age population—were recruited from Barbados to help build the Canal. Other smaller islands soon followed but Jamaica held out, imposing a tax of one pound on anyone wanting to go and work in Panama. As a consequence, those immigrating to Panama from Jamaica were largely skilled workers who could afford to pay the tax.

Evelyn remembers her grandfather worked for an American shipping company. It is quite likely he was one of those skilled workers.

> I never met my grandfather on my mother's side.
> We would write to each other. He was very kind
> to us. I always looked for my parcels and things.
> We were well-kept.
>
> He bought a house in Kingston, 3 Catherin
> Street, so that we would never be homeless. He
> was very good to us but he did not come back to
> Jamaica until after his second wife died. I was in
> England by then so I never met him.
>
> I've visited his grave twice since he died.
> Funny enough my mum died fifty odd years ago
> and he died not long after that. The graves are
> not far away from each other. You get to his grave
> before you get to my mum's and I thought: 'How
> nice'. So quite naturally when you visit Mum, you
> visit him.

Winifred's mother died in Panama. This is the reason why

she, her brothers and sisters were sent back to Jamaica. At the time of Evelyn's birth, Winifred is living with her mother's grandparents.

> I was a happy child in my early home, a very happy child.
>
> I did not know my grandmother because she had died. We lived with my great-grandmother, her name is Catherine. I had a happy time with her.

Following Evelyn's birth, Winifred left Mandeville to become a maid in Kingston, leaving her daughter in Catherine's care. Her stay in Kingston did not last long and she soon returns to Mandeville to help her grandmother on the farm. She then meets and marries Evelyn's new stepfather Harold Ellis. This is when Louise and Eloise are born. Evelyn's father, Benjamin, is still living across the road with his wife, Pun, and their five children, Evelyn's half-brothers and sisters.

During this time, it is her great-grandmother Catherine who becomes an important figure in Evelyn's early childhood.

> She was ninety-nine years and a few months old when she died. She had ten children and she buried every one.
>
> She was one of the slaves from Africa. She used to tell us slave stories and she dresses like Kizzy. You remember the character in the film Roots. She dressed all in grey material with the stripe. She wore a two piece—skirt and blouse with long

sleeves. She dresses like they did in slavery. You've never seen her ankle; her dress was right down to her feet. Her Peter Pan collar was always fastened up. She wore a frill over the skirt with five or six underskirts and she had a ballerina gathering on the bottom of the skirt. She also wore a wrap and she kept her money in her wrap.

She was about five feet ten or eleven in height. She had soft wavy hair and a very straight face. She was beautiful—jet black—but beautiful. Every time I see a tribe in Africa, I wondered which one she was from.

Evelyn remembers some of the stories Catherine would re-count to her whilst she was growing up.

My great-grandmother didn't tell us much about coming over from Africa as a slave. She told me mainly about when they were working in the cane fields, the hut they lived in and how hard they had to work in those days.

Sometimes when they go into the cane field there was a lot of snakes. She never calls them snakes, she called them nankas. So that should be the African word for snakes—I think.

'Nanka' could well be an African word for snake—there are a great many African languages and a great many snakes. However, in West African folklore there is a legendary creature known as a 'Ninki Nanka' reputed to be a reptilian, swamp-dwelling, extremely large, dragon-like creature. Parents would sometimes use 'Ninki Nanka' stories to scare their children: "If you don't behave and do what you're told, the 'Ninki Nanka' will get you."

Evelyn continues and recalls some of the other things her great-grandmother told her about the 'Nankas'.

> She said so many people died from snake bites in the field. Sometimes when she got out of bed to use the potty, there were snakes curled up in it. That was the reason why mongoose is in Jamaica because they brought them there to kill the snakes.

Catherine was right. The mongoose is a small carnivorous animal native to Southern Eurasia and Africa. They were introduced to some Caribbean Islands and Hawaii to control the population of snakes on the plantations.

Snakes and mongoosees aside, we cannot be sure that Evelyn's great-grandmother was 'one of the slaves from Africa'. Catherine died when she was ninety-nine. Evelyn was nine years old at the time which puts the date of her great-grandmother's birth around 1842. Slavery was abolished by Parliament in 1833. However, Parliament also decreed that abolition had to be followed by a period of transition during which 'freed' slaves would undergo an 'Apprenticeship' which could last up to six years. There was not much difference between outright slavery and Parliament's 'Apprenticeship'. So, for all practical purposes, slaves during this period remained slaves. In Jamaica, slave 'Apprenticeships' did not come to an end until 1838.

It is therefore likely that Evelyn's great-grandmother

Catherine grew up in an environment not that far removed from outright slavery. Her surname and that of her husband's was 'Senior', which Evelyn thinks they got from their slave master.

The bond between Evelyn and her great-grandmother was very strong.

> She was one of the most loving persons I ever had when I was growing up. So I had a very nice, loving, giving life at the time.
>
> She was such a sweet person. I got a lot of love—a lot of love. That has made me really, really caring for older people. I hate it when anybody is trying to hurt older people—I don't like it. I'll defend them because I grew up with one and all my memories are so nice.

Evelyn's father, Bolas Spence, and her great-grandmother, Catherine, are relatively prosperous.

> Both sides of the family had a lot of land, so you have a run. But with my great-gran it was a lot of land with paddocks and things.
>
> We had a small holding where they use to grow corn, sweet potato, yam and Irish potato—which we call spuds here but we use to import it in barrels in Jamaica. She used to grow strawberries. We had a lot of fruits so we never went hungry.
>
> She paid people to come in and work the

land but it was fun for us to go and pick fruits—soursop, nisberry, oranges, grapefruit—the citrus that they export. We had another one called sweetsop. We use to climb the tree, bore it so that we could eat it and tell them that the birds ate it.

We had horses and a buggy. We also had donkeys and mules. When we were small we use the get the horse up by the veranda and climb on its back.

We had a lovely, lovely, happy life in my youth.

There are two houses on her great-grandmother's land.

One was like a cottage. The other one was L-shaped, built of concrete with a zinc top roof—one side was lower than the other. The tank was behind, away from the veranda. We use to go on the lower side, run round the L bit and jump off the high part—that was fun. There was a pimento tree with a swing and we use to swing in the evenings.

I could ride a bicycle when I was about four—without any brakes. I rode the horse and the donkey but I did not ride the mule because he would jump and kick. We even rode the pigs. Some were big, so we jump on the back. As children you do anything for amusement.

We were allowed to go to the pictures once a week in Mandeville. We had to go to the matinee. You were never allowed to go to the late show. We

went to the six o'clock and came home while our
parents went to the late show.

Evelyn spoke at length about her relationship with her
great-grandmother Catherine before delving into the nature of
her complicated relationship with her mother, Winifred.

My mother was strict about a lot of things. She
would say: "As a girl you're suppose to learn to
cook."

Although we had helpers, we had to do house-
work. She would say: "You don't know what your
life is going to be like, so you must learn to do it."
I had to learn to clean the house, which I didn't
like. I had to learn to sew my buttons and I had
to learn to wash clothes.

She started off with our socks, we must wash
our socks. Then you got to your pants. The first
time I wash her blouse, I was so proud that I did
it and hang it out. I did not touch the collar or
the arm, so I had to go back over it. I thought: 'If
I wasn't at home I wouldn't be doing it.' So you
thought of running away.

Everybody got on well and the children on
both sides of the family grew up together. We
played and ate together, there was no animosity.
You played from one yard to the other.

Life, however, young Evelyn would learn, was rarely that simple.

I was never very close to my dad when I was young. I acknowledge him, I speak with him and I mingle with him and the other kids. But his wife use to let them call me names and tell me I wasn't their dad's child and things like that. So quite naturally I sort of distanced myself—not because of him, but he didn't stop it.

It's not that I hated my dad—I didn't hate him. I did not want to be very close to him because of his other children. It wasn't so much the children—it was more his wife. What she put in their heads is what they speak.

I thought it did me the world of good because it made me strong. I had his name. He signed my birth certificate and he didn't disown me. He did not disown me.

Looking back on her early childhood, Evelyn thinks she knows why her mother treated her harshly.

I think the reason for it was because her dad hadn't taken her back and she made the mistake of getting pregnant with me.

Sometimes I was accused of being the reason for her dad not taking her back. Sometimes she took some of her anger out on me.

If you do something and she said to you that she was going to punish you, you might as well stop and be punished. If it's until you go to bed, she'll never forget it. She promise you and she's going to deliver the punishment. It's no good running. Don't care how you cry and beg—she's doing it. I was one who was very scared of a beating. She only have to tell me that and I'll wet myself. It's not that she's going to hit you constantly, you just don't want it.

But my great gran was there for me every time. When my mum is raging, I get to my Gran and I'm safe. So you had protection and it cools down. She worked hard—my mum—to bring us up.

Evelyn is also not always getting on well with her younger half-sisters Louise and Eloise Ellis.

There was times when things is not very right. Because I wasn't their father's child my other sisters would sometimes call me names. I was lighter than them and they would call me 'mongoose'. They wanted to hurt me.

I got my colour from my mum. They were not the same colour because my dad wasn't as dark as their dad—so they're darker than me. Sometimes colour comes out in the genes. I have two children—one is light, one is dark.

I have no full brothers or sisters. I'm on my own and I'm not like any of them. I have my own personality and I behave in my own way—different from everyone. With my mum I am the eldest but on my father's side, I'm not.

Luckily for young Evelyn, her new step father Harold Ellis was a pleasant man whom she adored very much.

> My stepfather was such a lovely man. I love him even more than my own dad.
>
> He was the father of my two sisters and lived with my mum. He was such a lovely person. He was a lovely, lovely man.
>
> He was a Porter Indian. His dad was half Indian. He was a butcher by trade. On the weekends he used to kill pigs. On Tuesday he used to kill goats and sheep and things like that, which he supplied to traders in the market.
>
> The only fault he had was he drank on the weekend—he never drink during the week. If he doesn't drink, he's as beautiful as anything. When he drinks—he doesn't hit out or anything—but he behaved stupidly.
>
> I still love him. He's never hit me. If we do things he would hit his children but he would call my mum to me. He never hit me. That was a beauty and it made me love him dearly.
>
> So the love that I should have had for my dad went to my stepfather. He gave me a shoulder to cry on. He was there and he listens.

One of the most significant events in Evelyn's early childhood is the loss of her great-grandmother, Catherine.

> I remember when we were living with her and she

was very ill. That was coming up to her death. She was ninety-nine years and a few months old when she died.

She had a house that was L-shape and she was in that room in the L. We use to go and sit in there. Sometimes we use to sit on her lap and play with her chin because she was so old and her chin was very soft.

I remember she fell in a coma for about three days. She did not wake. We always go and watch and see whether or not she was still asleep or she had wake. Sometimes I would get a chair and sit by the side of her bed.

I was sitting in there this day when she woke and I said to her: "You've slept so long I didn't think you were going to wake up."

She said: "Well I was in a beautiful garden with lots of flowers and everybody was dressed in white." Then she held my hand and said to me: "Evelyn you're a good girl. Continue being a good girl and may the God of Heaven bless you wherever you go." I'll never forget that.

Later on she said to me: "Do you know the song 'The Lily of the Valley'?" I said: "I didn't know all of it." She said: "Will you sing what you know for me?" I did that. Then she said: "Can you get some water for me, I'm thirsty."

I went for the water and when I came back, she was gone.

I was about nine years old at the time and I'll

never forget it—ever, ever. Sometimes when I'm in a very low mood or something is not going right, I think nothing will touch me. My great-grandmother has blessed me on her dying bed. I repeat the words she said to me and I think: 'I'll get out of this'. And I do—I do.

IVY

Ivy is just six months younger than Evelyn and this is not the only coincidence in their early lives. Both are from the Parish of Manchester.

> I was born in Evergreen—April 1933. My mother's name is Estell Bishop and my father's name is Jamsey Parker. I was their only child.
>
> My mother was born in 1909—9th October. My dad is the same year. I can't remember what month was his birthday but I know they were born in the same year.

Evergreen is about thirty miles from Mandeville, Evelyn's birthplace. The circumstances surrounding Ivy's and Evelyn's births are remarkably similar.

> My mother left Manchester when she was quite young and went to live in Kingston where she met my dad. She had me out of wedlock. Once my mother got pregnant she came back to Manchester.
>
> I was born at my grandmother's house in

> Manchester, then my mother went back to Kingston. I lived with my grandmother from when I was born until I was nearly eight years old.

Evelyn's mother was born in Panama. Though Estell is Jamaican born, there is also an overseas connection.

> My mother was like somebody on the front of a magazine. I didn't think she was real or natural for a person living in Jamaica at that time. She was very beautiful.

Estell's mother came from Cuba—white Cuban—and her dad was a very dark person. She had eight brothers and sisters. Four of them were white and four of them were Black.

That Ivy's grandmother is Cuban is not surprising. Jamaicans began immigrating to work on Cuban sugar plantations and as labourers building railroads towards the end of nineteenth century. This was again a consequence of American intervention. The Cuban War of Independence from Spain between 1868 and 1895 disseminated the island's sugar industry, following which, American Corporations moved in, led by the United Fruit Company. It began sugar production on Cuban plantations in 1901. The Company was already well established in Jamaica and other West Indian Islands. Naturally, this was where it recruited additional labour to work on its new sugar plantations in Cuba.

Most likely Ivy's grandmother would have been one of the refugees fleeing the Cuban War of Independence. The majority of these were white or 'Brown' people who would have been welcomed in Jamaica.

Her father, Jamsey, is a building contractor in Kingston at the time of her birth. In hindsight, Ivy can only speculate on the reasons why her parents left her with her grandmother in Evergreen.

It's not because financially they couldn't afford to keep me, they could afford. Their lifestyle didn't involve a child. They wouldn't be able to go out. My dad used to play his guitar on a Saturday night and my mother was the star of dancing.

My mother used to come and visit me when I was with my grandmother. My dad didn't come. When she came I didn't think she was real—being dressed up and marvelous—coming into a district where people are shabby and did not wear clothes like hers. I used to think she wasn't real. I wasn't yet seven. I was still a young child.

Seeing her and being told she was my mother, I used to think my grandmother was my mother. We called my grandmother Dah. I don't know what it means but all the grandchildren called her Dah.

Though her mother and father were absent, Ivy remembers her early childhood in Dah's home with a great deal of fondness.

My grandmother's house in Manchester was made of wattle, wood and plaster—but it was a nice house. It was a big family house.

I don't know who built it. My uncles were big strong men who did building work and gardening and things like that. I think most of my aunties and uncles were living there. They were all married and had kids of their own.

As far as I can remember my mother was the second youngest and she had left there in her teens. All the others were still there but after a while they began to move out to different districts.

My grandfather was living there. I remember what he looked like but I can't remember important things about him. He also did building and he and his sons use to help build people's homes. My grandmother was husband and wife and ruled the house when my grandfather and the boys were away on building work.

He died when I was very young and my grandmother was left alone. After my grandfather died I reckon she just continued ruling. I think they were very obedient children, they would listen to her.

Ivy is nearly eight years old and still living in Evergreen with her grandmother Dah. It is around this time that Ivy's mother, Estell, becomes privy to a problem concerning her daughter that she cannot ignore.

My grandmother wouldn't send me to school.

I had asthma and she thought I was too frail to go to school and mix with other kids, so she didn't send me to school. I think my mother was upset about that and she came just before my eight birthday and took me to live with her in Kingston so that she could send me to school.

The transition from Dah's home in Evergreen to her mother's home in Kingston is not easy for Ivy.

I used to call my mother 'aunt' because everybody says Aunt Estell. Even when I went to live with her it was the hardest thing to say 'Mother' because I always think my grandmother is my mum.

The first year of living with her was the hardest of all with her taking me away from a loving home. Eventually I got used to it.

MELISSA

I was born in Montego Bay on the 24th January, 1948. I do not have any brothers. I do not have any sisters. I'm the only child.

I live with my grandmother from the age of zero. I live straight with my grandmother. I was born in my grandmother's house. My mother was living in my grandmother's house when she gave birth to me.

Melissa remembers what it was like growing up in Hampton with her grandparents. The area is dominated by banana and sugar plantations. She recalls the house in which she spends much of her early life.

I lived at home in a 'pan roof house' which we called 'zinc house'.

My grandfather has a lot of land. We all lived on this land in different houses but we're not far from each other.

Her family are known and well respected in Hampton. Melissa remembers her grandfather with great detail and reverence.

My grandfather was like the chief in the district and every next person you see in the district was a cousin—first, second or third cousin.

My grandfather was a very educated man because he was working for the government. He would go to the court. I suppose you would call him something like a Justice of the Peace. If there was any problem in the district, they would all come to his house. We use to call his house the 'Big House'. They would all come there and discuss what the problem was and try and trash it out before going to court. If it cannot be addressed there then it would go to court.

My grandfather lived in the same house as my grandmother. He used to buy bananas from everyone in the district and put it at his gate. Then a man would come from the government who would buy it from him. If they didn't come, he would take the bananas on a truck to the wharf and sell it to the government people there. They would cut the bananas into hands, wrap it, put it in boxes and then unto the ship to go to different parts like England, Germany—places like that. He was a trader. Bananas use to be sold on a Monday, Tuesday and on a Wednesday. On those days you're eating good because then you're going to eat fish or meat. When he's coming back, he's buying those things to bring.

Melissa also speaks of her grandmother very fondly.

My grandmother used to sell things in the market in Montego Bay on Wednesdays and Thursdays. We use to sell Cho-Cho, thyme, tomatoes, ochre, lime, yam, breadfruit—all the necessary things you use for cooking. Going around seven o'clock in the morning, we would walk nine miles to Montego Bay from Hampton with the goods on our head—oh yes. When she sold things, my grandmother used to tie up her money in a knot and put it in her bosom.

Not surprisingly, it is her grandparents whom Melissa remembers as the key figures in her early childhood.

Grandfather, I love him very much. His name was Jerome Williams, we called him Grandpa. When he comes back from court or whatever, my grandmother cooked. Sometimes there would be six or eight of us children and he would put each and every one of us on his lap.

My grandmother would give him his food. One plate with his meat or fish, the other with his hard food—that's yams, sweet potatoes, eddoes, tannias, dasheen and such. He would cut the meat, he would cut the dumpling. He would put piece in this one's mouth, put that one down, pick up the other and feed them. He was very, very loving—extremely loving. That's the family unit I missed.

My grandmother's name is Fergina but I call

her 'Doule' because her nickname was 'Doular'. I couldn't say 'Doular' when I was small, so I just say 'Doule'.

She was well-known in the Hampton district. She was like an angel. My grandmother was so good, so loving and so kind. My grandfather was very loving too but my grandmother was the greatest.

I never knew that children could have stress. What my grandmother use to do with me and my cousins was this. When we finish eating or when she's cooking, we would sit on the kitchen floor. The kitchen was a thatch-roof—outside—away from the house. For cooking you have your three stones, you have your firewood underneath and your pot. While the food is being cooked she would be there massaging our heads—it was relaxing. You know that in those days kids use to have lice, let's not deny it. She use to feel to see if you have lice. We use to push each other saying: "It's my turn, it's my turn." It was really good.

One evening when it started raining my grandmother said: "It's raining. You can't go outside to bathe this evening, so I'll wipe you down." She got water from a calabash, pour it into a basin, wipe me down and put me nightdress on. She did her tidying up and went to bed.

My grandfather was at the front of the bed, my grandmother at the back and I'm in the middle. I was about five. The rain on the roof, my tummy was full—heahhh! It is one of the happiest moments of my life. Whenever I am sad in England here and I remember that, it makes me happy again. It's a feeling I'll never get again—everything is perfect.

At the time of Melissa's birth, her mother Pengal is in her late teens and not married.

Young girls, they hanky-panky. My mother was very cheeky. She's was a very cheeky girl.

I was given the surname Bennett, the 'gentleman' who my mother say was my father. His name was Ferdie Bennett. He lives in another district. It was about eight miles from where our district was. It's a district they call Burnground where they had a massive plantation of bananas and mangoes.

We use to go to his mother's house in Burnground. The mango trees were soooh loaded with mangoes. You could full two, three baskets from those that drop and you still didn't touch the tree.

A couple of years after Melissa's birth, Pengal leaves Hampton for Kingston.

My mum went to Kingston to work as a domestic. She may have been about twenty years old when she went. Before that she lived with my grandmother.

Growing up, Melissa is allowed to visit her father, Ferdie Bennett, in Burnground. She then uncovers new information about her parents. Despite what her mother has told her, a man who lives close to her grandparents' home in Hampton tells her that he is—in fact—her father.

His name was Upert. That man used to love me. For years he kept saying to me: "I'm your father."

I never use to take any notice because we were living next door. His sisters, his brothers, his mother—they all use to love me like their own. They were very poor but they would take me round to their house when I'm maybe feeling ill or not too happy. It's the happiest time I use to have with them because they would put me in a bed.

In those days you put hay in your bed. You get what we call a 'jutta bag' and you full it up with banana dry trash or hay to make a bed. They would put me on that bed and make me a drink. I was very young but I can still remember it. They use to have a soft drink bottle and it had a teat. They would make sugar and water, put it in a bottle, put the teat on and give me. It was the sweetest thing. I would lay on the bed with them and I would jump from this sister to the next one.

While Pengal is away in Kingston, Melissa continues to visit her father, Ferdie. Overtime however, she gets to know the 'other' man who claims to be her father rather well.

> Upert—who said he was my father—he was
> always bringing me something. Let me see, in that
> family there was Pervis, there was Peggy, there was
> Girle, there was George. They were all the chil-
> dren of that lady.

Upert is earning his living nearby.

> He use to work on the plantation as one of those
> what we use to call 'Brackra'—that is a Plantation
> Chief. We call them 'Brackra' because they were
> the ones who give people in those areas jobs on
> big plantations.
>
> He use to work on a plantation which mostly
> grew bananas. They cut it, they put it on the truck
> and they take it to the ship. He used to work on
> there—pruning it, digging it, cutting it.
>
> He would bring me ripe bananas sometimes
> and sweets from the shop or cakes. I use to think
> they were just lovely people. He said he was my
> father but my mother said no.

Melissa's treatment at Ferdie's home is a little different to that
of Upert's.

> I would go to him [Ferdie] and his mother would
> say: "You no Ferdie pickney." She was deaf. I
> can remember that she was deaf. She would

say: "What's wrong with yer hair. You no Ferdie pickney. You brown skin, Ferdie Black." I never like her, never liked her.

Anyway my father was a tailor—Ferdie was a tailor. He used to make clothes for men and he use to have a small grocery shop. I didn't like him. He didn't show the interest in me as Upert showed. I was his first child and eventually he married another woman and they have two other children.

Pengal's stay in Kingston does not last long.

She didn't like what was happening, what she had to do. She wanted to go back home to her mother. She worked in Kingston for a while, then she came back to Hampton to live with my grandmother and my grandfather. She then found a gentleman from another district—not very far away—named Martie Macdonald. She married him. He built a house to put us in but I didn't want to stay with them. I would say: "Take me back to my grandmother." I would run away each time and find ways to go back to my grandmother's house. Then my mother came and says: "You're going to primary school. I think I should watch over you more now." Even though I went to live with my mother at twelve, every day I would go to my grandmother. Coming from school, I have to pass my grandmother's house before I got

to my house and I would still go to my grandmother. She would cook, leave my dinner in 'shot
pan'—it's a thing you can carry food in to workers
in the field. It would keep my food warm.

The church was a central feature of African Caribbean society
during this period. On Sunday mornings almost everyone
attended church.

My grandmother would take me to church every
Sunday. Sometimes three or four times a week we
would go to church. We're doing youth things at
church—drawings, crayon, recitations, we do all
those things.

That is one thing my grandmother believe in.
She didn't go to the hierarchy church. She went
to Pentecostal church where you worship Jesus
Christ and nobody else. I've seen my grandmother go into 'spirit' for three days—three
straight days—at the church. She would speak
into different languages. When she came out, she
couldn't remember a thing.

My grandmother told me: "Never steal, never
tell lies, never be boastful, never feel you're better
than the next person." That is what I've built my
character on.

Melissa's remembers another thing about her grandmother—
she was a very good cook.

Doule's food was the sweetest. All of us go to Doule to eat. My other four cousins—one is over here now, two is in Jamaica and one in America—we all use to go to Doule to eat.

When Doule do fish—especially sprats—she's not giving us half, she's giving us one each. She fry them Escoveitch. She's giving us one each in our plate with our rice or with hard food—banana or yam. She knew I never use to love rice. Each of us, we don't eat out of each other's plate. She has a plate for each and every one of us. Doule's food was the sweetest.

My aunty use to have a grocery shop at the junction of our district, stocked with everything—well stocked. She's making good money but—with all the chicken, with all the beef, with all the pork and all the fish—her children never use to eat her food. They'll get it, they'll play in it but they don't eat it. They have to go to Doule to eat.

When Doule make 'Rundown'. What is 'Rundown'? Coconut juice—the milk, you boil it down until it start becoming oil and it's got a thin sediment at the bottom when it's more or less like yoghurt. You put your thyme, your scallion and your spices in it—that is nice. In those days you use to do salt herring or shad. I don't see shad or salted herring any more but when you put it in that coconut milk and boil it down—hehhh! It's the nicest thing and you to eat it with rice or hard food and dumpling. Nice!

When Doule took Melissa to the market in Montego Bay to sell produce grown on family land, they would go to local cafes nearby.

> When you want to eat, there use to be little shops that make ginger beer and draft porter. It's a very strong drink. I don't know how they made that but I heard they get bark from trees and they put it in a container, dig a hole and leave it in the earth—then it ferments. You also put in sugar, cinnamon and other flavourings. When it is in the bottle, you have to make sure that the bottle is well corked because the strength of it is so powerful, it would explode—pooooh!
>
> I don't know, maybe the people who use to make it in Jamaica die out. You find a few of them here but they still can't make draft porter. That thing used to be nice. When I say nice I mean nice. It's soooh good to drink—heh the power, the power in it. They use three or four different barks to make it. I know there was one they called 'Strongback', there was another one they call 'Chainey Root'. It was nice. When you drink it, you feel you're iree.
>
> They use to bake hard dough bread. Not the one you see in the shops now, those are not bread. You never use to cut it man, you break it. When you break a piece of it, when you smell it—Ooooh—you know it's bread. I don't bake it

now because I don't think I would bake it as good as they use to do.

We use to have an old lady called Miss Fan and that was what she did in the district for a living. She used to bake the bread in a massive brick oven, wood blazing underneath it. They had a long stick to push the bread in—that is Jamaican style. I miss it.

Even at an early age Melissa is passionate about food and she is determined to learn how to cook.

I remember one day; I was about five but I can remember it. I think they kill a goat and give me some of the tripe. Me decide me ah cook me own soup.

I have the little fire stones, cooking my soup out of a Milo tin. I'll never forget it. I didn't know I wasn't to supposed to cover the Milo tin. Even if I put the lid on, I shouldn't have shut it down.

My dear, when the thing started boiling up you see, it hit the lid. It sounded like—well in those days I never know what a bomb sounded like. Thank God it didn't do me any damage. My grandmother said: "You see! This is what you get." I said: "But you're cooking and I'm cooking!"

I was learning to cook, I saw her doing it. She was making soup the evening too, so I thought: 'I'm going to do my own soup.' I never got any of my own soup because it all went, so I had was to drink her soup. So the very evening, it was about six o'clock because dusk was just about coming down—I'll never forget it. She cook, she took the pot off the fire and took it inside to serve it. While I ate mine, the rain started falling. You could hear the raindrops on the zinc roof. Oooh—the music it made on the roof.

EMMA

My name is Emma Alethia Thompson. My maiden name is Emma Robinson. I was born in Priestman's River, which is part of Portland in Jamaica, on Friday 25th January, 1951. I was the eldest child of Millie and John Robinson.

Priestman's River is near Port Antonio—capital of the Parish of Portland. By 1951 Port Antonio is already an important area for growing and exporting bananas. It is also developing as a Caribbean tourist destination.

At the time—shortly after I was born—there were five people living in my parents' house. My mother and father, Uncle George, my sister and myself.

It was only two rooms with a kitchen leaning off the back of the house, but in the eyes of a child it looked big. Later when I returned, it was a surreal moment—how tiny it was.

The family home is on land inherited from her father's parents. Emma did not know them.

They passed away before I was born.

I can remember dad's father's name was Richard. Can't remember my dad's mother's name. I've never seen a photograph of them because back in those days photos were taken for passports and they didn't have passports.

Much of what Emma has to say about the short time she lived with her parents in Priestman's River and her grandparents in Port Antonio is what she discovers later in life. Her father left Jamaica for England in 1952, just under two years after she was born. Her mum followed a year later.

My grandparents both felt disappointed because my mom was thirty-five when she had me as her first child. He and Mom didn't get married until after I was born. They could have got married before I was born but that's something else they shared in later life with me, my husband and a few other people. He and Mom could have got married a year sooner but she was very rebellious. He noticed such a change in her when she was expecting me.

Dad worked the land in Priestman's River where I was born. My parents grew stuff to sell in the local market. They planted bananas and yams which Mum sold. He was a Farmer and a Fisherman. It was a very resourceful home.

Before that, during the war years, my father also worked near the wharf in a warehouse as manager or something like that. He used to get a lot of flour bags that was given to people who make different things. I heard him talk about it. All that was before I was born and is what other people said to me.

My mum made her money baking—making cakes. She was a woman of many talents. I would describe her as like that woman in the Book of Proverbs that was gifted in so many different ways. She was the heart of the community. She was always baking cakes, making ginger beer— all those things. You name the food—Mum was always doing that—long before I was born and after I came on the scene. She was a woman of great hospitality. Everybody was welcome. She never cooked for just the people that lived in the household. I discovered that later on in life when we came to England.

Emma also discovers out other things about her mother, things that surprise her.

My mum was a twin; she was a twin girl. Her twin sister passed away when she was young. I didn't know this until I was about forty—a couple of years before my mum passed away.

My husband and I have been talking about the gaps that there are—the things we would have loved to have known about. This was a secret that our parents didn't want to reveal. Whatever the reasons, there are gaps and there's very few people left remaining of our parents' age who are in a position to actually tell us.

Emma continues to discover secrets about her parents. One particular secret was about Emma's mysterious illness as a child, and why her parents believed the illness to be linked to her cousin who fell ill at the same time. This cousin was someone Emma knew fairly well.

That was back then. I would spend time in Priestman's River because we were all family. We would probably go up there for maybe a week if it's holiday time. Grandma would leave me there with her sister.

Her sister's youngest child is my half-sister. She's my half-sister on my father's side. I didn't know then. I thought she was my cousin. I don't think she knew either because she's been brought up with her brothers and sisters who are older than her. She was a Reed and we were Robinson. My grandmother, her maiden name was Carr. My half-sister's mum, her married name was Reed but her maiden name was Carr.

When I went to stay with them I was like their little cousin. It was a big family but I wasn't treated in anyway differently. In fact, the relationship that I had with that sister was closer. We were tiny. She's about four months younger than me. She's the one that went to America and she's got two daughters. One is the spitting image, as she was growing up, of our daughter. The younger one, if you saw Emily and I when we were both young, her two daughters were like me and Emily when we were young. It's amazing!

Emma did not or could not explain how it came to be that John Robinson could be father to both her and her half-sister whose mother is, in fact, her great-aunt—her grandmother's sister. It can only be assumed that her great-aunt had to be significantly younger than her grandmother. Her father was thirty-eight at the time. To complicate matters more, her half-sister had older brothers and sisters. She is the youngest of them and was born only four months after Emma. That would mean that Emma's mother Millie and her great-aunt were both pregnant at the same time. Her half-sister's surname is Reed, which is the surname of the man her great-aunt married. Could this be the real reason why Millie was initially so unwilling to marry John? Emma thought it was because her mother was 'rebellious'.

Even though her grandmother lived a few miles from Port Antonio, presumably she would have known most, if not all, of this. So why would she send Emma to stay at her sister's house in Priestman's River during school holidays, once John and Millie had left for England. As far as Emma knew at the time, both she and her half-sister thought they were cousins.

All this is little no more than speculation based on what Emma was later told by different members of her family. As she said: "…my parents took their secrets to the grave." However, later in her life she wonders about something she noticed earlier.

I do recall in relation to my half-sister that Dad always looked after all of them.

Despite being young at the time, Emma remembers quite a lot about her early life with her grandparents at their home in Port Antonio.

The house was right up on the hill, the very last one on the top of the hill. There were like others going down.

Grandpa was a butcher. He was the butcher in the area for everybody else.

He was a very little man. My grandmother was tall, he was short. My mum was shorter than both me and my sister.

I'm trying to think what my grandmother use to do apart from giving me a hard time. Grandma, she was an Adventist and a seamstress—she use to sew. I can't recall her doing sewing for other people but she was always sewing, doing embroidery. Of course she helped Grandpa with the meat at the market but because of her religious beliefs she would have to get all her cooking done on the Friday evening. Saturday would be Sabbath school so I would be going through that ritual with her from Friday night. I've got recollections of going to the market in them days. Imagine the heat and the smell and what have you as a young child. You would finish school half-day on a Friday. Then I would go down to meet Grandma and Grandpa in the market—Port Antonio market.

My uncle on my mom's side—the eldest of the boys—he'd get me pet bread and some soda. Leave it every Friday, religiously. I'd just go in and help myself as a child.

We didn't lack in any way. We had our food but she'd never put that pot on the fire on a Saturday. Whatever we had, it wouldn't be anything that needed warming up on a Saturday—not until sunset on a Saturday. That was the ritual.

Growing up there it was just me, my grandmother and my grandfather. Well it was mostly me and Grandma because Grandpa he love him drink, doing butchering and other things. Most of the time it was she and I.

She never, ever hit me—so that bond was stronger. I had a wonderful relationship with my grandma. She didn't really want me to do anything hard.

Emma is actually named after her grandma Emma, whom she comes to love dearly. However, she also remembers her grandmother giving her 'a hard time' as a child.

My grandma was very, very strict. She had jobs for us around the house. My job was to wash the handkerchiefs—grandpa's handkerchiefs.

The washing, that was just a little task. She also taught me how to make a Katta to carry a little butter pan of water on my head. (*A Katta is a piece of cloth, folded in a circle and placed on the head as a cushion when carrying loads.*) Other people children would carry much bigger pans but my grandmother didn't give me that burden. She wouldn't let me carry anything that heavy. I was spoilt.

Because of her Christian convictions, she didn't tolerate swearing of any description. I knew that my uncles would swear at each other but away from her. I never snitched. I wasn't one for taking tales because that was something she would say: "When big people having a conversation, make yourself scarce. Go to one side."

Emma could not have known it at the time but her grandmother is to shape a great many of the values that will guide the rest of her life.

I can sit and recall some of the words that she'd used to me, or I would hear her using. It's just as if it was yesterday, they're so fresh in my memory. One such as: "If yer want good, yer belly have fe run!" In other words, if you want to do something good, it's going to take some sacrifice. Oh goodness, she had these little gems. To me they are little gems which I'm now passing on. Our children knows them and our grandchildren. It's impressing on them to do the best they can. She loved to read and there were several teachers in the family—not on my mum's side—on my dad's side.

When I was in Priestman's River spending time, they would have work prepared for us. It would be a book—not just an exercise book but where you had to do additional tasks. This was even before I started school. I could read before I went to school. My grandma and my cousin who was a teacher taught me. I love books. I love reading. My grandma didn't like dogs or cats and because of that I didn't particularly like any animals. If I saw a dog, I'd start running. She would say: "You mustn't run you know." My grandmother, she'd be there praying and reading scripture if anybody pass away. That sort of discipline and that way of life was already something imprinted in my head from a young age. As I grew up that just became part and parcel of who I was.

Even at an early age, Emma begins to wonder why she was separated from her younger sister when their parents left Jamaica.

My sister Emily was left in the care of my dad's younger sister with her husband. That particular aunty I haven't had much contact with for many years. At that time, I don't think she was married as yet but she did get married afterwards. She lived in Kingston, which was quite a way from where we were in Port Antonio.

I don't know exactly why my sister went to Kingston and I stayed with my grandparents when my parents went to England. I think it may have been because my sister resembled my aunt Isobel who lived in Kingston—it's amazing.

Emily is just over a year old when her mother leaves for England in 1953. Then in 1956, her aunt Isobel also leaves Jamaica.

When my parents sent for our aunt to come to England, my sister actually returned into the care of my grandparents.

That's when I really met her because we were both very young when one went one way and one went the other way. We came together as two strangers in a sense—two little girls as strangers. I wouldn't say thrust together. I was the eldest grandchild, then suddenly my sister came. It didn't really matter because it was companionship for me. For those few years from 1956 we were together until we came to England.

At the time the two sisters are reunited at their grandparent's home in Port Antonio, Emma is six years old and her sister Emily is five.

Before she came, we'd never met. We were both infants. All I knew, yes I'd got a sister that lived in Kingston, but Kingston was like the other end of the country from where we were. There was no visits that transpired. I don't know if any letters had gone from Grandma to Aunt Isobel. I very much doubt it actually.

Shortly after Emily arrives, grandma Emma ends up taking care of the children from other members of her family.

> So suddenly it went from two grandchildren to four. I can remember there was Maureen, Bing, my sister and myself.
>
> We were loved. After having your own children you realise how privileged we were. We didn't lack of anything. Our parents would send things for us. Then other relatives who was living in America—the Wright and Campbell family—would send things. My grandmother would give some of these things to other people.

Emma's schooling begins when she is seven years old.

> I said I was privileged. I went to a private school actually. Can't remember the name of the school or the Head Teacher. It was a small building. I didn't go to a school that had more than maybe fifteen or twenty children in it. This was in Priestman's River. It was a two-room school with the girls separated from the boys. I had private tutoring and Wilma Wright—a member of my family—was one of the teachers there. I'm trying to think. Yes! I use to go there before I started at the school in Beswork.

Whether attending school in Priestman's River or Beswork—Port Antonio, her father's cousin takes a special interest in her education.

> My schooling in Port Antonio was more peri-
> odic. It was like I spend half me time in one to
> the other. But Wilma, she was very involved in
> what education I had up until that point. She was
> another disciplinarian.
>
> When I came to England, I spoke the Queen's
> English because the people around me spoke
> very, very good English. My sister had more of
> a Jamaican accent than I did when we came to
> England.

Emma's dad, John Robinson, is a devout Jehovah's Witness. On
leaving Jamaica for England he left specific instructions that
both his children are to be brought up as Jehovah's Witnesses.
The problem is that their mother is Anglican, Aunt Isobel is
not religious and Grandma Emma is a devout Seventh Day
Adventist.

> On a Saturday we'd be at the Adventist Temple
> and on a Sunday we'd be at the Kingdom Hall,
> which wasn't too far away. As children you just
> did it—that was the way of life. Of course, my
> sister didn't experience much of this until after
> she'd come to us in 1956. Before that she'd expe-
> rienced a totally different way of life in Kingston
> where she did not have much to do with this
> double church thing. By the time she came to
> my grandparents' home, while I had a Christian

experience, she'd had none. That was difficult for Grandma. Grandpa wasn't in the church—he love him drinking. It was hard for my sister to adjust to that but she still had to try and comply.

Even though Emily is a year younger, it is not long before Emma is a little bit in awe of her.

Growing up with my sister in those days, she was certainly a rebel. I would say it was the environment she lived in and the individual she was with before she came to us. Oh my goodness! There was little things that she did around the house, which was amazing.

Some money went missing and it was me grandma's money. I didn't even know up until this time that her little stash—whatever she had—was in a mortar underneath the house. The house was on stilts. You can picture it.

My grandma couldn't find this money. Nothing like this had happened before, but Uncle Reynard—the same one who left food for me at the market—he apparently was always borrowing money from my grandma.

He twigged that my sister being new and seeing that she was a little rebel at the time, he must have said to her: "Go on. Look see if you can find where Grandma leave her money."

He put that in Emily's head. She went and found the money and gave some of it to him. The

story came out later but that was part of her lifestyle in Kingston, the way she was living and he
knew it. She didn't turn out to be that bad over
the years.

Emma and Emily's stay in Jamaica comes to an end when their
parents send for them and they board a plane on 13th June,
1959.

IRENE

Irene was born on 27th April, 1953 in Spanish Town—capital of the Parish of St. Catherine. It is not that well-known outside Jamaica but in many respects the town is central to the island's early history.

In 1534 Spanish Town was the capital of Jamaica. The island was then a Spanish colony and its capital was known as 'Villa de la Vega'. In the process of conquering the island in 1655 the British more or less destroyed the capital, which they renamed 'Spanish Town'. Most of its administrative functions had to be moved to Port Royal. The town was later rebuilt by the British and resumed its functions as capital of the island. Just as well, since Port Royal was destroyed by an earthquake in 1692. Spanish Town remained the centre of government in Jamaica until 1872 when Kingston was designated capital of the island.

Irene is an only child. When her mother left for England in 1959 she was left in the care of an aunt for a total of one year. Much of what she now knows of her early life in Jamaica comes from later conversations with her mother, Lucy, and other members of her family.

I can't remember the house where I was born and

I haven't been back to see it.

She got me late. I think she was thirty-six and she couldn't have any more children. My mum was single at the time.

Her mother died when she was quite young, when she was only twelve. Her grandmother was the one who brought her up. So all the things that was passed on to me was about: 'Granny told me this and Granny told me that.' I think she lived with her granny for a while. When she had me she was living in a tenant house from what I can vaguely remember.

My mother has always been a disciplinarian. I remember her being quite strict but still loving. She was always quoting different proverbs and stuff. Maybe not so much in Jamaica but in later years. I remember her saying: "If there is something going on and everybody is sitting outside in the yard, get inside. It's only old nagger sit out. If anything happen they'll call your name. Get yourself inside—go and read."

This was a mindset common in African Carribean household, that is, when adults are together talking, children should make themselves scarce.

She also talked about some people being quite jealous and you have to be careful what you say to people: "If you brag too much, people don't like it. They will think you're showing off and they will try to cut you down. Keep things to your chest. Watch your company. If you see a person company, you'll know what they're going to turn out like because they'll influence you." I do remember things like that.

She wasn't from a well-off family. My mother always worked, you would say she was working class. She was a nurse in Jamaica but she qualified when she came over here.

Nobody sent for her to come to England. I can't remember how she came here but she worked enough for passage and then to send for me. She was always saying: "I wanted to leave Jamaica because I wanted to do better and I wanted to do better for my daughter. My daughter must do better than me. I don't want you to land up like me."

Emma was also able to find out a little about the relationship between her mother and the man who was her father.

Yes, I've met my dad. My mum did speak of him. He was a womaniser.

I think he was a mechanic. I did have photographs. My mum is quite dark. He was very fair so I sort of got my colour from him.

She actually met him when she was working at the hospital and he swept her off her feet. Then afterwards she found out he was sweeping several other nurses off their feet as well.

She didn't feel good about that. She was quite hurt. When you think you're the one and you find out there's three others, it's not something that you laugh about.

When I was born, I think he was around for a bit. He must have shown a bit of interest then. He did acknowledge me as his daughter and I have his surname. His name was Webster Bryant.

I don't know if in those days in Jamaica men gave anything towards their kids like how it is in England. Unless they were interested, I don't think they gave anything. We've never discussed anything like that.

Irene starts school just before her mother Lucy sends for her to come to England.

My infant school was in England as well but I do remember school in Jamaica. We had school outdoors. I remember my aunt and other teachers. If anybody did anything wrong, the punishment was you had to stand and hold one leg up for a certain period of time. After that the teacher said: "Don't do that again. You can sit down now." That's all I remember. I can't really remember much else.

Chapter Three

Grow Up Early—
Grow Up Quick

EVELYN

It is 1939 and Evelyn is seven years old. She is living in Mandeville at the home of her great-grandmother, Catherine, with her mother, Winifred, her stepfather, Harold Ellis, and her two younger half-sisters, Louise and Eloise. Her father, Bolas Spence, is living across the road with his wife, Pun, and their five children who are also her half-brothers and sisters.

> My first school was Georges Valley School. I had
> a cousin who was older than me and we went to
> school together. We had a lovely time there—a
> very happy time.
> I use to go to school looking so nice because
> my clothes use to come from abroad. I had my
> little silver chain and everything.

Wearing clothes imported from abroad with her little silver chain, Evelyn would certainly have stood out at school. Evelyn's clothes were being sent from Panama by her grandfather. Though he strongly disapproved of his daughter Winifred becoming pregnant with Evelyn while unmarried—he did not abandon them.

My worse subject was maths. I hated it, especially long division. I was a slow starter anyway and I was lazy too.

I use to be singing all the time, my voice is not bad. My teacher used to always have me by the piano singing and doing solos.

After I got to a certain stage and with my reading and everything—she used to have me as a monitor helping other kids learn to read. She did all that for me. She sort of built me up. She gave me a lot of confidence—a lot of confidence.

There were quite a lot of us at the school. They start from the Junior class at seven right up to sixteen. I stayed at that school right up to sixteen. Both my sisters—Louise and Eloise started at the same school.

The Head Teacher at Georges Valley school is Miss Jackson and her relationship with Evelyn takes a dramatic turn following the death of Evelyn's great-grandmother Catherine.

My teacher—she used to love me that much. I had just gone into fifth standard and she had a lovely cottage at the back of the school where she lived. She had no children at all at the time. I just wanted to be with her because we got so close.

Amazingly—even at this age—Evelyn had ideas about the direction of her future.

I remembered I went to school and I said to my teacher—she was the Head Teacher at the time: "My mum wants to know how much you would charge to board me?" My mum never said it.

My teacher said she would be willing to do it because she used to love me and she had no children. She was on her own.

The pride of my mother! She wouldn't say no because she doesn't want to be looked down on. So I got to live there. I left home and went and lived with my teacher as a boarder. I was about eleven coming up twelve. My great-grandmother had died by then.

My mum agreed I would board with her because she would be letting herself down if she said no.

Given that Evelyn does not fit in with her mother's and father's side of the family, her desire to leave the family home and live with her Head Teacher is understandable.

When I was boarding with my teacher, I would visit home and sometimes stay overnight.

I was one who liked to be on my own. I don't know if it is because I had no attachment as a brother and sister—I was alone. Even when I was with them, I was on my own a lot.

I'll go away from them, don't play with them or anything. I remember there was a hill—more a rise but flat on top—with trees growing around it. There was a massive stone in the middle. Sometimes I would go up there by myself and sit on it. They would be calling and I'm not answering.

At this point, Evelyn's relationship with her father, Bolas, has not improved.

I knew him to the extent I wanted to know him. I didn't want to go too far in—even when I was young—because if I get too close his wife became jealous and it got worse. So I thought to myself: 'Keep my distance.'

I'll acknowledge him. I'll go to see him at his house and everything. We were neighbours but I never got close to him—not close, close.

While Evelyn is still living with her mother and just before moving in with her Head Teacher, the church begins to feature more prominently in Evelyn's life.

I was confirmed in the Church of England when I was ten. It's not that I wanted to be confirmed but Pastor Jones was our parents' friend. They grew up together and everything. He said I should confirm because I had to go to Sunday School and I had to go to church.

I didn't even study the catechism. The day of the confirmation when the Bishop came, if he had asked us singly to repeat the catechism, I wouldn't be able to do it. But he did it in a group and then just confirm us.

Evelyn could not have known it then but this would not be the only time Pastor Jones would play a pivotal role in her life.

Evelyn thought of her mother as very strict. At an early age Winifred insisted on her learning to cook, wash and iron her clothes, prompting a young Evelyn to consider running away. Before long Evelyn finds out that Miss Jackson, the teacher she's now boarding with, is equally strict. As she gets older, in addition to making her a school monitor and helping younger children learn to read, she is also assigned other tasks that seem to her a lot less like chores and a lot more like responsibilities.

The kids who couldn't afford meals, they provided meals for them. I use to supervise that. If they do a cook meal, I was the one who had to count the amount of children who has to have meat and I was the one who has to cut the meat so that everyone has a piece of meat.

If they're going to have sandwiches and things, I was the one who had to go with the boys to fetch the bread from the bakery. You wouldn't buy bread from the shop—you get a better deal from the bakery. We use to ask them not to wrap it, just put it in a bag. You get extra bread free if you wrap it yourself, so you have enough that the kids instead of having one sandwich can have two. I'm always doing that—organising. Unto this day, I'm very good at organising.

In addition to learning how to organize herself and others at an early age, Evelyn also gets her first glimpse of the world outside of Jamaica.

> When I went to live in Battersea we use to sit and watch them playing tennis at the Tennis Club. So growing up—tennis and all those things—I know them before I came here. Where we lived there were people of prestige and you get to mix with them and their children. They had just found bauxite in Jamaica and then they build this area where you have workers from Canada and other places. So we were sort of neighbours. You sort of see how the other half lived and you could mix with them. I remember Mrs Earl—she's a Canadian from Montreal. She has a son and we used to play. She said to me: "Evelyn have you travelled?" At that time I'd never travelled. I remembered I thought about it and one day I thought to myself I wanted to explore. I just grew tired of what was there—I wanted more. At an early age I was the one who wants to explore—go out and up.

The presence of significant deposits of aluminum ore in Jamaica was known as far back as 1867. However serious interest in mining did not begin until the Second World War when demand increased dramatically. Detailed surveys and preparations began shortly after 1942 with the arrival of three North American companies—Alcan, Reynolds and Kaiser. Alcan was originally a Canadian mining company and its mines were located in Kirkvine just outside Mandeville.

Evelyn remains at Georges Valley School boarding with her Head Teacher until she is sixteen. It is her mother's intention that she should continue at the same school in order to complete her junior and senior Cambridge exams over the next two years. She begins the first year but soon enough there's a problem. That problem is a boy.

> The teacher I was boarding with was a little bit like my mum. I was in the Guides and there was the Scouts. You get friendly with kids.
>
> I remember I use to like this bloke and he was camping down by the common and came up to get water. She suspected that I liked this boy and she made me give him the water through the window.

Shortly after, a more significant relationship develops with another boy.

> My boyfriend at sixteen did not go to the same school. Calvin was going to Mandeville school. He lived in the Lane and that is before you get to Mandeville. So we meet up halfway. I thought I was making a good selection because his parents was not badly off. I knew his sisters and everything. We all got on very well—we were friends.
>
> I remember his dad was the only jeweller in Mandeville and he was doing jewellery work with

his dad. He was the one who use to run the film projector at the cinema. He was older than me but he'd never sort of ask me to do anything wrong. I would go to the jeweller's shop sometimes. He's working, we're chatting and his dad is there. We're not doing anything wrong.

Despite not doing anything wrong, Evelyn knows there is no way a relationship with Calvin is going to sit well with her mother. After all, Evelyn is only sixteen years old.

I told her that I gave him up. I lied—I didn't. Somebody saw me with him and told her.

My mum thought: 'No you don't'. She said: "No, no, no, no, no—not at your age." She didn't want me to be with the boy I was seeing. She was frightened of me getting pregnant.

She knew that I like him and knew his parents and everything. He would come round to the house. I think it was fear of me getting pregnant because she got pregnant young. So she was trying to be over protective. She liked him and she was okay with him but she just didn't want me to have a boyfriend at that age.

It's not that she hated him or anything but to me she's using her own experience to protect me. At the time I didn't understand that. After, I realised that she didn't want me to go through what she went through because there was no surety if I got pregnant that he would be there for me. She was just protecting me from getting hurt.

When Evelyn's mother discovers that her daughter has in fact continued to see Calvin behind her back, she takes decisive action.

> She wrote to her sister Mavis in Portland and asked her to let me come over. She shipped me off to Portland.
>
> That was the end of it. Would you believe me, until this day I sometimes wonder what happen to him. He's never left my thoughts and I would love to see him or know what happened to him.

Portland Parish is on the north-eastern coast of Jamaica and Aunt Mavis lives in the capital, Port Antonio. As well as putting an end to Evelyn's relationship, going to Portland also puts an end to her education in Mandeville.

> I think I was just gone sixteen going seventeen. I was still going to the school doing my first year Junior Cambridge. In the evenings I use to go over to my Head Teacher's cottage to do the piano.
>
> I did not leave Georges Valley school with either junior or senior Cambridge exams.

IVY

Now eight years old, Ivy is living with her mother, Estell, in Kingston. She has just moved from Evergreen in Manchester where she has been living with her grandmother, Dah, since her birth. Estell left the family home in Evergreen in her late teens to live in Kingston. This is where she meets Jamsey, Ivy's father, and became pregnant at the age of twenty-three. She came back to Evergreen to give birth to Ivy and returns to Kingston shortly after, leaving her daughter in the care of her grandparents. Though her mother often comes back to visit her in Evergreen, her father does not. Until Ivy is eight years old, she thinks of her grandmother, Dah, as her 'mother' and calls real mother 'Aunt Estell'.

Though Ivy is very happy living with her grandmother Dah, there's a problem. Ivy is frail, suffering with asthma, and Dah is unwilling to send her to school. She should have started Junior school when she was seven years old.

This is the 1930's and I don't think parents thought much about what they wanted for their kids as long as you could read and write. Some parents did not send their kids to school.

Two of my uncles couldn't read and write.

They didn't want to go to school and my grandmother and grandfather didn't force them. It was easy to take them to work in the field or take them around and teach them building.

Most of her aunts and uncles, along with their children, are living in Ivy's grandparents' home. As builders, her grandfather and uncles are often away on business. As a result of this, Dah then assumes the role of 'husband and wife' in the family.

Away in Kingston, it takes Ivy's mother nearly a year to find out that Dah is not sending Ivy to school. To her credit, Estell has very strident views on this issue. She goes back to Evergreen, packs her daughter's things, and takes her to Kingston.

Ivy is too young to understand any of this. As far as she is concerned, she is being taken away from a loving home where she has lived happily for the past eight years to live in Kingston with her mother, a woman she does not know and regards as an 'aunt'. Plenty for an eight-year-old to cope with. Though, as Ivy soon discovers, her mother's new presence in her life will provide another challenge.

She didn't send me straight to school in Kingston.

She kept me home for a year teaching me to read and write so that when I went to school I wouldn't look silly for my age, which I hated.

I'd rather have looked silly than staying at home and being subjected to my mother's beating and teaching and beating and teaching, which brought so much fear in me.

When she goes out I'm fine—reading and

doing whatever. But as soon as I hear her come in, everything has gone out my head. If she comes and I can't remember what I've read, then it's a beating.

For a year I had that.

Ivy is nine when her mother finally enrolls her in Franklin Town Elementary School in Kingston.

My mother put me in school saying my age was seven because I wasn't that big, so I had two extra years in school.

The first day I went to school, I was able to read ABC and all the little bits that was written up on the blackboard and books I was given. As a new kid coming in, the teachers didn't have to teach me ABC or whatever as a seven-year-old. That's the age people use to send their kids to school. I was moved from the ABC class up to the third class because I could already read.

Given Estell's harsh approach to teaching, Ivy is grateful when she is eventually sent to school.

I was kind of glad to be in school away from my mother. It was like a refuge open up for me. I loved school. I loved to read and write.

Refuge it may be but when the school day comes to an end, Ivy must return home where her mother's rules apply to every other aspect of her life.

> You can't play, couldn't have friends. My friends couldn't come to the house and I couldn't be out. You have to study and do your homework. As soon as school was over, I had to be home and in the books—I've got to stay in books. So I got to kind of hate books.
>
> I just went through school doing what I'm told to do and no extras. Because I could read, I skipped a few classes and that got me up to the sixth form really quickly.

Ivy's mother, Estell, is still not married to Ivy's father, Jamsey. This eventually causes some more tumult in the household.

> My dad wanted to marry her and she didn't want to get married. My mum and dad separated. He wanted to get married and settle down, she didn't. He left and found another woman who would marry him.
>
> I was about eleven or twelve years old at the time. I remember on my twelfth birthday they wanted to take a picture of me and I didn't want a photograph. I didn't like the camera.

The separation of Ivy's parents triggers another significant change in her early life.

> They sent me off to the country to my aunt Mabel,

one of my mother's sisters, who was married to one of my dad's brothers.

They had a shop in one of the adjoining districts, Comfort Hall. They sent me there so that I could go to St. Paul's Church School.

I used to go and stay with her in my school holidays so it wasn't an upheaval. She didn't have any children of her own but her house was always full of kids. I think it was her husband's kids and other kids in the District, which she mothered.

Ivy's mother does not explain why she did not want to marry Ivy's father. She also does not tell Ivy why she is being sent off to live with Aunt Mabel just four years after being removed from her grandmother's home in Evergreen. She suspects it could have been something to do with the way her father took care of her.

I loved my dad. I loved him very much.

But a part of my life experience with my dad I blotted out of my mind. This is a part I wouldn't want you to publish but it doesn't really matter anyway.

From the time I went to live with my mother in Kingston, before my eight birthday, my dad started sexually assaulting me. He said that was the way fathers look after their daughters—take care of their daughters. Even though I loved him very much, I couldn't understand why I had to be hurt in that kind of way.

When I saw other girls with their dads and they're happy, I used to say to myself how come they can be so happy and having that kind of experience. I didn't know any better. I knew that wasn't something nice to be doing to your child or anybody else.

I didn't see him much after he separated from my mum and got married. It was nicer living with Aunt Mabel in the country than the life I was living in Kinston with my mother and father arguing. Then to get away from my dad as well, it was a new life for me. But even then I still carried the scar, which I could not tell anyone.

Ivy likes living with her aunt Mabel and 'all those strange kids' who were living with with them.

We use to go to school together. The kids didn't fight over her. She loved everybody and she was fair to everybody.

I was a bright child and I learned quickly. They tried to push me up to do things. I could do sewing, make hand-made garments, which won first prizes. So I became a favourite of the teachers.

Though Ivy is now away from Kingston, this does not bring an end to her father's attentions.

During my school holidays I had to go back to

my mother in the city. My mother had to go to
work and my dad use to come by.

I was glad when the time came for me to go
back to my aunt.

Ivy attends St. Paul's Church School in Comfort Hall until she
is sixteen and is reluctant to return to her mother's home in
Kingston.

I stayed on with my aunt Mabel. I was helping
her in the shop. My aunty couldn't read. My uncle
could and he did all the bookwork. Being there,
I was more a help to him. If people come in for
things without money, you would put their names
in the book and how much they owe. Things like
that was quite simple.

Helping in the shop, Ivy continues to live with her aunt for
another two years. Then at eighteen years old, she returns to
her mother's home in Kingston where she finds things have
changed dramatically.

My dad was married to another lady and he had
two other kids. When their mother died they
came to live with us—me and my mum. I didn't
know of my father's two other kids before they
came to live with my mother. They use to go to
his house to visit him. I never went.

I loved them because I was told they were
my brother and sister. I grew up as an only child

until they came into my life. We got on very well. Even now I still keep in touch with my brother in America, don't know where my sister is though. She was more wild like my mother and didn't want to be controlled, so she left early and got married.

My mum looked after other kids from other members of our family as well.

Though Ivy does not go to her father's house, he still visits her mother's home.

He use to come by.

I don't think my dad touched my sister because her temperament wasn't like me. She would fight for her life while I accept things the way they are.

Reflecting back, Ivy can only speculate on why her mother, Estell, broke up with her father, Jamsey, and why she was sent off to live with Aunt Mabel in Comfort Hall.

The worst part of that part of my life is that I think my mother knew what was happening to me and she did nothing about it. I think maybe that was the reason why she didn't want to marry him.

I didn't talk to anyone about it. The way I was made to understand it—the way my dad made me understand—was that it was a natural thing.

A year after she returns from Aunt Mabel's home in the country, Ivy's decision to put an end to her father's treatment of her comes from an unexpected quarter.

> I started going to church when I was nineteen. Well I didn't actually go to church at first, I was just at the window. We were always at the window watching them keeping the service. The windows were open and you could hear everything that's going on.
>
> One of the nights I went there, I didn't hear the preacher—I don't know what he preached. I just watch them. They were the 'Church of God' and I knew they're having an altar call. I didn't go there intending to go in the church or anything. I was just watching them.
>
> I don't know why but I answered the call to come in for prayer. I don't know how I got in there or the reason why I'm in there. Whatever was happening, I know I was crying. I don't know what I was crying for. I could remember somebody saying: "Don't cry—pray." Another person said: "Leave her alone, let her cry."
>
> That was it. Something had happened to me then that I couldn't really explain. I started going to church from then.

Aged 19, Ivy begins her new journey as a churchgoer.

> My parents didn't go to church and they didn't

send me to church. My grandmother lived in the country and they use to go to the Presbyterian Church—we all had to go. When I went to live with my mother in Kingston, they didn't go to church and they didn't send me to church. I didn't know anything about church. I use to read my Bible and that. I loved to read my Bible because it was nice stories in there. But it was just another story book, it didn't mean anything to me. I didn't know there was a God or anything until that night when something happen to me.

I was nineteen when I started reading the Bible again and that was how I knew that what my dad was doing to me wasn't right and I could get him arrested and locked up. That was the end of it because after that he couldn't come near me. I still didn't tell anybody. I couldn't talk about it then. I felt ashamed and unclean. I didn't belong or fit in anywhere.

At the church service there was a hymn: 'How willing he was to die in my stead that my unworthy soul should live.' I had never heard the song before but the night I heard that song it becomes a reality to me.

I got baptised and I felt washed clean.

Ivy's father, Jamsey, is aware of her sudden conversion to the church and before long other family members begin noticing it too.

I started going regularly and got baptized. I made friends. My mother didn't like it and she tried to stop me—sometimes dragging me out of meetings and taking me home. If we're on the street having a street meeting, she would come and grab my arm and pull me out of it. She wouldn't let go of me—going at ninety miles an hour—until she get home. I would only go out the next day— go back and back until eventually she gave up. I think she got tired and she realised that dragging me out each time isn't going to stop me going.

That strategy didn't work. Then she would wait for them in the mornings—Sunday mornings— when they come into church. She would throw water out there or sweep the dust on them and things like that. She called them 'Pokamania'— people who roll on the ground and wallow in dirt while in a trance worshipping. She must have seen that somewhere because these ones didn't really do them kind of things. They were nice decent people.

My mother was terrible. She could be terrible but that didn't stop them. They told me they loved her just the same because she doesn't really know what she's doing.

MELISSA

Melissa is living with her mother Pengal and her stepfather Martie Macdonald in Hampton near Montego Bay. It is 1960 and she is twelve years old. Shortly after her birth in 1948, her mother left the district to become a domestic servant in Kingston. Melissa is left with her grandparents, Doule and Jerome Williams. Pengal did not take to domestic service and her stay in Kingston is short—less than two years. She returns to her parents' home, meets and marries Martie Macdonald. The newly married Pengal and Martie then move into their own home when Melissa is three years old.

They later have two children, both girls. When Melissa is seven and going to primary school, Pengal insists that Melissa should leave her grandparents' home and come to live with her, her husband Martie and their two daughters. Melissa had not spent a great deal of time with her mother and does not know Martie Macdonald. Her sense of home and belonging is with her grandparents.

> If I stay one night at my mother's house, I don't stay two nights. The rest of the time I stay at my grandmother.
>
> They live maybe about three miles apart

from each other so I could walk—everybody walked. Three miles is nothing—nine, ten miles is nothing—because I use to walk about six miles from my home to my primary school.

Melissa's attachment to her grandparents' home is in part because she was sent to school nearby at an early age.

It was Sister Lloyd school or kindergarten. She was pastor of the church we went to. That is where we learned to read and write. She was a splendid woman. Every one of us in the district learn to read and spell our name from Sister Lloyd. We use to take our lunch in a lunch pan.

We had to go there from three and a half or four years old and she would keep us until we're about seven. All of us are in one big classroom. You want to go to toilet, she's got helpers who take you to toilet, bring you back, wash your hands and help you with lunch.

We had to walk to school at four, not on our own. Aunty Pearl—God rest her soul, she's now dead—would take us. That was kindergarten.

The most that I could remember is when I am coming home. How did I use to know that I'm coming home because I can't read the clock? We have a song that Sister Lloyd use to let us sing in the evening before we come home: 'Now the Day is Over.' When I hear this, I say: "Yeah! I'm going home." She was very caring to us.

Upon leaving Sister Lloyd's kindergarten, Melissa moves on to primary school. Her mother is working in a local shop at the time and her stepfather is working as an agricultural labourer.

> I think I was about seven when I first went to primary school. I was still with my grandmother and she send me to school. To me, as far as I'm concern in my head, I am still with her. Doule could read and she taught me to read books and the Bible when I was still at home.
>
> On Fridays now when we finish school, Doule and I use to go and buy all the things them that she was buying as usual. Then early Saturday morning—maybe three, four o'clock—we would get up, put our load on our heads and walk to the market in Montego Bay, nine miles away.

Melissa begins going to the same school as the other children of her father, Ferdie Bennett.

> They use to go to my primary school—Springfield School. They come from one side down there in Burnground to come up to Springfield school. I come from my side in Hampton to come to Springfield school. It's the main primary school for us.
>
> I use to walk with my cousins—Neil was the older one. He was going to that school so we all go together with him. When we finish Neil would bring us all back.

Melissa's time in primary school is filled with pleasant memories. There is one teacher in particular who leaves a lasting impression on her.

> I remember one teacher in particular at my primary school—Mrs Henry. She later became the Headmistress at that school. She's a brown skin lady. Hehhh—that woman is so tolerant. She marry a gentleman who was married before with four children. The first wife died and she married him—Mr Henry. He was a hygiene inspector. He would go round and inspect meat in shops to make sure that it's hygienically proper. Once he check the meat, he stamps it.
>
> Mrs Henry use to be the most fantastic teacher. We use to have two other teachers— Miss Floe and Miss Johnson—both also played piano. Every song that you hear on 'Praise On Sunday', they thaught us. Mrs Henry, she teaches the entire subjects—English, maths, Geography, General Knowledge—everything.

Melissa goes onto complete her schooling at Springfield Primary and it is now time for her to go to high school.

> When you pass your scholarship, the government gives you your education. Your school fees is not paid for by you—it's paid for by the government. You get your own books and you get your uniform. It's like comprehensive school here.

Melissa's mother Pengal eventually takes the view that it's time Melissa's father, Ferdie, starts financially contributing towards Melissa's education.

> My mother sent me to my father to say that I have passed the scholarship and I needed some money to buy books and my uniform. I stayed with him and his wife the weekend. While I was there his wife's niece, name Con, was there as well. She was one year older than me. I was twelve, Con was about thirteen.
>
> The Sunday evening, I came back. The evening when I was coming home, my father give me a letter to give to my mother.
>
> On my way walking home, I reached to a place where bamboo overhang the road and make it darkish. When I got there I wonder how much money he put in the envelope for me. I thought: 'Oooh, I'm going to open it.'
>
> I open it. There is no money in it.
>
> There is a letter and in it he says I am not his child and he is not going to mind any children that is not his.
>
> I burst out crying.

Melissa is twelve years old and this is the first time she learns that the man she regards as her father, the man who her mother insists is her father, does not think that he is her father.

> While I was walking, just about to go up the hill,

there was a policeman who everybody said was bad, name Humphrey. He's in his police uniform and everything.

He says: "Wah wrong with you? Wah that in yer hand? Yer nah frighten pickney?" Me say: "Yes." He say: "What's the matter?"

I show him the letter and he say: "Lord Jesus! Yer nah suppose to tell a pickney this man. Even if it's not fer you pickney and the pickney wah to go ah school—yer tak care ah the pickney school."

Ferdie's intention was of course not to have Melissa open the letter but Melissa's young curiosity got the better of her. Very upset, Melissa continues on her way home.

I gave my mother the letter and she was reading it. My mother name Loucella but nickname Pengal.

My mother's husband Macdonald says: "Pengal, me can't read. Me no going mak Melissa no able to read. Me no have the pickney with you but Melissa is my child. I took Melissa with you from she was three years old. You know something? She's never rude to me one day. She's like my own child."

At the time he was working on an Indian man's truck, loading it with cane.

The Friday evening, he got £5 as his salary. He came home and he said: "Pengal, here's the £5—take it. Go and buy Melissa's books and her uniform."

Shortly after, Melissa's stepfather leaves Jamaica for England. Melissa remains in her mother's home with her two younger sisters. Then in 1962, her stepfather sends for her mother. Melissa is fourteen years old and still in high school. Again, Pengal leaves Melissa and her sisters with Doule, their grandmother.

> When I left high school in Jamaica I have what they call Senior Cambridge. You had Senior Cambridge in A, B or C—just the same like 'O' Level's here. I was sixteen when I left high school.

Two years later, Pengal and Martie send for Melissa. The man across the road, who says he's her father, is concerned.

> When I was coming to England in 1964, £5 was a lot of money. Upert came and gave me £5. He said: "I don't know when I'll see you again or if I'll ever see you again but take this for your pocket."
>
> It was a lot and I thought: 'This man give me £5. He must have been rich.' He wasn't, it's what he had. He told his children—he has two girls and one boy—he said: "Melissa is my first child." Each time I go to Jamaica and go to visit them, they say: "Dad use to tell us, you're his first child."

Chapter Four

Then It's Who You Know

Chapter Four

Those Who You Know

IVY

Ninteen is a pivotal age for Ivy. She is back in Kingston living with her mother. This is the second time she is living with Estell. When she finally returns to her mother's home, there are two other children living there. Once they are introduced to her she learns they are her half-brother and half-sister from her father's side.

> My dad wasn't living with us but he still had authority.

This is also around the time she discovers the church, which helps her to find the strength to confront her father and refuse his advances.

Though her father is not living with Estell, her father is still, for practical purposes, head of the household. Once Ivy finishes senior school, it is her father who decides what is to happen to her next.

> My dad did ask me what I wanted to do and I told him I wanted to go to high school. I wanted to do shorthand and typing. I wanted to be a receptionist. I wanted to sit in an office and talk

to people. I took a scholarship for high school in Kingston because they thought I should go on and do some studies. I won the scholarship but then my dad said: "No! You can't go to high school, girls don't need education. They need to learn to make clothes." Strange how some things you don't forget. He told me: "You're too Black to be sitting in an office, so go and learn to do some machining."

Ivy begins to compare her father's treatment of her to that of her younger brother's.

He wanted my brother to go to college but my brother didn't want to go. He said he was not that minded.

My dad wanted my brother to be a carpenter like himself—a builder and contractor. But my brother didn't like that. When he got older he got a job driving buses as much as I can remember.

Reluctantly, Ivy accepts what her father decides for her.

I don't think my mother ever said anything about what she wanted for me. They decided for me to go and do machining. So I did.

Her father selects the person who he thinks should teach his daughter to sew.

My dad introduced me to her. I don't know how he found her but that's where he sent me. This was in Kingston.

She was a Chinese lady, a very nice lady. Mrs Chen we use to call her. She wasn't an old person but you didn't ask people their age then. She taught me to sew, not just make dresses, but any garment. I was like an apprentice learning the trade. I didn't get paid or anything.

I stayed with Mrs Chen for quite a few years. When I was able to master things, she use to go away to China and leave me in charge. When she came back, people's dresses would be done, ready to deliver. Those who would pay the money would be waiting for her.

Sometime later, when Ivy is about twenty-two or twenty-three years old, her relationship with her mother changes and Ivy develops the confidence to become more independent.

I moved out of my mother's home when I started getting paid for the work I was doing. I can't remember exactly how old I was.

Mrs Chen was encouraging me and I think she was the one who helped me to find a little place of my own in Franklyn Town in Kingston. It was just a room in a house with lots of other people living there.

Ivy remembers this period in her life as a time of change and recalls the impact it had on her family.

> By this time my mum had a little shop by the
> gate of her house. She was selling food: yams and
> bananas and things like that.
>
> By then my brother and sister had left home. I
> think my sister went to Old Harbour. She said she
> was going to look for her rainbow or whatever.
> My brother had a girlfriend. He left and started
> driving buses. My mother was left on her own
> because I wasn't there either.

Ivy's fraught relationship with her father goes on to impact
other areas of life.

> I didn't have any boyfriends then. I didn't like
> men because of my dad. I lived a lonely life.

When Ivy started getting paid, she decides that she wants to set
up on her own.

> I saved my money up and bought a sewing
> machine. I started sewing for people but I wasn't
> charging anybody for anything.
>
> I just sew and give it to them.

Ivy's approach means she is not making much money. So when
her friend, Jay, writes to her saying that she can make a great
deal more money in England doing the same thing, she does
not hesitate.

Ivy came to England in 1962. She told her mother and her father but no one else. No one came to see her off.

EVELYN

Evelyn is sixteen going seventeen when, Winifred, her mother, puts an end to her education at Georges Valley School. Evelyn's mother sends Evelyn to live with Aunt Mavis in Portland. Winifred gave birth to Evelyn when she was young and out of wedlock. She is therefore determined to ensure that the same fate does not befall her daughter.

It would not be an exaggeration to describe Evelyn as headstrong, or in her own words, 'stubborn'.

> I didn't look on Aunt Mavis as my aunty because she was young. We grew up like good friends. You could tell her anything and we would do things together. I wear her clothes, she wear mine. We wear each other's shoes—that's how we were. She was married and settled.

It may well be that her mother anticipated Evelyn's relationship with her sister, Mavis. Whatever the case, Winifred takes out a 'copper-bottom' insurance policy.

> Before I went, Pastor Jones was informed to keep a close eye on me.

Pastor Jones was previously a minister in Mandeville and a close friend of Winifred. Pastor Jones was sent to Port Antonio by his church. He knew exactly what Winifred meant when she asked him to 'keep a close eye' on her daughter. His approach was simple; as far as possible, keep her where you can see her.

> I use to have to go to church. I was confirmed so I had to go to communion six o'clock in the morning.
>
> I had to be in the choir and in the youth club. Whatever was going on at church, I had to be in it doing things. So quite naturally I was kept busy. It was more strict than when I was at home because of Pastor Jones.
>
> The funny thing is I never had a boyfriend in Portland.

Evelyn stays with Aunt Mavis in Port Antonio for about a year. Her horizons have already been expanded through meeting the Earls, a Canadian family living in Mandeville. Evelyn used to play with their son.

Whether or not it's the pastor's intention, Evelyn also comes into contact with what she regards as privileged circles in Port Antonio.

> I admit that because of my lifestyle and moving around in Jamaica, I met people of class.
>
> When I went to Portland from school, I was sort of mixing with Dr Ferguson and his son Earl. We were in a group with Dentist Harris, his

brother and sister. It was like all business people.

Then there was the Smarts, they were Jews. We were always in that group of people. You sort of not slip down and it keeps you going up.

It turns out that there were even more interesting people wandering around Port Antonio at the time.

That's where I met Errol Flynn, his dad, his mother and Patrice Wymore. I met all those people in Portland.

Errol Flynn had the island in Portland. His dad and his wife were living in Portland and they came to the same church as well. At Christmas we go to the hotel, sing carols and would be rewarded with things as young ones.

So you met people from you're small, growing up, which to me was a privilege.

Legend and the popular media had it that Hollywood's foremost 'Swashbuckler' made his first appearance in Jamaica true to character. Apparently his yacht 'Zaca' was forced to take refuge in Kingston during a storm sometime in 1946. He is said to have hopped on a motorbike to Port Antonio and immediately fell in love with the place, declaring it to be: "More beautiful than any woman I have ever known".

What is more certain is that after marrying Patrice Wymore in 1950, Errol Flynn and his wife spent a great deal of time in Port Antonio before he died in 1959. For a time, he owned the idyllic Navy Island where he was planning to develop an up-market tourist resort. This did not come to pass, but the island did serve as a private retreat: a harbour to moor his yacht and entertain his Hollywood friends. The movie star also bought other properties in and around Port Antonio, most notably the Titchfield Hotel, said to be one of the grandest in Jamaica at the time. He also bought a Cattle Ranch on the edge of the port where Patrice Wymore lived until she died in 2014. Almost certainly the Titchfield would have been one of the hotels visited by Pastor Jones and his church choir at Christmas.

Sending Evelyn to Port Antonio in order to get her away from Calvin did not mean that Winifred wanted her daughter's education to come to an end.

> It was intended that I should continue at school or learn a trade or something.
>
> My mum want me to be a stenographer or a teacher. She's picking what she wanted for herself and never had. To me, I'm just going to be wasting my time because I'm not going to do it. I don't want it. I don't like it.

Evelyn made a decision to not do what her mother wanted and to this day, she feels she made the right decision.

> All my family in our age group, they had to do exactly what their parents said. They didn't want to do it. I was one who wouldn't do it. Cynthia, my first cousin, was a stenographer and Patsy went into teaching. A lot of parents do that and their children actually go along with it and then

they leave it completely afterwards. So you've wasted those years as my cousin's did. Patsy don't teach. She did for a little while then gave it up. Cynthia did shorthand and everything. She work in an office for a while, then she gave it up. Later on she had her own business and even in her own business she don't do those things because she hated it. She did it because her parents said you must do it.

So how are you going to tell me I must do what you love. I'm the one who will have to live with it.

Having told her mother that she does not want to teach or become a typist, they eventually settle on Evelyn enrolling at the local college to do a course in Domestic Science. Winifred is reasonably happy with their decision; Evelyn, however knows she does not want to do this course.

I went to the college for a month then it fell apart. I did not like it because I had to clean the floors. I had to do everything.

Things fell apart when the Governor of Jamaica came to visit the college and Evelyn was informed that she would not be amongst the students chosen to meet him. That combined with the fact that the course was not what she expected, Evelyn decided to walk out.

My mum was fuming. To me, if I make my mind

up that I was not doing a thing, I'm not going to
do it.

Before leaving Georges Valley School, Evelyn had a clear sight
on her next goal.

> I had a friend who was a hairdresser in Mandeville.
> She was right down by the Manchester Hotel. I
> use to go there. Sometimes I use to go as a model
> and I just love it. It was artistic, it was creative and
> I wanted to do it. I wanted what I wanted and I
> was very stubborn. Even now I'm very stubborn.

A confrontation occurs between Eveyln and her mother
following Evelyn's walkout. Evelyn comes clean and tells her
mother of the career path she wants to pursue. She wants to be
a hairdresser.

> My mum said: "Over my dead body. You're not
> going to do it. No! You're going to get TB."
> I said: "My friend has been doing it and she
> hasn't got TB. That's what I want to do." My
> mum said: "I will not spend my money for you to
> do it." I says: "Fine! I'm not doing it."

For a brief period, Evelyn considers her options.

> I thought about nursing because I'm a very caring
> person and when I came here I went to work in
> a hospital.

> In Jamaica it wasn't easy to get into nursing. In
> the Caribbean, it's who you know. It's always who
> you know. Whether you're good at something or
> not, it's who you know.

Evelyn decides that there's no future for her in Port Antonio
with Aunt Mavis, or Pastor Jones for that matter. She goes to
live in Catherin Street, Kingston at a house owned by her mother's father who is still in Panama at the time.

> My aunty Lillian was living there and my
> great-grandmother, Miss Ester, was living there as
> well. So we were all there together.

Evelyn is now eighteen going nineteen and there's no way she's
going back to her mother in Mandeville. Moving to Kingston
gets her away from the control of her mother and Pastor Jones.
She has no idea how this move will help her achieve what she
wants to do.

During her time at Catherin Street, it is not Aunt Lillian
but her great-grandmother, Miss Ester, who makes a lasting
impression on her.

> I had spent time with her when I was younger.
> Miss Ester is white and she's a Jew. She was pretty
> good at making things. She make things for the
> stores: ornaments and broaches. She would even
> use fish scales, dye it and cut it into shapes. Even
> foul wishbone, she would paint it and use velvet
> to make leaves. She was very artistic but she only

wore black. I had so much black clothes when I came to England, sometimes I don't want to put it on. It's like you don't change your clothes. I've never seen her wore any other colour than black and I seem to inherit it.

Throughout the time of her stay with Aunt Lillian and Miss Ester, Evelyn ends up accidentally learning a new skill.

A neighbour use to make baby clothes. Miss Ester does a lot of hand embroidery and at school you were taught how to do hand embroidery and sewing. I could do embroidery.

The lady next door says to me: "You're not doing much, so will you do embroidery on the necks of the children's clothes for me?" So I use to do it.

I was there in Kingston for about two years. I didn't do a lot, I did not do a lot.

After leaving Aunt Mavis in Port Antonio, it will be a year before Evelyn goes back to Mandeville to visit her family.

I went back home to mother. I didn't enjoy staying, I just wanted to be on the move. When I went back I was nineteen, not far off my twentieth birthday.

I went on the Friday and on the Saturday afternoon I was sitting outside underneath an orange tree knitting a jumper.

I heard this motorbike coming up towards the house. This bloke came off the motorbike and stood in front of me, just looking at me. He never said anything. Then he went away.

I thought: 'This is funny!' So I asked my mom: "Who is he?" My mom said: "His name is Reggie Wallace and he has a shop out at the crossroads."

Reggie's shop is in the Broadleaf district, about a mile from the one her mother is now running.

It is curious that Reggie turns up at Winifred's home in Mandeville when Evelyn happens to be there on her first visit in over a year. It is even more curious that when he arrives, looks at her, says nothing, then gets on his motorbike and rides off.

It was through my stepfather why he met me. He and my stepfather was very close, they drank together.

Anyway, he came back another day and he says: "I like you and your stepfather said to me that if I want a wife, you will make me a good wife."

I didn't stay long with my mother. I left on the Wednesday and went back to Kingston.

Evelyn knows barely anything about Reggie and does not respond to what he has to say about her making a 'good wife'. Evelyn's nonchalance towards him does not bother him, he likes her and is not going to give up easily. He later follows her back to Kingston.

On the morning—eight o'clock—he was there. Came in on the early train.

He said he wanted us to be friends. I said, "Well I'm in Kingston now and I ain't coming down to live in the country." I had left there and I didn't really want to go back to stay.

I thought I'd had a chance to widen my horizon and I didn't want to go back to the same situation. It wasn't a bad situation but I was the one who just want to be out on my own, not with the family as such. Not that I hated them or anything. As I said before, I was more of a loner. I loved to be by myself and do things without others criticising me, calling me names or making me cry. I didn't like it.

Though she still knows little about him, she is interested, and tells Reggie that she will come back to Mandeville to visit.

I went back down on the following week. I was there for a few days just moving round. I'll go to the shop, he would come round. We talked and things like that.

Whilst she's there, she's also asking around about Reggie and is told something that totally changes her view of him.

I found out that he had two children. I thought: 'No! This isn't for me.' He didn't tell me he had two children, but around the area people talk. He had two children and he wasn't caring for them.

I said to him: "I don't think it would be wise. You have two children with two different women and you'll do the same to me." He said: "No I won't! I won't."

I went back to Kingston.

Reggie does not give up.

He use to have to come to Kingston to buy groceries and things so we'd sort of meet up. It took about six months or more for us to sort of get together.

Evelyn remains uncertain about Reggie. Besides the two children he did not tell her about, there are other issues.

I didn't like the situation. The business he was in wasn't his. It was his sister's and her husband. He was just doing it without pay or anything.

Well I thought if that's what you're doing, it wouldn't make any sense. He says: "Well, I'll give it up! I'll give it up because I don't want to lose you."

That cause friction between his sister and himself. Then they seem to dislike me because I'm causing trouble. But he was persistent.

Between Evelyn's visits to Mandeville and Reggie visits to Kingston over the next two years, Reggie and Evelyn's relationship continues.

At the age of twenty-three, Evelyn decides that her future lies in England. She presents Reggie with an ultimatum that will determine their future: either come with me or lose me. They agree to go to England together. Winifred does not approve of her daughter going to England and she certainly does not approve of Reggie. His family take a similar view but it makes no difference—the couple have made their decision.

On the morning of the 3rd October, 1955, Evelyn and Reggie board the TV Santa Maria.

Chapter 5

England, It's Not What I Thought

EVELYN

Evelyn is the first of the Five women in this book to set foot in England. She arrives on the 14th October, 1955 as a twenty-three-year-old traveling with Reggie—the man she hopes to marry. Both of their families do not approve of their move to England. They travel on the boat that was advertised as providing luxurious accommodation, excellent service and food. Upon leaving Kingston the ship takes them to Havana in Cuba, Tenerife in the Canary Islands, Funchal in Portugal, landing at Vigo in Spain where they complete the remainder of their journey by train and ferry.

At the time, the Santa Maria is one of a great many cruise liners taking European tourists to the Caribbean and South America on the outward journey. This cruise fills empty berths with West Indian passengers travelling to England on the way back. Both groups of passengers are often segregated aboard ship. Whether by luxury cruise liner or not, the standard fare by ship is £75.

Upon her arrival in London, the first thing Evelyn notices the next morning is the cold. It's only October but it's cold she's never experienced before. She can make no sense of her surroundings. Circumstances at the house they now live in only adds to her sense of disorientation. Evelyn is convinced she has made a terrible mistake and cries for days.

> It was a massive house on the corner of Gloucester Street, Langley. It was owned by Reggie's cousin and her husband.
>
> There was only three other houses we knew of in the area that was owned by Black families. One was the Duncan's in Langley, the Ferguson's in West Bromwich on the High Street and the Woolsworth's in Handsworth. Every Black person head for these houses because you couldn't get any accommodation from government.
>
> So you were piled in. They put in single beds—two, three or four in one room. There were about twenty or more people in the house.
>
> They use to charge like twenty-five shillings per week, per person. Then you have to give another three shillings for gas and you have to drop [put money in the meter] for your water to have a bath. Sometimes you would be told the gas is finished. You would give them money on a Friday and then on Monday you would be told the gas was finish.

Evelyn struggled with many things living in England and was deeply troubled by it all.

> You would have so many people cooking on a four burner [stove]. You would put a six pence in to cook your dinner, then when you would go

upstairs to do something, somebody take it and start cooking.

It was hard. It was very, very hard. I cried and cried.

The Asians, they're the ones who use to give Black people a room. I see people now sticking up their face against the Asians who gave them somewhere to live. They gave them credit to buy clothes. The Asians lost a lot of money because our people didn't pay them. Then I see our people them skinning their face up and carrying on. We could have got on as good as the Asians. We spoke English, they didn't. So you can't blame them. They see an opportunity and they grab it. It was there for everyone; it doesn't fall in your lap. You have to go out and get it and you have to work hard to get it. If you're not prepared to do those things, don't expect to make good. It's not going to happen.

Thinking back to her life in Jamaica, Evelyn felt she had just come down in the world, not up.

***

With the chronic shortage of manpower in the immediate postwar period, the Attlee Labour government of 1945-1951 was drawn to actively recruiting workers from British Colonies. The need is illustrated by the terms of a government Inter-Departmental Working Party established in 1948:

"Inquire into the possibilities of employing in the UK surplus manpower of certain colonial territories in order to assist the manpower situation in this country and to relieve unemployment in those colonial territories."

Whilst, at the time, the Attlee government was seeking to address labour shortages at home, the Inter-Departmental Working Party forsaw a problem. They drew attention to the potential impact of unrestrained inward immigration from certain colonial countries, noting the possibility of 'an inassimilable minority'. As a result, they recommended that ministers consider the introduction of controls that would limit immigration and the right to settle in the UK under the British Nationality Act 1948. Throughout the 1950's, behind the scenes, the government is struggling with the issue of restricting immigration and the right of Commonwealth citizens from the West Indies, India and other non-white British Colonies to settle permanently in the UK.

In the end however, it was the urgent need to address postwar labour shortages that prevailed and no definitive immigration controls were enforced until the Commonwealth Immigration Act 1962.

So, from as early as 1948, individual government departments began advertising job opportunities in Caribbean newspapers.

By 1949, the Ministry of Health, the Ministry of Labour, the Colonial Office, the Royal College of Nursing and the General Nursing Council have all launched campaigns to recruit staff directly from Caribbean islands. Staff members from the Ministry of Health even travel to the West Indies to promote recruitment. London Transport later set up a recruitment office in Bridgetown, Barbados where they regularly recruit Barbadians.

The desire to recruit labour from the colonies was not restricted to the public Sector. For example, in 1951 an article in the Manchester Guardian—picked up by the Daily Gleaner on 6th April, 1951—reports the views of a Mr R L Greenwood, Chairman of Craven Brothers, a large Engineering Firm in Lancashire.

There are literally thousands of vacancies in foundry and furnace work that could be filled satisfactorily by Jamaican workers of unskilled and semi-skilled qualifications with good prospects of their being able to rise to the category and pay of skilled workers.

Despite the concerns of the 1948 Inter-Departmental Working Party, legislation to control immigration is not introduced until 1962. Following this, it is only in 1965 that anti-discrimination legislation is introduced to prevent the creation of 'an inassimilable minority'.

In the meantime, both national and local government are doing very little to assist incoming immigrants from the Caribbean and other British Colonies. As Evelyn observes, "they had to find their own way."

For accommodation, migrants are largely dependent on a few of their countrymen who came before them. It is important to remember that this is the 1950's and early 1960's when advertisements for accommodation regularly stipulated 'No Blacks, No Irish and No Dogs'. The result of this hostile environment is the early residential concentration of Caribbean, Indian and Pakistani communities in the inner cities.

After their arrival Evelyn and Reggie move in with one of Reggie's cousins in her house on Gloucester Street. Reggie's cousin takes advantage of their need for accommodation charging them twenty-five shillings per week, per person for a single room. This would be the equivalent of over £40 today. In addition to this cost, they also have to pay for gas and electricity. To further complicate matters, Evelyn is not getting on with some of the other tenants living in the house.

> It was only two of us women. Most of them were men and they can be ruthless.
>
> They tried to touch you up—they had no women. So you've got to be very careful and very vigilant. You've got to be sharp to keep them away.

Reggie's cousin and her husband own the property Evelyn and Reggie are staying in. So excluding Evelyn, Reggie's cousin is the only other woman in the house. Oddly she takes it upon herself to report suspicions she has of Evelyn to Reggie.

> Even in the kitchen and one of the men talk to you, as soon as Reggie come from work, she would say: "Evelyn was talking to that man."
>
> She was nasty, she was nasty. I'm not joking, she was nasty. So quite naturally I had to be ruthless. Well I speak my mind and I just tell them what I think about everybody who interferes with me.

Evelyn does the best she can to treat Reggie's cousin with respect, helping her in any way she can. Yet despite this, Reggie's cousin remains committed to reporting Evelyn to Reggie. Evelyn struggles to understand why Reggie's cousin is behaving in this way.

> She had two children. I use to help her with her
> two children and comb their hair and everything.
> If she was sick, I would cook and give the children
> and her husband meals. If I was sick, she would
> never even heat a cup of water and give me.

Reggie found employment in a factory almost immediately. New migrants from the Caribbean had little difficulty in finding jobs. Evelyn however was up against a major challenge—her desire to be a hairdresser was not a career path that was easy to attain as a Black woman. The task of 'doing hair' for Black women at the time, was primarily domesticated. Most Black women did each other's hair within the house. This would be the norm in Jamaica—especially in rural areas.

> When I came, I went to Simplex. It was a factory
> in Oldbury. I remembered when I went there, the
> personnel officer looked at me and he says: "I'm
> sorry! I can't give you a job because you won't
> be able to do it." I was just tiny and so feeble
> looking. He says: "You can't do it."
>
> I was so sad, I turned away. Walking away,
> he looked at me and said: "Come here. I'll try
> and see if I can find something for you, but you
> can't do the factory work. I'll try and find you

something in the office." He did.

When I went in, I had to parcel up and post the door plates they did for solicitor's and doctor's offices.

At the time, an office job like the job Evelyn managed to get would have been exceptional for a Caribbean migrant in 1955, particularly when considering that Evelyn did not have any office skills or qualifications. Despite this, she is unhappy with her job.

Simplex made screws and brass plates. I never went into the big factory where they do the smelting of different iron and things. I hadn't done that sort of work or anything. It's hard to break into it.

Yes, I was working in an office. I didn't like the factory; I didn't like it at all because I've never done it. I didn't want it. It wasn't what I wanted and I knew I didn't want it.

Back at their room in Gloucester Street the situation is not improving and Evelyn wonders what, if anything, can be done to change this.

There was this lady and her husband, they were on Causeway Communal Road. I met her husband Mr Charlton when I went to Simplex.

He come up to me one day and he says: "You look so unhappy." I says: "Well the truth is I'm not happy and I'm a bit sad that I did come to

England because it's not what I thought it was. I would love to go back but I told my parents I won't come back. I'll fight—I'll do it. If I went back, I am going to be told 'I told you so' and I can't let them win."

He said: "Well OK. If you're that unhappy, what's wrong?" I just tell him about the situation at the house and the attitude of the woman. She had never worked and she was a nasty piece of work.

When I hear people say that whites had been nasty to them, I think our colour was worse. Our people were worse than the whites, believe me. Their behaviour and their treatment was bad, very bad.

He said: "Leave it with me. I will have a word with my wife when I get home." He came back the following day and he said: "I spoke with my wife and if you don't mind living with us, you and Reggie, both of you can come and live at our house. We'll board you."

I went home and tell Reg, but because his brother was living there and it's his cousin house, he wouldn't leave. So I told another bloke who was living there and two of them went to live with the Charltons.

When I was feeling very down, I used to go and sit at the Charlton's house.

Evelyn decides to leave her job at Simplex after just six months.

In May 1956, she gets a job as a nursing auxiliary at Edward Street District Hospital. She had briefly considered nursing while living in Port Antonio but couldn't get access to training because she didn't know the right people. In any event, it wasn't what she wanted to do, then or now. Reggie also leaves his first job around this time to become a bus conductor.

It's nearly a year since Evelyn and Reggie arrived in Birmingham, leaving against the advice of their loved ones. They then decide it's time to do what they have always wanted to do.

> We married not long after we came over. We got married on the 26th September 1956. That was another situation.

Evelyn refers to her marriage as 'another situation' because Reggie's relatives in Gloucester Street did not approve.

> When they realise that we were going to get married—she, her husband, his brother, and I think two others, took him in a room and tell him: "Are you going marry a woman like that? You should get a basin of water and wash your hand from a woman like that."
>
> She [Reggie's cousin] is the one who told me what they said because they weren't expecting it to last.

Evelyn never went into what she thought Reggie's family in Gloucester Street meant by 'a woman like that'.

Reggie's family make it a point to not help Evelyn or Reggie with their marriage arrangements. True to her character, Evelyn does her best to ignore the difficult environment created by Reggie's family.

> That was a very hard situation because you had nowhere to keep your marriage reception or anything. I had to keep it where I live, in the front room.
>
> You had no one to sort of help you. You have to do everything yourself. I remembered I went to the church—it was the Elm Church round the corner—to ask them if they would marry us. I started going round because you had to visit the church for them to do it.

Interestingly, Evelyn receives wedding help from an unexpected couple.

> I remembered this couple. They lived in Smethwick and their name was Leison. They were always friendly with us.
>
> They had suffered a lot because people call them 'Nigger Lovers' and all sorts. They were white. Mrs Leison said to me: "Evelyn, I will help you to do your wedding."
>
> She did.

Evelyn is then met with another problem. There are twenty people living in the house that Evelyn will be having her wedding reception at. All the residents are Jamaicans.

Unfortunately for Evelyn, the bane of wedding planning did not end there. The lack of help she received from Reggie's family causes, another obstacle for Evelyn.

I couldn't find anybody to give me away. Nobody would. They didn't like me.

Luckily for Evelyn, her distress is eased by Mrs Leison who gave Evelyn her word that she and her husband can help.

Her husband said to me: "Evelyn, I don't mind being your dad for a day."

So I went up the aisle on a white man's arm. He gave me away.

Those people I had respect and a love for right up until they died. The husband died first. Then the wife wasn't very well and I made sure she was OK, right up until her death. You do not forget people who have been kind to you.

As fate would have it, Evelyn was first introduced to the Leisons by Reggie's cousin at Gloucester Street, the woman who hated her.

EMMA

Travelling by air, Emma, age eight, and her younger sister Emily, age seven, are reunited with their parents—John and Millie Robinson—on 14th June, 1959. Their parents are living in West Bromwich. John came to England in 1952 and sent for their mother a year later.

Emma's memories of those first years in England are from the point of view of an eight-year-old child. One of the first things she learns upon her arrival is that life at home in West Bromwich with her mother and father is not going to be all that different from the one she had just left with her grandparents in Portland, Jamaica.

When I came to England, I can remember that very week Dad say: "Millie, mak dem start learn fe wash."

Mum would show us but that was a directive that came from my dad. Mum bought us two little wash pans—zinc bowls—one each. Our tasks was to wash the pillowcases, wash his shirts. Pillowcases first, then it developed to his shirts. This is by hand, we were taught the traditional way. She taught us to draw the starch—Robin

starch—to starch the clothes, wring it out and
hang them out. When it dry, damp it and put to
one side for ironing.

In Jamaica Emma's grandmother insisted that girls had to learn
to wash clothes.

Emma and Emily arrived in West Bromwich on a Sunday.
The following Monday morning they are both enrolled in
school.

My parents had some lovely neighbours, a Black
family that lived at number 13 Dartmouth Street
and a white family that lived across the way whose
daughter was in the same junior school. Mum had
already informed them.

Mum took us to the school on the Monday and
on the Tuesday the neighbour's daughter across
the way accompanied us. So we got company
straight away until we got familiar with the area.

Likely due to Emma's private schooling back in Jamaica, she
adapts rather well to her new school as does her sister.

I settled in well and from what I understood my
sister actually settled in very well.

When I came here and went to school, I was
ahead. I came at eight and a half into junior
school. My sister started in the infants because
she was younger than me. Now there are certain
words written the same in Jamaica that I had

to learn. I love the English language and I love English literature. I felt I had a good understanding of the English language and I found it quite easy because of that.

What we discovered, we both had spoken very good English when we came to England. For me, in particular—because of the teachers I had around me—I spoke very good English.

On her first day at school there are only two other Black children. Before long others arrive.

I can remember it as if it was yesterday. There was about six or seven of us in the infant's and junior school: my sister, Camille, Larkin, Stephen and the Henrys' children Joe and Alfonso. Joe was the oldest of the Henry's children. He came from Jamaica afterwards.

Emma attends this school until 1962 when she is eleven years old. Odd as it might seem, coming from the 'Colonies', she sees herself as academically advanced in comparison to her English peers at the time. She is not wrong. Up to the age of eleven or twelve, many children coming from the West Indies were in fact ahead on basic subjects. She is especially proud of her command of the English language. Nevertheless, for reasons she does not wholly understand, she is constantly being corrected by her teachers.

It was more a question of how did you know that?

Who told you that was the understanding of a particular word?

This was a challenge I had from a couple of teachers. Funnily enough, it was this person named Evans in junior school and it was also the Deputy Headmistress in senior school also called Evans.

Nor is this her only problem while attending early school.

Racism as it's known today didn't particularly exist. I wouldn't say it existed amongst us as children.

Well maybe it did because there was questions that they asked us. I look back and I think perhaps they were just curious or is it the parents ask them to say that to us: "Have you got a tail?" To me it didn't come over as being that 'word'. But in spite of that we had to sort of learn to deal with it.

My way of dealing with it was being the best I could possibly be at everything. So I was good at sports. I was good in the classroom. It amazed them, particularly in General Knowledge. My let down was History, that wasn't anybody's fault. I grew to embrace Geography more because the Geography was about England, most of it. But I wasn't taught History as a little girl in Jamaica, so I had to be working on that. I was above average in my stream in Geography but I was at the top of the class in English Language and English Literature.

166

In April 1962 the family moves house from Dartmouth Street to Beeches Road. Though it is less than a decade since people from the West Indies began to arrive in significant numbers, some are already moving out of their initial areas of settlement. Emma's memory of this period helps to shed light on the role of family and village ties in influencing early settlement patterns in England.

> In those days—if you came from a particular area in Jamaica—when folks sent for their family members, they sort of settled in that street and in that particular area.
>
> Our community were mainly from the same place in Jamaica. I know the people from Clarendon, those from St. Andrew's and St. Elizabeth. In our community everybody come together and over a period of time you know who's related to who and which area they came from in Jamaica.
>
> We were now moving from that area in West Bromwich, where most of the people were from the area in Jamaica where my dad was from, to a bit further away. We moved from the lower end of town to the top end of town in West Bromwich.

In many respects the two homes are not all that different.

> Both houses were big. In those days rooms were rented out. In some houses every room was rented except the kitchen. Mom and dad always had a

dining room that everybody use. They rented out rooms in the house at Beeches Road. It was a big family home and they'd run a business from there before we bought the house. It's now a care home because of the size.

It was a five-bedroom house, three storeys with three reception rooms and you got your own front porch. It was one of the smaller ones on that street, some were double fronted.

We had a dining room, a front sitting room, a back sitting room which led onto a patio with big French doors. There was a kitchen and a utility room—which was where the dog stayed, a down-stairs toilet and then the coal shed. The garage was at the bottom of the garden that looked like a bungalow.

It was bought for less than £3,000. It was a lovely home. Upstairs three bedrooms and a good size bathroom on the first floor. In the attic was a massive room plus a room that could be a dressing room and another small room which my cousin lived in for a period.

Early migrants from the West Indies buying houses with an eye to rent out rooms to family and other new arrivals was fairly common. Well into the 1960's it was still 'No Blacks, No Irish and No Dogs'!

Uncle Raynard, my mom's brother, occupied the attic. He got married about 1965 while he was in that house. The reception was kept at the house. My uncle Raynard, he stowed away to come to England. He just turned up on the door step at our first house. He got the address from correspondence. Of course, they took him in. I believe the name he used was George—my other uncle. If he'd used George's ID, he might have got it changed. I really don't know and it's not my business. That's another story and Uncle George is dead now. I never found out why he stowed away. He'd been devious all his life.

Miss Harris and Miss Simpson was living in the backroom downstairs, there was more than enough space. We'd got a front room that was always available to anybody and we'd got a dining room.

I had the small bedroom to the front of the house next to mum and dad. My sister was in the box room on the top level.

Mr and Mrs Stennett was in the back bedroom which in them days was called a nursing or mother's room because it had a wash basin. Mrs Stennett worked at a nearby maternity home.

In junior school Emma continues to excel academically particularly in English Language, Literature and at Geography. Emma sits her eleven plus exams and expects to pass.

I felt I was ready to take it even when I came to England. However, we had to do this Math thing.

I didn't believe I failed it. The standard that I'd been taught to in Jamaica, when I started senior school in England, I'd already done it. Yet I failed my eleven plus. That didn't quite make sense.

I realise now that it wasn't a matter of failing. It's just there were certain schools that you—as a Black person—would be allowed to go into. There was only one Black person which I discovered had been to the local grammar school. He'd been adopted, I think by some white people. His name was Stanley. He wasn't somebody we saw around town much but he'd actually gone to the grammar school.

With Emma's family moving to Beeches Road, Emma can not go to the same secondary school as her friends Camille, Larkin, Stephen, Joe and Alfonso. They went to George Salter Secondary Modern. She goes to Spon Lane.

So my secondary school existence was lacking those people. We'd only meet when we were at sports days, or in town, or socially.

When I started there was only two of us Black children in the school. Apart from myself there was an Indian girl name Barbara Singh. She was very thin.

It is around this time that Emma begins to notice little differences between her parents on how they wish her and her sister to be brought up.

I had nearly started senior school. When we moved from Dartmouth Street they had the Guides and Brownies, Cubs and cadets at Beeches Road Methodist Church. My sister was really keen so Mum took us down and signed us up, got our uniforms and everything, not saying anything to Dad. She did it behind his back. Although it was a weekly thing, we only went every other week when Dad was on his two-till-ten shift. I think we went along for maybe twelve months.

Dad found out and all hell broke loose. They had this big argument. That wasn't our part, that was between them.

He said: "No! It just can't happen. Not in this house." Why? He's a Jehovah's Witness. Mum thought: 'Well maybe if he see us with our uniforms on he might change his mind.' He says: "No! That's not worshipping God. That's worshipping man." Mum says: "What? You expect them to live in a prison! They're children."

But when my dad said 'No', there was no room for discussion.

Emma's mother, Millie, is not a Jehovah's Witness. She was brought up as an Anglican but did not become a churchgoer until fairly late in her life. Nevertheless, she makes a point of supporting a great many of her husband's religious activities.

She didn't attend the meetings but if there was a Convention going on, whether it was on a national or local level, she would accompany him. People would see us as a family unit supporting Dad.

There wasn't a Jehovah's Witness Convention that he was going to that she didn't support in doing something behind the scenes.

At the same time Millie is building her own relationships within the local Jamaican and wider African Caribbean community around her.

My mom was one of the first people in the area that did cake baking. She taught a lot of other people and because of that we got invited to many things: social events, weddings, christenings. We were even bridesmaids at weddings even though we weren't related to the family.

So there was that side that I was a part of and enjoyed. But I need to say, with most of these weddings and christenings, my dad rarely attended.

Emma's dad is not interested in events at other churches. He does not prevent his wife from attending but he is determined that his children are to be brought up within this religion.

The other part now would be when we were with Dad. It was basically centreed around the Jehovah Witness ethos and having a different set of friends or colleagues.

Though Emma's father is strict in his faith, he is also practical and ensures that his children are incentivised to enjoy attending services at the local Jehovah Witness temple.

> When we would go to church, he would make sure that we felt happy. We could have bought a whole shop full of sweets before going to church. This was a compromise, a sweetener as we would probably use the term. I loved the original Blue Bird's toffee and Dad would allow me to buy a pound in weight to sit and just eat through church.

Beginning with their early separation in Jamaica, tensions between the two sisters have not exactly gone away. Now, for different reasons, their parents begin to take sides.

> I don't know whether my dad actually noticed—he probably did—but I became his favourite.
>
> I already had that heritage of having books around me all the time and Dad enjoyed doing that as well. He would quiz us when we got home from school as to what we'd learnt. Mom wouldn't, but he took that as a role. He wasn't paying out for our education but he took an interest in our school life. So I learnt to tell Dad exactly what we were taught, and he was happy with it.
>
> Anyway, later I found out that my mum and my grandmother they didn't get on at all when she was younger. They just didn't get on. As I was

growing up, it was like Mum had got that pattern of behaviour that she had with her mum. It was creeping into the relationship that I had with her. Maybe she didn't even realise it, but it was a different relationship she had with my sister.

Emma did not elaborate on why her mother and grandmother did not get on. However, she has a ready explanation of why she and her sister, Emily, are treated differently—particularly by her mother.

We went to this wedding one Saturday. On the Sunday the two of them would be having this discussion like two grown-ups. I'm not condemning or anything, it was just natural. That was the way things had been between her and Aunty Isobel. She developed that behaviour then and it was still allowed.

I would like disappear from the room if we had visitors because that was how I was brought up by Grandma. But Emily would sit there, cocking her ears and listening. If anybody mess with anything it would be my sister—she's fast. That's the way she was. I never did that.

Dad knew it and he tried to do something about it. Then they would have this big argument. Dad had me on his side and Mum had Emily on her side.

The funny part about it is that Emily is 'red' like me dad and I'm dark like me mum.

It is 1962 and Emma has just transferred from primary school to Spon Lane Mixed Secondary Modern, which is in the catchment area of their new home at Beeches Road.

> I did begin with hardly anyone there that I knew.
> This new beginning with people who I had never
> met before, now I would use the word challenging.
>
> It wasn't a large school. It wasn't hard to get
> around compared to what schools are today. The
> classrooms were smaller—in particular the fifth
> form. I would say on average the classroom size
> in my day was probably twenty-five, twenty-six,
> maximum. We weren't talking about a school of
> three or four hundred people.

Though she is proud of her earlier grounding in English, she soon discovers that more will be needed if she is to get on with the majority of pupils around her.

> Before long I developed a Black Country accent.
> This was more in senior school than primary.

There are only two Black children at her secondary school when she arrives. Fortunately for her it is not long before this changes and she forms a number of new friendships.

> The group of girls that I went around with at
> senior school, there were eight of us later on.
> All were from Jamaica except two—Alberta and
> Teresa—they were from Trinidad. By the time I

left there were loads more. There were children coming into the school who were actually born in England.

Out of all that, I still have contact with at least five of them after all these years. We all lived in close proximity to each other. Even when we meet up now, it's like we've never been apart.

Of all the teachers at her secondary school, Emma remembers one in particular. It's her English teacher whom she does not like.

Miss Roberts was also the Deputy Head and she was very, very, strict. She was this very tough teacher that taught me English Language for so many years. She use to enjoy giving us the 'ruler'. She drummed it into us.

Later, however a single encounter transforms her view of her 'dreaded' Deputy Head teacher.

The other side of Miss Roberts I saw was when she had to deputise one evening on the Home Economics section.

We had to prepare a meal for two—you and a guest. Nobody gave you the ingredients or anything. You had to do it yourself from start to finish, lay it out and present it. She was like flabbergasted at my ability to do it with very little support or prompting from her.

We had to be able to use our own initiative.
She turned out to be this extraordinary person
that gave me such a good salutation. She wrote
that I had a flair for entertaining.

During primary school Emma develops a habit of telling her
father what she learnt at school each day, which she notices he
enjoys very much. As she goes through secondary school, her
daily accounts to her father become a little more circumspect.

I wouldn't tell him what we would get up to. At
lunch time in senior school you had to stay to
dinners in your first and second year. After that
you had a choice.

You could go and buy something from the
local shop and still sit in the canteen and have
your dinner in a separate area. Because we were
older we would leave the school grounds and
go up to the park. We'd never get back late or
anything like that.

But there was this part of our life which Dad
might have guessed. Boys would be there but we
were all just peers—we weren't doing anything. I
never, ever told him because he was so strict.

Before long, Emma's selectiveness when it comes to communicating with her father about her day to day experience starts to
result in significant consequences.

School and home in my teenage years were two

totally different lives actually. I was this individual
that was living one life within the home and one
life in school.

Going back to their earlier experience of joining the Guides and
Brownies, Emma and Emily are not the only ones in the family
not telling dad what's going on.

My sister and I had this external life. We couldn't
go out without each other. We would go to our
local youth club, which was at the Holy Trinity
junior school in their Church Hall. This wasn't
too far from where we lived. Everything was fairly
close because we would have to pass Holy Trinity
Church School Hall to get to Spon Lane School.
The youth club was done from a Christian
perspective, you know, doing something for the
community.

That was another thing. We could only go
to the youth club when Dad was on afternoons.
I don't know whether he ever found about that
because Mom allowed us to go when he wasn't
there.

By 1966 Emma is fifteen years old and in her fourth year at
secondary school. She is beginning to think about her future
career and the reasons behind her initial choice are not straightforward. In large part, this is to do with her dad and the religious control he has over the family.

I thought to myself I'm going to find a way around this. In my own mind I was plotting. I need to break through from this.

At the time Emma is in correspondence with a member of her extended family whose lifestyle attracts her, but may also be a way of confronting her father.

I had a pen pal, a young man who was a sailor. Remember I said about my half-sister? He was my half-sister's eldest brother name Roy. We were pen pal's for years. So the idea of him travelling and all that appealed to me.

By the time the careers team came to her school offering employment choices, Emma has already made up her mind.

I wanted to go into the Navy. I wanted to be a WRNS—the Women's Royal Naval Service—not the Army.

Remembering that her father took issue with the uniformed activities of the Guides and Brownies, Cubs and cadets, Emma is aware that her father will take issue to her career choice.

I brought all the information and paperwork home. I told Mom about it first. I said: "This is what I would like to become. That's what I want to do when I leave school." She said: "Huh! What you think your dad going think about that?"

I had to tell him because I brought the letter home from school to my parents. Part of the contents said I wanted to be a WRNS.

I already had a feel for what his response was going to be. He says: "You mean to tell me say, after all these years you're coming under the Kingdom Order and Blessings, you still want to be serving man?" I said: "It's my life. It's going to be my life, ain't it. My life is my own. Your life is your own."

Emma's father has different plans for what he would like Emma to take on going forward.

His idea was for me to become a missionary in the Jehovah's Witness.

Looking back, Emma reflects on her father's control over her life.

Life is a revolving door. Being a parent, you recognise that most parents want the best for you. But there's also parents that want to live their life through you. He wanted that my life should have been dedicated to what he believed in.

Realising she can't protest her father's parental reign, Emma attempts to appease her father's wishes.

I submitted. I gave what seemingly was a

submission. But in me, I was plotting a way of leaving home. How am I going to leave home? How am I going to be away from this?

Not thinking of what dangers or what was before me, I got pregnant at sixteen.

IRENE

Irene is just over seven years old when she arrives in England in 1960. She does not remember a great deal of her early life in Jamaica. From what she later learns, her mother, Lucy, was thirty-six years old at the time of her birth and not married to her father, Webster Bryant. When her mother discovers that he has been seeing other women, she leaves him. Lucy never discussed Webster with Irene. Irene had little contact with her father and almost no knowledge of him before coming to England.

When Lucy came to England in 1959, she leaves her daughter with an aunt—one of her sisters who is a teacher. Irene travels to England by air in the care of a woman she does not know. Leaving Jamaica is not an upheaval. She is not leaving any close family members behind. She is going to join her mother.

Lucy is living in London—Finsbury Park—at the time and working as an auxiliary nurse. Her immediate priority is to get her daughter into school. Irene had attended primary school in Jamaica for a short while and thinks she knows all about it.

> I went into infant school soon after I arrived. On
> the first day my mum was walking me to school,
> I says: "It's alright. I'm alright. You don't need to

walk me to school." You could see she was quite hurt, but as soon as I got near school, I ran off. I was trying to be tough.

In school, Irene is immersed in a completely new environment and instantly made aware that she is a minority.

I remember being in a class with all white kids which I'd never seen before in my life. There might have been one other Black child. I don't remember having a lot of Black people or children around.

Like most West Indian parents, Lucy is anxious about her daughter's education. Based on her own experience of growing up and school in Jamaica, this was one of the main reasons behind her coming to England and sending for her daughter as soon as she could.

She said money does help if you're struggling to buy shoes and other things to go to school. Her mother had died when she was quite young and it was only Granny and herself. Her granny said: "You can't go to school anymore, there's not enough money. You need to go and work."

I think she got to a certain level and she'd have liked to have gone on more. But because her mum wasn't around—it was her granny—she had to stop and get a job. She said when you haven't got your parents around to support you, it's Grandma

and the others. She had to leave school. That's
why she said: "You've got to make it in school.
You've got to do better than me. You've got to do
better than me."

Lucy takes her daughter's education very seriously and is taking
steps to ensure her daughter has a stable future.

My mum was always pushing education. It was
my mother who taught me to read, she loved
reading. From in Jamaica she said she was always
reading books to me all the time. She said she was
reading to me when I was in the womb and she
was doing one, two, three's with me once I was
born.

Irene credits her literary inclinations to her mother's hard work.

When I came to school I was quite bright. I was
able to read and I was always asking questions. I
loved reading.

There is, however, one problem when it comes to her love of
reading. Irene likes to read everything out loud as this is how
she was taught at school in Jamaica.

Later on, when I got to about eight or so, I
remember me reading everything and she said:
"Oh, I wish I'd never learn you to read. You
reading too much now. Keep quiet! You getting

on me nerves. Too much, too much!"

Irene cannot remember much about the house she and her mother lived in other than the fact it was in Finsbury Park. It could have been a flat or, more likely, a room. Irene did however remember what her mother did for a living.

My mum was an nursing auxiliary in a hospital. I remember her telling me stories about the Matron. In those days it was a Matron.

I remember her saying: "If Matron came to sit on your table at lunchtime, you have to eat fast. If Matron had come in after you, and you were too slow, you would have to eat up because by the time Matron is ready to go, you need to be ready to go as well."

I think it was an army sort of a thing. If Matron was eating fast, you better make sure you were eating fast as well. I just remember stories about that.

It's 1964, Irene is eleven years old and her mother decides to leave London.

I'm trying to remember the reason why we moved to Birmingham.

My mum was a born-again Christian; she went to a Pentecostal Church. That was the link for her coming to Birmingham. We use to have convocation. We use to come to Gibson Road in

Birmingham once a year and we'd stay in brethrens' homes for that period. It's sort of like a convention. That's how we knew of Birmingham. She knew some of the church people here in Handsworth, and that's how she found out about the prospect of a job at Dudley Road Hospital.

With getting the job and everything, we moved to Birmingham.

A year later, Irene discovers the reasons for her mother move to Birmingham.

Once we came to Birmingham she did actually get married. That was to a church person. I think she was going up to fifty when she got married. He was an older person as well. It was a mature wedding—a small wedding—at the church. She had bridesmaids and such but it was just a small wedding. I think I was a bridesmaid. I blotted that out. I don't remember.

Thinking back, I think she just had three ladies as her bridesmaids because it wasn't like a youngster's wedding. I don't remember her having any children as her bridesmaids.

When Irene is first told of her mother's intention to get married, she is not happy. By then she knew of her mother's previous relationship with her father. She also knows that her mother is the only person she can depend on and the thought of a man entering their life concerns her.

186

I thought he was going to upset the nice relationship that me and my mum had got.

She had to sit down and tell me that it
wouldn't make any difference—she still loved me.
He wasn't going to take her love away from me,
she still can love me.

At the time Irene and her mother are living in an upstairs apart-
ment of a housing association building.

You'd got one family downstairs and we'd got the
upstairs with an attic. So I had my own room,
my mum had her own room and then there was a
little dining area. It was a bit like a flat but it was
a massive house.

Irene's new stepfather is living on his own when him and Lucy
get married. He then comes to live with Irene and Lucy. This
is when Irene finds out a little more about him and his family.

He had some children of his own in Jamaica and
some in America as well. I don't think he had any
here. I never met any of them. I remember him
talking about them, but I never met them.

Now in Birmingham, Irene spends half a year in junior school,
before moving on to Handsworth Wood Girls when she is
eleven years old.

Handsworth Wood Girls was a uniform school. It

was very strict. I've still got my school tie.

I do remember the first day because you couldn't go to school without a uniform. They told us it was bottle green and red, with beret and jacket and everything. It was a grammar school before, and we had the boys' school behind us. We had a very inspirational headmistress, very strict on discipline and always talking about 'wanting my girls to do well'. She was awesome—a character. She's dead now.

The Headmistress at the time is a woman called Mrs Finchley. She is a strict teacher who takes the matter of school uniforms very seriously.

Mrs Finchley use to say: "When you wear the uniform—when you're outside of school—I am watching you. I have people watching you. So whatever behaviour you get up to, I'll know what's going on."

I remembered a particular day when the mini-skirt was in. It was quite funny. We use to have assembly and Mrs Finchley, for the teachers, would be on the top. Mary—a white girl—was a favourite of Mrs Finchley, who called her out: "Mary, I want you to come up unto the podium. Come up." At that time Mary was wearing a skirt up to here. Mary's walking up to the podium all nice and proud. When she got there Mrs Finchley said: "Stand up tall girl. Lift up your jumper

Mary." She lift it up and her skirt rolled up as well. The Headmistress said: "Now pull your skirt down Mary." Mary goes all red. As she stood there Mrs Finchley says: "Let this be a warning to you all. This uniform is not a mini. Anybody wear their uniform like that, I'll be doing the same to them."

To Lucy's joy, Mrs Finchley develops a slight affinity towards Irene.

I missed out on swimming because of Mrs Finchley. In the first year you go swimming. Not far, we use to walk it from school to the Grove Lane Swimming Baths.

Whenever it was time for swimming I was quite interested to go, but sometimes Mrs Finchley would say: "No Irene, I want you to stay back. I've got some inspectors coming and I want you to read to them. Come and read for me. Education is more important than swimming."

So I'd stay back and I would go home and tell my mum. Of course, my mum loved that. She would say: "Better than you going swimming, you read to the inspectors. If that's what Mrs Finchley wants you to do, you do that."

We had a boys' school behind but we couldn't talk to the boys. She banned us. That was a big rule: "You're my girls, those are the boys. You behave different." My mum loved that.

Needless to say, Irene and her friends soon find ways around Mrs Finchley's ban on talking to the boys next door.

> We had little boyfriends at a church in George Street called the New Testament Church of God. I think we met them in Handsworth Wood Park. Mrs Finchley found out about that and told us off about going in the park. She said: "There was a fight. One of the girls told me that they were involved in a fight." I didn't know anything about it.
>
> The church's ruling on boyfriend and girlfriend was quite tight but my mother—although she was strict—was happy for me to talk to boys. I had little boyfriends but it's not something I would go and tell a big adult about. So when we went to church meetings we'd meet up with our little boyfriends and after school we'd walk through Handsworth Park together. There was many relationships but nothing overly romantic. It was healthy boy-girl relationships.
>
> My mother knew of that, but then she also remembered the teaching of the church that you're not supposed to be going around with loads of boys and stuff like that. She didn't have to remind me because I had my own integrity by then.

Just like in infant and junior school, there are not many Black pupils at Handsworth Wood Girls.

The few of us that were Black, we got on very well in that school. I got used to that coming up from Finsbury Park. It seemed normal that there wasn't a lot of Black people around. In my class there was only two of us who was Black. We got on with the others, we got on with the majority.

I have to be honest with you, I don't remember being called names. I remember Mrs Finchley being strict but I don't remember racism at school, I don't remember it. She had no discrimination. Although we were Black, the teachers were there pushing us all the time.

Before long, the few Black girls at the school, all around Irene's age, form a little group.

There was a core group of us at school who were friends. We had like a fellowship at school. It's interesting—we do know white people—but there was no white people in our group. We were all Black.

Mrs Finchley is not the only influential teacher that Irene remembers.

Some of the teachers were quite inspiring. I'll never forget Mr Clements. Oh! Mr Clements. He taught us this one day about 'individuality.' I was in my element.

Mr Clements is Irene's English teacher and his lesson on 'individuality' comes at a time in her teenage life when she begins clashing with her mother.

> I think I was in the third year. and because my mum was such a disciplinarian, whenever we had discussions, my mum's way was always right. It was: 'This is the way and there's no other way'. That use to annoy me sometimes because I always had different thoughts.
>
> He told us that: "Yes your parents will say this and that, but you have your own minds, you have your own thinking." I thought: 'Yes! At last somebody says this.'

That day Irene comes home and shares the information Mr Clements imparted onto her with her mother.

> I went home and Mum said: "How was school?" I said: "Great! Mr Clements taught us about 'individuality'." She said: "What?" I said: "Mum, you know when you and I have discussion? Well Mr Clements says that we can agree to disagree. That I can have my own thoughts and I don't have to think what you think." She said: "You wait till I see Mr Clements. I'm going to talk to him about teaching 'individuality' what."

At the next parents evening, Irene's mother gets a chance to confront Mr Clements.

I was into acting and drama. I think he said to her: "Irene does really well in acting, drama and things like that. She could go to acting school." She said: "No! Irene is going to get a proper job. None of that for her."

By the end of Irene's fourth year at Handsworth Wood Girls, her group of friends remain close. Together they enter a new chapter in their lives.

As we all got into the fifth year, those of us who were Christians had like a School Union—a Christian Union. Instead of going out to play, we would stay in and read our Bibles.

We were all bright, so we were doing well. I think we were quite respected at school—our behaviour was good. I became a Prefect and there were a couple of others who were Prefects as well. So for Black people, we were on a par with other white people. We weren't victims. We could stand up for ourselves. That does help.

I had some good, good, white friends at school. But I don't remember going to their homes for dinner—not that close. We got on very well with the teachers. In the fifth year, one of the teachers—Mrs Hill—invited me to her wedding.

The girls in that core group are to form a lifelong bond. On each of their 60th birthdays, ten of them got together for a reunion. Not in Birmingham as might be expected, but in Ocho Rios, Jamaica.

***

Back in the house Lucy continues to re-assure her daughter that marriage will not change their relationship. Irene however, remains uncertain.

> I didn't like 'the man' my mum got married to. I tried to be as polite as I could but I just didn't feel I could trust him. Never liked him from beforehand. Didn't feel he was right for my mum. As a child I'm not sure how I know that but I was right. I was right.

Very quickly, Irene notices their marriage become toxic and worries for her mother.

> The marriage lasted about three years. I think the marriage didn't last because of domestic violence. That got me quite bitter.
>
> I remember getting involved one day. I said: "Don't hit my mum. Don't treat her like that." I think it happened once and then he said: "Oh, it will never happen again—never happen again."
>
> It did, and that was the final straw. My mum said to him: "Go! Go! You're no Christian. Go!" I know it's not everybody who goes to church is a Christian. Sometimes people use church as a cover. I'm wiser and that doesn't mean anything.

The first time, she thought that was a mistake. The second time it was never again, just go. She said it wasn't good for me to be seeing that, it could damage me.

In 1968, Lucy's marriage ends in divorce.

IVY

Ivy arrives in England in 1962. She is single, twenty-seven years old and travelling alone to Southampton to join her friend, Jay, who is married and living in Peckham.

As far as Ivy is concerned coming to England is about getting away, especially from her father who started molesting her from the age of eight

Ivy has no idea how she is going to earn a living when she arrives in England. Letters from her friend, Jay—who she is coming to join—assures her that England is a nice place and she could make a lot of money. It turns out that Jay is a housewife bringing up her kids and has never been employed.

Both Jay and her husband go to meet her in Southampton as she comes down the gangplank. Her first reaction on arrival is to get back on the boat and go back to Jamaica. It is not the "nice England" she has been told about in Jay's letters.

Like the rest of 'The Five', Ivy has difficulty adjusting to her new surroundings and her new home.

> When I first came and walked around the streets, people would stare at you as if they're seeing a ghost. Kids would say: "Mummy, what is that!" You thought, somebody calling you: "What?" It

wasn't nice but we've survived it.

Ivy observes what she feels is the mania going on around her.

> When people going to cook in the evening in the
> house where I was staying, they would all be in
> the same kitchen wanting to use the same cooker
> at the same time. There was always an argument:
> "I put a shilling in the gas and I have to do my
> cooking. I have a baby and the baby needs food."
> It was just chaos.
> Jay and her husband lived in a downstairs
> flat with two bedrooms and there was a shared
> kitchen and bathroom. She had a baby by then
> and the baby shared the room with me.

The relationship between Ivy, Jay and her husband is a far more complicated than it might first appear.

> Jay's husband was the man who had wanted to
> marry me when I was still in Jamaica. Jay did not
> know at the time.

Ivy first met Jay's husband—who she refers to as TT—when she joined the church in Jamaica. TT liked her, but because of her experience with her father, Ivy found it difficult to commit to relationships with men. When Ivy rejected him, he transferred his romantic interest to Jay. They remained friends and when he immigrated to England, Ivy kept in touch with him by letter.

He told me he wanted to marry Jay and I told her. So when he wrote to her to come and be his wife, she came without asking any questions.

We all got on OK.

Ivy stays in Jay and her husband's flat in Peckham for a total of three years. Upon arrival, as a matter of urgency, she has to find a job. This is London in 1962.

I had a hard time getting my first job. Nobody wanted a Black person in their place of work.

I was looking for work in places that made clothes because that was what I could do. That was my trade. Even though they would put up notices saying machinist wanted, when you go, they say the vacancy is filled. They would close the door in your face.

I went around and around and around— Peckham, Camberwell, Aldgate East. Jay's husband—we called him TT—used to take me sometimes. But nobody wanted a Black girl in their place to work.

Ivy's hunt for employment begins taking its toll on her and she begins to lose hope.

I remember one day when I was walking. I was so tired, exhausted and fed up, thinking this was the end and I can't take this anymore.

I knocked on this door. A woman came and as

she was about to shut the door. I held it and said to her: "You wanted machinists." She said: "Yes, but we don't want you." I started to cry. I was at my limit. I burst into tears.

I said to her: "You don't know who I am. You don't know what I can do, but you're ready to shut the door in my face like everybody else have been doing. Don't you think I need a chance before you can condemn me?" She looked at me and said: "Alright come in."

She gave me a bundle of items from a sample of a garment to sew. She didn't tell me anything else and she was gone. I was given an hour.

I opened the bundle, completed the dress and just sat there waiting for her to come back. When she come, she looked in and out, around and about to find some fault to say I cannot have you. But she couldn't find a fault because it was well done—so she took me on. That was how I got a job.

The job was based on piecework, so you had to work quickly to earn some money. I worked there for three or four years.

I was the first Black person employed in my first job but firms soon started to employ other Black people.

Ivy's first job is in Aldgate East and not all that far from where she lives in Peckham. She later finds a similar job closer to home.

The job in Peckham was also piecework, but they made a greater variety of garments. I could fit in to do anything I was asked to do because I learnt that from Jamaica. With dressmaking here you have to use a pattern to cut everything. They would put all the material on this big table and lay paper on top of it, then cut the pattern. I used to say to them: "What are you doing that for?" I could cut and make up a dress by just measuring the person. No pattern.

I was a very good machinist and I was fast, so I could make money on piece rates. I could usually finish by daily bundles, do more than was required and had some time to help other people. I could pay my way.

I could have moved up to supervisor in my job in Peckham but I didn't want that. I wanted to work on the machines. That's what I wanted to do. Didn't want to supervise anybody.

People came in that didn't know the work and I would help them and show them what to do so that they could keep the job. I did that off my own time when I could have been earning money, but I like to help people. I made quite a few friends that I have even up to today.

Ivy remembers one lady she met whilst working very fondly.

When I was working at Peckham, there was a lady who lived with her husband and had a child—eight

200

years old. The lady was very fair-skinned and she used to come to work with bruises in her face and on her arms. She used to say she fall down the stairs, or she walk into a door.

One day I confronted her and I said to her: "From the time I was growing up, I decided if a man hits me, I'll kill him. If I can't kill him face to face, I'd wait until he's sleeping and I'd boil a kettle of water and pour it in his ear." She looked at me, laughed, and went away.

She came back and told me the story of what happened. That she went home that night and her husband gave her a beating. She took it and didn't cry because she knew what she was going to do.

She was tidying up the kitchen and when she thought he was asleep, she took a kettle of boiling water upstairs to pour on him. But he wasn't sleeping. He was wandering why his wife was acting so strange all of a sudden which was a good thing, because if he was sleeping she wouldn't have been able to come back and tell me what happened.

When she went into the bedroom with the kettle, he saw her—jumped off the bed—call out for God Almighty and ran out. That was the last time. He never touched her again. They weren't married then but he took her to the registry office the next day.

She offered to help me buy a house for helping to turn her life around, but I wouldn't let her.

In 1965, Jay's husband loses his job in London and decides to move his family to Manchester, where he intends to live with his brother. Ivy urges him to buy his own house instead.

> I gave them £50 as a down payment on a house in Manchester. In them times that was a lot of money.
>
> He went up first to find a place and then he came back to move his family up. His brother got a van to move their things and I went up with them to see where they were. After that Jay and her family moved to Manchester.

Ivy does not stay on at their flat in Peckham. She moves into a room in Camberwell, where she reconnects with her church.

> When I started attending, they knew I could sew and I spent a lot of time making things for people. Like in Jamaica, I made things for people.
>
> Church people just think you're there to do things for them and never, ever say: "Here is a couple of pounds for your electricity or whatever." But it never bothered me. I never, ever, think about charging people for anything. I was just being of service, to be here for you and to do what you want.

This, along with her experience in her first two jobs, convinces Ivy of the true value of the skills she learnt from Mrs Chen back in Jamaica. Like many coming from Jamacia at the time, she learnt her craft through a prolonged period of apprenticeship. Ivy decides she wants to commit to the craft of sewing.

> I decided I wanted to do my own designing, so I went to night school. I wanted to learn to design my own garments. I was thinking maybe I could open a shop and have my own business. I thought I could do that. When I walked into a dress shop and see a garment, I could go home, cut it and make it. I could take two different garments, two different styles and make them into one. I could do things like that.
>
> The first night I got there, the teacher was explaining patterns to us and how you lay it on the material to cut. I was the only Black person there. The rest were all white girls.
>
> The teacher said: "Don't ever cut your pattern in the middle of the material. Start from the end." But she cut her pattern right in the middle of the material. I said to her: "Did you not just tell us not to cut it in the middle?" She said: "Oh my God!" So then I had to help the other girls to lay out their patterns and show them how to cut around the pattern, without cutting from the middle.
>
> I didn't go back to the class after that night because I knew more than what the teacher was telling me.

Ivy showed much promise when it came to fashion design.

She could have found another course in fashion, she could have also been promoted to supervisor within the Peckham firm, but she chooses not to pursue these avenues. As fate would have it, something unexpected happens, taking her life in a totally new direction.

> One of the girls I knew from the country in Jamaica where I and my friend Jay went, had a brother name Wesley. I used to like talking to him when I went to the country, he was somebody nice to talk with. Wesley is also Jay's cousin.
>
> He came to England but I didn't know until one day he turned up at my door. I was surprised to see him.

The church, for a variety of reasons, is still an important aspect of Ivy's life. It is the church that gave her the confidence to confront her father and it is through the church that she now keeps in contact with the Black community in Camberwell. Wesley is also religious.

> I liked him but there was something between us. He was a Christian going to the Pentecostal Church and I'm a Christian going to the Church of God.
>
> The Church of God didn't have any confidence in the Pentecostal, and the Pentecostal didn't have any confidence in the Church of God. We could talk but that was between us.

Nevertheless, when Wesley asks her to marry him, she says yes.

> But after, I didn't feel like getting married.
> I did love Wesley, but I didn't feel I wanted
> to settle down. Thinking back to my childhood,
> marriage was always a big stumbling block for me.
> So I moved away from my home in Camberwell
> to another house where he couldn't find me.

After she moves from Camberwell, she believes, at least for now, Wesley will not be able to get hold of her. However, to her surprise, this is not the case.

> Purely by accident, I met Wesley one day on the
> bus going to Clapham.
> That day he said: "You're not going to get away
> from me again. I want to marry you and I want to
> marry you now." I said: "OK."
> We went straight to the registry office and got
> married without telling anybody. One of the staff
> at the registry office was the witness. This was in
> December 1966.

Most of Wesley's family, at the time, are in England. This includes his stepfather who Ivy becomes aquainted with.

> He brought his stepfather to introduce me as his
> wife.
> His stepfather told me off. He said the
> wedding was my idea because Wesley would never

have done anything like that. He didn't want me to marry Wesley because I wasn't in their category. I think they loved him and wanted somebody nice, rich and fair with long flowing hair. Anyway, it was already done so there was nothing they could do.

Jay knew we got married because Wesley was her cousin.

MELISSA

Melissa is now living in London with her mother Pengal and stepfather Martie Macdonald. She distinctly remembers her first few memories of England.

> On a morning when I wake up, I hear the birds chirping in the garden. This is what I will always remember when I came to England, the birds chirping that day.

Melissa recalls in decent detail, memories of the house they used to reside in.

> We had a cousin here prior to my stepfather coming. That cousin had a house in Croydon—88 Oakfield Road. That was the first place I lived in when I got to England.
>
> It was my mother's cousin's home. He came from our district in Jamaica. He was living there with a companion of his—a lady friend. I think the house was the lady friend's house. All of us who came from that district in Jamaica went to that house. That's where we started.

We use to live in one room.

It's a fairly big house. I think it was four bedrooms, one kitchen, one bathroom, one toilet. Because we were all relatives, that was alright. We cook for each other although it was sometimes more than five.

At the time, Melissa's mother is working at Mayday Hospital in Croydon.

My stepfather used to work with a firm building houses for the council—Waites. He worked for them for years. He used to wear Donkey Jackets to keep warm. He used to get a bit more money than my mother, so he was the one who saved up the £89 for my fare.

Melissa arrives on a Tuesday. She has not seen her mother for two years and her stepfather for five. She is not given time to get use to her new environment. Her mother, who took time off work to meet Melissa at the airport, has to be back to work on the Wednesday. She leaves instructions with her cousin's lady friend to get Melissa officially registered, so that she is able to get a job.

Though she is just sixteen years old, Melissa already knows what she wants to do in England. She wants to enroll and train to be a nurse.

She [Pengal's family friend] took me to the Job Exchange that morning.

> I told them my name and address when I went and gave them my passport. They gave me a number—that is your National Insurance Number.
>
> They said there was a job in a Button factory nearby. I said: "But I want to do nursing." They said: "Well you can't go into nursing because you're only sixteen. You can't do it until you're eighteen."

Upon receiving this news, Melissa is disappointed but accepts that there's little choice in the matter. This is her second day in England and getting a job—any job—is what her parents expect of her.

> I went to the Button factory in Gloucester Road, Croydon. I work there until I was eighteen years old.
>
> They made all types of buttons at the factory— small, medium, large. You have like silver buttons, you've got gold buttons. They've got different drums with chemicals that they put the buttons in to add colour. The buttons then went into an oven on a rack to dry. When it is dry they put it on an assembly belt. Then we put the buttons into boxes, six or a dozen. These are then loaded up and they send them off to different distributors.
>
> There were three brothers who use to work there. One of the brothers, he was the foreman— the headman—an elderly Jew. His other two

brothers work with him. They were the ones who have to spray the buttons. I can remember the fumes because the two brothers use to drink bottles of milk. I said: "Why are you drinking milk?" They said: "We spray in the spraying room and we drink the milk to get rid of the chemicals we're inhaling." They would wear a mask, sometimes.

Three Black girls use to work there at the time. It was quite nice there.

Working at the button factory is 'nice' but it is not what she wants. Nevertheless, Melissa continues to press on with it, after all she *needs* to have a job. Melissa soon learns that having a job gives her a degree of independence, separate from her parents.

I use to get £5 a week. A pound in those days was a lot. It was a whole heap of money.

I give my mother one pound towards the rent of the place and one pound for food. I would keep £2 for myself to buy clothes or maybe go to the cinema—you could get a skirt or a blouse for a pound. Every other week I use to keep one pound so that I could buy my lunch.

That was how my life begin in England.

Soon after their arrival, some Caribbean migrants caught on to the value of setting up businesses that sold imported products from the West Indies.

We use to have this food shop on Spurgeon Bridge in Croydon. The little shop is still there but it's not owned by the same man anymore. He was a Jamaican man. The only things we could get there was plain or self-raising flour, rice, corn beef, tin sardines and somehow he use to have red beans. I don't know where he got red beans from.

I remember when my mother wants to cook, she gets the red beans like mid-week day. She would get ham hock and spuds—then it use to be Irish potato, the Irish use to have nice dry potatoes. The best soup in the world was ham hock with red beans, Oooh! Red beans and ham hock soup, nice.

We use to credit from him. He would credit every one of us until Friday when we go in and we pay him. Every person goes there, all us Caribbean, whether we were Jamaican or not.

His name was Mr Kelly. His wife [Sislin Fay Allen] was the first Black policewoman they have in England. She pass the police test and went into policing. She use to police around Croydon. They've now gone back to Jamaica.

***

Once Melissa is eighteen, she applies to train as a nurse.

I went into cadet nursing at eighteen at the Royal Marsden Hospital—the cancer hospital—up towards Sutton. Later on they open another one down Knightsbridge.

The selection process involves your certificates from school but you have to do a test. They gave you arithmetic, an essay on why you want to be a nurse, what experience have you got. Then you have to wait for the result.

When you go further on into student training, you still have to pass what they called the General Nursing Council test to enter into nursing itself.

Due to Pengal's absence Melissa was not especially close to her mother in Jamaica.

Now that Melissa is in England, it would be fair to assume that Pengal's and Melissa's relationship would have improved, however, Melissa soon learns the busyness of life in England takes its toll of family life.

I think I was closer to my mum when she was in the West Indies than when she was here. She was always busy working when she was here. I saw very little of her. I find that it was a distant relationship.

On Sundays sometimes I would see her when she cooks—we sit down, talk and laugh. We use to have this Blue Spot Radio, they're the big ones. Yeah, my 'dad' use to have one of those radios. On a Sunday morning we use to listen to Jim Reeves. Every Black person—if you walk on the road where they're living—you would hear Jim Reeves playing. My favourite for Jim Reeves was 'Deck of Cards'.

During her time with her mother, Melissa grows fond of her stepfather Martie. Melissa is still not sure who her biological father is but now that Melissa is living with Pengal and Martie in Croydon, it is her stepfather whom she comes to regard as her father.

My 'father' [Martie] was very nice to me. He was extremely nice to me. As I've told you, he use to work for Waite's the builders. I think they use to build a lot of social housing for the government, so my dad was always in work.

He use to ride a little bicycle, oh my poor 'dad'! He would ride the bicycle and sometimes it's so cold, it's so dark. I'm always worrying in case traffic would hit him because in those days it was dark.

He saved and eventually got himself some money. He decided to buy himself a car, well he was taking driving lessons.

The first car he bought was a Rover. Oooh! My 'dad' use to clean that car. You would think the car was his house or his baby. He started driving around and he was wearing one of those round hats, dem Caribbean style hats. He's stepping, stepping with his car and with his cigarette. He'd puff out his chest—that's him stepping. They'd say: 'Mr Macdonald is a rich man. He's got a car'.

The family remain in Croydon—88 Oakfield Road for a few months before moving elsewhere.

> We went one road away from Oakfield Road to 2 Kidderminster Road. It was a stranger's house. He was Jamaican, Mr Simms. Friends lent him the money to buy the property. That's what we use to do to get money to pay down on a house. Sometimes you don't get the money from the bank, it's your friend's money. In those days houses use to sell for about £2,000. You would borrow money from your friends and use the rent money to pay them back.

At the time, Melissa does not know why her parents decide to move out of their house. Whatever the case, the conditions at the new house are significantly worse.

> It was him, his wife, a baby and three other people living there. We got one of the rooms.
>
> At this house you had to have a routine in bathing. You pay a shilling a week for gas for your bathing. If you feel you wanted a bath more than once a week, you go to the public baths.
>
> When we're ready to cook, there were four burners and four families living in the house— one burner each for each family. If you were doing your stew, you have to cook that down first before you cook your rice, yam or whatever it is. You can't use the next man's burner. You're responsible

for your burner. When you finish, you clean off your side.

In those days there were bright yellow cupboards with work tops, so you had to clean that. You took turns in cleaning the kitchen floor. Then the house—the passage and common areas—you have a rotation. This one clean this week, the next person clean next week. That's how we kept the house clean.

I use to have a folding bed. My mother and my father was in one room and I have a folding bed which you fold in the day. It looks like a table because it's got a narrow wooden top and then at night you open it out and sleep.

That was our life.

Understandably, Melissa's parents do not want to stay there long and decide they want to become home owners.

During this period, although whole families sometimes lived in a single or a couple room in a house owned by a member of their extended family or someone from their country of origin—as soon as they could, they would move out into their own homes.

After living at Kidderminster Road for a while, my 'dad' started seriously saving again. My mother was working and I was also bringing in something.

Then he decided to get a house in Thornton Heath, I'll never forget it. My 'dad' bought it for

£4,000. It is a semi-detached house on a very famous road in Thornton Heath—87, Melfort Road. Everybody knew of it.

I remember we had a pear tree in the garden. We have gooseberries and I use to make gooseberry juice, it's tasting like Soursop juice. It used to be nice. You can get Soursop juice here now from Rubicon in box drinks. You buy the juice, get your sweet milk, get your nutmeg and vanilla and mix it with the Soursop juice.

Melissa is delighted with her new home but she also has to adjust with the method in which it has to be paid for. It was very common, back then for Caribbean migrants to house other people in their homes as a means of income or for paying the mortgage.

My mother, 'father', myself and a teacher—a man who came from Jamaica—lived in that house. The teacher's name was Lloyd. Then Lloyd met Leona who was a student nurse. They became friends and Leona came there to live as well. Then another lady from Ghana—Julie Mensar—came there to live as well.

I was living at the back in a small room downstairs. Julie was living in the middle room. My mother and father was living in the front room. Leona and Lloyd was living in what you would call the downstairs sitting room.

We didn't have dining room then. You want

216

to eat, you go and eat in your room, or you go in
the kitchen and sit down and eat. We lived there
for a long while.

Melissa remembers those days rather fondly. She remembers
very clearly the sense of community that was fostered around
her.

It was nice in those days. Why it was nice? Because
we use to unite a lot. Today we're like strangers.
Even us Black people, we're like strangers to each
other.

In those days on a Saturday, people use to have
bottle parties. If it's your birthday or whatever it
is, you have a party. You don't have to have the
money to buy the drinks, each person bring a
bottle. It was really nice in those days.

You could find a little bit more Caribbean food
if you go down Brixton. Things started coming
in gradually. In those days all we use to eat was
spuds. I love my food. I mentioned Strongback
and Chainney Root and Blood Wist. Strongback
makes a strong potent brew. If you go to most
of the shops now and ask for root beer they will
give you a lot of that. The men reckon that when
they drink it, it boosts their libido and helps with
blood pressure.

Even though Melissa is nearly eighteen, working and making
weekly contributions to the family budget, her mother and

stepfather are still keeping a close eye on her.

My parents were very strict.

Funny enough, I use to have a white friend and she use to come to visit me because we both worked at the button factory. My mum would allow me to go to the cinema with her.

I remember the first time I went to the West End with her. Didn't know how to get there. We got the bus—the 159—and it took us to Baker Street. From Baker Street we got another bus into the West End—Leicester Square.

We were walking around and then we happen to go towards where the Chinese Quarter is. Never seen so much Chinese in my life. I use to see them in Jamaica but not so many. Then we realize this was China Town.

We walked further and got lost. Guess where we got lost in? Warren Street! Oooh, you're got all the porn shops there. We eventually found our way back down into Leicester Square. It was exciting, really exciting because we've never seen that before in our lives.

While I was walking with her a man came up and says: "You're got lovely long legs. You're good for modeling. Here's my card." I don't even know what I did with the card because he was talking gibberish to me. I didn't know anything what he was talking about.

I don't know where I would have been now.

Maybe I wouldn't have been as fat as I am now because I would have taken caution, but there you are. In those days I didn't think about all those things. I was just thinking about a profession—nursing. That was it.

Melissa continues her training at St. Lawrence Hospital, Caterham in Surrey. When she moves on to Mayday Lady Hospital in Croydon she decides to leave the family house in Melfort Road.

I would come home so often to visit. I would come home for food and stocktaking and go back to the hostel.

Melissa is especially pleased with the new freedom she has attained, away from her parents' home.

When I was in the nursing home we were going to parties. It was a group of us from different parts of the Caribbean, so we all amalgamate together. You find that the Africans were there. Even then there were Africans and they were together with us.

She recalls this period in her life in much detail and remembers it as a time full of fun and spontaneity.

When we're going to parties from the hospital, we would finish working nine o'clock at night and get dressed quick. Usually it was one of the boyfriends driving.

We are coming back in the morning, sometimes at six-thirty, and we have to go on duty at seven. When you finish working, you dash in the canteen to get something to eat. You finish eat quickly and you gone up to your bed.

When you're young, you're able to do that. I did enjoy those days; you make a lot of friends. Then when you finish your training, you all go your different ways. Sometimes you keep in touch, sometimes you don't.

As one might expect, Melissa soon has a boyfriend.

I don't want to talk about this. Charlie, who was from Barbados, was a very nice person—but very hyped.

One day we were in the cafeteria and we were arguing. I can't remember what it was about but he went and hit me. Oooh! Who tell him fe do that? Hey, Hey! I was drinking from a glass and I just pick up one of the glass and wedge him. The glass splinter, cut me and cut Charles. I said to him: "You like to hit! I'm not into this hitting business. Let's call it a day and just be friends. You can talk to me but you don't ever put your hands on me." That was it.

Melissa maintains a relationship with Charlie long after their romantic relationship is over.

> Charlie and I still keep in touch. It's about five years now I've not heard from him. His wife who he married, he used to beat her a lot.
>
> One day he beat her and she passed out. When she came to, she says: "I'm going to do you like what Melissa did to you." He hit her again and she 'blood' him. He never hit her again.
>
> He rang me one day and he said: "You know, I hit her and she passed out. I was so frightened. Then she took up something and gave me one lash. Since she lashed me, I stopped hitting her because I remember what you did. She says, 'I'll blood you like Melissa did.'" I said: "That is good because it's not nice to hit someone."

Melissa is twenty-two years old in 1970 when she passes her nursing exams and becomes a registered nurse. She then goes on to do eighteen months of additional specialist training before going into full-time employment. Shortly after, the family receive urgent news from Jamaica.

> My grandmother Doule died in 1972. I'd just about started at Mayday Hospital. I use to keep in contact with her, very, very, often.

The death of her dear Doule saddens Melissa deeply and this becomes a particularly challenging period in her life.

My mother didn't go back for the funeral but we sent money to help bury my grandmother. I felt sad because I'd just started working that month for a salary which was going to be £40 for the month and I thought I will give Doule a monthly income from that. Just as I start to work, that's the time she died. It was kind of sad because I wanted to take care of her. My cousin, the midwife, the first thing she bought out of her midwifery salary was a radio for Doule.

That I wasn't able to take care of her, my grandmother's death hurt me very much. She cared for me and that I was not able to go to the funeral, it's like a part of me still isn't complete. I missed her a lot.

Doule died of renal failure. Although there is a history of kidney problems in the family, Melissa—now a qualified nurse—is deeply suspicious of the circumstances. Her suspicions are provoked by one of her cousins.

In the Caribbean when you die now they have got funeral parlours. Then, if you're up in the country and you die, usually they put you on a block of ice from the ice factory to keep you.

My grandmother dreamt to my cousin Creighton: 'I wasn't dead. I was in a coma. It's the ice they put on me kill me'.

She had renal failure. She went to a medical doctor and the stu-pi-di-ty of Dr Roberts. She was in a coma. He catheterise her, then remove the catheter. If he didn't have a bag to put on her, leave the catheter in situ. All you have to do is spigot the catheter. Each time you want her to pass urine, pull the spigot out and let the urine drain out. He took the catheter out and her stomach bloated up because all the fluid was there and couldn't come out. She went into renal failure—it was a coma.

Thanks be to God that these days these things won't happen anymore because people are too sensible now. Those things will never happen again.

Chapter Six

Getting On!

EVELYN

It is September 1956 and Evelyn has just married Reggie. The newly married couple is now living at Gloucester Street, Langley, with Reggie's brother and one of his cousins, both of whom objected to the marriage and did their best to dissuade him. To Reggie's credit, he did not listen. Their wedding is rejected by Reggie's family. On the day of their wedding, Evelyn walks up the aisle on the arm of an Englishman, a friend, who offered to be her 'Dad for a Day'.

After Evelyn and Reggie's wedding, the house they reside in remains grossly overcrowded. There are about twenty people living there, sometimes three or four to a room. Evelyn has grown extremely frustrated with the nature of her and Reggie's living situation. For one, despite the fact the home is owned by Reggie's cousin, Reggie and Evelyn are still paying exorbitant rent. Evelyn is one of only two women in the house and is still having difficulty keeping the men in the house at bay. To her absolute dismay, the wife of Reggie's cousin, the other woman who owns the house, still dislikes her and continues to provide a hostile environment for Evelyn. As a result of these issues, Evelyn desperately wants to leave the home and tries to persuade her husband, Reggie to leave and board with an English family—the Charltons. Evelyn meets Mr Charlton while working at her first job with Simplex and confides in him about her circumstances at Gloucester Street. Despite Evelyn's request and unhappiness Reggie refuses to move.

Shortly after getting married Evelyn begins to feel unwell.

> I never even knew I was pregnant. I was so ill, so ill. I had to ask the doctor to send me to the hospital. I went to the hospital and my husband came once. No one else came to visit.
>
> I was at the hospital by myself and I started to get worried. I remembered I was feeling a bit better and the doctor came round. I asked him if I could go home. He said yes, but I must visit my own doctor.

Evelyn develops severe bodily pains and is struggling to manage. The advice she remembers being given by the doctor does not prove helpful.

> I think coming over here, I was having terribly pains. I seem to pick up a cold. My tubes were blocked and I had really bad pains and things like that.
>
> The doctor said to me: "You came over here and you're wearing all these thin knickers you wore at home. You got to wear cotton!"

Discharged from hospital, Evelyn goes back to her home in Gloucester Street.

I remembered I got dressed. I had some money and
I paid my fare and come off in West Bromwich.
I stopped at the butchers and bought some meat
and I went home.

When I went home, Reg was ill in bed and
no one came to see him either. It was hard. It was
very, very hard.

Evelyn has her first child in 1957 when she is 25 years old. It's a
boy, Garry. The couple are still at the house in Gloucester Street
at the time of the birth of their newborn.

I was ill all the time with the baby.

The house was so cold. I managed to get a
little box room and the place was so cold. I had a
little paraffin lamp and you had to dry the nappies
round the lamp with the baby. You couldn't stand
in the room. You had to go outside in the snow,
stand out there and wash the nappies.

The wife of Reggie's cousin made Evelyn's life particularly difficult during this time.

That woman [the wife of Reggie's cousin] was
hard. The baby got pneumonia. I remember the
doctor came round because he was only across the
road and he said: "I'm sorry. I can't leave the baby
here. He'll die by morning. He's got to go straight
into the hospital."

Reg was at work. I started to cry because I had

to go by myself with the baby.

I'll never forget the words of that woman. She started laughing when I was crying, and she said to me: "What a way you have your baby wrap around your heart string. I have three and none is wrapped round my heart string. What frighten me, stop train!" I'll never forget it—ever. I've never, ever knew a woman so hard.

I took the baby to the hospital and straightway they put him in a room by himself. They had to get a kettle and steam boiling for him to inhale. It was sad. I couldn't go in. I had to look through the window and when he sees me, it was so sad.

I said to Reggie when he came home: "You know what, we've got to move. We have to move. I can't live here." He said: "Well, the best thing is for you to go home with the baby." I said: "If you want me to leave you and take the baby home, that's the end of us. So you might as well say goodbye. It's either that or we ride it out here together. I'm not leaving you here and go over there because that would be the end. The distance between us will be too far."

Reggie is persuaded. If Evelyn goes back to Jamaica with baby Garry, it would be the end of their short marriage.

We had a bit of money in Jamaica, so we decided to send for it. We had to save a little bit more, so we tried.

It was towards the end of 1957. I looked in the paper and I saw a house in Trinity Road for sale. We decided that we should go and have a look at it.

I went and had a look at it and I said to them: "We're going to take it. We want to buy." They said: "You really want to buy it?"

They never took the keys back so I moved in. Without signing a piece of paper or anything, I just moved in.

At least I had a bit of peace. If I didn't get out of that place, I'd go mad because she was a nasty, nasty, nasty piece of work. Nasty!

Evelyn, eager to push things forward, goes to view the house alone.

It was one of those terraced houses, but it was beautiful. We have a front and backroom and a long passageway. Then we have a veranda in the middle. There is a dining room, then the kitchen.

It had different things carved in the wood in the archway and we had a massive mantel piece and a mirror right up to the top. There was a very long backyard—all the way down—and we had a well with a pump that you could get the water out.

It was absolutely beautiful. It was really a nice house.

The cost of the house is just under £3,000.

> In those days that was still a lot of money. We had the deposit and then West Bromwich Building Society gave us the mortgage. We had no trouble whatsoever and I'm with them until this day. I still keep an account with them. I never had any trouble with them.
>
> We had to go to the second-hand shop to get things because we could not afford new ones. But it was good furniture. Even now, if it was left with me, my house would be packed with second-hand things because they are better than the new ones. At the time I paid three shillings for my dining table. Later on I paid £90 to have it stripped down and polished.

Evelyn and Reggie are the first Black family to move into Trinity Road.

> I didn't get any hassle. My neighbours and I were very close. I got to know them, we speak. We used to come out in the morning and sweep the street—stand up with our brooms, chatting.
>
> The funny thing is I couldn't tell my white neighbours that I had a very hard life. Some of the things I think we created for ourselves because we kept ourselves to ourselves. They want to talk to you but sometimes we're frightened.

By this time Reggie has left his job at the factory and is now a bus conductor. Evelyn left her first job at Simplex after six months and is now working as an auxiliary nurse at Edward Street District Hospital.

> I remember when I was working in the hospital, a patient came in once and he didn't want me to see to him at all because I was Black. I insisted because he couldn't say no and I've got to do it.
>
> He was nasty. He says: "Go back to your trees. Go and swing in your trees where you came from." I said: "Where I came from we don't swing in trees and I don't know anywhere where a Black person swing in trees. So don't call me a monkey."
>
> He looked at me. I said: "If you do that again, if you call me that again—I'll eat you!" He jumped out of the bed. In the end he relented and after that he was very nice. He let me do what I had to do. At the time I had to pull his pyjamas down. You've got to do his bum and everything to prevent him having bed sores. All he could say was: "Oh nurse, if you get a penny for everyone you see like this, you'll be rotten rich." We were good friends after that. So it's how you handle things that happened that makes it get out of hand or it just comes back to a normal way.

Despite her constructive attitude at work, Evelyn is not enjoying her job at Edward Street.

I use to find it hard, especially when you're on night duty. You need to sleep in the day and you can't sleep—you got to look after your kid.

On one of her night shifts, Evelyn refuses to undertake a task because of the way the charge nurse speaks to her.

She reported me and the following morning I had to wait to see Matron. You're on from eight o'clock in the evening, all through the night. You're supposed to come off at eight and you have to wait until Matron come on at half past eight. So I'm getting angry because I need to go home and see to my kid. I couldn't. I was off.

I was supposed to come back on that night. I realise Garry was ill and I couldn't go in. I call from in the morning to tell them that I wouldn't be able to come on duty, so they could get some-body in place. Matron called me in to tell me off that the patients was my family and I'm supposed to be there to look after them. I told her plainly that my child come first—my immediate family come first.

The patient is her family because she is not married or attached to anyone and that was her choice. But in my case, my family is my choice.

Following this disagreement, Evelyn makes her decision.

I came off duty and I never went back.

I went into nursing after leaving Simplex because I felt I would be happier doing it—you're helping somebody. The nursing profession in those days had a bad reputation with most of them that come in and with a lot of the Black girls. The wages was very low and they just flirt with men. My husband didn't want me to be there because their behaviour was not good. In a sense I think he was glad that I came out of it.

I never went back. Even my superannuation, I never went and collect it until years afterwards.

Evelyn was in her first job for only six months. This one lasted for about a year. After that, she didn't work for a while.

Evelyn then becomes pregnant with her second child when she is 27 years old.

Janice was born in 1958. Garry was only a year and six months old at the time.

Then I decided, no more babies. I was so adamant, I said to my husband: "I'd rather my marriage break up. I'm having no more babies." I never had any more. I just couldn't.

From the time I got pregnant with Janice I was so ill. When I was carrying her sometimes I couldn't stand up. I couldn't walk. Sometimes even to get to cook something for him [Reg] coming in, I'm on my knees to get into the kitchen. To move about I had to go on my hands and knees. If I stand, I'm wetting myself from the way the baby was lying. Everything I eat, it comes back. I couldn't keep anything down.

I remember it wasn't the nurse that delivered Janice, it was the doctor and he said to me: "I don't ever want to see you back here again."

She was so tiny. She was only five pounds, five and a half ounces. I was in hospital for eleven days before I could come out when I had her.

I thought to myself: 'No more! I am not going back.'

Desperate to not get pregnant again, Evelyn resorts to an interesting method.

I lied to my husband. I told him the doctor said: "I must not have any sex until I come back and see him."

We had terrible arguments because his friends are telling him it's not so. I told him: "They weren't there. That's what the doctor told me. I have to go back and he has to tell me." So we had horrible, horrible arguments. No hitting—but arguments.

I wouldn't go to bed sometimes. I'll do my ironing and things when he's gone to bed to catch the four o'clock start bus. In those days you never had any contraceptive, so you have to make you own way not to get pregnant.

Evelyn is living through a testing period in her life. She has given up her second job and survived her second difficult pregnancy.

Yet she is still determined to push through.

> I went shopping one day. I was walking, going
> back home and I noticed an advertisement in
> the window of the South Staffordshire Laundry:
> 'Assistant Manager Wanted'.
>
> I applied for it and I got it. All you do is take
> your clothes in to be done, they sent it away and
> you come and collect it.
>
> No Black person has ever worked there. I was
> the first Black person who ever work on the High
> Street in West Bromwich.
>
> My job was to take the laundry coming in,
> check how many pieces, give them a receipt and
> put it in a bag. The van pick it up. They laundry
> it and bring it back. Then you give it out. That's
> all you had to do.
>
> It was only up the road from my house.

Reggie is still on the buses at the time but he has stopped
conducting and started driving. Evelyn is now in her third job
since arriving in the UK. This job unlike her previous one allows
her to take care of her parental responsibilities.

> At the laundry I could take both Garry and Janice
> to work. I could take my babies with me.
>
> Nothing was going on there to harm them
> because the laundry come in, it goes in a bag, goes
> out and comes back in a bag, then you give it out.
> So it was fine.

At the time, most African Caribbean parents would have left their children with a carer they knew—most likely a friend or family member. Evelyn, however refuses to do this. By the age of sixteen Evelyn had lived in four different households and she doesn't want the same fate for her children.

> My kids come first and I'm not letting anybody else care for my children because I didn't want them to get confused.
>
> I'm trying to bring them up this way and then you send them to somebody else, they're doing it a different way—so the child gets confused. A lot of kids got so confused and they turn out badly. It's because of them going from pillow to post from they were babies. They didn't know which way to turn.
>
> I decided no. Nobody is looking after my kids.

By any measure, Evelyn's job at the laundry is a good one. It satisfies all of her requirements, except one—her career goals.

> I worked there for a while. Then the manageress and I had an argument. They have a window cleaner and one day he didn't turn up. She's telling me that I must go and clean the windows. I said: "I ain't cleaning no window. If you want to clean it, you do it. Clean the floor, do whatever you want to, but I'm not doing it."
>
> We had an argument and I just took my coat and walked out.

It turns out that the area manager is a little more understanding than Evelyn's boss. They offer her an alternative.

> The area manager came and ask me if I would go as a supervisor—relief manageress—to other laundries. I said: "No, I'm not travelling. I've got children, I'm not doing it."
>
> It would have been a good job.

Shortly after leaving South Staffordshire Laundry Evelyn tries her hand at something totally different.

> I went to theatre school. Yes, I went to the Old Rep Drama School in Birmingham. I did drama there. Donna Carroll was there, she's from Coventry. You're seen her on telly. She made famous from doing *Hair*—the musical. I remembered we went to see her at the Hippodrome. It was a sort of a hippie show and she had to strip on stage. The first time they did *Hair*, they did the strip scene and they didn't floodlight it. But when they did it again and she was in it, they floodlit it. I thought: 'Oh my God! I hope your parents is not in the audience'. Her dad was a minister in Coventry.
>
> Toyah was there as well, she's a singer now. We were all in the same group. Toyah was picked from Birmingham Rep. She was a punk. The first thing she did, she said: "I don't know how I got the part." They were doing this Punk thing in London and she got the part. She said: "I read it.

I was a mess, but I still got the part."

While I was there, I think I appeared in nearly every episode of *Angels* when it came to Birmingham. At first I was selected to start in *Empire Road*. I didn't like the script and I didn't like the bloke who wrote the script. I think he never wrote anything to uplift Black people.

He did one script for a TV play with [a well-known Black actor] which I thought was disgusting. It was about a Christmas meal that Black people were having—'Black Christmas'. There was quarrelling and things in the script, and I challenged him about it. I said: "I'm not against you writing the script but you couldn't even see Black people doing one good thing. I don't think you should go down to that level just to get your script accepted." I didn't accept a role.

I didn't like [that actor]. He was a nasty piece of work. I thought I ain't kissing him on screen, no way. I remember we were at Pebble Mill and the police arrest him. They come and take him off the set and everything. He never looked after his children. He was a drunk, he drinks like a fish. He would go round some of the girls and ask them to sleep with him. Then he would come back and tell everybody. He was filthy, not a nice person at all. I thought I'm not going to act with you. I don't have to go to that depth. They paid hundreds a week but I thought no. I could have gone and done quite a lot.

Her brief foray into the world of acting is not sustained. Unlike most of the young students around her at the Old Rep Drama School in Birmingham, she is around forty years old. She is not getting the roles she wants and she has issues with the management. Though she recalls the venture with a great deal of nostalgia, getting roles on a regular basis is far too uncertain for it to be regarded as a real job.

> After I walked out of South Staffordshire Laundry I thought: 'You know what, I ain't working for anybody else after this. We're not going to get along'. So I decided to go to college and do hairdressing.
>
> The West Bromwich college was not teaching it, so I had to go to Wolverhampton College. I called to make an appointment.

Although it's the 1970's, getting into a hairdressing training course is not as straightforward as Evelyn assumes.

> When I went and they saw that I was Black—shock! They said: "Will you reconsider because we don't think you will be able to do it." I said: "Excuse me? No! I'm not going to reconsider, I'm not reconsidering. I came here and I'm supposed to have a test. If I pass the test I'll be here. If I fail it, I promise you I won't bother you."
>
> I don't know why they thought I couldn't do it. They said they've had never had a Black person before and all their customers is white.

I went in and I pass the test.

You had to do three years. A lot of people don't realise the depth of hairdressing. Three years you had to do it. After that you had to go and work in a hairdressing salon before you should open your own shop. That was more training—advance—and you learn business management as well.

When Evelyn is accepted for the hairdressing course, she is forty-three years old.

The principal of the college was Scottish. I went in and I started to do it. After that I just blossom. If I see something once, I get it. I only have to see it happen once.

I was the only student in that college who pass the perm theory exam one hundred per cent. The morning I was going in, I got to top of the stairs. The secretary was standing there and she said to me: "Trust you! It had to be you who done it, nobody else. It had to be you." I thought: 'What have I done! I haven't done anything that I know of'.

I went up and my name was there, a hundred per cent. Everybody came in and I heard them saying: "We've heard of ninety-seven, we've heard of ninety-eight, but we've never bloody heard of one hundred per cent."

I was so embarrassed I left college midday. I always wanted to do hairdressing. It's exactly what

I wanted to do.

Evelyn's tutors think she's an exceptional student.

I did the course in a year and a half instead of three years. I was offered a job there to teach.

I said to the principal at the college: "Do you think I'll succeed if I open my own salon?" He said: "Evelyn from what I see here, you can." He use to test me. He use to test me a lot. He'd give me something to do or he'll give me a virgin head and say you do this or you do that, and I'll do it. He said to me one day: "I'm not teaching you anything new here."

I went on to the Nectar College to do colouring and everything. I was offered a job in the Nectar Company to go the London for three days a week to doing training, naming my own price.

I couldn't do it because I had my kids.

Evelyn continues to aim high and takes the next step in her career.

I decided to open my own salon. I opened my first salon in the second week of December 1978. It was in West Bromwich on the Ringway.

God has provided me with a husband that understands. If he tells me he doesn't do this, I'm doing it as long as it's not something wrong. If it's going to be good, I'm doing it and he understands.

I always say: 'God gave me my brain and if you have to think for me, I shouldn't have one'. We talk about it out of respect, but don't you insist that I have to do what you say. It's my decision. My life is my own.

IVY

Ivy and Wesley are now newlyweds. Upon getting married Wesley moves in with Ivy at her room in Camberwell. Shortly after, Ivy, at the age of 33, becomes pregnant so the couple decides to move.

> We had to find a place to live and that was some-where in Balham. Can't remember the name of the street, but it was somewhere in Balham.
>
> My first child, Simone, was born in 1967, a year after I got married. Then we moved to some-where in Streatham. That's when my Daniel came along in 1968.
>
> When we moved to Streatham, we wanted to buy that house because the landlady was my second child's godmother and she was going away to Canada. She said we could still live there and just pay rent, but my husband didn't agree with that.
>
> We then moved to Tooting Broadway and my Charles came along in 1969. The boys were bigger than the girl and called her their kid sister.
>
> We were in a tenant's house. We had the

middle section of the house. The owners wasn't living there yet because they were waiting to sell their own house. They were friends of ours and we lived there until they sold their house. They had the top floor and the bottom floor. Their kids were on the top floor.

***

Before getting married Ivy had been trying to send for her mother, Estell.

After 1962 you couldn't just come and go between Jamaica and England. I went to the Home Office and they told me she couldn't come to England because I had to have a home or house to put her.

Around the time of Charles's birth in 1969, Estell becomes seriously ill and the need to resolve the issue of her visa becomes more urgent.

I was sending money home to Jamaica for my mother. By then she had got sugar diabetes and was in hospital for a long time. One of my cousin's had moved in with her to look after her. I was sending money for her care and support, but my cousin was spending the money on herself and my mother wasn't being cared for.

A next door neighbour of my mother wrote to me. I don't know how she got my address. She

told me my mother is going to die because she's
not being cared for. She wrote: 'Unless you come
and get her, she's going to die.'

Ivy, now a mother of three and aged 37, knew something had to
be done for her mother, Estell.

I went out to Jamaica to see her, I think it was
1970. That was the first time I went back.

I saw my cousin and she said she was looking
after my mum, that she was cooking food for my
mother and buying her clothes. But my mother
didn't have any more clothes than the ones I
had sent for her. She, my cousin, had loads of
clothes—earrings, nice things and such.

I just told her that it was okay. I'll continue to
send money until I can get my mother to England
with me.

Ivy is determined to send for her mother and keeps on trying
to get a visa for her. She knows her mother has already spent
a great deal of time in hospital and the cousin Ivy is sending
money to on behalf of her mother, is apparently spending it
on herself. It is 1976/7 before the Home Office finally grants
permission for Estell to come to England.

I booked her fare. By the time I got back home
from the travel agent, there was a letter for me
saying that my mother had been given a visa and
had to travel by a certain date.

> I sent my mother a telegram to say get ready as
> I would be sending the ticket.

Ivy does not explain why she was so determined to send for her mother. Ivy is open about her mother's lack of commitment to her upbringing and at the time. When Ivy left Jamaica in 1962, she wanted to get away from her abusive father, but she also wanted to get away from her mother.

Just before Ivy sorts the visa issue for her mother, her and husband Wesley manage to secure a mortgage to buy their first home—a three-bedroom house in Canal Road, Barkingside.

> My husband was working for British Rail. I had
> stopped working as a machinist. I was fed up of
> dressmaking.
> When we came to Canal Road School my
> youngest was seven, so it was quite a while since
> our last move.

When Ivy's mother, Estell, arrives in England, she stays with Ivy, her husband Wesley and her three children.

> My mum came while we were at Canal Road, so
> then I could go out to work while she was here. I
> left her and I went to work.

Once Estell is in England, Ivy feels she is now responsible for her mother's wellbeing.

She was going to stay with me for good.

She didn't really need treatment. She just needed her diabetes taken care of. She didn't know how to, so she was always getting sick while she was out there and not getting proper food and all that.

Ivy finds that the relationship between her and her mother improves immediately.

Once she came up where I could look after her. It was different and we became much closer than we've ever been.

I didn't accept her as my mother when I was growing up. We were never close until when she came to live with us. She had changed a lot from her young days when she use to be like a princess or whatever. She was more mature.

Ivy, however, cannot avoid noticing that her mother's attitude towards young children has remained—particularly with regards to her approach when educating young children.

When she came, she still didn't want my kids to play. She wants them to get down to their books, read and study.

I told her one day that: "When I was growing up, I vowed I would never grow up my kids the way I was grown up. I would let my kids know that I love them and I would show love to them.

I stopped her from putting any pressure on my kids, the way she did to me."

Ivy is now standing up to her mother in a way that she couldn't in her youth. Having previously given up her dressmaking job, Ivy goes back to work as a dinner lady in a school, leaving her mother to see that the children get to school every day.

I can't remember any major problems with the kids at school. The only thing I had to sort out at school was with Charles. They put him on daily report because he was lazy. He didn't do his homework and things like that. If you ask Charles: "Have you done your homework?" It's: "Yes, Mum." "Bring it, let me see." "Oh I did it at school and I left it at school." So they put him on report and then I ask them to make sure he do his homework before he come home. Even then he was on report for quite a while. Otherwise than that, I've never had any problems with the other children at school.

Ivy's and Wesley's three-bedroom house in Canal Road is too small for a family of six, so the family take out a mortgage on an ever bigger house in Rockhalt Road.

Despite all her initial uncertainty, Ivy is now settled in England. She is married with three children in school and is back at work. Her and her husband have just bought a larger house and her mother is living with her, taking care of her three children when she is not there. Things seem to be going well.

My cousin in America send me a fare to come and
see her. My mum was here so I could go to see
my cousin. Before that I couldn't leave the kids
to go away, so I took the opportunity when my
mother came.

That cousin was maybe a few years older than
me when I was growing up, but she didn't act like
that. She act like we were the same age. We could
talk about things, subjects which I couldn't raise
with my mother. She was like a big sister.

She left Jamaica and went to America and got
her own place. She was moving to Florida when
I got there so we went together to view the house
she wanted to buy.

Ivy's trip to America—sometime in 1981—is not one she
thought she would be making but when the opportunity arises,
she takes it. Little does she know that this trip will be the beginning of a very challenging time for her and family. At the time,
Ivy is forty-eight years old, her daughter Simone is fourteen and
her sons Daniel and Charlies are thirteen and twelve years old.

It all starts with what is a seemingly innocent suggestion by
her cousin when they are together in Florida.

She wanted me to buy a place there as well and I
did pay down a deposit. When I came home my
husband said "no way," even though it wasn't his
money. Maybe I was silly to listen.

Ivy does not go into detail on why, out of the blue, she

251

considers investing in a property in Florida. Though she must have given her decision serious consideration, as she puts a deposit down on the house. Maybe Ivy thought her family might actually want to move to America. Other Jamaicans in England were doing that at the time.

> My husband thought he was only going to be in
> England for five years. Then we were going to go
> back home to Jamaica. I didn't think the same
> thing because I didn't have a home to go back to.

A likely explanation of why she considers investing in property in Florida is to do with what her cousin tells her. While Ivy is in America, her cousin brings up the troubling issue of the sexual abuse Ivy was subject to by her father.

> That was the first time I spoke about it. She told
> me that she knew because my mother told her.

The impact of her cousin's revelation on Ivy is huge. Up until that moment, Ivy had believed that her mother knew nothing of her father's abuse. Ivy is in shock particularly as she took steps to ensure that her mother was cared for while ill in Jamaica and could come to England. She wouldn't even be in America if it wasn't for her mother looking after her kids. Now that she knows her mother knew all along, she is unsure what she is to do.

When Ivy's trip to Florida comes to an end, Ivy and her cousin return to New York.

Understandably, Ivy is unable to get the news of her mother

out of her mind. Though she has a stable and relatively happy life in London, she is seriously considering not going back *home*.

I was introduced to a lady who cuts up dead people. I can't think what you call that. She does post-mortems.

I was recommended to her and it seemed that we had kindred spirits. She had a boy and a girl and she said: "Come and stay with me and look after my kids."

It was in Chappaqua, that's just outside of New York. The place she lived, it had a big house and a lot of land. Her clothes closet would have been bigger than this room.

***

Ivy returns to the family home in Rockhalt Road.

When I came back from Florida I had to face my mother. I told her what my cousin said.

I told her that I couldn't forgive her for knowing that something like that was happening to your only child and you didn't do anything about it.

She started crying and said she didn't know.

But my brother also knew. He told me later when he came to England to visit me and he told me he was going to kill my dad. I told him I'm glad he didn't.

Even though Estell refuses to admit to her daughter that she knew what Jamsey was doing to her, Ivy later tells her that she forgives her.

Once again, the family is on the move. Ivy and Wesley sell their house in Rockhalt Road and buy a flat in Chadwell Heath. Wesley goes to live at the flat in Chadwell Heath. Estell gets a council flat in Rockhalt Road and Simone, Daniel and Charlie move in with her. For all practical purposes the family seems to have split up. Ivy does not explain why this happened.

Ivy then decides to go back to America. She's going to look after the children of Dr Gatt—the coroner in Chappaqua.

> She gave me a big room which she saved for her visitors when they come along.
>
> My daughter and my husband came to visit while I was there at this lady's place but the boys didn't want to come.
>
> She found out I could do dressmaking and freehand sewing. She would go to the store, buy a dress and the material, bring it home and ask me to copy it. Then she would take the dress back to the store. I did quite a few dresses for her, just copying them. I did her some lovely jumpers— knitted and that.

Ivy's daughter Simone brings Ivy's stay with Dr Gatt to an early end sometime in 1984. Simone is seventeen years old and comes to visit her mother in Chappaqua.

She said she was homesick and wanted to see her brothers. So she came back and ended up in a mental home.

I had to come home. I came home to look after her. I think she was in her teens, but she wasn't working or anything.

The doctors did not ever say why my daughter got ill. She was a book pest and they thought she was studying too much and that it affected her brain. That's all they could think of. There was nothing visible to say.

Looking after Simone while she's mentally ill is far from easy and it has a profound effect on Ivy.

I was going to the mental home two, three times a day. The way she was harassing me like a little baby—jumping on me, pulling me around.

The doctors at the hospital were telling me don't come that often. They told me it wasn't good for me. But I couldn't sit at home and know that she's there and I don't go and see her. So I kept visiting until I got sick myself. I had a minor nervous breakdown.

By her own admission, Ivy is far from mentally stable herself yet she decides that Simone is not being helped by the doctors and chooses to take matters into her own hands.

My daughter came out of hospital after because

I took her out. I shouldn't have because I wasn't well at the time when I took her home.

She was a handful. She couldn't settle down. She was like a toddler then.

The difficulty of caring for her mentally sick daughter takes a serious toll on Ivy.

I couldn't cope.

We were at the flat that we bought in Chadwell Heath. That's where my husband was living. The boys were with my mother in the council flat, but I wouldn't let Simone go there. So I was looking after her.

Unfortunately for Ivy, Wesley is not particularly helpful during this time.

My husband wasn't one to show that he cared about anything. He didn't want to know and carried on his life as usual. He go to work, come home, expect his meals and that.

I looked after her the best I could while I needed someone to look after me as well. I had to look after myself and her. She got better in the end. She got a job and went to work. She was fine.

During this time Dr Gatt wants Ivy to return to Chappaqua and continue looking after her children. Dr Gatt is aware Ivy has her own family in England and that this might affect her decision, so she attempts to persuade her by telling her to bring her family along.

> The lady in America started getting out papers for me to stay in America—get my Green Card and all that. They sent the card over here and I could go somewhere in the West End to get it. I had a couple of weeks to go and collect it.
>
> I didn't have to leave my own family to go and work in America. Dr Gatt was saying: 'If I come and be permanent there, then I could bring all of my family out as well'. That was the idea of me getting a Green Card to settle down. She even promised that she would help me get my own place.
>
> But her kids didn't need any looking after. They were able to look after themselves. I was just there to see they get off to school and be there when they come home from school. They were kids that does everything for themselves.

Ivy contemplates going but in the end it is her daughter who helps her decide what to do.

> Simone said: "Don't go." The time pass for me to go and collect the Green Card, so they sent it back to America.
>
> I just couldn't go. I couldn't leave Simone.

Dr Gatt however refuses to give up. She is determined to get Ivy back to America.

She sent me my fare to America.

When Simone got better, I wanted to go, and I didn't want to go. Everybody was saying, she sent you the ticket, you have to go. I was tempted.

The boys are old enough to make their own minds up. I reckon they just carried on the way they use to when we all lived together. They didn't give my mother any problems and she was happy with that. She never complained, and they loved her because she was their Gran.

I decided to go.

Ivy boards the plane to New York using the ticket Dr Gatt bought her.

She was waiting for me at the airport. I didn't go out.

I just think what if Simone gets sick again? I would have to keep going back. I asked them if I could get back on the next plane out.

I got the next plane back home.

That was it.

EMMA

It is 1967 and Emma is sixteen years old. She is attending Spon Lane Secondary Modern School in West Bromwich and she is pregnant.

Understandably, when she discovers that she is with child, Emma is especially anxious to tell her parents. By then, most of the other tenants had left the family home in Beeches Road.

> The only people that was living in that house at the time I had Samuel was my uncle Raynard and his wife, who was pregnant.

Uncle Raynard is Emma's mother's eldest brother, he got married while living at the family home in Dartmouth Street and moved in with the family when they bought the house in Beeches Road. Emma does not like his wife.

> She had never worked since she'd been in the country. By the time she had children for my uncle, she already had four children who were in Jamaica.
>
> She was the person who first noticed that I was pregnant. She was pregnant herself at the same

time, so she knew about a woman being pregnant and she was observing me.

She was actually instrumental in letting the whole area know I was pregnant, and had been saying it outside our house before saying it to my mom. That's how it came back to my mum and Mum was very annoyed.

I look back on all that now and I think: 'God was on our side and the power of her tongue has worked back on her in different ways.' Uncle Raynard is divorced from that lady now.

Emma's mother is furious about the way she finds out that her daughter is pregnant, as is her father.

She would say: "It's only a prostitute would have gone out and done that."

Dad went absolutely ballistic and wanted to know who was responsible.

I went and contacted Mathew. I was waiting at his house one day. When he came home from work I told him what I was there about. I think he knew.

Anyway, he came back with me to my parents. Dad asked him if he was responsible and he said yes. Mathew was very calm and Dad says: "Well! What you're going do about it?" He said he would take on whatever the financial responsibility was.

I thought it was commendable of him to have said that. Around me there were other friends

who fell pregnant and the fella's they just didn't
want to know, or they took off. He stayed.

Emma's father remained furious and made the decision that
Emma would have to get married.

> My wedding dress was bought. This wedding was
> being planned quite hurriedly. It would have been
> called 'shotgun wedding' back in them days.

Fortunately for Emma, there is a divine intervention of sorts.

> Dad said one day he had a vision from God that it
> wasn't the right thing to do. That wasn't the words
> he used. He said: "I was going to get married to
> gallows!" In other words, this man would beat me.
> Whatever the conception was behind that, he
> felt that the marriage wouldn't have worked.

Concerns about the proposed wedding are also being raised by
others.

> Mathew's parents got involved. No, it was more
> his aunt, because his aunt had raised him.
> Anyway, his aunt was against the marriage.
> If she could have got him to marry somebody
> else she would have done that because she liked
> this woman. That was the person his aunt always
> favoured that he should have married. I never
> knew her. It turned out that this woman married

somebody else. His aunt didn't realise that she'd got married.

Our wedding plans was scrapped. We didn't get married. I remained at home.

The next few months can only be described as a period of 'high drama' in the life of the pregnant sixteen-year-old.

After all this initial shock, my parents must have felt reasonably happy because Mathew was still visiting for a couple of months. This is the stupid bit. My dad then said he doesn't want for anybody to be saying that I'd got an association with him. He stopped him from coming to the house. He wanted the relationship to end.

Luckily for Emma, her mother feels bad for her and when her father is not at home Emma's mother helps her and Mathew see each other.

I didn't see Mathew for about two or three weeks. Then he sent a message to me so I'd be seeing him secretly, which didn't really matter anymore. We kept in contact and my mom allowed him to visit me, but not when dad was there. It was like deceit in a sense.

My mom knew his aunty who raised him. They were the same age group and they use to meet at different things. So there was already a connection of some sort.

Though Mathew is now supposedly banned from the house, he stands by his original promise to take care of the baby.

> He said he would support me and that he would take financial responsibility for the child. He faithfully brought money and gave it to me. As far as I was concerned, he was keeping his side of the bargain.
>
> Folks who I knew within the family would give me ten shillings or something like that, and I would save little bits for myself. I handed it all over to my mom, assuming she's going to be putting this money aside in preparation for when I had the baby. I felt there would be some security. I was naïve. I was young.

Emma's mother Millie is accepting money from Mathew, intended to be put aside for the baby. Secretly and against the express instructions of her husband, she is also allowing Mathew to continue seeing her daughter. Then, to Emma's shock, Millie changes.

> Oh my mum, she beat the hell out of me. She started hitting me, especially in my stomach. I can only imagine that was her way of dealing with the shock. Then afterwards she cried when she realised what she was doing. She was really hitting my stomach. My feelings was: 'Well typical. They really hated me anyway'. That was what I was thinking. 'So here she is now, trying to kill this child'.

Emma becomes withdrawn in the house. She now distrusts both her parents.

> I even stopped eating from home although I was pregnant. I didn't give up eating. I just didn't eat anything that was provided by my parents in the home because of the different names I was being called. Mathew would bring me stuff. He would come and meet me but we wouldn't stay in the house. Dad knew by this time that I was still seeing him but I was already pregnant, so what's the point.
>
> Mathew, he took the abuse for me. He held me when I'd cried. He called my dad 'The Vicar', so I was Vicar's daughter. That was so painful for me when I was pregnant with Samuel. I was thinking: 'How could he be a Vicar and he was treating me like that'? That's our private story.

Emma's mother finds other ways of demonstrating her disapproval towards her daughter.

> I told you that we were highly favoured in a sense because we had relatives that got skills. One relative in particular—living in England—was the first cousin of my mom, on my grandmother's side. She had about nine houses in London, so she was a woman of substance. Her maiden name was Louise Parkes and her married name was Bell. We call her cousin Lou. She's deceased now.

She made clothes for what is Harrods today. She had teams of people that she employed in the cotton industry—mostly Asian people. She was like the original in our community that did that. But I didn't know all that at the time. All I knew was that she made these clothes.

The clothes use to come from London by the boxful. It was like the ones which wasn't stitched quite right. They would come to my mom. They wouldn't be fully completed. They might have had the darts put in the sides because of miss stitching, so they wouldn't be acceptable. They come up and we had the first choice of all this. We were privileged.

Up until I was pregnant, I had loads of clothes from my mum's cousin Lou. When Mom found out I was pregnant, she gave everything away— coats, everything. It was very painful. All Mom left me with was my underwear, two smock dresses and other maternity clothes that was bought. She said I wouldn't have any use for these other clothes anymore. All that was how she displayed her anger and her dismay. She gave everything away. I was left with just my underwear and these two dresses.

Anyway, OK. I lived with all that.

Somehow, Emma manages to continue with her education.

I have five GCE's. I completed some of my studies

265

at home whilst I was pregnant, I managed to get five 'O' Levels. That's not bad at all.

There is also sympathy and support from some of the tenants still living in the family home.

The Stennetts—they lived in the back room on the first floor. She was a lovely lady because she experience the turmoil I was actually going through being pregnant. She was that kind face and encourager.

She worked at the maternity home that I actually had Samuel in. There was lots of people who she knew that knitted and gave things to the maternity home. She had things knitted for me, although I use to knit myself. She brought me this little knitted matinee coat—in yellow because it could go for boy or girl—with a hat, bootees and mittens. She wasn't a midwife but she worked in the maternity home. She was the first person that ever brought me anything.

She moved out of our house before I had the baby.

It is October 1967 when Emma's baby arrives; she is 16 years old.

I had Samuel on the Thursday morning. Mathew came and visited me in hospital and I said to him: "Well you need to go and see Mom now because she has the money you have been giving her weekly." He went to see my mom on the Friday evening. She says: "What money you talking bout?" He came back and told me. I didn't realise that the money he was giving was suppose to have been paying for my food when I was pregnant.

He had to go and find money from some-where. We had already selected what we'd get for the baby and it was like the best they had in the shop—the bath and stand. I had already bought nappies and nightgowns and stuff like that, I had a start. Whether the baby was a boy or girl, you wore a nightgown anyway back in them days. So the basic necessities we need now would be his cot and some cot blankets.

Mathew had a bit of money, not a great deal, but enough to have bought those things and buy them for cash. He went and got them and had them delivered. He told me mom they would be delivered. He had to go in the house and set it up.

Oh! That created tension. The fact that he had to go in my room which was in the attic and set up the cot and that. I was still in hospital, but contention was being created out of this.

Anyway we overcome.

When she leaves the hospital with her newborn baby, Emma has no idea what her parents are going to do next.

You would not have believed it! There was a

celebration. My mom did this big cook-up. People came from all over the place and local people from the neighbourhood. I only see these people in the street and they were being entertained.

Well it was their first grandchild but that wasn't the side I saw. She's invited them. There was cake, curry and rice, in celebration. I was like flabbergasted! How I was meant to feel because that was contrary to how things were.

I think she threw the party as a way of letting people see that they were glad to have a grandchild. I look back on it and I say: "That was just a show for the community."

Things didn't really change. Things didn't actually change.

The next challenge for Emma is learning how to look after baby Samuel.

The midwife would come and carry on teaching me what I needed to know. Although she'd moved out of the house, Mrs Stennett came and visited me. She worked at the hospital and she gave me tips and what have you. Mom was cordial to her but the reason why the Stennetts moved out was because of the way Mom and Dad was towards me.

Looking back on it all, it was a very painful time. Anyway, I forgive them for all that.

Emma is allowed to remain in the family home.

> Samuel was registered in his father's name. Our parents did not interfere. Both Mathew and I went and registered him as Samuel Thompson.
>
> Because I had a faith, which most Caribbean people were brought up with, I knew that he needs to get christened. My mom knows everybody. She knows the Vicar at St. Phillip's, our local Anglican Church, and I asked her if she could make an appointment with the Vicar to have him christened.
>
> I expected her to come back and say she'd made the appointment. Anyway she did. She says she speak with the minister and he needs to see you. Reverend Daniels his name was. She told us where his address was and when we went and saw him, we set a date for the christening. It was December 1967—the day before Christmas Eve.

As Emma learns, nothing involving her parents is ever going to be that simple.

> My mom bakes and she had baked lots of cakes for Christmas. So I says to her: "Mom, which one of them cakes is Samuel's?" She says: "Samuel what!" I says: "Samuel's Christening cake." She says: "You ah christen Samuel?" I said: "But Mom, you got the appointment for us to go and see the minister." She said: "Did you go and see

him?" I said: "I come back and I told you." She says: "Out ah street me hear it."

When I think about what I went through, it brings the pain back without a doubt. I said: "OK." I went and bought fruits, flour, sugar—all the bits and pieces I needed to bake a cake. Mathew had a word with his landlady, asked if I could come down there and make the christening cake. I made two cakes. This was less than two weeks away to the christening.

I didn't give my mother that responsibility. It's our child, so we're going arrange what we were going to have. Me and Mathew spoke with two of my cousins and a friend of his on becoming godparents. Samuel was christened at St. Phillip's church.

The only family member there from Mathew's side was his dad. Some of his friends came. The godparents were Canute and Lobby, cousins of mine who have passed away now. My cousin Leyman and his brother-in-law came, but no one else from my family—not even my little sister. The reception? We had the reception in the bedroom where Mathew lived. The cake was cut downstairs. That was it.

Around this time Emma's grandmother in Jamaica becomes seriously ill. This is the person she spent the first eight years of her life with.

Emma has a great deal of respect and admiration for her

grandmother. As far as she was concerned, before coming to England in 1959, her grandmother was her 'mother'.

I kept in contact with my grandma periodically. When I heard she was sick, I said to my mum: "Can we go and see Grandma?" I didn't have the finances to have gone, but I knew Mum had. If she had decided to have gone, I would have asked her then: "Could I come with you?"

My grandma died and my mother said: "She not going go look pon no corpse." She didn't say why.

I must say in those days I was never one for questioning. I was very introverted, I didn't say much. I very much bottled-up my feelings. No one really knew what my true feelings were, I tend to just bury it. I realised in later life that I buried quite a lot.

I just left it as it is. Later I realise that was a hurt I had buried inside me, against me mum. I internalised those words that she said and I didn't realise that it had gone so deep. I held on to that resentment for quite some years.

I still loved her, I was obedient to her. I didn't ever say anything to her except by my actions. If there was any mention of her mum, I would mutter under my breath: "You don't care about her. You don't care about your mom." If she'd heard what I said, she probably would have hit me. Because of that there was this void that

started happening between her and I. But she was
civil towards me and I was civil towards her.

Even though Emma is living in the family home, she is estranged
from her parents. Yet they seem to know a great deal about what
is going on between her and Mathew.

I discovered that anything Mathew and I had to
say in conversation and my sister heard, she would
take it back to Mom and it would get distorted.
That's how it was for a few months. Well it was
happening before I had Samuel.

I'd made me mind up before that I'm gonna
get away from here. I've got this child and I'm
gonna get away from here.

Baby Samuel is four mouths old when Emma decides to leave
the family home in Beeches Road. She has every intention of
concealing her plans from her parents.

Mathew had moved to West Bromwich and he
was planning to move back to Smethwick. Now
whether he was moving back to Smethwick to get
away from me, I don't know. I'm saying it as I saw
it at the time.

On the night that he was moving from this
rented room in West Bromwich, I said to him:
"Tell the man to come and get my bits and
pieces." I left home.

Obviously, most of the things in my suitcase

was Samuel's. I had a couple of dresses and a coat that Mathew had bought me. So basically, in spite of being privileged and had all these beautiful clothing, I left with just my underwear, some towels and my son—not even a sheet. I did take two pillowcases, I think I still have them.

It turns out that her parents knew of her plans to leave the family home.

My sister Emily—God bless her—had heard. She heard part of our conversation but she didn't get all of it. Before I actually left home she told my mom. My mom tackle me one evening and says: "Hmmm! What's this me hear say you ah move go ah London?" Then another day it would be: "Oh! You not going so far again. You going ah Handsworth." I am saying to her: "What yer talking about?"

It is January 1968; Emma is aged 17 years old when she leaves her parents home for good. Emma's father, thanks to Emma's younger sister Emily, follows the van Mathew, Emma and baby Samuel are in.

On the night when I did leave home, my dad followed the van. But he followed the van to the first house where Mathew was going to be moving into which was in Smethwick. When we were moving in and the family who owned the house

Chapter Six

see there's a cot, a baby and a woman coming they said: "Oh no! The room is only for you."

So there we were. We're in transit. We got nowhere to live.

Emma, Mathew and baby Samuel are stuck. They had not anticipated that they would not able to stay in Smethwick. Luckily for them, the landlord is able to help.

The same landlord that was a friend of Mathew's, who said that there would be a room, he says: "There's some Indian houses up St. Paul's Road."

This is the house that we actually went and lived in. Her surname was Kaur. Her first name was Maggie, can't remember her husband's first name but it started with an 'A'. She said: "Yes, there's a room."

Emma, Mathew and baby Samuel finally have a home.

The family that took us in, they'd got four sons of their own. The youngest son was the same age as Samuel, so there were two little boys in the house. The other ones were older and there was four other lots of tenants in the house. It was a massive, double fronted house—big. Our rent for our first room in that house was £2 fifteen shillings a week.

Dad had followed us to the first place. When he saw the van pull up and things was going

274

in—which he would have done from a distance—
he went back home and assumed that's where we'd
moved. He didn't see that we moved somewhere
else. So he went back with that news.

It's not Emma's father but her mother who quickly discovers the
couple's new address. Emma and Mathew are now living less
than a mile from the family home.

I was speaking to cousin Leyman who was at
Samuel's christening. Leyman was somebody we
could confide in. He's also the half-brother to
my half-sister, so his aunt was my grandmother.
But I still look on him as a big brother—not even
realising. He would also bring food to the house,
nearly always fruits or cakes and what have you.
He knew where we were living and he told me
mom.

Mom came to visit after a few weeks. She just
turned up. She found us, met my landlady and
told her who she was. Not sure if she met the
husband. The landlady sent one of her sons to call
me and I invited her up.

She says: "Me tell you say you going end up
in telephone box." I says: "Yes, thank you for
coming Mom." She says: "You need anything?"
This is February 1968 and I've left home now
nearly a month.

Following her mother's 'visit', perhaps for the first time, Emma comes to realise the full implications of her situation. She is now almost totally disconnected from her immediate family.

> I didn't get this enfoldment that perhaps I felt I should have had because they thought I was probably being rebellious. The message coming over to me now was that there was really nothing left for me to live for. I didn't feel suicidal then but I felt suicidal later on down the line.
>
> The love I know that my parents had got for other people was there, but unfortunately I didn't feel it. I was a teenager, maybe rebellious. But I'm not blaming them for everything.

Emma's room in St. Paul's Road may be little more than a 'telephone box', but the rent still has to be paid, so Emma needs to find a job.

> After I had Samuel, I got a job at our local Woolworths store in Smethwick—my first proper job. The building itself now is actually a market, but it use to be a Woolworths store on the High Street. I was a cashier.
>
> Then I left from there. I heard that they'd got a job at the co-op laundry where I knew a number of people. You could just turn up at the place, have an interview and you start the job. It was more money you see. At the co-op, I was a laundry operator. I didn't work in the dry cleaning department. When the clothes had been washed, they

had this big machine which was like a giant iron really. It was called a collinder. You would feed the clothing through it and it would come out ironed. I stayed there for over a year.

Emma, Mathew and baby Samuel are to remain at St. Paul's Road for almost two years, then something happens.

I found out I was pregnant again. Before we had Donna, we'd planned to get married. We had our second child living there and we got married a couple months after that.

Their wedding plans following baby Donna's birth are modest.

We planned a small wedding, what we could afford. We went and sought our parents blessings. We did get his dad's and stepmother's blessing and we got my parent's blessing as well.

With the unexpected approval of Emma's parents, their wedding plans gather momentum.

Mom took it to another level. She's now very excited and said: "It can't be no secret, hush, hush, something. You're only going get married once." She took me and bought my wedding dress. I choose the dress. She was going to take care of the cake. We end up having a six-tier wedding cake and eight more, what they call a fourteen-tier. It was spectacular, really beautiful.

Their wedding is held at St. Phillip's Church and conducted by Reverend Daniels who christened Samuel.

> We had a lovely wedding. We had a big wedding. My dad gave me away. Yeah, he actually came in the church.
>
> Mathew's aunt gave us £30. Back in the day that was an awful lot of money, it was a month's wages. I think it was the first time I saw a twenty-pound note. Looking back on it all, she loved him. She didn't have any children for herself.
>
> We paid for the flowers but a relative gave me the money back for the flowers. Listen to this, we saved just over £200 on the wedding. That take some doing.

Shortly before Emma had her second child and before the wedding, her mother Millie came to visit her bearing some important family news.

> It was a Friday when my mom came to say that Emily had a baby yesterday morning. I'm saying to her: "What you talking about? Are you trying to shock me into having my baby because I'm big here. Emily was with me two weeks ago. How can she be pregnant and I never saw?" She concealed it well because she was stocky.
>
> Anyway my sister had her first baby ten days

before I had Donna. That's another story. She was
seventeen at the time. She was working at an old
people's home over in Acocks Green, Birmingham.
If you've heard of these surprises—women having
a baby not knowing they were pregnant—it was
a scenario such as that. I think she knew, but that
was a surprise to me.

There was no preparation but Mom and Dad
helped her. She got things.

Emma's sister had her first child while still living at the family
home in Beeches Road. Emma cannot avoid comparing how
Emily is treated by her parents with how she was treated on
becoming pregnant at sixteen.

I don't know what life would've been like for her
there, she never said. But everything seemed OK.

The circumstances surrounding her being
pregnant with this child was somewhat different
to mine. The father accepted that he was responsible but they'd broken up and he was going out
with somebody else. When he heard that she'd
had the baby, he didn't leave the person he was
living with but his parents took responsibility.
They gave Emily, or my parents, money for the
baby's upkeep.

How the two daughters' pregnancies are handled by Emma's
parents is to become a divisive issue within the family. In
the meantime, even before having a second child and getting

married, Emma and Mathew are trying to find a way to move out of their single room in St. Paul's Road.

Let me rewind. Mathew had taken out life insurance with United Friendly before we got to live together. After I moved in with him, we took out a life insurance for myself that would have covered Samuel also.

The man from United Friendly said: "You could get a house through us." We didn't know this. That would be going on February 1968 and we're now in summer 1969. Anyway, he said they've got a two-bedroom house off St. Paul's Road which suited us down to the ground. I didn't know whether it meant rent? He says: "No, to purchase. If you could get your deposit, the insurance company could help you."

We don't understand about these things, so we went and saw Mom. I knew Mom had got the money. She says: "Let's hear what your dad have to say." We go to Dad. He says: "What! You going buy a house? You can't buy a house." He repeated the same words again, twelve months after.

What he was saying to us was maybe for the right reasons. He didn't think we were responsible enough. We were too young blah, blah, blah! He was telling us how old he was when he buy the lumber to build his house. But the answer was no. So that was an opportunity we felt slipped through our fingers.

Emma is disappointed by her parents yet again. Nevertheless, the couple still look into other ways to find a bigger place to live.

> Still living at St Paul's Road, before we got married, we'd put our names on the housing waiting list to get a council property. We didn't know how long we'd have to wait. It was maybe six or seven months when we got the first offer.
>
> They offered us a flat just a few weeks after we got married. It was on the sixteenth floor up, so we didn't even go and look at it. Within a month they offered us a maisonette which we just went and signed for the keys without even going to look at it. It was a low rise, on the third or the fourth floor. We took it.

Emma remembers the spaciousness of the place.

> It was like going into a mansion. Imagine, you're coming out of one room into your own space. You've got your own kitchen, you've got your lounge, you got your downstairs toilet, three bedrooms and a bathroom.

Emma and Mathew are now married with two children. Emma's mother organised what was a big and very public wedding. Her father gave her away at an Anglican Church—against his devout Jehovah's Witness beliefs. Mathew's aunt even gave them £30 towards the wedding. Though Emma's parents refused to help with the deposit to buy their first house, Emma hopes her parents will at least help her and Mathew move into their new council maisonette.

> We paid either a week or two weeks rent in advance because we needed to secure it. We needed furniture. Our landlady at St. Paul's Road, Miss Maggie, gave us things. We had a wardrobe, dressing table and a bed. We didn't have anywhere to keep our food. We didn't have a fridge. Not many people had a fridge in them days. We went and saw my mom and dad. Again Mum says: "Well let's hear what your dad have to say." It was the same thing he said to us about the house. He says: "What unno doing? You know how old I was before I buy my first house and how I had to go to second-hand shop to buy furniture and things for it." We weren't asking him to give us. We were asking him to lend us some money.
>
> So the answer was no. Now if you going to a second-hand shop, you need some money to go anyway. I think my parents sort of resented me leaving home and marrying Mathew. They had an expectation that I would have been running back to them. Thank God, it didn't happen.

After Emma's parents refuse to help her and Mathew with their move, the couple move forward with acquiring what they can for their new home.

Alright, we go to the gas board—this is like the following Monday. It was called West Midland Gas Board at the time. We bought a three-burner cooker, brand new, for £75. We got the money from what we had saved from the wedding, so at least we could have a cooker. We couldn't afford the four-burner, that would mean hire purchase.

We didn't have much bedding. What money we had would have to do different things. So we went and spoke with Mathew's dad. His dad couldn't help much but he had an account with Woodhouse. We went to Woodhouse, choose what we wanted, and my husband's dad stood the guarantee. We had a dining table and four chairs, brand new, in teak. We had a double cupboard— which match the small one that we had—a coffee table for the living room, two wardrobes, a dressing table and our bed. We had a carpet for the living room and carpets for two bedrooms. We went and bought a carpet for the stairs from somewhere else, for cash. Pots and pans? We had lots of pots and pans for wedding presents.

When I did ask for some help from Mom— well I didn't actually ask—she says: "Don't worry about curtains and that. I'll sort out your curtains." I had earmarked some money for curtains, but I didn't have to buy any curtains— not new ones—because me mom brought me some curtains down. Curtains she'd had before. They weren't new but they were OK.

In her own way she was like saying sorry
without ever using the word.

Though the hostility from her parents remain, Emma notes the
slight change in her mother's attitude.

They said I'd got this 'boasty man'. That was how
they described Mathew. You got this boasty man.
Me got millionaire.

My mom mellowed but she showed him great
indifference. She only mellowed a little bit. We
would go out socially and she'd be there. She'd
ignore me and she'd ignore him for many, many
years.

By contrast, Emma's younger sister—who got pregnant at seventeen while still living at home—appears to have a completely
different relationship with their parents. Emily broke up with
the baby's father before she had the baby. At the time, he is
living with someone else. Though he had accepted responsibility for the baby, it is his parents who are making the financial
contributions towards the baby's upkeep. In Emma's view, it is
her parents who end up taking care of her sister's baby.

Then Emily got pregnant again and had a little
girl, a year and a bit afterwards. By this time now,
she and the father of her first child were living
together. Emily tells him that the child is not his.
That's a nice soap opera there, I'm telling you. She
tells him that's it's not his, but that's not my story.

The first child my mom and dad helped to raise. The second one Mom and Dad said they adopted. We can only take their word on that. I don't think it was a formal adoption for one minute.

My sister's two children were treated differently to my children. I realised that the indifference wasn't that they didn't care. It was the fact that I'd proved them wrong. Mathew stood behind me and I never had to go to them for anything. So really, they felt I was alright. They adopted my sister's second child, they raised them both. They were grandchildren and they were always there. So no room was actually made to accommodate my children.

Mathew had been brought up by his aunt. She did not give her approval when it was first proposed that he should marry Emma because she wanted him to marry a lady she knew and felt would be a better match for him. It was only when Mathew's aunt discovered that this lady was already married that she approved his marriage to Emma.

For many years she [Mathew's aunt] used to basically taunt me. This was after we were married. She would call me up about something and she would say: "Why can't you be like Jones's daughter?" If you can imagine, it was like 'a fly in the ointment' which wasn't a good thing.

One day I just had to say to her: "What you

trying to do? You're trying to raise this woman from the dead to me?"

That was my experience. It was a bitter situation.

IRENE

It is 1969 and Irene is sixteen years old. She is just about to leave Handsworth Wood Girls School in Birmingham where she's been a pupil since 1964. It is a uniformed school and very strict. There are only a few Black girls at the school but for Irene it is a positive experience. She is a 'favourite' of the formidable Headmistress Mrs Finchley who takes a special interest in her progress. She does not recall being called derogatory names by other pupils or being treated differently by teachers. She is also part of a small group of Black friends bonded by their Christian faith.

It is 1968 and Irene's mother's marriage ends in divorce because of domestic violence. Irene witnesses some of these incidents and on one occasion beseeches her stepfather to stop hitting her mum. She reflects on that time.

> That was a nasty period in my life, I didn't like it.
> It was a disgrace on the church as well. In the end,
> after they got divorced, he moved to America. I
> think he had got some family there. He didn't get
> married again. Then a few years after, he died.

Irene cannot help but wonder if her mother's short marriage

and what happened with her father, affected her own attitude to men.

> I don't think it's damaged me, but when I've had relationships, I've been very hesitant. I always thought to myself: 'No man will ever treat me like how they treat my mum—no man. You can't treat people like animal. No man! Never!'

Irene remembers he mothers advice when it came to men.

> Mum always said to me: "One of the important things is make sure that you're not depending on a man to get a house or a car. If you meet some-body, that would be nice, but you're not saying I need a man to get my house. Be independent." Some of my friends have got married because of that and some of their relationships have broken up. You should get married for love, not getting married for the wrong reasons.

Irene remembers a lot about her mother and the two had a lovely relationship, one that Irene cherishes.

> My mum was very modern in a way. The church I was going to before was very strict on makeup and my mum use to like to do her face up. She said one of the church officers looked at her and say: "You wearing powder and makeup?" My mum came home and she was going on: "Who

she think she is telling me about making my face up to look good."

She always dressed well. She put a little powder on, put a little makeup on. She said: "I don't know. Just because them old nagger them nah know how to powder them face or straighten them hair."

My mum would tell me all this: "Make yourself look good girl. Don't follow them. Don't follow what them say. Make yourself look good. Put on your powder. Dress up yourself." She was before her time like that, she wasn't old fashion. She would say: "Look good. Look the part. You have to make sure you look good in front of them white people. Make them look up to you and see that you look good." So not oldie worldly.

She would say other things like: "Be careful. You don't want to get pregnant. Don't let no man fool you. Remember your integrity. Get married— do things properly. None of this partner business. Mak sure the man have some property. If him don't have anything else, he must have ambition. You don't want to come home, you work and him just sit down there look up at you."

I'm telling you the truth, I got all of this. Of course, I was keen on individuality so I spoke my mind to my heart's content. When I didn't agree, I said I didn't agree. But it was bantering, we had a good relationship.

Irene is now sixteen years old and will be leaving school. The issue of what Irene is going to do after leaving school becomes a matter of contention within the family. Irene is not sure. Her mother, who is a nurse, is a great deal more certain.

> I was very good at drama at school, loved English and poetry and that sort of thing. But Mum said that was out.
>
> My mum use to talk to me about her job all the time. She used to take me to the hospital and say this is my daughter. In those days you weren't paid through the bank. If she went on a Saturday or I was not at school, she would take me along to the hospital and we'd pick up her wages because it was all cash. She would introduce me to the people she worked with.
>
> She said to me: "You either go into further education or you get a job." According to my mother, the ultimatum was either further education or look for a job with training prospects like nursing—hint, hint! I'd seen that hospital environment quite a bit and I knew I'd like working in a hospital, but I didn't take that hint. I just thought: 'I don't like blood. I don't want to be a nurse'.

When her school days finally come to an end, Irene is distraught. She is about to be separated from her best friends.

> I remember the day when I had to leave school.

We cried our eyes out because it was such a close bond. We really cried.

With only a few GCSE's, Irene is not particularly well qualified. However, as a pupil of Handsworth Wood Girls, she has high expectations and aspirations.

I started looking for a job in the local paper. Then I saw an advert for a pharmacy technician at Selly Oak Hospital where on-the-job training would be given. I applied for the job and received an interview. My mother prayed with me and said: "We're leaving this day in God's hands."

I was sixteen then. I attended this interview with the chief pharmacist, Mr Owen. He told me that the position I applied for was for a qualified person with a Diploma in Pharmaceutics and Dispensing. I looked at him. I was very nervous and embarrassed. I told him: "My mother worked as a nurse. I like the hospital environment and I'm eager to learn."

He hesitated, then he said: "Well, if you're interested, we could give you a placement at this hospital and send you to college. We'll get the local authority to pay for your training."

I was flabbergasted but quickly said: "Yes please! I'm very interested. I want to learn more about medicines." I went home with a skip in my step, told my mother the good news. She said: "That's God. You're now on your way with a small salary and they're paying for your training. Couldn't be greater."

So I started my placement as a student and then started college doing Chemistry, Physiology, Maths, Physics and all of that. I didn't like Physics but Chemistry and the other subjects, I loved. Once I started those subjects, I loved it.

What was blessed about this? The chief pharmacist at Selly Oak said to me: "It's just a placement. After the three years training I can't promise you a job here but you'll be qualified to work in a chemist or at other places as a pharmacist."

This is Irene's first job after leaving school. Whether by good fortune, the reputation of Handsworth Girls School, or God as her mother would have it, Irene is extremely pleased. She does, however, have one reservation.

When I started training on my first job, I was the only Black person there again.

Irene spends three years training as a pharmacy technician. When she was appointed as a trainee by the chief pharmacist at Selly Oak.

When I did qualify he actually said: "There is a post going here if you want to apply for it." I thought this is another God incident because when I said I was willing to apply he called me into his office and says: "Irene you've got the job."

I said: "What!" He says: "You've got the job." I said: "Oh! OK."

My mum use to say: "Sometimes you go on too intelligent." I'll tell you how this fits in. Before I qualified, I'd pick her up at the bullring in Birmingham. Sometimes when I was with her, the store-holders are giving her extra meat and I'd go: "Why are they're doing that Mum? It says it's so much a pound." She would say: "Shut up your mouth. You're too intelligent. If the man giving me extra, shut up your mouth."

I learnt that. So when the chief pharmacist said you've got the job I didn't say: 'But I have to apply'. I shut up me mouth. I could hear my mum's voice saying to me: "Just shut your mouth. The man say you've got the job. He must know you don't have to apply. Don't be asking him stupid questions." I just said: "Thank you very much Mr Owen. Thank you."

Irene is twenty years old when she qualifies and secures her first job at Selly Oak General Hospital in Birmingham.

That was great. Every year an increase in salary. It was a good footing to be on. I was there for a while. It wasn't always easy. There's not a lot of Black people in pharmacy. You had to work hard.

Before long Irene discovers that in order to progress, hard work is not going to be enough. She is in need of more qualifications and more experience.

I wasn't wasting my time. Once I'd qualified the next thing I wanted to do was to be a senior. So I did loads of different courses that you need to do for promotion.

One of the things I learnt is that for a senior position you needed to be able to drive because these jobs weren't close.

Irene applies for an after-hours job with a high street chemist.

How did I get the job at Boots chemist? Hmmm.... that's a good question. I'm glad you asked me that. pharmacy is quite incestuous. We had a staff of about forty at Selly Oak Hospital and you talk to people. A lot of the pharmacists there work in chemists, everybody was trying to get extra. When I talked to people and I said I wanted to buy a car, they said: "Why don't you try Boots? Boots do six-till-ten. You'll be able to get money for your car." What the hospital was paying you in those days, the chemists always paid much more.

I rang up, applied, and showed them my certificate. Because they were so busy I got the job. This was the big Boots in Birmingham town centre. I didn't have an interview or anything. I went to see the person in charge and said: "I'd like to buy a car and I'd like to do some extra work. Here's my qualifications." She said: "Come Monday night, you can start." So I did. It was great because you get ten percent discount at Boots as well.

I was the only Black pharmacist there as well. That's been my life, so I don't find that strange. When I have other Black people around that's a bonus. It's nice.

After a full day at Selly Oak, eight-thirty to five, Irene would take the bus into the town centre to start her evening shift at Boots. She soon finds out that her experience of working in a general hospital is nowhere near what is required at a high street chemist.

The six-to-ten shift I did at Boots, the chemist was harder than the whole day I worked at the pharmacy in Selly Oak. People who work at the chemist, they're faster than us who work in hospital. You have to move fast. You had prescriptions coming in from doctors all over. You had private prescriptions. You had to be on the ball, know what you're doing. That was another experience. I had to learn to pick up my speed in dispensing.

I learnt and got on with it. When I got in at night at half-past-ten, my mother would say: "Your dinner is in the oven." I'd never worked in a chemist before but I did it until I got the money to buy my first car, a little Ford Escort for £200. It took about six months. I was able to buy the car right out. Went with a friend—a guy from church. We looked the car over and bought it. When I got my car, my mum benefitted as well.

Irene is extremely busy at this stage of her career. In addition to her extra shifts at Boots, she is taking courses that will to add to her qualifications in the hope of a promotion within the NHS. She also has other interests that she pursues.

Apart from the church, I was a Youth and Community Leader. I'd always been interested in working with kids. I got all my counseling certificates and was actually volunteering at youth clubs in my spare time.

It is 1976 and Irene is twenty-three years old, earning a good salary, no kids, and she has her own car. She decides to go back to Jamaica on holiday.

After starting work, I kind of saved up and had enough money. I just thought it was a good idea to go back. My mum thought it was a good idea me going to see where I was born, but she wasn't interested to come.

Irene was only seven years old when she came to England in 1960. She is an only child with few immediate family connections to the island of her birth.

Up to leaving school, neither me or my mother had gone back home to Jamaica to visit family—we couldn't afford it. My mum was always writing my uncle. They wrote like once a fortnight by the time the letters came through. She was very close with my uncle. Not so much with my aunt, the teacher—there was a lot of jealousies and stuff going on there. But she wrote to my uncle. We always knew what was going on. He was an inspector of police and always telling us about the political scene. None of my family came here to visit.

It is actually Irene's uncle who requests that Irene visit.

My uncle—my mother's brother, who was an inspector of police—had been inviting me and he said to my mum: "Let her come over and see where she was born. I'll look after her, no problem." He was like a father figure, he was beautiful. I decided to go and see him, get to know him. It was my idea. Since I had left Jamaica, this was the first time I was going back and I couldn't remember what Uncle looked like.

When she decides to visit Jamaica, Irene is working her full-time job, and also doing an 'A' Level Sociology night time course. She doesn't need the qualification. She finds the subject interesting and that is a good enough reason for Irene.

I went for about three weeks. I was halfway through my course when I went. I think it was in

July when the college had broken up.

When Irene arrives in Jamaica, she goes to meet her uncle.

> His wife was in America but he'd got a maid anyhow. He said there would be no problem. He didn't have to do any cooking or anything like that.
>
> He lived in Kingston. I think it was in Kingston 17. It wasn't as bad as how Kingston is now from what I can remember. It was a nice area. The house was nice and everything.
>
> Of course, Uncle had taken some time off— but because he was inspector of police—he still had to go to work. He'd organised different things we were going to go to in the evenings, but he still had to go to work.
>
> Joyce, the maid, looked after me during the day. Uncle said: "Joyce will take care of you. You'll get the experience of going on a bus and going into town, but you must go with Joyce. Don't think you're in England and can be independent, do your own thing."

Irene accepts her uncle's advice and goes to Kingston with Joyce.

> Then this one day now, we're going into town. I stepped out of the house with Joyce.
>
> I was quite socialised in the English way of thinking. I was standing at the front of the queue

at the bus stop waiting for the bus. Joyce was somewhere down the road there. The bus comes and I can't get on the bus. Joyce said to me: "You don't need to queue here like you're in England. When the bus comes everybody just pile in."

There's me like a good little English girl queuing up, and then I ended up not getting on the bus. She said: "No! We don't queue here. You stay with me. When the bus come, we just run on."

I thought that was quite funny because I was in the middle of doing sociology. There was my uncle saying about the maid and there's me trying to be a good little Black English girl, queuing up because I had been trained that way.

Uncle told me not to talk too much either when I was out. They can recognise the clothes and if I open my mouth people would say: 'You come from England'! The fares would go up in taxis, so if I could just keep my mouth shut it would be better. I usually like to talk a lot, but they said it's best if you don't. People can tell if you come from England anyway—from your clothes—and they think the streets there are paved with gold.

This is not the only time that Irene's English upbringing clashes with her uncle's cultural expectations.

When it came to meal times there was myself,

299

Uncle and Joyce. I tried to be helpful because you're modern English. I'd set the table and I'd set a place for Joyce.

Uncle said to me: "What are you doing?" I said: "It's just the three of us." I'm doing Sociology, Marx and all that. I said: "There's the three of us." He said: "No! You need to understand what's going on Irene. No, No. No! Joyce eats in the kitchen, she serves us. We eat in the dining room. Joyce doesn't eat with us. She's the maid."

That kind of blew my mind.

Nevertheless, Irene is getting on with her uncle who is making every effort to ensure that she gets to know Jamaica and her family.

I took in all the sites. We did the Blue Mountains, Dunn's River—all the excursions that you do in Jamaica. It was good for me.

Then he took me up country. He said we'd got some land there. I think it was St. Catharine's— Spanish Town. He took me up there, introduced me. I met Mum's niece, her sister's daughter. I'd not met her before. I think I actually spent a day there. We've got half Chinese in the family. He took me to meet them as well.

Here's a picture of me when I first came here. Can you see the Chinese in me? Got the Chinese eyes. That was a nice trip.

I think there was a Ball or something and I

had to dress up for that because Uncle was introducing me as his niece. That was quite a social occasion. Then he was saying to me, had I got a boyfriend? He was going to fix me up. It was quite funny but it was good, a nice family moment.

We did a lot of talking. I actually found out that he and his wife were separated. I didn't realise till I got there because he just use to write my mum. His wife was living in America at the time. It was a trial separation and they'd got one child as well, who was with the mum. The girl was a little bit older than I was.

While there, Irene also gets an opportunity to see her uncle in action as a police inspector.

It was election time and he took me out to one of the election nights. It was totally, totally, different to politics over here. People carry rice and peas and they sit on the top of their cars. They make loads of noise and they blow their car horns. They were very excited about the PNP and the JLP, I think it was. It was a big thing. People would start shouting at each other if they were in different factions.

He was kind of half on duty but he couldn't turn a blind eye. I remember him using his baton a couple of times.

***

Irene and her mother are living in a council flat which is on the tenth floor of a tower block.

> It was just the two of us, so there wasn't a lot of money. After a while I thought: 'Why are we paying all this money? Let's buy a house." I sat down, got the calculator out and said: "Look mum! This is how much rent we've paid for the year. We could have bought a house with that."
>
> Like any Black family will tell you, we lived in some tenement houses. Before we got the council flat, we lived in a tenant house. I do remember how you're treated—that will never leave me. You can only use the cooker at certain times and then they want you to clean the whole house.
>
> That's some of the worst memories I have because of what my mum had to put up with. They were supposed to be friends, but the landlady would have certain rules. Mum would clean the cooker, then people would come and use it—leave it messy—and she'd have to clean it again. That stuck in my mind. So when we moved to the council flat, we had our own little place, it was nice. When I worked out how much money we were paying for rent I said: "We could buy a house.
>
> She was still working at the time, but she was getting ready for retirement. Remember she had me late. I kept getting an increment in salary every year and even though Mum was thinking of

retiring she said: "Well, if you paid the mortgage and the bills and I did the food, we could do it." So we bought the house I'm living in now—in Perry Barr.

Lucy, Irene's mother, is working as an auxiliary nurse in a mental health hospital.

> She used to tell me bits about that and it was always interesting. After a while in mental health my mother became ill. Like all nurses her back wasn't very good. She stopped for a while, she was off sick with her back.
>
> She was also a diabetic. She got maturity onset diabetes when she was sixtyish. That was in our family because Uncle had insulin diabetes, so we weren't too surprised.

Though she is not in the best of health and approaching retirement age, Lucy decides its now her turn to visit her brother, the police inspector in Jamaica. This is after Irene's visit to Jamaica in 1976.

> She went to Jamaica on holiday. I think she was looking to see if she could retire there. She didn't want to live in Kingston where Uncle was living, so it would have to be up country. I think Uncle said there was land up country we could have, but he was fighting with our relatives out there to get the land. They were lazy and rented out the land

anyhow.

My mum came back and said: "I don't want to be involved in all that."

Sometime after returning from her holiday in Jamaica, Lucy starts looking at other places where she might live in retirement. When she decides, Irene is utterly confused by her choice.

She use to get the Jamaican Gleaner and she saw something about Belize. I think she'd been praying and she'd got some dream about Belize, so in her mind it was all tied up. That's why this Belize thing came up. It was in her dream.

She'd now retired but she was diabetic, so I was a bit worried. I was saying to her: "But Mum, you're on medication." She just told me she had written to somebody and they were going to meet up with her. She was going to go to Miami and then go on to Belize.

I was very concerned. I got 'involved' with the letters to see who these people were that she was writing. They said they were going to meet her at the airport in Miami, and then somebody was going to meet her in Belize as well. Other people from England was also going over to see this land. She had seen something in the Gleaner and had put a deposit down on a plot of land in Belize. She wanted to see the land, see her plot.

I was very anti. She was sixty-five when she told me she was going to go to America—first to see a friend—then go on to Belize.

In Irene's mind, her mother has always been independent and self-reliant, but also a little too conservative and cautious. Now, all of a sudden—without asking for her daughter's advice—she wants be adventurous. Irene felt this was a cause for concern.

Given her mother's age and ill-health, Irene is against her mother's intention to buy land and build a house for her retirement in Belize.

> It was some Chinese guy who was running the land deal in Belize. She said it was alright but I know you need to watch what they're doing to make sure. It's like if you're buying land in Jamaica, you need to be going over there and overseeing what's going on.
>
> For a woman to be trying to build a house in Belize, you'd need somebody that you know very well over there. It's not something that is straightforward and I wasn't over keen. I made some noises and said I'm not sure. She felt it was right because she'd prayed about it.
>
> After, I told her straight out: "I wouldn't want to live there." She said: "That's alright." I still liked the idea of Jamaica, so we agreed to disagree, but I encouraged her to do what she wanted.
>
> The plot was cleared and all that. No it wasn't a scam. It was a genuine offer.

Irene continues to actively pursue her career as a pharmacist.

It is now ten years since she started at Selly Oak but she is not happy.

> There were a lot of chiefs there. I was doing senior's work and not being paid. I was training a lot of students and stuff like that. It was: "Oh Irene will do it. Irene's good at that. We'll leave Irene to do the students." Some of the times I would speak up and say: "Hang on a minute. So and so is a senior. Why am I doing all this work? I'm not a senior." They'd say: "Oh, but you're good at it. You've got away with you. You can motivate people. You can do it."
>
> I did feel a bit bitter thinking I'm not getting the salary. This person's getting the salary. I really do need to get out of here because I was getting fed up. I'd got the training for doing the senior anyhow because a lot of it is training students.

Irene has some very clear ideas on how her career ought to be progressing.

> Once I'd qualified, the next promotion is to be a senior. I was looking for a senior, I was looking for promotion. I was doing various courses that you have to do in pharmacy. If you want a promotion, it's better that you'd got a piece of paper—a certificate.
>
> It was hard in those days to get to a senior position—especially as a Black person—because

everybody who had senior positions was white. I applied for jobs, couldn't get any. You had to be good to get a senior position. It took time.

Maybe this is the first time I faced a little bit of racism. There wasn't a lot of Black seniors around and the interviews for those jobs were pretty tight. It was just one of those things in those days. You couldn't just get it like that.

Irene then gets a call from the chief pharmacist who notifies her about a job opening.

The pharmacist that was at Selly Oak got the chief pharmacist post at Rubery Hill which is a big mental health hospital. It's closed, well it's Rayside now. She went there as chief pharmacist and we kept in touch. She rang me and said: "I think you ought to apply for the senior pharmacist post going here." I applied, went for interview, and I got the job. That was my first step out into senior.

I think the only thing that frightened me was not being in mental health before. I sort of asked around and looked at questions that I might be asked about mental health. To be honest, I was ready for the challenge because of what was happening at Selly Oak.

It is 1983 when Irene starts at Rubery Hill as a senior pharmacist.

I think I was about thirty. The salary structure was good and also it was good for your self-esteem to get there because it was so difficult. As I said, in those days you couldn't just get a senior position like that. It took a long time—ten years.

The people I went to college with, we met up. I didn't feel too left out because a lot of them didn't get senior pharmacist positions although they were white. They were struggling for positions as well, which made me feel better because it would always have been in the back of my mind that: 'Is it because of my colour—the colour of my skin'! Sometimes you have to be in the right place at the right time, but the colour of your skin does matter.

Irene quickly settles into her new job.

It's quite funny. I'm now working in pharmacy in a mental health hospital and once I left general hospital I never wanted to go back. It's more satisfying to see somebody with mental health problems—all down—and to see their depression lifted, if not cured.

It's so different to working in a general hospital because if it's diabetes you give them your medicine: It's hello and goodbye. With mental health you've got to work on the mind and we're involved with the patient. How you treat the patient that's really fascinating. When you go on ward rounds and you hear all the case histories and the abuse, sometimes you're thinking: 'Thank God my childhood was good.' Some of these people, sometimes you don't know what's been in their background but working in mental health is so satisfying.

It was a smaller hospital than Selly Oak. Where Selly Oak had a staff of about fifty, this only had a staff of fifteen. That was good. It was smaller and more family orientated as well.

Of course, I'd got a car and it's eleven miles by car from my home. Otherwise it would be nearly a two-hour journey—I'd have to take two buses, a bus into town and a bus from town to Rubery. Part of my early strategy was buying a car. Once I got the car I knew if I got a senior position I can drive to my job. It made quite a difference being able to drive to Rubery Hill.

Even though Sociology was nothing to do with pharmacy, it's something else that in the long run helped me with going into a mental hospital because Sociology and Psychology were intertwined with mental health.

In her previous job at Selly Oak, Irene felt her managers were taking advantage of her by asking her to undertake supervisory roles which were not part of her job. Now, however, she occupies a much more senior position and she is grateful to be undertaking these tasks.

Managing staff at Rubery Hill was fine. As I said,

I'd been doing some of that at Selly Oak without getting the salary. One of the management things was we had a lot of students coming in from university. You have to do the rota. You have to manage the students and manage the staff where they are on the rota.

I was kind of doing that at Selly Oak so I'd got me in-house training at Selly Oak without getting the money. To be honest when I went to Rubery I didn't find it challenging as such because firstly it was a smaller hospital. It was easier to manage fifteen people than when you had fifty. I think the only thing I didn't do at Selly Oak was I wasn't involved in doing the staff rota. Even when they'd ask me I wouldn't do it—I didn't get paid for that. You have to draw a line somewhere.

That was new to me when I went to Rubery— doing rotas, organising people and delegating the work.

Approach is very important. How you speak to people is very important. You can be a manager and you can delegate and say: "James I want you to do this." But sometimes you have to say: "James we have quite a task for the day. We need to get all these things sorted out. I've got something else to do but I'll like to delegate this to you and see how you get on. So you see I'm kind of challenging you. I'm here for you. If you're not sure, if you need my help, you can call me. If you need other people to help, fine. I think you're capable—I'll leave it to you."

My supervisor at Rubery Hill was the chief pharmacist. She was the one I knew from Selly Oak who recruited me and who I reported to.

When I had my first year appraisal she said that she knew I was the right person for the job, that I was able to motivate and delegate. I needed to keep on doing what I was doing but I needed to keep the error rates down.

I pointed out that sometimes the busier you are, the more mistakes you make: "I think we need some more staff because as the work goes up and people are stressed, they'll make mistakes with prescriptions." She did listen to me and we got more staff.

In contrast to her experience at Selly Oak, Irene is less concerned with the issue of race in her role as senior pharmacist at Rubery Hill. Nevertheless, at times she does feel threatened from an unexpected quarter.

All the way through my professional life, I've always been like the only Black or the only one of two Blacks. As the Black person and dispensary manager at Rubery Hill, I got on alright with the people around me. However, the Asians really don't like you in a managerial position. I have got on with them but you can see they'd rather it was them. So I've always got to fight for the position that I want. There were not so many Asian nurses

at Rubery Hill when I went there because of
where the area is. A lot of them had to train there
but it was mainly a white area.

Upon getting her promotion Irene decides to give up her voluntary youth work.

As a senior, if the work wasn't finished you would
have to do it. As a Junior, when it comes to five-
thirty, you're finished and it's bye—gone. As a
senior there were times I should finish at five-
thirty and many nights I was still there at seven
o'clock—that's responsibility. So when I did get
my senior post I did pack in my work with youth
clubs because I couldn't just walk away from the
pharmacy and go home. I couldn't fit in the youth
clubs because they were starting about six o'clock.
I just couldn't do it but I still did the church
youth work.

Irene does, however, continue doing youth work at church.

My church is Shiloh Apostolic—it's an Evangelist
Church.
    Church was Sunday all day including Sunday
School teaching. Then there was a meeting on
Tuesday night at church but I didn't go to that.
Thursday night was the youth meeting and I'd be
organising. Instead of just me, I'd get different
youth leaders to run different nights with maybe

a youngster along as well. I'd do a rota for that so I wasn't doing it every single week. I'd have about four or five people on the rota. Then if we had meetings that we had to attend on a Saturday, we could be involved with church on that day as well—but the fixed days were all day Sundays and Thursday nights.

For Sunday School, children are taken out of the church congregation for separate lessons instruction and are returned to the congregation before the end of the service. Irene is in charge of the youth Sunday School at her church. She uses her experience of voluntary work from the Birmingham youth clubs to inform her Sunday School lessons.

Sunday School teaching was round the back of our church. I was doing something a little bit more radical that some of the senior people didn't like. I had the teenagers and once we'd done the rote of saying bible verses, I'd then apply it. I knew some of the youngsters that were going to leave the church—some of them were talking about having babies. You could see where things were going, so I'd be more radical in my teaching—stretch it a bit. I'm very much a twenty-first-century-person saying let's look at behaviour, how would we look at this.

Sometimes we never did get back into church. Some of the senior people, they didn't like it: "What's Irene round there doing with the youngsters dem? They should be in church hearing the word." That caused a bit of friction so I did give it up eventually.

Irene remains at Rubery Hill until the hospital closes in 1995.

We moved to a purpose-built psychiatric unit at the bottom of a big complex at the new Queen Elizabeth Hospital. I just moved with the rest of the staff.

It was a bit larger but I was doing the same job. There was more management involved. We had to start doing more appraisals. When I was at Rubery, it wasn't so top-heavy with management. You would get on with it—you'd organise and do your rotas. At the QE there was more management. You got to do appraisals, staff monitoring. You got to do this, you got to do that. The job got heavier.

Irene's mother, on the other hand is still pursuing her dream of having a retirement home in Belize.

There was some problems with the land. It didn't kind of work out. She realized she'd got a piece of paper that said she had land there, but land alone isn't enough really. You have to pay the tax and if you don't pay the tax there are problems. The land went to rack and ruin.

It didn't happen in the end. To be honest she

did lose the land. The trip to Miami and Belize was her last. We found out that she had ovarian cancer.

MELISSA

It is 1972 and Melissa is mourning the passing of her dear Doule. Unbeknownst to Melissa, the next few years are to be life changing for her.

Melissa's mother Pengal and stepfather Martie have done reasonably well in England. They have managed to buy their own house in Thornton Heath, but England is not where they see their future.

> She and my stepfather went back to Jamaica in 1973. She just wanted to go back to Jamaica to live because she'd had enough of England. She said: "You get no rest. You work, you work. It's always seven days a week."

Melissa continues working at Mayday Hospital for several years, then moves on to London Chest Hospital. For some reason Melissa has very little to say about this period in her life.

In 1980 she decides to go on holiday and, unusually, it's not to visit her family in Jamaica.

> I went to Nigeria with a friend, Beverley, who was Jamaican to. This government man, who was

an MP in Nigeria, fancied my friend and took her over there. When you're a government man in Nigeria you have money. The man wanted my friend—who was what you call a 'Yellow Woman'. He wanted to marry her as his second wife.

Before going on holiday to Nigeria, Melissa gets in touch with her mother who is now in Jamaica.

"I rang her and told her that I was going over to Nigeria. I use to speak to her like every other day. She says: "I'm not too well. I'm having a bit of pain in my tummy." I said: "You're sure?" She says: "It's only a little griping pain I'm having around my navel, but I'll be alright." I said: "Mum, you sure? You want me to come over?" She says: "No. Go on your holiday. Don't let me bother you."

Funnily enough, I didn't give her the telephone number where I was going to go because I thought: 'Well I just spoke to her before I went so everything would be alright. When I get there I'll phone again'.

While Melissa is on holiday, her cousin Nell, who is living at Oakfield Road in London, rings her.

Good job that I'd given her [Nell] the number where I was going. She rang me to say: "Your mother is desperately ill. Where are you? Your mother is in hospital."

Beverley and I went out the day. When we came back the houseboy who got the message says: "Madam, your cousin in London phone. Your mother is in hospital in Jamaica." I said: "Oh Lord!" I thought: 'How am I going to get back to England'?

In those days Shehu Shagari was in government and they had just found oil in Nigeria. Nigerians were travelling like there was no tomorrow, so you couldn't get spaces on the plane. It was British Caledonian Airline then.

Luckily for Melissa, she has a friend who is able to be of assistance.

There was a friend of ours that was working for British Caledonian. We phone him and I said: "Timmy, my mother is very ill and I want to get to England." He said: "Leave it to me, I'll get you a seat. Get your things pack. The minute I phone you, make sure you're ready to come to the office." I said: "Alright."

Whatever he did, he got me a space on the plane, so I said: "How did you get it?" He said: "Never you mind. We've got ways of doing it. I told someone we had no seats for them and they'll have to go the following day as the plane was full. I gave you her seat." That was how I came over.

When I came to England, I rang my cousin Nell from Heathrow. I says: "What happening?"

She says: "Your mum is very ill." I rang my mother's house in Jamaica. My father answered and
says: "You're mother is desperately ill in hospital."
I said: "Alright, I'm coming."

Melissa stays over in England for one day, just long enough to
pick up some money and supplies.

I bought some night dresses. Not that she didn't
have night dresses but I know she likes Marks
& Spencer's night clothes. I thought let me get
some more bed slippers, Complan, gauze, cotton
wool—the necessary things. I bought everything
that I know a sick person would need.

I rang the hospital in Jamaica the morning. I
said: "Tell my mum I'm coming to see her. I am
back in London and I'm going on the plane now.
I will see her this evening."

The plane from Heathrow took me to Miami.
I got into Miami that evening. I think it was in
June 1980.

I rang the hospital again and said: "Tell me
mum I'm at Miami Airport."

Flights from Miami to Kingston usually go smoothly, but not
this one.

I am waiting because the plane that I should have
caught to come to Jamaica by seven o'clock that
evening has been high-jacked by Cubans. It was

the time when Cubans were running away from Cuba and they were high-jacking planes to take them where they want to go.

I rang the hospital again. I said: "Tell me mum I'm still at Miami Airport. I am waiting for transport because the plane that I should have come on has been high-jacked by the Cubans. They have to find another airline. They said I have to wait until tomorrow morning so I'm at the hotel at the airport."

The Miami Airport authority have told passengers that their flight has been hijackd by Cubans. This is in the middle of the infamous Mariel Boat Lift when some one hundred and twenty-five thousand Cubans fled the island between April and October 1980. A great many ended up in US refugee camps controlled by the military. The conditions the refugees lived under led to rioting. As a result, there were a number of aircraft hi-jackings that year. One week in August there were six cases of plane hi-jackings from US airports—including Miami. Despite what she may have been told by the airport, Melissa's flight was not hijacked by Cubans. However, her flight could have been distrupted by the threat of a hijacking in a connecting US airport elsewhere.

In any event, Melissa is delayed.

When I rang again later that day the nurse says: "You spoke to me this morning and I told your mum you're coming. Everybody she see passing her hospital bed, she say, 'Is that Melissa? Is that

Melissa?' But I'm sorry to tell you your mum died a little after I told her that you were coming."

I didn't cry because if I'd cried I would have been broken. I didn't cry. I rang a friend of mine in Jamaica who's a solicitor, Carl. He was even in the government at one time. He was a Minister of State. I rang him and said: "Carl, you know mama died?" He said: "Melissa, you're joking! When?" I said: "I spoke to them in Jamaica just this minute. Then I put the phone down and I phone you to tell you." He says: "Lord! You want me to do anything for you?" I said: "No. I'm coming, don't worry. I will be there in the morning." He said: "Alright, I'll come out and pick you up at the airport." I told him what time the plane was going to land.

He came and pick me up. He said: "Melissa, you're not crying!" I said: "Carl if I break down now, I won't be able to do nothing. I need to concentrate on what I'm going to do." A cousin of mine—Evelyn—who is a midwife, she had to sedate my father Martie because he went to pieces.

Upon her arrival in Jamaica, Melissa takes care of her mother's funeral. She has been in continuous employment since 1972 and like a great many Jamaican women, she is a disciplined money saver.

I arranged everything. I took money with me. I buried my mother and I felt good that I was able to bury her. I gave her a very, very good send off.

But the funny thing is this. I didn't know that you're supposed to bury the dead in the usual clothes that they wear. When I went to the morgue at the hospital, I put one of the night dresses that I bought at Marks & Sparks on her. I didn't put on her bra. After she was buried she came back and dreamt to my cousin—the one who I told you is a midwife. She say: 'Why you and Melissa forget to put my bra on'?

The following night she came to that same cousin who was staying at the house and she say: 'Eh, Evelyn! You can't clean the fridge top? The fridge top dirty'. Evelyn told me when she woke up the morning, went up and do like this on the fridge top. She says: "Oh my God!" So you know, sometimes they say that when you die you're going to a different dimension and you don't have anything to do. But I'm not sure whether it's true. They're watching over us.

Melissa was haunted by the fact she was not able to go back to Jamaica in 1972 when her grandmother Doule died. She felt it was a great tragedy that she couldn't be there.

When Melissa goes back to Jamacia in 1980 to bury her mother, she decides that something should be done to pay due tribute to her dear grandmother.

I tombed her grave. That was the part I felt I should do. My mother is buried next to her. It's the vault I put my mum in. It's a family burial ground.

The funny thing is this. When I was a small child—if I go out and I feel afraid at night—the minute I get to our family burial ground, the fear is gone. I don't know why. I wasn't the only one, my cousin Evelyn said the same thing. There's my great-grandfather, my great-grandmother, my grandfather, my aunties and uncles. All the family who died are buried there. So if I die now, I don't know where they're going to put me because there's no space left. I'm not going up to the pig's crawl, that's the part where we use to raise pigs. They'll have to break mama's tomb and put me down there.

Melissa's trip to Jamaica comes sixteen years after Melissa left Jamaica for England. She notes the stark changes in her home country and is more than a little surprised by what she now sees around her.

There were lots of changes. Jamaica was like America. The Jamaica that I remember when I was small, wasn't there. It was much more advanced like America—especially Montego Bay. I thought I was visiting another country.

There were beautiful buildings and the people dresses well. What I remember is that we used to wear different coloured clothes, but now it was all colour co-ordinated. The children took pride in wearing their school uniforms. There was electricity in every house. I remember when we use to use thinning lamp with kerosene oil in it and a wick. The fumes use to go up your nostril. When I went home everybody have electricity, everybody have fridge and everybody have television. To me that was advance. If you go to Jamaica now, you think you're in America. Some parts of Jamaica are even better that America.

Impressed with how Jamaica is changing and its rising prominence as a tourist destination, Melissa decides to invest in property. With the assistance of her friend Carl, she buys a property in Ironshore, Jamaica with the remainder of the money she brought with her and a loan from Lloyds Bank in England.

It had a swimming pool and a maid's quarter. It was a beautiful place. It was a Chinaman's villa and he was going to America. He used to work in the tourist trade. When Manley was in power in Jamaica, everybody was running away.

Like the previous owner, Melissa intends to rent out the villa to people going on holiday—mainly from England, America and Canada. Responsibility for letting and managing the property is left in the hands of a local estate agent, Mr Daly.

Upon Melissa's return to England she struggles to settle back into to her usual life.

It was very painful and I decided I'm going to

go away for a while. I was working at London
Chest then. I just didn't want to stay in England
anymore. I thought: 'Let me go away somewhere,
I need a break from the white world'. In 1981 I
went back to Nigeria on holiday for a bit because
my friend, Beverley, was there. She was second
wife to one of the MP's who was the Minister of
Telecommunications.

As the guest of Beverley and her husband, Chief Etang Okoi
Obuli, Melissa is moving in exalted political circles.

The President of the Senate was Joseph Wayas.
Myself and my friend, we would go down to his
house. All the MP's, they use to live down by a
certain area in Lagos they call 'The Marine'. I
don't know why, but all the MP's live in that area.
   Now the first time I have ever seen a 'flat
screen' television it was at Joe Wayas's house. It
was like a cinema screen, it was that big.

Melissa, however is a great deal less impressed by what she sees
and hears at his house.

While I was there, Joe Wayas was speaking on
the telephone to someone on the Spot Market
in Holland, that's where they sell the oil. I turn
around after he finish his conversation and I
said to him: "Joe, you mean you are selling the
oil of Nigeria privately. It is not yours. It doesn't

come from your backyard. It's the nation's oil."
You know what, he turn round and says to me:
"Ah, Melissa you are in Africa, enjoy Africa. Leave
Africa politics alone."

Elected in 1979, the Shagari government (whom Joe Wayas worked for) is plagued by allegations of corruption. Re-elected in 1983 amidst further allegations of electoral fraud, the government is to be overthrown by a military coup led by General Muhammadu Buhari on New Year's Eve 1984.

Still mourning the death of mother, Melissa is still not settled. Though she is disillusioned by the corruption she sees within the Nigerian government circles, Melissa is still drawn to Africa.

I stayed there in Nigeria for about a month on holidays, and I then came back to England.

I did a bit of work again and got some money in my hand. Then my friend Zina—we did student nursing together—said she's going to Sierra Leone. I says: "Alright, I'll go with you." We bought some goods—handbags, dresses, shoes, earrings—which we took to Sierra Leone to sell.

We travelled on British Caledonian. That was 1982 and one of the air hostess's was a Black Sierra Leonean. After they announce in English with the English air hostess, the Sierra Leonean girl came on the mouthpiece and started announcing: "Boh, ah say. Nah put de heavy load up dey. It go fall down. It go conk yer head." I rolled up laughing because what she was saying to them was not to put heavy baggage in the overhead lockers, it could fall down and hit you in the head. But the way she said it in that Creole, I just rolled up—eh!

There use to be this hotel in Freetown name Paramount Hotel. It's no longer there now. When they were having problems in Sierra Leone the other day with the killings, the soldiers took it over as their barracks I've been told. But when we went to that hotel in 1982, it was a beautiful hotel."

When considering the items, they have taken with them, Melissa's choice to go on holiday to Sierra Leone with Zina doesn't seem at all impulsive. So what are Melissa's first impressions of the country?

From the airport to get into Freetown, you have to go on a ferry. You've got a lake, they said it's a river, but to me it's more like a lake. The ferries are big—like what you see down at Dover—and they are usually full. We cross over from the airport on the ferry. It takes about an hour to cross.

When I got to the port and I looked around I thought: 'Oh my God, what a desolate place'! The old pan roofs. We have some of them in the West Indies, that's why it reminded me of Jamaica. When you go up in the rural part of Jamaica, you find like the old plantation masters' houses. They use to have the pan roof—galvanized iron—but they're rusty, so they kind of have this brownish colour. That's the first thing you see coming from the airport going into Freetown, the houses were like little shacks. Coming from the developed world, I thought they should have done better to develop it. What you see make your mind feel: 'Oh my God! What is the country like then?'

The Sierra Leonean air hostess reminds Melissa of Jamaica, as do the pan roof houses she sees on her way from the airport. Then someone tells her the story of how the first Creoles settled in Sierra Leone, which also sticks in her mind because of the connection with Jamaica.

There's a massive cotton tree in the middle of Freetown. I was told that during slavery days, when Marcus Garvey ask for a ship to bring slaves back from Nova Scotia to Jamaica, you have to travel down the African coast to come to the Caribbean. The slaves from Nova Scotia—who was freed—were going back on a boat that sailed near to Sierra Leone. They saw greenery, beautiful trees and dry land. They said to the captain: "We have no water, we have no food. Let us stop here and see if we can get water and food."

Although it was the abolition of slavery that was taking them back to Jamaica and freedom, they were still chained in the ship. The captain took them off the ship with the chains still around their necks and ankles. He took them into Freetown to get the water and the food. He saw this massive cotton tree in the centre of the town, so he chained all the slaves around the cotton tree.

The captain of the ship was British. The slaves saw the people. The native people of Sierra Leone were Blacks. The slaves chained around the cotton tree were Blacks as well, because they were from Jamaica originally. The natives of Sierra Leone says: "Ah! These people are Black people like us. They look like us, but they speak the white man's tongue. Teach us to speak the white man tongue."

The Jamaicans who were around the cotton tree, they are the original people what they call 'Creole'. The natives ask the captain of the ship: "Please, can't you let them stay to teach us to write and speak like you?" The Jamaican slaves who were around the cotton tree said: "Yes. It's a beautiful place. It looks like Jamaica, it's warm like Jamaica. The Black people are like us. Let us stay here. We don't mind staying here." So the captain says: "Alright, let the natives take me to their chief." The chief of that land at the time in Sierra Leone was called King Tom.

The natives took the captain down to see King Tom. He says: "My cargo is slaves that I was taking back to Jamaica because of the abolition of slavery. But they want to stay in your country because they said it looks very much like Jamaica.

Have you got any land I can buy so that I can put them?" King Tom says: "Yes."

Why it was called Freetown? When the captain of the slave ship bought the land from King Tom, the slaves were released from the chain. So that is why the capital of Sierra Leone is called Freetown, because the slaves were freed there. Now the people who were released, they speak Creole. It's very similar to Jamaican patois.

The story that Melissa is told is part fact and part fable. At the end of the American War of Independence, escaped slaves who had fought with the British—called either 'Black Loyalists or Black Pioneers'—were given their freedom and resettled in Nova Scotia. Unhappy with discrimination and racism in what was then a British Colony, over a thousand of these ex-slaves choose to go to Sierra Leone when the opportunity arose. Sailing on fifteen ships, they arrived early in 1792. There was a large cotton tree near George Street in what was then Granville Town—a settlement on land originally granted to the British by King Tom.

According to local legend, on landing, the freed slaves walked up to the cotton tree and held a Thanksgiving Service. Shortly after, as a result of a new agreement between the British and King Tom, the settlement was renamed Freetown.

There is still a large cotton tree in the oldest part of Freetown today. Sierra Leoneans regard it as a scared symbol of their capital city and often go there to pray and make offerings to their ancestors.

There is also another connection between Jamaica, Nova

Scotia and Freetown around this time, which can be more closely linked to the story that Melissa was told.

In 1795, the British were fighting their second guerrilla war with Maroons in Jamaica. Maroons were escaped slaves who were determined to put an end to slavery on the island. They were not defeated, but after that war some six hundred—mainly from Trelawny Town—were deported from Jamaica to Nova Scotia. Later in 1800, they were again 'removed' by the British from Nova Scotia and sent to Sierra Leone. At the time of their arrival in Freetown, American ex-slaves—Black pioneers—who had fought on the British side in the American War of Independence were in rebellion against the British. Somehow, the British managed to persuade the Jamaican Maroons to help them put the rebellion down. As a reward they were granted their own land to the west of Freetown, which became Maroon Town.

Though Melissa is technically on holiday in Sierra Leone, she and her friend Zina are also trying to make some money by selling the items they have brought with them.

> It was so fascinating. I went there and what I saw of Sierra Leone was impoverished, but the people were lovely.
>
> What was happening at that time? There was one boy in the hotel by the name of Lloyd Beserve. Now he used to take our goods around to the boutiques—the handbags, the belts, the dresses—to ask who want to buy them from us. When he makes a sale, we give him a commission.

There was nothing to indicate it at the time but the boy at the hotel, trying to sell their handbags to boutiques, is later to play a far more significant role in his country's history.

> I'm going to cut to something which has nothing to do with this, but it has. During the war in Sierra Leone, one night I was here in this house. I turned on the television and there was a documentary on BBC, I think it was BBC 2. It was a reporter who went to Sierra Leone during the war. When he came back, he was showing documentary proof of what was happening with al-Qaeda coming into Sierra Leone. They showed a photo of a man and when I looked, it was Lloyd Beserve. He was on the ferry coming into England, and he had to go back on the ship to France because they detected him. Do you know it was Lloyd Beserve that we met at the same hotel? Lloyd Beserve met the al-Qaeda at that hotel.
>
> He was the one who took them to Kona. Kona is the area where the diamonds are. It was Lloyd Beserve who took them there. For a pittance Lloyd Beserve destroy his country and his countrymen. He wasn't a Muslim, he was a Christian. He wasn't a Muslim but in Africa, people who do not have, will do anything to make money.

Melissa's brief holiday in Sierra Leone makes a huge impression on her.

I made quite a few friends while I was there. It was so nice, I thought that I wouldn't mind going back there. I use to correspond with a friend who was in the government. I said to him: "I wouldn't mind coming over to Sierra Leone for a while because since my mother died, I just feel I don't want to go to Jamaica, and I want to leave England for a bit." He says: "Come over. I'll get a flat for you.

In 1982, I decided to go back. I went to live in Sierra Leone. He got me the flat. I use to live in Acton. I had a house in Winchester Street—very famous street. I took all my furniture, shipped it over. He cleared it for me. We became very good friends.

As you know I'm a nurse and I use to work for the United Nations at Wellington General Hospital in Sierra Leone. But I do quite a bit on my own time. I would go in there and help the nurses on a voluntary basis.

Though this is her third time in Africa, she is still having difficulty getting used to the food. After some time, however, Melissa begins to see connections between Sierra Leonean food and the food she grew up with in Jamaica.

When I first went there I couldn't eat their food because the palm oil was like cotton wool on my tongue. I would eat gradually—little, little, little—until I get use to it. Now, even when I'm here, I will cook with palm oil. At times, I will cook the stew.

Most of the fish is dried. You put a mesh over it, put wood underneath and set the fire so that the fish is smoked and dried at the same time. In the remote parts of the country, where they wouldn't have fridge, that is how they kept their meat and fish. When they're ready to cook it, they soak it overnight in water—very nice flavour.

They eat a lot of greens leaves, sweet potato leaves. They will cut it up like spinach or callaloo and cook it with meat or fish, very nice. There are two types of cassava, the bitter one they don't use. The sweet one, they'll get the leaves put it into a mortar and pound it. If they've got a grinder, they grind it. It makes the most beautiful stew. You cook it with meat—pork, beef or cow tripe. Nice flavor, especially when you cook it with tripe. Nice, nice, nice!

They've got a thing what we children in Jamaica use to call 'Shake-Shake'. It's a long shell thing that comes off this tree and when you pick it there are beans inside. Yes, you can use it as a musical instrument. They use the seed and pound it in a mortar, very nice flavour. When they're cooking that stew, they put it in—beautiful! Gives it Ummmh. But it stink! When it's done, it stinks like sore foot, but nice flavour.

Ochre! If you see when they cut up the ochre and cook it with dry fish, dry prawns and palm oil. They eat it with rice. Oh it's wonderful, 'Wunderbar', as the Germans would say.

There are lots of things there that we eat in the West Indies. But Ackee, they don't eat Ackee. They have Ackee trees but they don't eat it. They would pound the Ackee in a mortar and fishermen would throw the pounded Ackee in the sea to catch fish. The fish them would just float up on top because they're drunk on the Ackee. You know if you don't allow the Ackee to open—if you force open it—it will poison you. That's what they use to drunk the fish, and the fish will come up to the surface.

Nursing is Melissa's profession and she is well qualified. However, she is ambitious and you can only get so far as a nurse. On her first trip to Sierra Leone, she and her friend Zina saw an opportunity to make money by bringing in goods that could be sold for profit. On her return, she meets someone who shares her ambition to go into business.

I became very friendly with Malamah Thomas and we started doing Import-Export from Switzerland. We would import Peak Milk, it's evaporated milk. If you bring Carnation Milk to Sierra Leone, they wouldn't buy it as much as they buy the Peak Milk because all West Africans prefer Peak Milk. I tell him let us start something and he did. He was doing Import-Export with my money.

His friends them were Lebanese. There we've a lot of Lebanese in Sierra Leone. He use to be an accountant with one of his Lebanese friends who was bringing in stuff as well. His Import-Export business was good.

Whether in Jamaica, Nigeria or Sierra Leone, Melissa seems to have a talent for befriending people with influence and power.

Malamah Thomas's ancestors in the early 1800's were very rich. His great, great, great-grandfather was so rich that they named a street in Sierra Leone after him—Malamah Thomas Street. If you want to be vulgar, they called it 'Sourpit'. It's a commercial area, all shops and hagglers selling goods from one end of the street to the other. It's a very long street. You've got clothes shops, hardware shops, cement shops. When you go up to the very top, then you can get foodstuff. You name all the things you can sell, it's on Malamah Thomas Street.

They had a house which was called Malamah Thomas House. That house has been there from slavery days. I hear that just below the house was a wharf and ships used to dock down there.

I heard that he made his wealth during the time of slavery. You see slavery in Africa starts with the Arabs. The Africans used to sell their native people to Arabs. The Arabs in turn take them on a ship to another port to sell to the whites—the English,

French, Portuguese and the Spanish. Those were the four how ruled the waters in those times. He used to be allowed to go on ships in those days. He would come to England, buy things like a merchant, and go back to Sierra Leone. Don't ask me how. I don't know what arrangement they had why he wasn't sold into slavery as well. He used to buy wares because I've got a vase right underneath here—which is a Japanese Warrior vase—and that was one which he bought.

So the Malamah Thomas's have got a history in Sierra Leone. I don't know how they did not take him as a slave as well and how he was able to travel on their ship—that would be the British ship—to come to England and buy stuff and to go back.

They said that he was so rich that when one of his daughter's was getting married, I was told that he bought a red carpet for his daughter to walk on. It stretched about three miles from Malamah Thomas House to the church.

As might be expected with stories passed down orally generation to generation, facts become mixed with fable. The great, great, great-grandfather referred to in the tale told to Melissa was in fact John Henry Thomas. He was born in Hastings, Freetown to Creole parents—formerly slaves. His father died when he was three years old. Starting school in 1845, John Henry spent much of his time helping his mother to make ends meet. He left school at the age of fourteen and was employed as a clerk by a number of different employers. He later set out on his own and started his first business with a loan of £100. This was a factory on the Rokel River at a place called Malamah. This is where he acquired the name by which he became known.

Melissa was told a completely different story on how Malamah Thomas acquired his name.

> The Mende is one of the traditional Sierra Leonean native tribes. Their word for Malamah means 'lazy'. He thought well, I'll put 'Lazy' Thomas. So he just called himself Malamah hyphen Thomas. That was how the name came about.

John Henry Thomas was anything but 'lazy'. When his factory in Malamah closed, he took up employment as an agent of the 'Comagnie Francaise de L'Afrique Occidental' (CFAO) in 1882. Before taking up the post, he opened a small shop in Freetown, left under the management of his wife. Six years later he resigned from the CFAO and returned to Freetown to take charge of his business. Bringing his twenty-three years of commercial experience to his business, it quickly expanded and prospered. Malamah-Thomas eventually became one of the leading merchants in the city.

He traded mainly in cloth fabrics and patented his own brand of cotton which was known as 'Malamah Baft'. The beautiful 'Malamah House' he built in East Street—Freetown, still stands today as a monument of his commercial prowess and success. He served as the Mayor of Freetown eight times and became an unofficial member of the Legislative Council in 1907. John Henry Malamah-Thomas died in Freetown on 18th

January 1922.

Malamah—the great, great, great grandson of Malamah-Thomas and after whom he was named—is not just Melissa's trading partner. Not long after she arrived in Freetown, they are living together and end up having a baby.

> I had Cantrice in Sierra Leone. She was born in December 1983 in a private hospital there by the name of Neglan. I think the man who owns it was called Dr Frasier, he's dead now. He was a very nice man, trained in England here, went back to Sierra Leone and opened his surgery. His sister who did midwifery here with him also went back, and both of them set up the private hospital together.

Zina's friend, the one who found a flat for Melissa in Freetown, stood as a candidate in the May 1982 Parliamentary elections and won a seat. He must have been a member of the 'All People's Congress' Party. By then, Sierra Leone was for all practical purposes a 'One Party State', with President Siaka Stevens—aka 'Pa Shaki'—using the army to crush all opposition.

Through her contact with Zina's friend, a week after the elections, she gets an invitation to a social event at the president's home where she meets the President of Sierra Leone, Siaka Stevens.

> He say: "Eh! I'm going to speak now Creole."
> That's what the President Siaka Stevens say. He say: "Eh! I hearie say Jamaican titi [girl] deh,

nyah? Eh! You play you part in the election, no so?" I say: "No Shaki." He say: "I don't like you Jamaicans so. Eh! You know why I don't like you so? You talk and you talk weh you mean. We African, we no talk. We keep it inside here and we go kill the other man. But you—you go talk. If you're going lick em, you then lick em. You done, done." I say: "Pa! Ah so we Jamaicans stay."

The president is asking Melissa if she played a part in the recent election when he was re-elected. She replies 'no'. The president then says he doesn't particularly like Jamaicans because they say what they mean. He says that 'we' Africans don't do that. 'We keep it inside' and eliminate our political enemies.

He say: "One thing with Manley. Manley, he could get more coup help. But you know, Manley mouth too free. Because Manley mouth free, like he no get all dem charity so." I say: "Pa! We Jamaicans were slaves, as you lot call us, 'slave children'. We have to fight for ourselves and stand up for ourselves. From the age of nought we've been doing it. We don't want to be fed with a bottle." Him look me up, him look me down. He say: "Eh titi. Ah wish I had a dozen women that behave like you, stand up like you and talk like you. Eh! We would control the better."

According to Melissa's account of her conversation with the president, he tells her that Norman Manley—the then Prime

Minister of Jamaica—talks too much which undermines his ability to attract internal support and international aid. Melissa responds by saying 'we' Jamaicans—who you call 'slave children' have been fighting and standing up for 'ourselves' from the very beginning. Apparently Siaka is impressed and says his party would be able to lead better if he had a dozen women like Melissa.

This is not Melissa's only social meeting with Siaka Stevens.

Pa Shaki, he's a very nice man, but also a very wicked man. I went to see Pa Shaki twice. The second evening when I went there to see him, he was drinking his favourite whiskey—Chivas Regal. He asked me if I want some. I said: "No Pa. I'll have wine." He say: "Alright, this is my favourite." We were drinking and we were talking.

I say: "Pa, I go ask you something. Pa, whey mek you listen to gossip? Mek say you hear de ting from the first man and you don't hear it from the second man or the third man. Eh! Wen you don't hear it Pa, the person whey they talk against you—you go pull on. You go tell de police and your special men them. You go pull on, go put dem pon Padamba Road [Prison]. The next ting you deh kill em. That no right oh! Eh—no right. If you wah put me down ah Padamba Road, you can call your men them, arrest me, put me in ah prison, but I did tell you the truth. None of your women, none of you men will tell you the truth." He look me, he look me. He shake him head. He

say: "Titi, nah me you deh talk to." I say: "Shaki—
Pa Shaki—nah you ah deh talk so. Stop draw your
own countryman blood—enough, fine. If you
live by the sword, you go die by dem. Pa, ah no
wan hear say revolution start and dem done kill
you and machete you. Stop it!" He get up. He
come shake me hand. He say: "Titi, ah love you
spirit—I love you spirit. Not true because sometime you're hearie—now you hearie." I say: "No
Pa. Don't do that. You've got your own way of
judging, so no do dah one deh." He say: "Eh! Nah
sense, nah wisdom you dah give me so. Others
go talk me fey go kill de next man. I say no go
do dah."

Here, Melissa bravely challenges Pa Shaki on what she's heard
about him arresting people and sometimes having them killed
based on gossip. She appeals to him to stop. Of course Pa Shaki
does not admit any of this and tell her she does not understand.

It is utterly amazing how quickly Melissa comes to understand and speak creole. Though there are some similarities it is
a long way from Jamaican patois.

While we were there talking, Pa Shaki said to me
that in Parliament—when he has a plan, or when
he's going to announce something in his government—he doesn't tell his MP's. He doesn't call a
meeting and tell them. So I said to him: "Why
don't you do that Pa? Don't you think you should
more or less do what you call consultation?" He

say: "Ah titi! This ah Africa. Dem go sabotage with voodoo, so you no tell dem. If you got plan, no talk um." If you have a plan, don't talk it.

So I said: "Why Pa?" He say: "Nah evil world we live in so? Even the evil weh deh pass in the air evil. If you deh talk something and a evil one deh pass—he go tek em, he go tear em, he go raga, raga, raga em, he goin proil. Even in the air, evil passes by. You've got good evil in the air, you've got bad evil in the air if you speak something at the time an evil person is passing by. Evil person like goblin. We cannot see it in what you call the natural world. It's in the abnormal world, right. We can't see it but it will take what you're saying and destroy it—it will become void. So void or avoid, it will come to nought." He said: "If you want to do something, do it first and then announce it in Parliament." He said this is why whatever you're going to do, keep it to yourself until you do it. He told me, even business—if you're doing business—it's the same thing you must do because you see someone's face, you don't see their heart.

Just before the conversation between Melissa and Pa Shaki ends, Pa Shaki explains the way he handles business in Parliament. His approach is to make the changes first then announce them in Parliament, telling as few people as possible beforehand, including his own MP's. His belief was that MP's talked too much and there was no telling who would attempt to sabotage his efforts.

In Sierra Leone, when Melissa told the story of her conversations with Pa Shaki, people were amazed because she was a foreigner.

> Yes Pa Shaki was a very good man—fantastic man he was, in the sense. If you see Pa Shaki drink him Chivas Regal! When I tell people they say: "What! You foreigner come and you see Pa Shaki?" I say: "Ah! Pa Shaki nah look pon you." He even signed a book he wrote and gave it to me. I left it in Sierra Leone with a friend.

The book is *What Life has Taught Me: The Autobiography of President Siaka Stevens of Sierra Leone*.

In many ways Melissa's new home reminds her of her earlier experiences in Nigeria.

> Corruption in Sierra Leone stinks as well. If you have money, you can get anything.
>
> They believe a lot in voodoo, a lot in voodoo. I don't know—maybe it works—but because I don't believe in it, I don't worry about it.

Melissa's recalls an interesting interaction she had with a man who practised voodoo in Sierra Leone.

> One of the native girls took me to one once and tell me that this man is a wizard. I said: "Which part of him is wizard?" Wizard mean witch, the

man witch. He said: "Oh yes I am!" I said: "Which part of you?" He says: "Oh, if I drop something in your eye!" I said: "You're not dropping nothing in my eyes, nothing!" He said to the girl: "Oh dear! You know something? This woman, she's Black but she's a white woman! She nah believe in nothing. Eh! I going show you." I say: "You're not showing me nothing, it's rubbish!" The girl say: "Oh, he's good," I said: "To your mind, not to my mind."

He look me and look me. He say: "Eh! I didn't realise. Your skin is Black but you've got a white mind." I said: "It is called psychology what you're doing. You are psycho-analysing these people. When they tell you their problems—you put two and two together."

Melissa is skeptical because the 'wizard' reminds her of a story she was told in Jamaica about 'Obeah'—a version of voodoo derived from Africa. The tale is about a woman who used to argue with her husband and in the hope of resolving the tensions in her relationship, the women consults 'An Obeah Man'.

When the women went to the Obeah man he say: "Tell me wah ah go on with you and your husband." The woman explain. The Obeah man say: "Alright, ah go give you something simple. Ah going give you this water in a bottle and when you and your husband quarrel, just put some of the water in your mouth."

Melissa recites the story and explains that the Obeah man gives this woman a bottle of water instructing her to drink it the moment her husband starts arguing. This woman goes home and does just that.

> The woman went back to her house and her husband started to quarrel. She opened the bottle and put some of the water in her mouth. The husband is still quarrelling, quarrelling, quarrelling. He don't hear no sound from the woman. Him stop. The next day him start to quarrel with her again. She put some more water in her mouth for a week. When the week done the woman go back to the Obeah man and say: "Lord! Me nah know what this you give me, but it good you see. Me husband stop quarrelling."

Melissa feels the woman in the story is far too gullible and refuses to believe that the couple's arguing stopped because of the water.

> Of course him stop quarrelling. Him no have nobody to quarrel with. He quarrel with himself because she can't open her mouth. If she open her mouth the water come out. It's psychology—it works—but its psychology. So these people are psycho-analysing people. They hear your weakness and use it.

Melissa makes use of this story to confront the voodoo

man in Sierra Leone.

> So me say to the wizard: "Rubbish! All what
> you're doing is nonsense. You can say all these
> things work, but it's nonsense." He said to me:
> "You think it's nonsense but a lot of people don't
> think it's nonsense because these things work
> from Bible days."

The voodoo situation aside, Melissa fits in with people and culture of Sierra Leone. She is employed as a nurse at a hospital funded by the United Nations. She is living with a descendant of one of the country's most famous men with whom she has a child and together they are both working for and investing in an import and export business. As well as this, she also has access to the Sierra Leonean elite—including the president. However, underneath the surface, things are not going as well as she hoped.

> I was not making money in Sierra Leone. I was
> hoping that I would. I survived, what you called
> survive. But becoming rich? No!

Not that long after arriving, Melissa sets out on an extraordinary path.

> I got involved in digging for diamonds outside
> Freetown.
> In Africa or the West Indies, you can be doing
> four or five things. Nobody checks up on you.

Once you going do what you're to do, you can be gone in one or two hours—nobody kind of check up on you. If you're going to do a project up country and it's to do with health, that's that. You have time to do what you want.

The chief in the area was my good friend and he use his men dem to dig for me. But your diggers, they're thieves—they will steal your diamonds. What you do is you don't pay them. You give them food. I would supply them with rice, dried fish and palm oil. When they find a diamond and you sell it, then you give them a part of it. Yes you give them part of it.

Odd as it might seem for someone who was born in Jamaica and is a qualified nurse, Melissa seems to have acquired a fairly good understanding of the business she's getting into.

You have got different types of diamond. You've got the 'bluey-white' which is the best. In Sierra Leone it's called 'chop-chop'—or as Naomi Campbell called it—'dirty diamond'. You've got 'yellow' diamond, but that's not as valued as the 'bluey-white'.

You've got another one which is called 'black diamond'—[carbonado]. It's something that they use in machinery for cutting. Then you've one they call 'candlestick'. It looks like diamond but it's not diamond. If you see those in the earth, big long pieces, you will know that diamond is there.

A lot of people take those out of the earth—say that's diamond—and sell to people who don't know about diamond.

Some diamonds are good and some aren't, although they are 'bluey-white'. When you hold it up, it's got sparks like a star if you look in the centre of it. If it's good you will see this. If it's not good, although it's 'bluey-white', in the centre of it you will see little fissures or marks. That mean if you cut it—the minute you use your tool to cut it—it shatters. It's no good, you can't cut it. So when the diamond cutters in Holland see that, they put it down—the value is very little. You can buy it maybe for even £50 a carat because it's no good. It will shatter.

Melissa quickly realises that the business of diamond mining is far more complex than she initially anticipated.

The diggers will steal it. They will swallow it. They will put it up their bum. They will do all kind of things. They will also kill for it.

Melissa remembers a specific instance that causes her to make a pivotal decision regarding her involvement within the diamond mining industry.

We were digging one day and as I told you, when you see those things they're called 'candlestick', you know that diamonds are there. The main guy said: "We kept digging, digging. All we're finding is Johnny Stones. You know that diamond is the devil and the only way we will get diamond is if we kill someone. Ah go go ah village where man whey drink Omalay. Just get him to come here for rum because he will follow you anywhere to get that rum and kill him."

Until then she did not understand the true nature of diamond mining.

I say: "Ah! If this is what you're on about, I will not dig diamond anymore. I'm finished." I stop digging. I tell the chief: "I'm sorry. I won't come back." If this man has got this mentality, that mean all of you will. When you get diamond, I don't want it because it's blood! So I left.

Melissa decides to leave the diamond mining industry behind. Looking back, she laments about the nature of that sector.

What they did not realise, people are dying each time you dig in a diamond mine. When you dig diamond, it's deep down. You dig earth and you bank it. When you bank earth, the earth gradually slide back down. If you are deep down, it going to slide over you. That is why they usually die because of health and safety. They think that when that happen—when someone dies in there—you will get diamond. It's not, it's due to health and safety. If they get posts, put in the earth and then put boards cross that, the land can't slide back down—nobody would die. But they feel that because they die every time they dig, somebody has to die to find diamonds.

During this time, Melissa still finds time to see more of Africa.

While I was in Sierra Leone, I went to Liberia. You know it's on the border with Sierra Leone. I know Liberia very well.

The same white car I told you I use to have— the Mazda 323—I use to drive it over into Liberia. Liberia is beautiful. Of all of West Africa that I've been to, Liberia was the most developed.

I didn't try to do diamonds in Liberia, I just visited. How I know so much about Liberia? Malamah's cousin, name Joe, use to live in Liberia. I've been to Liberia a few times and stayed by Joe.

By chance, through one of her neighbours in Freetown, Melissa also makes other connections with Liberia.

I use to live at number 15 Carlton Kerry Lane in Sierra Leone. Taylor's girlfriend live at number 17 Carlton Kerry Lane. I knew Taylor, he's from Liberia. Taylor's driver use to come and park the car. Taylor would come out, he'd see me, we'd talk and he'd go inside. But I never knew that Taylor was that wicked.

The Taylor whose girlfriend lives next door is Charles Taylor. He will later lead a guerilla war in Liberia, overthrowing the government of Samuel Doe to become the 22nd President of the country in 1997.

Melissa may have left the diamond mining industry, but she's not ready to give up on other parts of the diamond industry.

There were times when I use to go to Conakry in Guinea. They've got a diamond area they call Banankoro. I use to go up to Banankoro to see if I could buy diamonds. It's a massive diamond field—massive.

The funny thing is this, it's out in the wilderness. You would think that native people are stupid because they always give away their diamonds—their gold. But when you go in these countries—like the diamond area, the gold area—they're smart. Hey! They're smart.

I stayed a week in Banankoro. It's funny, there was a guy there from Liberia but he lived in America for years. He was in Banankoro as well. They use to have like a log cabin, that's where we stayed. The toilet, hey! Even now today, the Africans in the country, that's what they do. They dig a round hole and you have to go and stoop over the hole if you want to pooh or if you want to pee. That's how you have to do it. I had constipation there for the week because no matter how

I stoop, it wouldn't come. I'll pee, but that's about
it.

Like in Sierra Leone, diamonds in Guinea are still being mined
by local people digging in the ground with hardly any equip-
ment. This activity is financed by foreign fortune hunters. If
and when they find anything, which is rare, it is traded in the
busy diamond street market of Banankoro.

I didn't buy any diamonds there. Those 'chop-
chop' stones were the black ones, so I didn't want
them. Remember I told you the black ones are
for cutting machines. I wanted the 'bluey-white'
diamonds.

Whatever can be said of Melissa's life in Sierra Leone, it is most
certainly not dull. On her return from Banankoro she's in for
a shock.

At the time I use to have a 323 Mazda sporty white
car. When I came back, my houseboy says to me:
"Mam, while you were away—you know when Pa
Malamah died—I see Mr Malamah driving your
car with a white woman in it." I say: "Really?"
He says: "Yes. You want to see Mr Malamah on
the phone ah talk to this woman. I hear, they talk
English, so I know what they say."

Pa Malamah is Malamah's father. In the week before Melissa
went to Banankoro, she had been caring for him in hospital.

Chapter Six

He dies while she is away. To make matters worse, she also gets news of Malamah's adulterous activities.

> I have a very good friend who comes from the diamond area in Sierra Leone—a Kono woman named Maybell. She said to me: "Melissa, I went to casino last night and I see Mr Malamah in the casino with this white woman." I say: "Ooh! Alright. At least you tell me. Me houseboy tell me, so it can't be wrong."
>
> He didn't come home the night. He phone say: "Oh, I get work. We have to finish because inspector they come, come." The morning, he came in the car of the Lebanese man he was working for doing the accounting. So anyway, I said: "Malamah, do I look like a fool to you?" He say: "Eh! Whey you deh talk bout?" I say: "You and I do not breathe the same air. I'll pack your clothes for you, alright!" He say: "Eh, weh you deh talk, weh you deh talk?" I says: "Look, I've packed your clothes. You see those three black bags on the veranda, your suits are on top of it. Take them and go. We don't breathe the same air." He say: "Eh! I no know anything." I say: "Just take them and go. We're not quarrelling."

After Melissa tells Pa Malamah to leave, she notifies him of some important news.

> While he was going through the side door to go

on the veranda, I says: "I think I'm pregnant but it doesn't matter. You don't have to stay. Go!"

Even though Malamah now knows that Melissa is pregnant with his child, he does not return to their flat. The reason why soon becomes clear.

Do you know Cantrice [Melissa's daughter] was born on the 17th December, 1983. Malamah had a child with that white woman who use to work in the British Consul. The child was born on the 29th January 1984. She is one month younger than Cantrice. So that was the separation of us.

Despite breaking up with Pa Malamah, Melissa remains in Freetown for a further two years.

I left Sierra Leone in 1986. I left because I didn't like what was happening in Sierra Leone. Cantrice's father and I became kind of dislodged so there was no reason for me to be there anymore. Cantrice was three years old when I left. I wanted her to pick up some English before she's too old, so I brought her back. Her surname is Malamah-Thomas.

My grammar was very thorough when I came to England, but since I went to Africa to live and came back, I found that my accent is totally different. Even if I'm speaking Jamaican patios, I tend to put a bit of Creole in the patios.

Chapter Seven

A Place to Belong

EMMA

Now living in West Bromwich with their two young children, both Emma and Mathew are working.

When I first knew Mathew, he was working at different places. Then he got a job at a company in Tipton, shortly before I had Samuel. In all the years I've known him, he'd only worked for two places.

After I left the laundry, that was '69 when I was expecting Donna, I went back to Woolworths. I worked there up until the Christmas. It was only a Christmas job. I started there September/October and finished the Christmas.

Then a local bakery called Scribens—the name changed to J. Lyons—you must have heard of J. Lyons Bakery. They were advertising for people to work. I think I went on the morning shift when I started at J. Lyons.

When I had Samuel, he was in a day nursery round the corner from us, so I could work full-time. With the two little ones, I went from doing the morning shift to doing ten o'clock in the night till seven in the morning. I never got much sleep until it was the weekend. A lot of women did it. I did that for a couple of years.

After that I did some stints at a metal closure company. They did bottle stoppers, pressed out the caps for the bottles and what have you. I was part-time there on the evening shift. I nearly always worked when our children were young— whether it was mornings, evenings or night work.

Ethan, their third child, is born in 1973 while they are still living in the council maisonette. By this time Emma and Mathew have fully integrated into their community and become close with the people they live with and by.

I think there were maybe about eight families living in the block. My husband and I, and the couple that lived in the flat directly beneath us, were the only two families that were African Caribbean and who had a father or their husband living with them. All the rest, they were single parents. But the community we lived in, all the Black people looked after each other's children or spent time with one another.

In one instance there was a father caring for four sons. He raised those lads hisself. That's somebody else's story. I was like a surrogate Mom for them, his four boys. His youngest was the same age as our eldest Samuel, so they were peers. Most of the children that lived round there were roughly the same age.

My husband was the only African Caribbean man out of the group that got a car, so the boys use to wash his car. My husband would treat them, take them for a drive out, get them some sweets and stuff like that. I use to bake cakes as well, so our home was very popular when our children were growing up.

Now when I left home and lived at Miss Maggie in St. Paul's Road, she made cakes. When I made Samuel's christening cake, I bought two cake tins. Those I got as a start. I never asked my landlady to borrow her stuff. I remember buying a bowl and I bought a whisk. I didn't take anything from my mom.

Just as well. Though Emma thought her mother had 'mellowed a little', Millie continues to ignore her daughter and Mathew at social events. She often referred to Mathew as 'this boasty man' who thought he was 'a millionaire'.

I was very independent. This is what I realise that me mom must have thought: I was a 'big head' as well as him.

I do know that they [Emma's parents] both loved us in their own way. I wasn't a burden on them, even when we didn't have it when I was married. I know there was times that we're in deep dire need and if we ask Mom, she would have given us. But we never did. So her words to the

community were: 'Me got me big shot. Me got
me millionaire'. Of course, that sort of affected
people minds and what they think.

There had been little communication between them at the time,
but looking back Emma is convinced that both her parents
loved her in their own way. In fact, there would appear to be
little communication between them for some time.

Emma speaks about her time in Jamacia with her two aunts
Wilma and Lynette, who both played a significant role in her
early education. Aunt Lynette later immigrated to England and
lived close to Emma's family home in West Bromwich.

Aunt Lynette was related to my dad. She reminded
me of my grandmother. They were teachers Wilma
and them. She lived on Birmingham Road which
is not far from here. She had a massive house.

The only thing I was sad about was that whenever she returned to England from America,
nobody inform me. I wondered whether something had been said, or she was deliberately
avoiding me. She'd visit England because her son
still lived here. She didn't come to visit me when
she visited England. Maybe because she didn't
know where I lived.

This is not the only instance of Emma feeling shut out of the
family by her parents.

There was other family weddings and events that

happened. Even when I was in my twenties, I was not invited. I never heard nothing about it and it wasn't that I wasn't in the community. I wasn't wrapped up in my family, so I was excluded.

Emma remains upset with how her parents responded to her pregnancy especially in comparison to her younger sister Emily's teen pregnancy.

They didn't show that understanding to me and, in actual fact, they did not ever show that to any of our children. That is another story. You know they were not the favourite grandchildren—the three of them weren't. The eldest one Samuel, he looked so much like my dad in every way.

When the time comes for Emma's sister Emily to get married, Emma remembers something her father does.

He didn't come in the church for my sister. I couldn't understand it. Dad posed for family photographs with Emily, but one of my cousin's had to give my sister away.

Emma's father is a strict Jehovah's Witness and strongly objects to going into other Christian churches. Yet he came into St. Phillip's Church to give Emma away at her wedding. Why he didn't do the same for Emily, Emma doesn't know.

Shortly after the birth of their third child, Emma goes back to work. Samuel is seven, Donna is five and Ethan is just a few months old.

It was an engineering company, one of the Brockhouse Group. I was looking for temporary work and that fitted in nicely. It was only for six to eight weeks, again from the job centre. I started there in January 1974 after we had Ethan.

Our department did shelving in banks and offices. This is from start to finish, from the raw metal right up. I worked on the conveyor belts, that was assembly work. It was hard work once you've got the skill. Then they offered me a permanent full-time job. I was there for ten years. My mom use to care for Ethan.

Though they were getting on with their lives, Emma and Mathew want to move out of their council masionette.

The story behind us actually living in this house? We wanted to get a move somewhere and tried to get a transfer from the local authority. This is really important for people who are going to hear this. Prejudice existed to the extent that if new homes—council properties—were being built, Black people never had them when they were new. We watched these houses being built when we lived in the maisonette. They were called townhouses. A family would move in and it was never an African Caribbean or Asian family that got one of these properties.

In 1979 and Emma and Mathew finally find a way of moving out of their council maisonette.

Our maisonette wasn't really that old but they were badly designed. They got structural problems with them as well. Furthermore one of our children had got asthma and then the younger one developed asthma as well. So three flights of stairs was not gonna be any good.

I was working for a company in the Brockhouse Group. It was across the road. My foreman at the company gave me the addresses of vacant council houses on this estate, which would have been easier for me to get to work. He lived in the area. Of course, we needed a garden as well for the children.

My husband and I went and saw our local councillor at her surgery back in early 1979. I gave her these two addresses. This one was empty and next door. She got in touch with the Housing Department and I had a call from them to say I could choose this property, but it would be about three months before it was ready. Next door I would have had to wait six months. Three months was going to be long enough.

It was the February. After, we actually came down to have a peek in because they wouldn't give us the key. Couldn't come inside, obviously.

We liked what we saw. It had got a front garden. I started hounding the council because they had said yes. But after a month, we'd come down here and we couldn't see if they were doing any repairs to the property. It had got a damp problem as well, but we found that out later.

We waited three months to actually move in here and it was like a palace. We had our own front door before, and my experience of moving from one room to a three bedroom maisonette with your own living space, was wonderful. This was even more so because in the back of our mind we wanted an old council house to buy. That was our remit.

To cut a long story short, we moved here and straight away we put in to buy the property. It wasn't the council's policy cause Labour were not one for wanting housing stock to be sold. We persisted and we bought the property.

They have just moved out of an area with a substantial Black and Asian population, and into a locality which is predominantly a white working class area.

When we moved in we were the only African Caribbean family that lived on the street, and that's how it remained for a year. Then another African Caribbean family moved in three doors away. They purchased their house from the person who was the foreman at the company where I

366

worked. There were others on the estate but not many.

That didn't make me nervous. It wasn't a particularly strange environment to have moved into. Handsworth is just up there. I worked across the road and my parents are just three bus stops away. That was another reason. I wasn't driving back in those days, but it was easy for us and the children to go and visit my parents.

Moving here wasn't a bad experience for us. It's always been positive.

Emma and Mathew find that settling into their new community turns out to mirror much of their experience back in West Bromwich.

The children were the ones who in a sense helped us to, because they were friends with some of the children that lived on the street when they started school. One family we became very close friends with was a white family. The wife was Scottish and they had a child the same age as Ethan. Our older kids would take Ethan to her house and she took him to school, kept him afterwards and I'd pick him up. Plus, I'd got my foreman who lived three doors away.

One of my neighbours had three boys—Timmy, Richard and Allan. We took them under our wings. We didn't plan to do it. I baked and the relationship began with me and then it was with the parents.

Even when our children were much younger, we always had other children around us.

When we lived in our previous home because I baked cakes, the other children who lived on the block—children of African Caribbean descent and also the white children—would come. They'd be there before the cakes were done. Because of that, there was always groups of children visiting our home.

It was like a continuation then of all these children who our home was open to when we moved here. Although I worked, we both worked, other people's children were still coming and going. I could show you photographs with dozens of children together in this house. It's a birthday party, but the children in the community would be welcome as well. Our home was popular with children.

While this is going on, members of Emma's family are sniping and stirring from the sidelines.

Me and my husband had a period of separation. It was necessary, and we discovered after two weeks we'd made a big mistake, but it needed to be done. People were like surprised. Our children would have known. Ethan would probably not have remembered that but the two older ones did.

It happened for a very good reason because we

can still be talking about it years after. We'd got all sorts of different pressures going on around us and it wasn't everybody that wanted our marriage to have lasted. There were tale bearers and what have you. I have to give it to my husband, he wasn't one for listening to rumours, but I use to be like a mop. They would carry rumours to my mom—regularly. My mom wouldn't even question what they're saying and she would ring me.

The rumour that leads to the couple's brief separation is about her husband.

One Sunday afternoon I had a call from me mom at this house: "Hah! Me hear say him dey ah Sportsman Club last night and white woman dem ah fight over him." That was the words she used. Mathew said: "Emma, what you going on bout? Where was I last night?" I says: "You was here." He says: "So why you bother respond to what your mom say for?" That's what somebody said, phoned her or visited her, and she phoned me for there to be contention to be in my home. But she and her mom use to be always having contention, which I found out later.

Important as it was in getting their new house, Emma's job with the Brockhouse Group is under threat. She started with them in January 1974 and remained there for ten years.

My hours were slowly getting cut, from full-time down to twenty-five hours a week, because there wasn't sufficient work. I was like doing mornings, eight o'clock till one.

Emma's hours are being cut because established metalwork companies in the West Midlands are in decline in the 1980's. Emma and Mathew begin to consider other options.

We'd been talking about it for quite a while. The Sunday evening—can't remember if we were at a christening or at some function in this pub. Anyway, he and I started this conversation yet again about these children we see on the TV. They'd been battered and what have you. Can't we do something?

We came home and I said to Mathew: "I'm going to find out about us doing something about this." So I got the Yellow Pages, the two directories, and looked up Welfare and social services. Children Services it is now.

The person I spoke with had only just started the job. He came from Southampton but he was originally from Ireland. I told him what I was ringing about and he says: "Oh, that's interesting. As a matter of fact, we've got some seminars coming up." They'd being doing a promotion for prospective foster carers and adoptive parents. We hadn't seen that.

Eager and willing to learn, Emma and her husband attend training sessions.

He invited us to the first meeting on the Wednesday. We went along and there were many other people there. They were going to set up some training for all the people who were showing an interest. It was over a period of five or six weeks.

We were the only couple who was there from the first week to when the training finished. People would show an interest, then didn't. We were the only self-motivated couple.

When this training got set up, we were the only prospective foster carers who hadn't been doing the job. All the other people, white people, were already fostering. They'd never had any training.

It was called 'Parenting Plus' and it was based on an American model. Some of the people were always grumbling: "What's all this in aid of? We've been doing the job for ages." It was an eye-opener for us but I was sort of feeling the same way. We've got three children, so what do we want this training for? I had swallow my pride— well both of us did—because it open our eyes to things that our own children would never have ever been exposed to.

You could have had twenty children, but caring for another person's child—especially if their parent is a local authority—it's a whole new ball game. You're only an agent for them. The training gave you an understanding of how to do the job—what these children would be feeling when they come into your home, that sense of loss. I can identify with this feeling of loss and bereavement in speaking with folks because I've actually been there.

Part of what that first training was, one of the first things we were asked to do was to try and remember as far back as we could—a favourite or a sad time. I did that. I went back as far as the sadness I felt on leaving my grandmother and coming to England. Other people said different things. It was more how sad you felt than how good you felt, because a child wouldn't be coming to you feeling good if they're leaving their parents. They'd be kicking up: 'I don't want to. I don't want to'! That was just the starting point because they would not just be feeling bereaved. You would be taking them from an environment which they're familiar with into this strange environment.

You needed that training because number one: corporal punishment is not allowed even to this day. If one of my grandchildren steps out of hand, there's no authority going to say to me I cannot reprimand them. But you can't do that, there are other ways of dealing with it. Even though you might feel like hitting them, that you couldn't do.

We were already sold on the idea. They now set up, for the first time ever in Sandwell, a requirement that foster carers had to have training. My husband and I were the only prospective foster carers that had any training before being on the job. All the other people on the course—I am talking about thirteen couples or more with single parents—had been doing it previously, without any training.

You've got to want to do it and this is where the people who would go into it for monetary gain, gratification—whatever you want to call it—fail.

It is 1984. Their first child Samuel is now sixteen, Donna is fourteen and Ethan is eleven.

When we started fostering, our children were growing up and it was with their consent. We wouldn't have been able to have done that without the support of our children. They had to be interviewed and if it was detected that they were not going to be happy with it, things would not have gone along.

We'd come to a stage in our life that we felt really, really grateful for having our children. They were with us. We were reasonably happy and we felt we wanted to give something back.

We got assessed and everything, and didn't expect to have had a child for probably twelve months because there weren't that many Black children that was in care. But I found out that it wasn't the case that Black children were not in care. White carers got them. They didn't want to release them from the white carers to give to a Black person, although you did the training. I'm talking about what I knew. You talk about institutionalised racism? You've got foster carers who didn't know how it was to care for a Black child properly. Hair and skin care was just two items, never mind diet. You're a Black person that's got some training, but it was still as if the white person was more superior to you. However, it is true that fostering was less common within our community.

The family is living in a three-bedroom semi-detached house when Emma and Mathew are assessed and approved to foster two children at a time. They ask to foster children who are eight years old or over and do not expect to be allocated a child for at least a year. Given their concerns about institutional racism within the local authority, they have no idea how the allocation system will work for them.

I was at work this Monday. Came home from work the evening in January when social services rang—just as I was coming in—to say they had a child that needed a place of safety.

It was Jacob that social services was on the phone about. He'd spent Christmas with his grandmother. This was the 6th of January and situation didn't improve. They had to get a court order to find a place of safety for him. I said yes and within about an hour or so the social worker was here with him on the doorstep, just with what he stood in.

Jacob, the first one that we fostered, was three. He's thirty-two now. The next one, Joel, was seven months old. He was twenty-nine yesterday. He's getting married soon. Joel and Jacob were our first two. Jacob was full Black. Joel was dual heritage—both his parents were 'half-caste'—so he was like quarter, but that's still classed as Black. Those were our first two foster placements. Jacob came in January and Joel came here in February.

Jacob shared a bedroom with our two sons. It wasn't an issue in them days but it's an issue now, he would need to have his own bedroom. Joel was in our bedroom.

I never returned to that job with Brockhouse but my foreman knew what we were considering doing.

Now, having been allocated their first two placements, Emma and Mathew are faced with the circumstances surrounding why children are placed in local authority care in the first place.

We saw it almost immediately with the children who came into our care—the hardships, the difficulties some of the parents were going through— hence why their children come into care. We tried to have an understanding of what the parents had been going through. Some of the children, it's just unfortunate that they do come into care. The longer they're in the system, sometimes the worst it is for them.

Helen, who is Joel's mom, had grown up in a children's home. She'd been in care. She herself was one of these children who was dumped. Abandoned as a child, she doesn't know who her mom and dad was. The only parental figures she'd had was the husband and wife who ran the residential where she lived.

Helen had Joel basically because she thought that would have made everything perfect in her life, but that wasn't the case. The young man himself, he'd got a similar background to hers, didn't live with his parents and had been in care. They came together because they'd got a similar experience. He wasn't able or ready to be a father. Unknown to Helen, he had got another girl pregnant almost at the same time. So she was trying to pull him one way and this other person was pulling him the other way. Eventually he married the other person, but it didn't work out. We became Helen's mom and dad.

She was the youngest mother and she was the most caring. She would ring up every day whilst Joel was here, checking on how he was, and she visited. He was here for about twelve months.

When she first came here and saw us, the second day she says: "Can you keep him forever." But within two weeks she was saying she wanted him to go for adoption. I said: "Helen, what if you don't have any more children? This might be your only child. Think really hard about it. Don't consider adoption yet, give yourself some time." She listened to us. She wanted him to go for adoption because it was a short term placement and she didn't think she could cope when it came to an end. She did though, we encouraged her to. She got a council flat and we went to see her in it. She would phone us and we use to go down most Sundays to see her.

Mathew is working full-time and Emma is responsible for looking after two foster children who she has been told will only be with the family for a short while. She decides to accept an opportunity to go back to work.

It wasn't planned. One of my neighbours was working across the way and she came and says: "Emma can you help me?" I says: "Depends on what it is." She says: "I've been helping this company across the road doing some cooking and I've got to go back to my own job." She was getting on at that time and couldn't do two jobs, so she says: "Can you come and do it?" I says: "What is it?" She says: "You enjoy cooking, don't you?" I says: "Yea." She says: "It's only cooking meals for some blokes in the canteen." So I says: "OK, when do I start?" She says: "Can you start on Monday?"

Now I've got two foster children here. She says: "Don't worry, I'll help with the children if there's a need to." She brought me the keys. I went and open up this canteen on the Monday morning, half past seven.

Emma eventually has to abandon the job because some of the new foster children coming into her care are challenging to look after.

The emotional baggage that they were carrying, you had to sort of get that understanding. We're normal, we go to the toilet. Some of them they would hold on to that solid because that was the only thing they felt belonged to them, that nobody couldn't take from them. They would hide it.

Having that training certainly helped us because we had a child in our care who was just like that. The training told us the places they would hide it. Carers would have smelled something in the house and they could not pinpoint where it was. It would be hidden like in an airing cupboard.

All those sort of things was good in preparing you because your own children wouldn't display that sort of behaviour. That was an emotional thing which they carried, buried in them. But if you become aware of a child who might display behaviour like that, then you start looking up what may be the reasons.

In the meantime, Emma's own children are growing up.

Well you can see around you, I love books, I love reading. I love to study and all our children were encouraged to. We supported them as much as we could at home and going to parents evenings when that was necessary. We kept up a dialogue with the school. The teachers always saw us and it wasn't just Mathew or me—they saw us as a couple.

When our daughter was a teenager an issue came about. You bring your children up with a certain standard and she saw something that happened at school which was not of the same standard. It was actually in the Domestic Science class. This teacher repeatedly brought her pet dog to school and it was in the kitchen all the time.

My daughter took her on. She told her no, it shouldn't happen. She refused to go into the lesson. Maybe the school had never been challenged before. Well she challenged the teacher. This teacher was not expecting Donna to refuse because previously to this, she'd kept that to herself. I had a call. I can't remember whether she came out of school but I was summoned to school to go and see the Headmistress. I think Donna came and fetched me and explained that the teacher was bringing her dog into the classroom.

We threatened to take her out the school altogether because of that. I says: "Well, I will make
an issue of this. I will let the press know about it
because a dog should not be in the kitchen." This
was at senior school.

Other than that, up until then, we'd never had
any issues with our children in school. They never
said that a particular teacher picked on them.

When Emma and Mathew hear of Donna standing up to her
Domestic Science teacher, both parents see this as testmament
to how they have raised her. They are proud and luckily for
them, Donna is not the only child who makes Emma and
Mathew proud.

I remember the time Samuel was out cycling and
he found this man's wallet. He brought it home.
Mathew took him down to the police station to
hand it in, not to be a thief.

Mathew recalls a similar occasion.

Samuel when he was growing up, broke a car
window. Somebody called him a 'Black So and So'
and he threw a stone and broke the car window.
He didn't run off, he came and told us. He bring
the person home and he said: "Dad, I've just
break this lady car window. I throw a stone and
break it." I was thinking to myself: 'Why didn't
he just run off?' He brought the lady home and

he was shaking.

Just over there, that was a garage at one time that fix cars. I just took the car over there and told them to fix it. They put the windscreen in and I paid for it because I told him: "Get into trouble, come home." That's what he did. Even though it cost me, I live on that principle. I couldn't say to him come home and when he come home I say to him: "Bwoy, why you no run off."

Later on however, their eldest teenage son comes under other influences—his peers.

We would ask Samuel what did he want to be when he grow up. It was always somebody's mate. It would never be that I'll be an electrician, I'll be a plumber, I'll be whatever. It was always somebody's mate. That's what he'd says and basically that's all he did.

Consequently, he got himself into trouble with another group of children when he was about fourteen. One Sunday afternoon there was a knock on the door and he came in. He and a group of them went into this bicycle place and stole some bits and pieces. Sunday afternoon! We couldn't believe it. Anyway, there were four of them. Two were brothers, they got cautioned. That was the first time he got himself into trouble.

Mathew has his own theory on why Samuel got into trouble.

This story is not long. You see, when you got children—in my opinion—you've got two children.
You've got the one that you see and the one that
you don't see. You got the child that organise the
friend to meet them down the street. So when
they meet with the friend, they're a different individual from when they're in the house.

Emma deemed Donna's prospects to be far more hopeful.

Honestly, I would say that the only person—
academically—that came out of school well was
Donna. When she left school, she went to a local
college. I think she did personnel.

She got a clerical job with Sandwell Local
Authority and she developed to a point where she
should have been offered a particular role, more
as an assistant manager than a manager. She was
being overlooked. Repeatedly, they would employ
someone who supposedly had the qualifications
for the job, and yet they weren't qualified for the
job role. Donna was expected to show them what
the job was.

Donna learnt her job from college and then
on the job. These people come from university—
didn't know the job—but they got the university
qualifications. They give them the job and then
they wanted Donna to train them up.

She came home one day and she says to me:
"I'm leaving the job because if I'm not good

enough, I'm not training somebody else." That was exactly what I would have done.

She got a job with Birmingham City Council who sent her to the University of Central England to do a degree in public Administration."

This is 1989 and Donna is nineteen years old, now doing her degree at the University of Central England.

She had a raw deal in the men that she choose. She met Isaac when she was still at home. Well it was secretly and she fell pregnant. She was nearly twenty and we all wanted to see him. He didn't come. So we got her to take us to meet his family. It turned out to be his mom and she wouldn't invite us in. When she saw Donna she said: "Didn't I tell you to leave him alone." That was his mom's response.

Now naively, she didn't realise that he'd got another child. Maybe she did because she loved him. He also got another woman pregnant at the same time. Whether his mom knew or not, her response was I told you to leave him be. She wouldn't even invite us in, wouldn't entertain any conversation.

Donna always had our full support. Anyway she left home. She went to live with Mathew's dad and his stepmom. She then moved in with her aunt Gloria, then she got a flat for herself.

Though Emma insists that their daughter always had their full support, Mathew admits that after Donna became pregnant the parental bond was not the same.

> She left home because the relationship was strained.

Having been prompted by Mathew's assertion, Emma goes on to explain things in greater detail and cannot avoid drawing parallels with her own earlier life.

> Even before she fell pregnant Donna was always headstrong. She was setting a plan. I look back and thought well maybe I was setting a plan—I don't know. Maybe she wanted to be pregnant so that Isaac would choose her. We actually heard a conversation. If they've got their friends around, you can hear more about them—what's going on in their life—more than what they'll ever say. I remember hearing her say: "I'm gonna get him. I'm gonna get him!" This was about the November or December. We didn't know what it was about.
>
> Lo and behold, a couple of months after that—on my birthday—she went and got herself a pregnancy test. She found out that she was pregnant and told me. That was my birthday present. She was what, nineteen? It became a strained atmosphere in the home. She was back-chatting me. Before she was pregnant, the face that she showed her dad was a different face she would show me

when he wasn't around. Very challenging behaviour it was. But she left home.

She cut us out of her life at this time. That was another low point for me, her being pregnant and leaving home. Mathew, Ethan and myself—the three of us was left at home with Jacob—that's our adopted son. Jacob had his own problems. He's still got his own 'demons'. The three of us were on sleeping tablets from the doctors. That's how it affected us because she was having nothing to do with her brothers, me and her dad. The only people she was communicating with was Aunty Gloria and by this time Mathew's brother-in-law and his wife. Everybody else was out of the picture.

The period what she was going through, I suppose we've all experienced something similar. Everything that she bought her dad as presents, she demanded them back. I can remember this pink shirt, it sort of brings things back. Not that one is holding on to these feelings, but it's just what it brings back. She'd got a portable television—hadn't she—which we had in the dining room. Of course, she took that when she went. There were so many other things.

Through family connections Emma and Mathew are able to keep track of the birth of their first grandchild.

When she went into labour, Mathew's younger

brother whose wife was a nurse and they lived fairly close to where Donna was staying, kept a close eye on her and reported to me in a sense. So we knew how she was getting on. When she had the baby, she had a really tough time.

As a mother—before I was told she was in labour—I was experiencing her labour as well. I was at work and I was in excruciating pain in my back and my legs. When I got home I was told she'd been in labour for how many hours. I threw up. I says: "No wonder, I've been feeling it." We didn't go and visit her.

The decision not to visit her daughter may well have reminded Emma of what happened when she was in hospital having her first baby as a sixteen-year-old. It is not long before she changes her mind.

The baby was a few days old, about five days old. One of my cousins says: "Oh the baby's gorgeous." I says: "Well the way she's acted, part of us want to but part is holding us back."

We went and saw her. In her whole body she wasn't recovering as they expected her to. She was there maybe five or six days but after we went and visited, her condition started to improve.

So her own well-being—not just having the baby—got better. I still kept our visits up. I kept that line of communication going until slowly— through my brother-in-law and his wife—she gradually came back into the family fold.

Donna moves into a housing association flat where her and her newborn son are to remain for the next two years.

In the ten years between 1984-94, Emma and Mathew are responsible for fostering seventeen children. Some stayed for two or three years but most are short term.

The length of time the children stayed with me varied. The shortest anyone stayed was forty-eight hours—a young boy—pushing thirty now.

As I said to you earlier, children came into care for a whole host of reasons. In one case the responsibility of getting this little boy to and from school was left with a friend of his mom. The friend asked somebody else to do it and that person didn't do it, so the school got in touch with social services.

When I had the call from social services about this little boy, they said: "Emma, we don't know how long it will be, but it's an emergency." When the social worker pulled up with this little boy, we knew his grandmother. It's part of being in the community, knowing people. He came in and— of course—we knew him.

We told the social worker: 'We know his grandma'. So that was a nice ending to that. He had to stay for twenty-four hours. By that night social services had to make the mom and the nan aware of where the child was. The following day when the grandmother came outside—she recognised this house. When she came to the door, she says: "I'm turning back. If I did know! Mak me gwane bout me business."He returned to them the following day because forty-eight hours had to take place. He was here the shortest time but it is still an experience because it showed again the reasons why children end up being in care. There wasn't any proceedings to follow, apart from form-filling and for his mother—Jennifer— to realize her mistake, promising not to let that happen again.

Emma remembers a young Black boy who came into her care around this time.

Then there was Dexter who was about six going seven when he came. He was here for three weeks. Mentally he was twisted up emotionally from before he was born basically.

Dexter is a Black child and had to be fending for himself. His mom went out to work and left him. He'd eat what he saw. He didn't turn up at school, yet he was seen on the street. Then they found out that he had been in the house several days on his own. So he came into our care for three weeks and—boy—I wouldn't wish it on anyone.

When I say that, the local authority had got an eye on the mom and him. There wasn't a close enough eye because the mom was fourteen

when she had him. She had a relationship with
her stepdad and Dexter was the product—right.
She'd left home by this time. She had a younger
child who she always had everywhere with her,
but he was left in her house. It was only when he
came into our care that it was recognised that he'd
been left on his own for long periods. The lad was
taking himself to school and school hadn't picked
it up until this period when he weren't turning up
at school. Then something got done.

The mess! He'd filthy himself three times in the
three weeks. That was an emotional disorder. Part
of our training was to understand why some of
these things happen, but until it actually happens,
it's then it hits you.

Dexter is only in their care for a very short while. Somehow
they manage to keep track of him long after he leaves.

He died. They found him dead in his flat. How
long he'd been there for? He was decomposed. I
read it in the newspaper and I didn't realise it was
him. That really, really saddened us although we'd
only shared his life for three weeks.

After he left us he went back to his mom,
temporarily. Then he was moved on to long-term
carers. I could write a book on this. The carers he
had, they were older than us at the time. So he
would go for respite in a residential accommodation once a month and he was sexually abused by

staff there. The child came back home and told the foster carers and they whipped him away and put him into a different children's home."

Dexter is followed by another difficult case.

We had a Black lad—Calvin—in 1991. He came from a children's home—a number of them came from children's homes. The idea was to integrate them into living with families if you came from a children's home.

This lad had got a good role model in a Black social worker—Andrew—who went through hoops for this lad. So many people went through 'hoops' for him but he just knocked everyone down.

When he was in care he use to keep absconding. He kept running away, he'd got a history of it. Calvin came to us when he was fifteen until he was about seventeen. From birth, his mom gave him up and his father's parents raised him. Within him, he was still searching. He wanted to find the mother that rejected him. He found her because she lived in the area, but he was getting this rejection even as a teenager. She didn't want to have anything to do with him, basically she'd had enough.

We tried to put him on the straight and narrow. I wouldn't say that we failed but he kept rejecting it. Whenever he couldn't get his own way, he'd run off—even if it meant climbing through a window. He did that when he was living with his grandparents. Now the grandfather fell ill and things got worse. I think his grandfather passed away, he had got a firmer grip on him than what the grandmother had. When he ran away from us he went to the grandmother's. The grandmother would allow him to do whatever he wanted. She encouraged him in a sense. I'm not talking about running away for two days, he would be gone over two weeks—sixteen days. That sort of period.

What he would do, he would present himself to the police because he feel, well it's time I went back home. You'd buy new clothes and he'd go and sell it. Shoes, he would take a razor or a knife and cut it from one side to the other. Very destructive.

He was well-known by the police. Say if he'd absconded for a couple of weeks and it was West Bromwich Police Station that brought him back, the next time he go missing, he'd present himself at Smethwick Police Station. He got us all running round after him like a 'blue ....'—you know what.

The last but one time he ran away, I said to him: "Calvin, I've had it. If it was left up to me you wouldn't be coming back." Mathew said: "Yes, we'll will have you back Calvin but I'll deal with you."

Of course, Calvin runs off again. This time there are consequences which Emma and Mathew could not foresee.

Every time this sort of thing happen, a review would be had. He'd gone now for good. We said we weren't having him back and they had this review. Went along to the review and there were about a dozen people in the room. We didn't know that when he returned to the children's home—he made an allegation against Mr 'T'. He said Mathew tried to strangle him—grabbed him by the throat. We didn't know anything about this and months had passed.

We're expecting to have had another place-ment. We didn't know that that was something in the review. We had the review notes and there was no mention—not even in the discussion—that Calvin had made an allegation. This happened about mid-September. So come December, we both said to our social worker: "Don't you think it's time you got your finger out." He didn't answer. This allegation is there pending but we didn't know anything about it.

In our training we were told that troubled children might make accusations. We were also told in the event that anything like this happens you would know within twenty-four hours. So the allegation which Calvin made to Andrew—although we said he was a good social worker—his hands were tied because it was the department against us. Andrew was Calvin's social worker. If anything we expected Andrew to have told us that he'd made this allegation—but the department, they change the rules to suit themselves.

So we're coming up to Christmas and we organised a foster carers Christmas party. All the food—the fish, the chicken, the curry—we did it all here, then after we went along to the West Indian Centre. Our car was playing up, it was like telling you we shouldn't be involved in this thing. Anyway we got there, this was the Saturday evening.

The following Monday evening we had a delegation come from social services to say an allegation had been made against my husband. It wasn't just one allegation, it was two. By this time we're Christians and my husband actually said to them: "If he wasn't a Christian, he would kick them out the house."

This allegation was made by a sister of one of the social worker's who worked in the office. She claimed that my husband had an erection against her. Now this would have happened at the party that we'd laid on the Saturday night.

Mathew speaks up and tells the story as he remembers it.

Me and Tina (our social worker), was standing there speaking together and she (the person from social services making the allegation) was sitting on a chair when some lads rushed by from that room into this room. So they kind of pushed me onto her. She was sitting down. When the lady from social services came to interview me, I actually took a chair out and ask her to sit down. I said to her: "Now you tell me, if you're sitting down and I rub up against you, how can you tell that you aroused me?" That was part of the interview—there was nothing to prove.

We threatened to take to them to court—Sandwell social services. We went and saw a solicitor about the whole matter. They're not placing any children with us because of the allegations hanging over our heads. Even so, our solicitor said we should go along to all the carers meetings that take place. We were not to say anything to anybody—neither carers or social services. We went along.

Anyway, when the independent social worker lady finished her report she said we could talk to other carers about it. So we went along to the next support group meeting and we just let loose on what we'd gone through. People were numb. The other foster carers, they were numb because of how long ago it had been since we were suspended with allegations pending over us and what the allegations were. They lost a number of foster carers through it.

In the meantime, Emma and Mathew are still registered and approved foster carers but Sandwell Council is not placing children with them. Not sure if or when the matter will be resolved, they try a different route.

We bought *The Voice* newspaper each week and three different authorities—Lewisham, Westminster and Southwark—were advertising for children to be cared for. All Black children.

I contacted all three authorities and in less than a week two authorities came down—Southwark and Lewisham. God is so good. The first social worker that came down to interview us, her name was Sue Fleet. I think she was from Lewisham. I remember her to this day because she was the first one to come down. We told her that something had happened with us and Sandwell. In fact, we told her all about it. After she made an appointment to go and see Tina our social worker. She was told over the phone: "When something like this happen, we don't expect anybody else would want to touch them with a barge pole."

In the end they did dismiss both allegations against us. Oh yes, we had a wishy-washy letter saying they're sorry. That was it! By this time, we were already speaking to other authorities. All three of the London authorities came to see us and we settled with Southwark.

That was a side of fostering which was unpleasant and we realise it wasn't something that happened rarely—it wasn't a rare thing. That happened quite frequently to other carers. They expected people to fade away, you see.

Mathew for his part is also far from pleased with the way in which the dispute was eventually settled.

I'm one hundred per cent for the legal way—
written down and dated. I like the legal way.
What annoys me most is that social services were
supposed to pay our legal expenses. When those
allegations were made against us, they did not pay
our legal bill. We had to pay it ourselves. That still
grieves me. There's a lot of people in an official
capacity who do not keep their word. That's what
annoys me but people like my wife and myself, we
never take things lying down. We recognise that if
you don't stand up you will be trampled on.

EVELYN

Evelyn has just opened her hair salon on the Ringway in West Bromwich. It is December 1978 and she is forty-six years old. From the age of sixteen in Jamaica, this is what she has always wanted to do.

Evelyn's children Garry and Janice are now in their early twenties. Evelyn thinks back to when they were younger during their secondary school years.

> I followed their school reports and I was always at the school—parent's day and things. If anything is going on, I'm at the school. They went to music lessons. They joined the Brownies and the Cubs, right up into Scouts and Guides. They were in everything. Whatever the school was doing, they were there. If there was a trip the school was going on, they were in it.
>
> They went to George Holton School in West Bromwich. The only thing with the school was that they were very strict on uniforms. Other kids could go to school without uniforms. My kids could not turn up without uniform—they sent them home.

I went down the school one day and I thought: 'Look how many other kids were going there without uniform. I am going to find out from the Head Teacher why they send my kids home.' I said: "I'm not coming here to make a fuss or anything but I'd like to know the reason why you send Garry home? He came today in ordinary clothes and he was sent home." The Head Teacher said: "Well the reason why your child was sent home is that I know Garry has a uniform. I know everything in the school, so he must turn up in his uniform. The others who don't have uniforms are the ones who are not in your position." I didn't make an argument because he has a point and it's the rule of the school. I just wanted to know why.

My kids had no trouble at all going to school.

***

It is 1974. Garry has just left secondary school and Janice is not long behind. This is a year before Evelyn decides to apply to Wolverhampton College to do a hairdressing course.

I sort of looked back on myself and I thought: 'What I would want them to do is maybe what I would have done. Let them choose. I'll guide, but I'm not going to insist'.

Evelyn is resolved not to treat Garry and Janice as her mother Winifred treated her. She is going to 'guide' them not 'insist' on what they do next. It is after all, their lives.

Garry, he wasn't good to go to college. Garry was more a hands-on person. When he was doing his woodwork and metalwork, he was good at it.

I thought myself: 'Let him go into engineering because he can make and fix things with his hands. Let him go into the jewellery quarter.' So I rang one of the firms and they said: "OK, bring him in." When I brought him the person who opened the door saw that he was Black and said: "There's no vacancy." I said no, can I speak to such and such—I can't remember his name. I said I'm not talking with you, go and get Mister so and so—your boss. He went and they took Garry on.

Garry trained there. He did everything right down to the tiniest. He was there for about two years or more. After Garry finished with the jewellers, I took him out. To me—at the time—there were different areas that was prejudiced. I wanted him to have a scope of choice. If he was struggling in one area then he has a choice.

I thought to myself: 'You know what. I want you to go into big industry. Metal closure is a massive industry. They do right up to a thirty-four ton.' I got him into metal closure. I put him into a factory to do tool setting.

There can be little doubt that Evelyn is acting with the best of intensions. Nevertheless, there is little difference between

Evelyn's understanding of 'guiding' Garry's future and 'deciding' Garry's future.

> Janice started out as a telephonist and she does typing and whatever. She didn't like it, said it's boring. She went to college and got certificates in hairdressing and beauty. She followed in my footsteps.
>
> She came into my salon—well she had to. I paid her and I work her harder than the others. When the others could have a day off, she's not having one, unless it's important or sickness. I was strict with her more than the others. She worked pretty hard and she's very good at her job. She's very disciplined.

Evelyn's hairdressing salon is now up and running. Though her mother, Winifred, never approved of her choosing to become a hairdresser. It is her mother's upbringing that instills the values within Evelyn that allows her to attain success in her chosen field.

> My mum started me off saving with the Penny Bank when I was growing up going to school. I remembered when I had £3 in the bank, I thought I was rich. She always say to me: "Evelyn when you grow up—if you're working and if you even get married—always have an account by yourself apart from the one with your husband. You don't even need to let anyone know that you've got it.

Keep that to yourself because it gives you certain amount of flexibility and if anything happen, you've got that to fall back on."

I had that account. I started off in a small way, then I built it up. I wanted to invest it and I took it to my lawyer in town. It was a big firm and I ask them to invest it. So when I wanted to do the salon I went to them and I said: "Listen, you've invested my money. You've got the books and everything. I need so much and I don't want to go and take it out and lose all my interest." I took some of that money and opened my salon.

A lot of people thought my husband gave me the money for the salon. No! I did it myself. I've always said: "I don't want anybody to say that they made me what I am. I must make myself. I must not owe it to anyone." I never did.

I had to fit it out. I was at the salon until two o'clock in the morning to finish off and open for nine.

Evelyn begins to encounter sceptisim within her own community.

Everybody was saying to me: 'You'll never survive. You'll never survive because of racism.'

The funny thing is, the first person waiting for me on my doorstep when I got to my salon at nine o'clock was a white person. My first customer was white.

Evelyn also notes how people within her community began treating her after the salon was open.

> I used to do a little bit of hairdressing at home before that. The ones who used to come to have their hair done at my home—even my husband's relations—when I opened the salon, they stopped. One of them said: "Think I going come here for you to do my hair and then when you get rich you come boast pon me!"
>
> You see, that's our mentality.

To be fair, at the time most African Caribbean women are accustomed to getting their hair done for free by a friend or relative. Evelyn knows this.

When Evelyn opens her salon, she has no intention of specialising exclusively in Black hairdressing. She would not have excelled at college if she couldn't do all kinds of hair.

> At one point if it wasn't for whites, I would not have a business. There was not one nationality that came in the salon that I couldn't do—especially the ones who worked factories nearby me. Whites use to come in. One of them—Margaret—she use to come and help me shampoo hair and everything.
>
> Blacks used to come in. Sometimes when they do come, they go round after and tell people that I don't do Black hair. That was the propaganda that they spread because they see whites at the

salon.

The salon was set out so lovely that three-quarters of the customers didn't even know it was a Black shop. I remembered one day a Black woman push the door and she said: "Heh! Yer still there? Me think you close down long time." I said: "I'm still here. I'll close when I want to, not when you want me to."

Little by little Black customers start coming back. But sometimes if they come in and I'm doing a white hair, they would want me to leave that white and come and do theirs.

I remember this lady—she was my husband's friend just over from Jamaica. She came to the shop and she was feeling the cold—it was in October. I gave her a coat and a cardigan and everything. She was the first one who was very nasty to me. She said: "Yer think me a beg you for these things? Me going pay yer." I said: "You know what Miriam, take yer coat, put it on and get out my shop. Don't ever come back here." Her behaviour was so nasty. Even now I have whites who are still friends and have been coming to my shop for forty years and their children.

I'll tell you this, it was whites who kept me open. Not my own.

***

Evelyn loves her house in Trinity Road. She and her family

have been living there for over twenty years. They paid just under £3,000 for the house which is now scheduled for demolition. A bypass is being built—Trinity Way.

I had to do a compulsory purchase sale to the council. I said to them: "You see how nice my house is? I'm not having no rubbish. I haven't seen anything I want to buy so you have to re-house me."

Everybody on the road got the same money from the council. I think I got two thousand something pounds. I thought my deal was bad but there was a man who live in Overon Street who had a leasehold and he got £30 for his house. He still had a mortgage—he didn't pay it. He went off to Canada—I don't blame him. Compulsory purchase was horrible, horrible.

The council gave me a house to live in while I was waiting to buy something. It was a new house. They said: "Do whatever you want to do with it." I built a garage and I put in central heating because I didn't know when I'm going to find something. But I disliked the house—I hated it. In the end I went out and bought a solid bed because of what was going on next door. You could tell if they were going to the toilet or whatever was happening next door. It was a semi-detached. I thought: 'No, no, no! If they pay me I wouldn't buy it. If I buy a new house it would have to be a detached, not anything adjacent to another house. You have no privacy.'

Evelyn begins searching for a new house. The only requirement is that the new house is similar to the family home in
Trinity Road. Interestingly this desire ends up triggering a longstanding aspiration of hers.

> I remembered these houses from down the Park
> Gate to the top end. They were specially built for
> a family who owned the Maybris Glass company
> and these houses were designed and built for
> them. I always say when I was passing: "I'd love to
> live in one of those houses. I'd really love to live in
> one of those houses."
>
> It so happened that I was passing one day on
> the bus and I saw a 'For Sale' sign. I later found
> out that the sister of the family who was living
> there had died.
>
> The estate agent was in Carter's Green, West
> Bromwich. When I went down there to see him,
> he said: "I'm sorry but the house is sold." I said:
> "But the sign is up and it doesn't say sold." He
> said: "It's sold!" They didn't want any Blacks to
> live here. That was not just the estate agent but
> because the rest of the family was still living there.
> I didn't argue. I waited and then I saw it back in
> the papers.
>
> At the time I was involved in setting up the
> Race Relations Board in Sandwell. I went back
> down to the agent and said: "You told me that the

house was sold. Here it is back in the newspapers. So how is it in the newspaper if it's sold? If you don't let me have a look at this house I'll be taking you to the Race Relations Board."

He gave me the keys and said I could have a look at it. This was a few years after I opened the salon. As I walked in and saw the design and character of the house, I thought: 'I'm having it.' I just loved the character of the house—the oak staircase, beautiful garden, your own drive at the back and the private garage. 'I'm having this house.'

Having shamed the estate agent into releasing the keys so that she could view the house, the manner in which Evelyn goes about purchasing the property is reminiscent of how she acquired the family's first home in Trinity Road.

It was just under £12,000 when I bought it. I didn't even discuss it with my husband. At the time he was more with his friends and his family. I thought: 'No. I'm not even going to discuss it because I can do it on my own.' I told the estate agent I would have it and I spoke to my lawyer. I had money there, plus I had money in the bank which I could have used. I just bought it.

Before the family can move in Evelyn has to tell Reggie that she has bought a new house.

I ask him to go and get the keys. He went and got

the keys. Then he went to Edgbaston and pick up his family and everybody to show them 'his' house. I didn't say anything. I didn't want to hurt his feelings.

I thought about it. Six months after, I put his name on the deeds. He was my husband and the children's father, so I went back and put his name on the deeds.

The lawyer wasn't very happy about it but it's not his due—it's not his business. It's a decision I made and I haven't regretted it.

***

Evelyn immigrated to England in 1955 and it's over twenty-five years before her first trip back home to Jamaica. By then she has already opened her hairdressing salon in West Bromwich.

In the intervening period Evelyn is looking after her family in Jamaica—her mother, stepfather and particularly her half-sisters Louise and Eloise.

None of my sisters made anything of their lives. I had to help look after them, I didn't have a choice. Both of them were living with my mother when the last one Eloise got pregnant. I had to help to support her and the baby—paid the hospital fees and all sorts. It was very hard. It was weighing me down.

When her baby son was six months old I thought: 'You know what, let me send for her. If

I bring her here I don't have to care of both her and the baby—she'll be able to look after her own baby.'

Like everything else where her family is involved—things are not that simple.

She came to live with me in Trinity Road. When she arrived I had to tell her take a taxi from the railway station because I am not sure I would recognise her. Her son Alexander was left in Jamaica with my mum.

Eloise came here three months pregnant. The baby was born at my home in Trinity Road. That was when we were in a depression like we are now. You couldn't get anything and I had to look after her and the new baby. In the end I had to grow up the baby Eunice like my own.

I grew up the baby with Janice—they grew up like sisters. Eunice calls me mum and everything. So there was a jealousy between Eloise and me because her daughter calls me mum. If Eloise is in my house and Eunice walks in and says: "Hello Mum." I say: "Why didn't you answer your daughter?" She says: "I don't know which one she's talking to."

Louise didn't come to England. She's still in Jamaica.

On her first trip back to Jamaica, Evelyn has little choice but to meet with her father, Bolas Spence.

> He came to see me twice and he said: "Evelyn I do love you. I do love you." I said: "I love you but not to the depth I should because when I was younger you didn't stand up to your wife to protect me."
>
> That's a mistake a lot of men have made and they lose out with their kids. When he died, to me he was just another man that died. It wasn't as though I missed my father. I didn't keep contact with all my brothers and sisters on my father's side.

As expected, Evelyn cannot resist going to see the Head Teacher with whom she boarded as a teenager.

> Miss Jackson had married by then—she's very old. When I went to see her, I remember she was living in Brumalia in a house they called Jackson Heights. Oh, she was so glad to see me. It was like she won the pools.
>
> I spent the day with her and she took me down to the hospital in Mandeville and everywhere to see her friends. She was still going to Richmond Church. I was saying to her: "You use to teach me to sing and we use to sing solos together. I'd love to come and sing with you one Sunday." But I had to go back to Kingston and I never get to do that. I left her my photos. She was so happy how I've turned out because I had my own business and

everything. She was so happy how I turned out.

Growing up in Jamaica, Evelyn had a great deal of affection for her stepfather Harold Ellis. At the time of her visit, he is not doing very well.

My mum had left him by then and he had sort of given up in a sense. He was living in a house owned by a member of his dad's family who just let it deteriorate. Parts was falling down and brace up by planks of wood.

When I went there grass was growing in the driveway and there's a moldy smell in the house. I thought: 'No, you can't stay here.' If you're ill or something, it's hard for the doctors to get to you.'

I decided when I was there to do something. I asked his cousin—who had some land by the road—how much he would sell me a quarter of an acre for? He told me £60. So I bought the land, it was a very good price.

Another of his cousins—Les—was a builder and I said to him: "If I send you some money—I can't send a lot at a time—but can you start building a house for him? I am trusting you and will send you the money to do it." I did and he did. I built him a two room house with a veranda and toilet—a standard house.

Then he met this other lady. They got married and lived there. I used to send him his clothes and everything from here.

> In his family—up to now—no one says anything bad about me. The neighbours—the people around—no one say anything bad about me because I cared for him. His other children never did.

Unfortunately for Evelyn, not everyone agrees with looking out for her stepfather in this way—especially her mother Winifred who had broken up with him after Evelyn left for England. Winifred made her views known long before Evelyn's first trip back home.

> She was so bitter. She didn't want me to have anything to do with him. I said to her: "Listen, you can do what you want but you will never tell me not to have anything to do with him. He's never done me anything. You and him fall out— that's you and him. I look after you and I look after him. If you insist that I shan't, then I won't. So it's either both or none. Make your mind up where you want to go."
>
> She shut up about it.

In the end the reason Evelyn's mother stops berating her over this is because Evelyn continues to look after her.

> She use to work in a bar in Kingston and then she said the bloke was selling it. I says: "Ok, if the bloke is selling it, I'll buy it and let you have it. If I do that for you, I don't have to maintain you so

it's easier for me."

I did it.

Evelyn is able to go back to Jamaica because her hairdressing salon is doing well. She looks back on her salon with joy particularly the opportunities she gave to budding hairstylists.

I never moved off the ring road. I changed shops but I never moved off the ring road. I got bigger. I had an upstairs as well as a downstairs.

I employ white and I employed Black in my salon. Then I started to train people. Sometimes I had seven or eight working in the shop—top and bottom.

I trained a girl who went to Bermuda. I had this call from this English bloke in Bermuda because I'd joined the Afro-Caribbean Hairdressing Federation. That's gone to the dogs now. I used to go to all the meetings and functions and things in London. This bloke, he went over to Bermuda to open a hairdressing shop, solarium, the whole thing. He wanted a Black girl to work in it and who did he call—me. One of the girls I trained, I sent her out to Bermuda. She's still there. She's married to a pastor. Every now and then her mum brings me a bouquet and she says: "Mrs Wallace, if you didn't do that for my daughter, I don't know what would have happened to her."

This other lady I trained—she's now retired in Jamaica and we've never broken contact. She has a beautiful house in Jamaica and she said to me: "Evelyn, thank you love. If it wasn't for you I wouldn't be in the position that I am now."

I had one girl that I trained as well and I realise that she just didn't want to be a hairdresser. She was very interested in scalps. I encourage her to go in for a trichologist course because we did not have a Black trichologist. She started at a clinic in Birmingham and then she moved on to London. She comes down every now and then to see us. She's done well. She's now travelling. She teaches and does seminars all over the place.

My trainees did not come from Wolverhampton College. These were people I took in as apprentices and paid them while they were here. They have their certificates. They've done really well white and Black. One day the Express and Star came up and said: "We didn't know we had somebody like you in this area." My wall was covered with certificates and awards.

Garry—who with Evelyn's 'guidance' on leaving school had trained as a jeweller and later as a tool setter—is still to some extent dependent on his mother.

I told him: "If you're desperate and it's something really bad that you've done and you need shelter, you can come home for a period. But apart from that, no!"

He was out of work once and I said to him:

"Garry, you have to go and get yourself a job. You're not staying here." After they get to a certain age, they have to leave home—that's my philosophy. If you keep your children over a certain age, they're not interested to go—especially if they can just give you a pittance.

I notice he wasn't looking for a job so after the first week I said: "Garry, have you found anything?" He said: "I ain't looking." I said: "Garry, do you think I'm joking? I'm not joking. You have to go." He went because I wasn't joking. If I hadn't stood up, he wouldn't have. Responsibilities, you must take it on at a certain age. If your parents is willing to carry you—no! Boys like that will make very bad husbands.

Later on, Garry is out work and living at home and Evelyn decides it's time to take matters firmly into her own hands.

When I noticed he was out of a job, I said: "Garry go and find yourself a job." He goes out every day but he's wasn't looking for one. He come back and says: "I didn't find anything." I thought: 'OK you didn't find anything, I'll find it for you.' So I bought the *Express and Star* and I sent him to Wednesbury to this job because they wanted a fitter with experience and he had it. He had his certificates because he went to college to get his certificates. He came back and said he didn't get it. I thought: 'No! I'm not taking your word for it.' I called the factory and they said: "The job is there." I came home, got his certificates, went to them and said: "Here you are."

He got the job.

So Garry is back at work but still living at home. As per the house rules, Gary is contributing to the family budget.

It was his dad who found out and said to me: "Do you realise how much Garry is earning?" I said: "No." His dad had found Garry's pay slip and said: "He's earning more than me."

I said to Garry: "From next week you'll have to give me more money." He says: "No. Why?" I said: "Garry, you're earning more than your dad. You're not living off him." He said: "Well if I have to give you more money, you have to give me a rent book." I said: "What did you say to me? Garry you know what I'm doing now? I'm giving you notice. You have two weeks to find somewhere and move. Go and pay the rent out there. In here you get your meals, you get your clothes wash, your get your electricity paid, water—everything. Go and take that on—that's responsibility."

I don't mess, I honestly don't mess. When I tell them they have to do something, they have to do it. I don't argue. I don't shout or anything. But I have my own way of letting them realise that they have to do it. Don't depend on me.

From the day he started work he had to give

me his keep—same for Janice. They didn't know
that I didn't spend it half the time—I put it into
an account. But they had to give me their keep.

Always on the lookout for new opportunities for her hairdressing business, Evelyn is branching out. She comes across a
company based in Atlanta, USA, that specialises in hair products for African American women.

I got involved with Sofn'Free. They had just brought
out a hair relaxant—a perm that was liquid. You
put it on the hair to straighten it and it just runs off.
I use to go out and help arrange seminars.

Then the representative from Sofn'Free—J.C.
Douglas was his name—invited us to go to
Atlanta. He arranged it. I think it was only myself
from Birmingham, the rest was from London—
all hairdressers. It was M&M [McBride and
McKenzie] Cosmetics at that time. They had not
developed the Sofn'Free products as yet. It was in
progress but it was not developed. He arranged
the trip and it was a beautiful trip—a really beautiful trip. They laid on everything to receive us.
They took us around.

We went to the Martin Luther King Centre. I
visited the Martin Luther King Centre about three
times. We went to a church run by the Bronner
Brothers—they're one of the masters of business
and churches and they have business from Atlanta
to New York. We met Andrew Young [then Mayor

of Atlanta] and all them. It was absolutely beautiful. We really did the whole thing.

Beautiful as the trip was, the primary purpose of M&M
is to develop a market for its hair products amongst Black
hairdressers in the UK.

> When we came back from Atlanta I suggested to
> Sofn'Free that they should thicken the perm and
> turn it into a cream because it was just running
> off the hair. I also got them to test the water here
> to see if it works with the perm because the water
> here is different. So I did give some proper advice
> and they thanked me for it. I had the letter for
> years.
>
> It's after that they started the hair show in
> London.

Evelyn's trip to Atlanta is to establish a longstanding relationship with M&M and—in particular—it's Sofn'Free products.
For reasons that she could not foresee, her trip to Atlanta also
has a significant impact on the next stage of her life.

Meanwhile, Reggie is not happy with his job.

> He came off the buses and went to work for Delta
> in a factory. I know he remembers when he come
> off the bus but I don't hold those dates in my
> head. It's a good while.
>
> One Saturday he was at work with another
> worker. I don't know whether he did not put up

the door properly or what, but it fell and hit him on his head. It affected his nervous system and he was in hospital for a while. He was ill for years—it started out with his nerves. From this year, I think it's twenty-six years he hasn't worked. He hasn't worked since 1987.

IRENE

Irene is still living with her mother Lucy in the house they bought together but Lucy is not well. Irene is now working at her new job as senior pharmacist at Rubery Hill mental health hospital in Birmingham. Lucy is now in her mid-sixties and in addition to her diabetes, Lucy suffers from chronic back pains.

Lucy's health issues do not stop there. Lucy arrives from Belize to England where she finds out she has ovarian cancer. Undergoing treatment Lucy is confined to her home.

> We had home care people coming in but it was getting difficult. My mum would look through the window and if the home care people weren't dressed right she would say to them: "I'm not letting you in here until you dress yourself properly to come in my house." You laugh but it's not funny when you're at work.

Lucy's health is not improving. Possibly as a consequence of her medical treatment, she is also becoming increasingly disoriented.

> She would have home care people coming in

during the day. As long as they dressed okay and looked alright, she would let them in.

The final straw for me was when Rubery Hill had been closed down and moved to the Queen Elizabeth Psychiatric Hospital. I'd have to get up early in the morning, do the rota sheets for work and half my mother's dinner before I left because it was nine till five-thirty.

Then one evening I got in from work. I don't know if she'd didn't let the home care people in. As I stepped in I could smell gas. I thought: 'Oh my God, what's going on?' It was a busy day at the pharmacy and this was after six now. I rushed into the kitchen. The gas was on. Me mum wasn't there. I don't know whether she was upstairs or what was going on. All the stuff was out of the freezer and on the floor. I said: "Mum where are you? Open the windows. Can't you smell gas?" She said: "What? What?"

I said: "Why have you taken everything out of the freezer?" She said: "You work so hard. I thought instead of you coming home to do the dinner, I'd get the stuff out of the freezer and decide what I'm going to cook but I couldn't decide what I was going to cook."

I couldn't get upset. A lot of the food had to be thrown away. So then I thought she was getting signs of dementia. I got the gas people to put something on the cooker so that only I could turn it on and off. She could use the electric kettle for making tea.

Then I got her to go to a day centre at Wesleyan Holiness Church. They picked her up, so she was out of the house and couldn't turn on the gas. She said to me: "I tried to turn the gas on and no gas coming out." I said: "Oh, I don't know what's happened." I thought that's fine. I'm happy with that.

Irene is told by her mother's doctor that Lucy has to have an operation for her ovarian cancer.

I didn't think she should have had the operation. I said to them: "I don't think she's strong enough." But the doctor said to me: "Your mum said she was strong enough."

After she had the operation she lost her mobility. She couldn't walk and ended up in a wheelchair. They came and looked at the facilities at our house. They're saying: "With you being the only child, she needs to be in a nursing home. If it was just the home help she needed, you could do it Irene. But because of her diabetes and the cancer, she needs nursing care and you are not able to give her nursing care at home." I had to make the very horrible decision to put her in a nursing home. You can imagine how I felt, it was quite heartbreaking. That was very sad for me because I wanted to bring her back here.

This decision still haunts Irene today.

I still feel sad when I think about it now. I didn't really want to put her in a home. I always thought that I'll be able to look after her. I knew I'd have to keep working because she'd retired and it was just my salary paying for this house. You had to be sensible, I think she understood that.

It was a nursing home in Kingstanding. That was close by but there was only two other Black people there. I was concerned about her getting 'proper' food. I use to go up and take her 'rice and peas'.

God is good. It so happened that some of the nurses at the home knew my mum from years back when she worked at Dudley Road Hospital. They said: "We'll bring in food for her. She will be alright." So she was getting the Black care. That's what I wanted.

Then as she got dementia, sometimes she didn't recognise me. It would come and go. At the nursing home they'd say there are times when she frightens us and there are times when we don't know. There are times she'll say to us: "Oh you nurses are so busy. Would you like me to help give you a hand?" But then at other times when we have to give her pills, she would say: "My daughter do pharmacy. Don't give me no bogus pills. I'll tell my daughter and she'll sort you out. Make sure you give me the right pills. I know what unoo do in these homes." She'd say it in that kind of authoritarian voice. They said she would go into patois and she don't normally speak patois. They said: "Your mum is a character." I said: "I know."

Lucy's dementia ends up altering the mother-daughter relationship between her and Irene.

Towards the end we were like sisters. I use to call her Lucy by then and encourage her by saying: "Come on Lucy." One time before her dementia set in she said: "Just remember, I am the parent and you are the child. There are times when you are acting like you're the parent. Can I just remind you who is who." I said: "You don't have to tell me mum—I know, I know."

Sometimes I took her to the botanical gardens in Birmingham when it was her birthday or some other occasion. Then I would take her out for a meal.

Irene remembers the time where the staff at the nursing home thought Lucy was going to die.

She'd got some sort of flu. They rang me and said: "I think your mum's going downhill, we've taken her to Good Hope Hospital." I went to Good Hope and I thought: 'Is this it?' But she fought back, returned to the nursing home and was fine.

Then she just deteriorated. I was at work on day when they rang me and said: "Your mum's not very well. Can you come?" I rang Erma—one of my best friends at work. She was like a second daughter to my mum. She said: "I'll meet you at the home." By the time we got to the nursing home my mother had just died.

It so happen that the day before, there was some church people there. They'd gone to the home to visit her. I think my mum knew she was going because the Deacon said that my mum said she'd had a hairdresser come in and do her hair the day before. She liked her hair to be just so. He said when they were there that day she seemed fine but she asked him to read a Psalm. The Psalm was: 'Now I lay me down in safety to sleep, cause the Lord giveth me rest.' He'll never forget that. The next day she died. It's like she was preparing herself to go.

She died in February 1995, when she was seventy-nine. She lived her life. She enjoyed her life. I had to handle all the funeral arrangements but the church people were good. I had some good support from them and from some of my best friends.

Phyllis is one of Irene's best friends. They both went to Handsworth Girls school and went on holidays together. Phyllis is concerned that Irene is having a difficult time mourning the death of her mother.

She said to me: "Oh, I'm going out to Jamaica this December. Would you like to come?" She'd got family in Jamaica.

I can't remember my reason for agreeing but that first year after my mother's death I didn't think I wanted to spend Christmas in this country—so I said yes. I spent Christmas in Jamaica that year.

We booked somewhere in Ocho Rios—one of these big apartments which people loan out. She'd got friends in Brown's Town. Christmas Eve we went to see Phyllis's family and friends. We went into town where they have different dances and people carried their rice and peas and cars blowing their horns. Christmas in Jamaica was very different—it was so different.

On Christmas Day we went to this big posh hotel. Not the one we stayed at—I forget what it was called. This was a top five star hotel in Jamaica, they did Rum Punch and they did Limbo. So we sort of had a bit of both worlds.

My mom's brother—the police inspector— had died by then. I tried to ring up one of the family members that was there but couldn't get hold of her. It really wasn't a trip about visiting family for me. There wasn't really many family members left alive in Jamaica. I did try but it wasn't a big thing for me. It was more about me unwinding the first year Mom had died and me being the only child. To be out of England and experiencing something quite different in Jamaica was nice.

Irene thinks back to her other holidays with friends.

I always go abroad on holidays two times a year with my friends. It was mainly Europe. I've been to Italy about four times—Venice, Florence, Rome. I love Italy. The Italians I love very much. The first time I went to an Italian supermarket there's loads of noise going on and they're doing things with their hands. We were only the Black people in the supermarket and I said to my friend: "I think we better come out of here—it's a bit loud." This Italian must have heard me. He said: "No! This is how we are."

Italy reminds me of Jamaica because you know in Jamaica they blow their car horns. Italy is worse. They're blowing their horns all the time and you just feel like you are in the West Indies. They've just got no patience and the horns are blowing.

In a year, usually I'd do a holiday with Phyllis and then do a holiday in the half-term with my teacher friend. She was the director of education in The New Testament Church of God. I've done Prague, Lake Garda, Portugal, Cyprus, Greece with her. One August we went to Atlanta and Florida as well. She had to go and give a lecture out there, so I joined her afterwards. We did the Martin Luther King things in Atlanta—that was inspiring.

I have no method of selecting holidays. Phyllis and I have a joke. When we first started going on holidays we both weren't earning much. We'd go to two star, three star hotels. As we both progressed up the ladder it got to be four or five star. We haven't got a man or children.

It's holidaying but we're not sitting around. Whatever area we go, we usually do all the cultural things—museums and what have you. We do try and spend one day on the beach but that's it. We're not beach people—I do not swim. I like to see how local people live, see what's going on. It's about life experience and meeting other people.

Wherever I holiday, I always have a go at the language. I never do much English translation. I try and get a background of the language before I go. When you're in a hotel and you can say 'No', 'Thank You' and 'Good Morning' in their language—they really do appreciate that. They feel that you're making an effort. I'd never go abroad and be wanting English food. We always eat local dishes—whatever it was.

After Irene's mother dies, the nature of Irene's annual holidays change.

One year God said to me: 'It's time for you to start your mission.' I thought: 'Mission? I'm not ready to go on any mission. Where am I going to go? I've never done this before. How can I do this? Lord, you're going to have to provide and tell me.' It was a vision that the Lord had given me about Gambia.

Through my church I get all these letters coming saying that they want people to go on mission but I've never taken any notice. When I got this vision I thought I'd better do something about it. There's all these different charities and trusts and I'm thinking: 'I've never done anything like this before.'

It is only until Irene takes a weekend trip with Phyllis that Irene decides to take action regarding her vision.

My friend Phyllis said: "Let's go to Lemington. Let's have a long weekend away." I think it was a Bank Holiday weekend and we could also go to the Isle of Wight. I told her about my Gambia vision. My friend goes to the New Testament Church of God—she's their director of education. I said to her: "Can you pray with me about this Gambia vision?" She's sort of like my prayer partner.

We decided to go away—Friday till Monday. It was a guest house. While we were there having breakfast one morning, the owner of the guest house spoke to us. She said to me: "I go to The Gambia every year. I do charity work there. Would you like to come with me Irene?" She's

Catholic. She got to see that we're Christians but I'd never met this woman before.

I thought: 'What! Where's this coming from?' I said: "Why do you ask me?" She said: "I heard what you were saying. I just thought you might like to come." I said: "I need to go back and pray about this." I thought: 'I've just gone on a weekend away—where's this coming from? Is it the Lord directing my steps?' Phyllis said to me: "Irene, I think this is it." I said: "We better pray. We only stay in this woman's house. We don't know anything about her."

I went back home and prayed. Then I rang her up and said: "Yes, I would like to come with you." When I told them from work that I was going to Gambia the reps gave me pens, books, paper and loads of stuff—my suitcase was full. They said if you're going to do that sort of work we'll give you things to take.

So, Irene makes her decision and off she goes to Gambia.

That was my first trip to Africa—it was for two weeks. The only thing I didn't like was taking all the tablets for malaria beforehand and after. We stayed in a hotel. She'd been before doing charity work, so she'd organised the hotel and everything.

There's no traffic at nights. You wouldn't go out at nights. There were no road lights in the area where we were at, it was dark. We were not in the capital—I can't remember the name of the place. Although we were staying in a hotel, you'd catch your water in the mornings. They'd turn off the electricity, they'd turn off everything. If you had to stay in the hotel all day, they wouldn't switch on the electricity and the water till six o'clock in the evening.

We went to schools in Gambia. We also went to some of the malaria hospitals. Because of my pharmacy knowledge I got some medical books. When I was going my boss said to me: "Those are out of date. They'll be out of date for Africa. Why don't you take the British National Formulary with you and give them to some of the doctors and nurses there."

As I told you, I didn't like taking the malaria tablets but when you see how bad conditions and malaria can be, you're thinking: 'Take the tablets—take your tablets.' malaria is a horrible disease so I gave out the medical books.

We have a thing in the Bible that says: 'The steps of a righteous man are ordered.' I did write a piece about it. I couldn't have planned it. I thought: 'That's exactly where the Lord wanted me to go.' It was good. It did work out.

Irene developed a love for The Gambia and ends up returning.

I went back two years later, the pastor invited me back. He still rings me up now and again. I went on my own.

Between you and me, I could have been married several times over in Gambia. Although the woman I went with the first time was white and middle class, I found out she'd got her young boy over there. That's why I didn't go back with her the second time. It's the way over there—the older white women and the young boys. I had to watch myself but I handled it alright.

***

Irene has now been working at the Queen Elizabeth Hospital for three years. She moved there in 1995 when Rubery Hill Mental Hospital closed, the same year her mother Lucy died. Though she's doing the same job—senior pharmacist—the workload at QE is much heavier.

I was managing forty-five people then and appraising seventeen yearly. I was struggling to see my staff over the year. If I manage to get all seventeen in for the year I feel I've achieved. Now they're saying you need to see them monthly and look at their behavioural profile. They're just putting more and more on you. It's just top-heavy.

Nevertheless—as she has done throughout her career—Irene still somehow finds time to pursue other outside interests.

I became a school governor, it was in response to

a local authority advert. You had to do a Criminal Records Bureau check because you're working with children. Then you had to write like a little essay saying why you want to do it. Every five years it's renewed.

There's a school that is all Black and Asian just there across the road from where I live. I thought that's the school I'd get so I was shocked when they said you've got a school in Kingstanding. I know my sociology and I know Birmingham. Kingstanding is one of the most racist places you can find. I thought: 'My God! Why have they given me Kingstanding? I'd only have to walk to the school across the road there.' I had no choice in the allocation—the local authority decided.

They had to give me time off work to get to evening meetings. Because of my work I couldn't make a lot of the two o'clock meetings and had to give my apologies to the school. When I did attend, colleagues would ask me if I'm leaving now? Most of the time we were too busy and as a manager I just couldn't walk out and say: 'Oh I'm going to a school governor's meeting now.'

When I first went to an assembly there were just four Black kids in that school. But kids are kids, they love you once you give into them. They don't always see the colour of your skin.

One of the times when they did allow me from work, we were doing a questionnaire at the school and we had to ask the children various

432

questions. It was quite a whitey school because Kingstanding is quite a racist area. I was asking the kids different things and this little blonde girl said to me: "Miss, can I read to you?" The teacher said to the little girl: "Listen, Irene has got to get back to work now. She only came here for the questionnaire." The child said: "Miss, I'd like to read to you." I said: "Go on, read. I like reading. You read to me—you read to me."

She was reading and reading and I thought: 'Yea, I'm enjoying this because way back I liked reading.' I got really good feedback when we got to the next governor's meeting with the Head Teacher.

I was, and I'm still, the only Black governor there. That's been good for them actually. The school has changed now—there's more Asian and Polish. I've been a school governor for over ten years now.

Nor is this her only outside interest.

The Trust Choir is through work. That's a choir that we have at work called the Birmingham and Solihull NHS Trust Community Gospel Choir. It's a bit different—a well-being choir: art and music can be so uplifting for patients. It's mostly members of staff but also patients.

The choir was the idea of someone at work who circulated an e-mail on the computer. I didn't see it. At work they know about of my church and that I sing in the church choir. Somebody said to me: "Irene they're forming a gospel choir for the Trust, did you see the e-mail?" They sent it to me.

I applied and they accepted me. There's about thirty of us—I sing soprano. We practise at the Trust headquarters in Ladywood. The Trust buy our uniforms and everything.

We're good—I hate to say it but we are good. We sang at the Symphony Hall in Birmingham. We went in for the BBC 'Choir of the Day' and actually won it. I've got the CD.

IVY

Ivy has just returned from America. It is 1986. Having taken
a flight from Heathrow to New York a day earlier—without
leaving the airport—she simply boards the next flight back to
England. Now that her American adventure has ended, she is
back in England and in need of a job.

> I went to do the lunch at London Transport—
> Loughton Bus Garage. I worked there for twelve
> years.

Ivy cannot recall her children having any problems at school.
This is the next phase in her childrens lives—they are entering
employment.

> Charles had the best brain out of all our three
> children but he was lazy—didn't want to do much
> at home. He went and did computers. He used to
> work in a bank and did computing.
>
> Daniel was clean and tidy. He use to like pulling
> apart my watch, clocks, my radio. Anything elec-
> trical he could get his hands on, he would pull
> apart to see what was inside and what it's made of.

He would use his pocket money to buy old radios and things. The basement was packed up with old rubbish. Daniel was always pulling apart and fixing things so I thought he's electrical-minded and I send him with one of his dad's cousins to do electrical work. He wanted more than that. He got himself employed as a trainee and he would go away to Bristol and different places.

Simone, my first child, she's good at anything she puts her hand to.

Ivy, now working as a lunch lady in the canteen at the London Transport Bus Garage in Loughton, is not in the best of health.

Whilst I was working there I had a heart attack and I ended up in hospital. I had high blood pressure, didn't know and it wasn't treated. That damaged me and gave me an enlarged heart. When I came out the hospital after eleven days, I couldn't go back to work. I was advised not to go back to work lifting anything heavy.

To make matters worse, her relationship with Wesley is not going well.

At the flat where we lived in Chadwell Heath, my husband came in one day and said he's moving out. He didn't say why but if I want to come with him I can come. So I said: "Where are you going?" He said he was going to a church sister who had a big house and just her son and daughter lived there. She had a couple of big rooms vacant.

So I said to him: "I'm not leaving here because this part is ours and I'm not leaving here to go and live in somebody else's place. If we leave here, then we could get a flat and be together and still have part of the house here." He said: "Ok. Go get a flat then!"

Wesley moves into the church sister's house anyway.

So I went and got a two-bedroom flat—painted it, made curtains, cushions and had it all ready. I told him the flat is ready and he said he don't want to move from where he is. So I gave up the flat and I went back to live in Chadwell Heath.

That was the beginning of our separation.

Despite their ongoing problems, Ivy remains hopeful about her marriage. However, Wesley is growing increasingly embittered.

He decided he wants his money off the flat we had bought in Chadwell Heath. We had put £30,000 into the property. He said he wants his money back. It wasn't long when we had bought that place. I think we went and took a second mort-gage to pay for his half.

He said that I wasn't going to get anything from that. I said to him: "We put £30,000 in and I want half of that. Whatever you get from the sale, that's up to you but I want back half of the thirty thousand we put in." He said I'm not getting anything.

So I went to a solicitor and I stopped them paying him. They were going to pay him £45,000. I stopped them paying him that much. Take out my fifteen thousand—give it to me—and give him the rest. That's how I could got my half.

I did not know the reason for him wanting to leave the flat in Chadwell Heath. He went to live at the house of a church sister in Ilford—I can't remember her name. He lived there for some time. From the time he was living in Ilford, he rarely visited me.

Ivy is now on her own. The children have long left home and the flat in Chadwell Heath has been sold. She needs to find a place to live.

When I got my part of the flat sale, they told me I could stay there and rent but I didn't. I didn't think it was right for me to stay there so I got myself a flat in Ilford.

Ivy knows Wesley is living in Ilford and does her best to re-establish contact with him.

I used to see him on the road. I would stop driving sometimes and say: "Hi Wes. How are you? Are you OK?" I never passed him on the road but that was how I see him.

Our children would go and visit Wesley all the time or go to his work place. They would go out for a meal and talk.

Once I went to his workplace. I took the Smiths' kids because he was godfather to their two younger children—Adrian and Charlene— who had grown up with our own children when we lived at Rockhalt Road. I was godmother to Adrian. Both children were pining after him because they loved him so much and asking when is he coming back. They hadn't realised that he had left.

Eventually one day, I had to take our kids down to Victoria train station to see him. He wasn't expecting them and he was like lost. He just stood with his hands at his side staring at the kids. When they saw him they run and jump on him. That kind of bring him back to the family— to visit the kids as it were. But the visits wasn't for me, it was for the kids. He never come up to my room and say anything to me at all. He would just stay downstairs with the kids until he go away.

Though Ivy is not sure why he left her in the first place, she still hopes to be with Wesley. Despite his belligerent behaviour toward her, Wesley has not asked for a divorce.

As life moves forward Ivy eventually loses track of Wesley until one day—out of the blue—he gets in touch with her.

I didn't know when he went off to Jamaica. I

didn't know he had gone to build a house out
there until I got the phone call from him to say
that the house is finished.

He asked me when am I coming home. I said:
"I can't come because my mother is here. I haven't
got another brother or sister here to look after
her and it wouldn't be fair to leave her at her age
and to come and just go sit down in Jamaica. I'm
sorry."

Despite their marital problems and separation, Wesley still
sees Ivy as his wife. Perhaps building a home for his family in
Jamaica was the reason he wanted the money from the sale of
their flat in the first place. It is possible that may have triggered
their separation—Wesley saw their future in Jamaica, Ivy did
not. Irrespective of this, it is Ivy who decides that their marriage
is now over.

Until now our kids haven't been to Jamaica to
visit him. They don't know where he lives. The
kids knew we had separated from when he had
moved out, but they didn't know why. They said
whatever I choose to do, they're fine with that.

Ivy gives up her flat in Ilford and moves to another one in
Hainault.

While I was there my mother got ill. She wasn't
ill, ill. She butt her toe on the fire door and she
didn't say—she kept it to herself. One day I was

taking her out shopping and she was limping. When I look at her foot, her toe had changed colour. She got very sick and couldn't walk about. She couldn't do anything for herself.

I decided I need to have my mother near me. Where I was in Hainault was not appropriate. It was a one-bedroom flat that wasn't appropriate. So I told Redbridge Council I needed a place to accommodate my mother. They wanted me to go to Walthamstow where my mother is living to get a place there to accommodate her because she wasn't their responsibility. I told them she's my responsibility, I am Redbridge's responsibility and I want a place in Redbridge to accommodate me and my mother. So they gave me this flat in Barkingside.

She lived here with me for a while but she didn't want to go back home. She didn't really like it here in England but I don't think there would be anybody there want her to come home.

Ivy remembers her mother's disapproving attitude towards church in Jamaica. Now, in England however, it seems Ivy's mother has had a change of heart.

I was going to church from Jamaica and she didn't like going to church. She use to tell me they're dirty people, wallowing in dirt. She'd do everything to stop me going to church. I wanted to because it had changed my life. When I came

here I was still going to church. When she came
up and she happen to meet some of the church
people, eventually she become one of them. She
become part of it and she loved them.

Ivy's mother is then admitted into hospital due to the issue with
her toe.

She went into hospital with that bad toe and they
found out that she got gangrene. The gangrene
got in her blood stream and poisoned her. She
was in hospital for many years. She never came
out. She died. She is buried in London Cemetery.

***

Having left her job with London Transport following her heart
attack, Ivy goes back to work.

The job was in the papers. They were looking for
summer workers and it's not many people want to
go all that way to work. They couldn't get people
from in the city to work for them. I saw it and I
applied. I got it as a summer job.

Ivy's new job is at Kensington Palace in Chelsea where she is
now working as a security officer.

Basically, the work was just security for that part
of the Palace open to the public. They can go in

and look at furniture and how the other half lived. People would come in and spend hours walking around from room to room looking at things.

443

MELISSA

Melissa is thirty-eight years old in 1986 when she returns to England having spent the last four years in Sierra Leone. On returning to England she has little money and a three-year-old daughter. So she has to start all over again.

When I came back I didn't have a house or even a flat. I stayed with a friend up in Roehampton. I also had a friend in Newham and I was going between her and my friend in Roehampton. I stayed with the lady living in Forest Gate, Newham Thursday, Friday and Saturday.

When I was in Roehampton I went to the nursery school and I said to the teacher: "I've just brought my daughter back from Sierra Leone. She doesn't speak English but she can understand some things said in English." The teacher says: "That's alright, it doesn't matter." Within six weeks of going there, one day the Head Teacher approach me. She said: "I thought you said Cantrice didn't speak English." I said: "She doesn't. From when she was born I spoke English to her but all around her everybody speaks this broken thing you call Creole. Her Sierra Leonean nanny spoke Creole to her, so she was in between both languages." The Head Teacher said: "But she speaks English fluently."

There was a BBC children's programme that use to come on in the 1980's about 3:30—no not 'Bill and Ben'. They would go to children's school and observe them, how they played—they do stories with them. Then they came to that school where Cantrice was and she was involved in it. I remember the teacher saying to us that we should watch the BBC at such and such a time. Maybe it's in the BBC archives now. I can't remember the name of the programme and I don't know if Cantrice would remember it. But nevertheless, she was it in. She was very proud, very, very proud.

The issue of finding a place to live with her daughter is still at the top of Melissa's priority list.

On the Thursday while I was with my friend in Newham, she says: "Why don't you go to the Housing Department?" I said: "I don't know anywhere round here." She says: "Come, I'll show you where the Housing Department is."

On the Romford Road is Forest Housing and I went in there. I had Cantrice with me and the lady said to me: "I'll put you on the housing list." She put me on the list. There were about four, five people after me. I sat there with Cantrice and I thought: 'Oh God, it would be really lovely to get somewhere. I'm just getting fed up going in between.' When they finished the last person the lady said: "Oh you're still here." I burst out crying. She said: "What's the matter?" I said: "I've nowhere to stay. I've nowhere to sleep tonight with my child."

She call her manager and her manager came round and she says: "Alright, I'm going to give you a letter—take it to Dagenham. There's a hotel down in Dagenham, right by where the Ford's car plant is. There's a hotel down there." I got a bus. She told me what bus to get and I went down there. When I saw where the place was it was like off the main road in the deepest part of hell. I thought: 'Me stay down here with my child? They're joking.'

I waited until the weekend. The Monday morning I went back and I says: "I'm not staying there. I can't get down there—there are few buses. When you get off the bus, to walk down there with a small child of three?" She says: "Alright, I tell you what I'm going to do. I'm going to send you to Earls Court."

The man who has the hotel in Earls Court was working with Newham Borough Council. He use to be a council worker, then in the eighties he noticed how lucrative things were with the government putting up these homeless people in

hotels who were charging a fortune. He decided
to buy this little place in Earls Court. He made
a contract with Newham and they were sending
clients directly. I was one of them. Beautiful place,
I stayed there for three years—loved it. I wasn't the
only one. There were lots of us who were homeless
living there, some without children.

Though Melissa 'loved' the hotel in Earls Court, it was always
going to be temporary accommodation. In 1989 she finally
finds somewhere a little more permanent.

You use to have to phone your housing officer
and eventually one day she says to me: "Oh we've
found a place for you, it's in Forest Gate. As
your friend lives in Forest Gate, we won't send
you away. But we've got somewhere—some new
flats in Beckton. Would you like one of the new
flats?" I think it was in the west part of Beckton
but I heard the National Front was around that
area. I went and I look at the flats. I thought: 'Me
living here, where the National Front is? My child
can't walk down the road!' Not only that, they
were reclaiming that area because it was a swamp.
When I saw the amount of fog that was down
there, I thought: 'Me living in this area with my
child? When it's six o'clock in the morning, you
can't even see your hand because of the fog. No
way am I living there.'

I came back and I said: "No, I don't like it." She

says: "Alright, that's one refusal. There's a second place in Church Street in Stratford." I went down there and look at the flat—it was a tower block. I says to her: "Me live in this—no way." She said: "It's the second refusal." I said: 'Yes, but I'm not going to take what is not nice for my child to grow up in'.

Then one day she rang me. She says: "Oh, we've got a place and I'm sure you'll like it. It's two-bedroom and the rooms are very big. It's a tower block but it's very close to the road. You can just walk a hundred yards from there and you're out on the main road and the buses." I went and looked at it. That was Brassett Point in Abbey Road, Stratford. I looked on it. It was perfect, just a hundred yards to the bus stop. Also the GP surgery was just at the top of the road. I thought: 'That's ideal. There was a school just down the bottom at the end of the road—beautiful, beautiful.' So I got it. Within ten minutes from there, if I take a 262 bus, I was in Stratford—it was ideal. In those days—in the eighties—Stratford was like a sleeping town six o'clock in the evening. You would never believe it. I've never seen a place so desolate and dirty.

Before I went away to Africa I use to live in Acton, Winchester Street—very famous street. When you go into Hammersmith, Acton, Ealing—beautiful houses. When I looked at the windows in Stratford, like the shops, they were

dirty, dirty. I thought: 'Oh my God, what is this?'
But at that time—in the eighties—when Stratford
was like a sleeping town before the re-develop-
ment. Ah!

On returning from Africa, Melissa has little difficulty finding
a job.

When I came back from Sierra Leone I was
working as a registered nurse at Chest. I would
have to pick up my daughter from school. I
thought I had to find a way round this because I
didn't want anyone else to pick her up or take her
to school.

There was a job going with a care provider
which is a care agency. I saw the advertisement. This woman was opening a care agency in
Wanstead. She didn't know much about nursing.
It was her and her friend—two white ladies. They
use to do cleaning in Redbridge and Wanstead. In
those days it was very easy to set up a care agency.
I was a fool. If I had done that, I would have been
laughing. Maybe God has something more in
store for me.

When I went there and I told them that I
was a nurse, they said they're looking for carers.
She explained to me what it's all about. After I
start telling them what I do, she says: "But you
know all about it. Would you help us to set up the
agency." I helped them—Christine and Carol—to

set it up and run it. Then they wanted me to be a supervisor. So I says: "Look I've got a child. I take her to school in the morning by nine o'clock and I have to pick her up by three." They said: "Be the supervisor. When we've got a problem you go around and monitor. When we have new carers, you supervise them and show them how to do things. At the end of the day and the following morning you report us." So I thought: 'This is ideal because then I can take care of Cantrice at the same time'. That was that.

Melissa is still living in her two-bedroom flat in a tower block at Brassett Point. At first, she thought the place was ideal for commuting to work and picking up Cantrice from school. However, her flat is within a high-rise neighbourhood built in the 1960's and she is becoming increasingly concerned with the safety of the flats.

> Living in tower blocks is an estate business. The government give you a house but it's not safe living in tower blocks because you cannot do health and safety on your own. You may try but the person above you might have no regard for health and safety endangering your life—which did happen to me at Brassett Point.

Having worked in hospitals for most of her adult life, Melissa's concern with health and safety rules is not all that surprising.

I was on the fourth floor. This white lady—she was Irish—lived on the fifth floor with her boy. I think her son was about eight-years-old. I don't know what caused it—whether she was smoking, whether she was cooking—but a fire broke out in her flat. Then obviously she panicked. None of us could use the stairs. I went out on my balcony when I realize that it's her flat and there were people congregating downstairs saying: "Throw him." They were concerned about her eight year old son. I shouted: "Don't! If you throw him you may hurt him. Stay still. Is it smoke or is it fire coming up?" She says: "It's smoke but fire is coming up and it's spreading." I said: "See if you can go out in the corridor. If you can go out in the corridor take a blanket to cover you and your son. Try and feel for the stairs and walk down the stairs because you won't be able to use the lift."

Well people outside keep telling her: "Throw your son over, we'll catch him. Throw him over." They went and got a blanket or a sheet—I don't know which—and they held it. They said: "Throw him. He'll drop in it." Well the little boy didn't drop in it. The boy fell on the ground and broke his back. The newspapers and the television came that evening and the tower block was on the news.

The fire and drama at Brassett Point—sometime in 1996—attracts considerable attention from locals and the press. It is reported on multiple television channels and in local newspapers.

> That was how Cantrice's father knew where we were. He came back to London before us. I bought over Cantrice in '86 when she was three. I think he may have come to London in '83 when Cantrice was born. I never corresponded with him and he didn't correspond with me, so he never knew that I was here with Cantrice. I knew that he was here because he's got a cousin who is like a sister. When I came that's the first lady I phone to say that I was here, so I kind of more or less knew where he was.

They are not directly in contact with each other but—one way or another—Melissa seems to know a great deal more about Malamah's life than he knows of hers.

> He and that 'white woman' he had the child with, they got married here. They got a flat down Phoenix Road in Kings Cross. I don't know what happened because I wasn't taking an interest. They didn't last. I don't know why, I never asked. The next thing was his cousin down Lewisham say to me: "Oh him and JR mother, dem don divorce." I say: "Good luck to them."
>
> Then his cousin rang me one day and says: "Ah Malamah, him don get one lady. Him father a child with a woman in Essex and this woman nice so."

He found me because of the fire. When Malamah saw the news and saw me on television he must have phoned his cousin. The lady came over to see me and says: "Malamah would like to see Cantrice." I says: "Well, I didn't tell him not to see Cantrice. He choose not to see Cantrice."

Anyway one day Malamah came to the place where the fire was and he says: "Look Melissa, I'm asking you to forgive me. I've got a lovely wife now and I would really like Cantrice and I to grow together." I said: "Cantrice is grown up now, she is thirteen."

There is a way the Sierra Leoneans say: 'Eh Bo! You no ah go beg?' Bo is boy and when they beg they bend down asking you to forgive them. I says: "Alright, you know where we are. From here it's entirely up to you."

Malamah is now married to his second wife. Her name is Jessica; which Melissa learns from his cousin. However, one of the many things Malamah and his relatives in England do not know is that Melissa is growing closer to someone else—Dennis.

I'll tell you how I met him [Dennis]. I told you that I use to be a nurse here and the mother of his uncle was a patient in the hospital. I use to nurse Uncle John's mother and Dennis use to visit her in my hospital.

Melissa first met Dennis in 1971 through her friend John

who lived in Luton. She was caring for John's mother in the hospital where she worked. Dennis also a friend of John's would visit John's sick mother in hospital. Though John is a friend Melissa often refers to him as 'Uncle' using the title as a term of endearment.

> I knew Dennis and Uncle John before I went to Africa. When I came back from Africa one of the first person I communicate with was Uncle John to say that I am back in England and I've got a little girl. He in turn communicate with Dennis—who was in Norway—to say that I am back here. So Uncle John told Dennis that I've got a little girl and she's about three.
>
> I met Uncle John the week I came back. He came straight down from Luton to see me. He says: "How are you going to manage? How are you going to do nursing with this little girl? She's only small." I said: "I don't know but I am going to have to try." He told Dennis what I said.

Dennis is a petrochemical engineer then working in Norway.

> He rang me at the house where I was staying in Roehampton. He said: "Uncle John told me you're back and you have a child. I'm coming over this weekend. I'm going to stay at the Bedford Hotel in Euston."
>
> He came to see me and Cantrice who took to him like a duck to water. He thought that was

wonderful but asked: "How are you going to cope?" I says: "I don't know." He says: "Alright, we'll have to find a way. First of all, you need a car." He knew that I could drive. He gave me £500. He said: "That five hundred is for the car." Then he gave me another five hundred: "You have to get insurance and road tax. When I go back to Norway, I will start sending you an allowance. I will give you five hundred a month." I thought: 'Oooh! My boat has come in.'

Why would Uncle John contact Dennis working abroad in Norway to ensure that he knew of Melissa's return from Sierra Leone with a three-year-old child? After all, Melissa was only one of the nurses taking care of his sick mother in hospital over twelve years ago. Even more curious than that was why would Dennis on his next trip back to London take extraordinary steps to ensure that Melissa could support herself and her daughter?

To complicate matters further, it turns out that Melissa has another child—a daughter who she is very unwilling to talk about.

Cantrice is my second daughter. My first daughter—Jean—was here all along. She was born in the 1970s before I first went to Africa. She would be in her forties now. There are bad seeds which I want to forget. If you see my other daughter, you think she is Dennis's child. Everybody see her think she's half-caste.

Dennis is white and Jean—Melissa's first daughter is light-skinned. It is for this reason people believe Jean is Dennis's child. Melissa strongly denies this but provides only the barest details on the birth and father of her first daughter.

> She's not half-caste. She's a Black man's child. He's
> in the West Indies—he's still in the West Indies.
> He's got about three or four sisters here. He went
> back to the West Indies because his parents have
> got land, land, land.
>
> He's a lazy good-for-nothing. It's bad genes
> but there you are. Just leave it at that! Finished!
> You've heard enough! Leave it at that.

Jean would have been born sometime in the first half of the 1970's. This is certainly within the time frame of Melissa qualifying as a nurse and meeting Dennis for the first time while caring for Uncle John's mother. Insisting that her daughter Jean is a 'Black man's child', she did admit to having a relationship with a West Indian man while still training as a nurse.

> I don't want to talk about this. Charlie—who was
> from Barbados—was a very nice person but very
> hyped.

At the time she goes off to Nigeria on holiday for the first time in 1980, then went on to live in Sierra Leone from 1982 to 1986. Jean would have been around twelve or thirteen by 1986, so who was looking after her from 1982 and 1986? Certainly not Melissa's mother and stepfather—they returned to Jamaica in 1973. Nor does it seem likely that Melissa would have left Jean with the 'lazy, good-for-nothing' father.

Whatever the case, Dennis is in Melissa's life.

Dennis is an English man. I think he was born in Wandsworth but I think his descendants are more from Wales. Traditionally his name—'Paquette'— is associated with the French. Between the world wars they use to come across.

Dennis was loving. He was very, very, very nice—not only to Cantrice but to my 'other' daughter. He use to work like in Iran, Iraq, Bahrain. He worked in all the Arab countries that you can think of. When he got his leave he would come, stay three weeks, then he would go back to work.

We got married in October 1992. He was faithful and honest. Dennis was good to Cantrice. She use to have terrible, terrible colds. She was always blocked up, always coughing. Dennis use to get up at night, go to watch over her, rub her back, rub her throat with Vicks. As morning come he would be off to the chemist. He would bring back all different types of drugs. He would go and take Cantrice to the park.

It's a pity I didn't have a child for him because he was the most wonderful father. But you know, life is as it is.

Dennis is sixty-two years old when he marries Melissa, who is forty-four. The couple are living in the flat in Brassett Point with Melissa's daughter, Cantrice. Dennis is also helping to support Jean, who is now in her late teens and not living with the family.

At the time of the fire in 1996—when Malamah discovers where Melissa is living, he turns up on her doorstep—Dennis is also there. He has been a stepfather to Cantrice's for four years and part of the family for ten years. Belatedly, Malamah—now married to his second wife—begs to be forgiven for deserting Melissa when she was pregnant in Sierra Leone and promises to look after his daughter. Melissa points out that Cantrice is now a teenager, she is thirteen.

> Malamah says: "Oh but I've got three properties. One for Cantrice and one for JR." My husband Dennis say: "I don't care two hoots. I am taking care of her. Do you know anything about Cantrice? What is her favourite food? Where are you when she's crying in the night or when she can't breathe?"

The answer to Malamah's request is an emphatic no. However, later that same year Dennis becomes ill.

> As I told you he used to work for oil companies. He went to Bangladesh—a place named Sylhet in Bengal. One Sunday he rang me. I was at the tower block then and he said that he's not feeling too well. I said: "If you're not feeling well, don't stay there and get worse. Come home." He said if the Monday he was still not feeling well, he would

ask them to come home on sick leave. Well he
wasn't. On the Thursday he got a flight and came
out.

One of the reasons why I like living at Abbey
Road was because the surgery was just not even
fifty yards from the tower block. He went there
to see the doctor. They did some tests on him and
sent off his blood. Then he went and did some
more tests.

When the tests came back, they found he's got
cancer of the bladder. Straightaway he went to see
this Australian doctor name Dr Taylor. She says:
"You're a petrochemical man?" He said: "Yes." She
said: "That is a petrochemical illness." Dennis said
that when they are in the oil field, sometimes to
cool down the rig when the oil is burning, they
have this freeze thing. I can't remember what's
it called. It's a chemical—you have to put on a
mask and protective clothing to spray the fire and
sometimes they inhale it. That's what sets it off.

Mercifully Dennis's illness is short.

He died of cancer. Dennis died on 26th March
1997. He was about sixty-seven. He's buried just
down the road there. There's a cemetery down
there. He's buried down there. God rest his soul.

Melissa and Dennis were married for just four and a half years.
Before Dennis died they were thinking about moving out of

Brassett Point.

One day I came home from work and I saw a little note put through the door. It says: 'Do you know you could buy your own place? If you're earning up to thirteen thousand, give us a ring.' When I look I notice it was from the housing association that had given me the place. I thought: 'That's funny.' I was paying £60 a week for the two-bedroom flat then.

So I give them a ring the following day and they said: "Fill out the form and send it back." I did that. About three, four days after a young guy—who was my housing manager—came over to see me. He was very nice, his name was Corey. He said: "Melissa do you know you can get £20,000? The government can subsidise you £20,000. You know why?" I said: "Why?" He says: "Because you're not living on income support. You are paying your own rent. That money that you're using to pay your rent, you can use it to pay a mortgage." I said: "Really!" He said: "Yes! The government could give you twenty thousand." Anyway I kept thinking about it. How am I going to cope?

A year goes by and Melissa now has clarity on the matter.

I let a year pass by, then I phoned Corey again. I said: "Corey, I'm interested." He said: "You see! When I was telling you to do it, you didn't do it. Now it's only thirteen thousand." I said: "I'll take it, I'll take it." The year before when it was twenty thousand, one of my neighbors—an Iranian family—living on the floor above me had taken it. They've got two little boys. One of the young ones—Ashkon—was Cantrice's age. They were going to the same school. Sometimes when I'm not there on time, Ashkon's mom would pick up Cantrice or I would pick up Ashkon—so we became very good friends. They took the £20,000 and went over to Christchurch in Essex. They bought a three-bedroom house with the twenty thousand.

I thought: 'Well I've lost seven thousand, I'll take the thirteen.' But they do not give you the thirteen in your hands. They sent me a letter saying get yourself a surveyor. I got a surveyor. The surveyor came and survey this house. I went to the estate agent and they told me about this house. I said: "I don't want a big house. It's me and my child and I want something which is not too expensive." He says: "Alright, I know where's there a beautiful little house, just right for you and your daughter."

When I came round and I looked at it, the first thing that caught my eyes was the lawn. The lawn was like a tennis court. The man who owned it was a retired gentleman—a white man. My dear, I think he use to use a ruler to cut the grass, nothing was out of place. I loved the garden so much I said: "Yes, I'll take it." When I took the place, I brought my daughter Cantrice. We came here on the 8th June 1997. When she came and saw this house, she was just thirteen. She says: "Mom this is the ideal house." I says: "Why?" She says: "Have you seen the name of the road that it's on? Godgold Road—God is gold! It's a quiet road. You will never, never lose in this house. This house will be of value one day, Stratford will rise." I said: "How do you know?" She says: "Yes I know Stratford will rise."

Melissa and Cantrice move into Godgold Road within three months of Dennis's death. Shortly after, Melissa changes her mind on Malamah having contact with his daughter.

Was it she or I who phone and tell him that we moved from Brassett Point? He came over to see her and ask me if she could accompany him to his house to meet his wife because his wife was pregnant.

He had a second wife—Jessica. She is very nice—very nice. Cantrice would go down there and see them. When Cantrice go there she said that Jessica did care for her.

Then Jessica had baby Betty—a little girl. When she had Betty, Cantrice and I would go down there to see Betty. Jessica and I became quite good friends. At times, if Malamah and Jessica was going to go out—like on a weekend—she would ask me if Betty could stay with Cantrice and I. She would until Betty was about ten, the last time we had her. Then it kind of tailed off and Cantrice didn't bother. Cantrice kept saying: "Oh he doesn't care for me like he care for Betty or JR." I would say: "No, don't worry about that. Dennis cared for you dearly, so the love that Malamah didn't give you, Dennis gave it to you."

In the meantime, Melissa is still working as a supervisor with a private sector care agency. Aged twelve, Cantrice has transferred to secondary school allowing her mother a great deal more flexibility in her hours of work.

When it's holiday or when it's in the evening and the office is closed—everything is handed over to me. I was their on-call care co-ordinator. I will divert the office phone unto their mobile and I will take the calls whether it's social services, the carers, clients or their relatives.

The nature of Melissa's job is hectic and rather intense.

Whatever the problem I have to deal with it. I had to make my own assessment of the situation. If it is something that I feel very strongly that I cannot let a carer do, then I will go out to see the situation. If the daughter, the son, or the next door neighbour phone up and say no carer turned up—I would have to sort it out. Sometimes the carer couldn't enter the house, the person isn't answering the door or answering the phone. Your most obvious course is to check the neighbours—left and right—and ask: "Have you seen so and so? Have you seen an ambulance come by? Have you seen the relatives of that person come by?" If they have not, then quite likely that person is ill inside. If you haven't got the keys then it's either that you'll have to ask the next door neighbours or the family if they've got a key. This is what you had to do. Now they've got a way where they put a key safe at the door.

Melissa recalls a specific instance at work as an example of the problems she would sometimes have to resolve.

Once we had a carer I sent to Tower Hamlets to do a job and she couldn't get in. She said she ask the neighbour but the neighbour said they saw that person two days ago. Now the carer hadn't phoned to tell us that she can't enter and what the neighbour said—she waited until the afternoon. She rang us about five, just as the office was about to close. We close at five-thirty. She rang at five so say that she couldn't get in. So I said to Steven, the manager of the company: "Steve, I will drive and go up there." When I went up there the carer was by the door. I ask one of the neighbours and they said they've seen the woman two days ago.

The other neighbours said they've not seen her. I said to Steve: "Look to see who her relative is." He phone the relative who had not seen her. I said: "Steve, you know what I want you to do for me now? Phone the police for me. I'll wait here for the police."

Two policemen came and one kicked in the door. The policeman wouldn't go in. He said: "You have to go in with me." I went in. We look in the front room, we look in the kitchen, we look in the toilet. She wasn't there. He says: "Now we'll go upstairs." We went up the stairs, there were two rooms. The room on the right was her bedroom. When we look, she was laying across her bed like this. She was about to pull up her clothes because you could see her knickers was half way on. She was dead.

The policeman call the doctor. The doctor came and certified her dead. Then the policeman started asking who was there? How many carers? We have a book that carers have to write in. He look through the book and says: "Oh, nobody came to see her this morning—what happened?" I said: "A carer did come but the carer couldn't get in and the carer could not find anyone who'd seen her during the day. The carer rang us." Because it was a domestic the carer was doing, you could play about with the time. That's what covered us because it was domestic she was doing. If it was morning care, that means she should have been there from eight or nine o' clock.

Eventually the ambulance came and took her away. This is why I tell my carers that whenever they go anywhere, they must not be later than fifteen minutes. If you're too late, you don't know what will happen within the time you were to be there and then you are in problem. It could be a problem for the company and a problem with the law and insurance.

Chapter Eight

As It Turns Out

EVELYN

It is 1984 and Evelyn's hairdressing salon is doing well. She has recently returned from a trip to Atlanta, Georgia, as a guest of M&M—an American cosmetic firm specialising in African American hair products. Most of the other Black hairdressers invited to Atlanta are from London. She is the only one from Birmingham. At the time M&M—later to become better known as Sofn'Free—is developing a new hair relaxant perm for Black women. The reason why Black hairdressers from the UK are invited to go to Atlanta—all expenses paid—is to develop a market for their products over here. Between seminars, Evelyn and other members of the group from the UK are taken on tours of the city. They visit the Martin Luther King Centre and meet the mayor—Andrew Young. They are also taken to see other Black-led businesses—in particular those owned by the Bronner Brothers.

Evelyn is impressed. She describes her trip to Atlanta as 'absolutely beautiful'. On returning to Birmingham, she gets in contact with M&M, urging them to explore the possibility of developing their new hair relaxant perm as a cream rather than as a liquid. They thank her for her advice and she still has the letter to prove it.

Demonstrating what is to become a longstanding

commitment to using and promoting their products, in 1994
Evelyn wins the Sofn'Free Hairdressing Customer Award. In
1995 she wins the Sofn'Free Industrial Leader Award.

Evelyn's trip to Atlanta inspires her in ways she did not
expect. Having been taken on a visit to the Martin Luther
King Centre by M&M, she goes back on her own account—
twice. She becomes interested in the lives of African Americans.
Evelyn notices that African Americans are making a great deal
more progress than the African Caribbean community in the
UK. As a result, she becomes particularly interested in how the
African American community handle the obstacles they face.

> I thought when I get back I'm going to try and
> take the example from Atlanta—set up a little
> organisation and see if we can get a centre. The
> organisation was called ACA [African Caribbean
> Association]. There were six of us: Mr Barber, he
> was a social worker; Mr Stennett was a bus driver;
> Mr Neilson, he owns a pub; Mr Williams, he
> was working at the church in Beeches Road and
> Mrs Jones, she lived locally on Herbert Street just
> below the church.

> They already had a West Indian Association in
> West Bromwich. For years and years, they tried
> to get a centre and could not get one. They tried
> and tried.

> There was nothing. We had nowhere that
> we could have a function, a wedding—nothing.
> It was important for people to have a centre. A
> building where you could meet, where people

can go and entertain themselves instead of having 'house parties' because that was a headache associated with drugs. I never went to any 'blues parties'. I don't like loud music. I never went to any of them—it was not me. My husband would be there but I never go.

Even now I just like peace and quiet. I don't like loud music or anything. If the telly is on and it's on six or seven—that's fine for me. Above that and it irritates me—I just don't want to hear it. I can't stand anything loud—I don't like it, I have to leave. Even when I go out when I was younger and the music is so loud, your heart is going like that. If you've got to talk to somebody you have to shout or you have to go outside. That's not entertainment. You need to socialise. I pay a lot of money and go away. I rarely ever go to anything local.

Evelyn is determined to make the African Caribbean Association (ACA) a success.

So quite naturally when I came back from Atlanta we put a little organisation together. I was in business and I had a lot of relationships with the Sandwell Council. They know me all the way from the top-down.

We drew up a constitution and everything. Then we started having meetings with the council. They looked at our application. I don't know.

> Maybe it was because it had the Martin Luther
> King principles that it hit the board.

The ACA wins provisional approval from their local council. However, Evelyn soon realises that this win causes tension with other similar groups.

> It caused a lot of arguments with the other African Caribbean associations. There was a lot of associations—some were very political. That's why the centre was not called the Martin Luther King Centre because of the political bias of some.
>
> We had a meeting with the council one night and they said that they will give us money for the centre. But because there are so many other organisations they haven't got the money to give them all.

Initially, local authorities with a significant immigrant population were reluctant to fund different community and resource centres dedicated to a specific national group. This was due to two main reasons, 1) some saw this as likely to be politically unpopular 2) some felt that if the local authority were to fund one ethnic group, it would have to fund them all. When this approach did not work, most local authorities were willing to fund community centres and projects directly related to their main incoming immigrant population at the time—this was Indian, Pakistani or African Caribbean. While this was an improvement on previous policy, it was also defensive. The local authorities did not want to get involved in funding projects based on differences of nationality, ethnicity, culture or religion across each of these three populations.

This is the position taken by Sandwell Council. They are only willing to fund one centre for the whole African Caribbean population, irrespective of the fact that many migrants at the time were coming from different countries in the West Indies.

> We were told that what we have to do is take two representatives from each of the African Caribbean associations to make up the committee to run the centre.

Evelyn is practical and she is also a successful businesswoman. She cannot see how this political compromise is going to work in practise. After all, it is her group that have won council approval to fund a centre while all these other associations have failed—despite years of trying. Evelyn believes this is a reciple for failure.

> I thought: 'This is not going to last.' I said to Councillor Marsden: "Well you've given us the money. But the reason why is so you can say you give us the money and we either use it wrongly or couldn't agree with each other, so the centre had to close. Then we can't say you did not give us a centre." He said: "Well that's it—ain't it." He did—he did.
>
> I knew what was in their heads. I've been around them enough in meetings and in their offices—enough to know what was in their heads.

I thought to myself: 'You're not going to win.'

It is now the night of the important meeting. This meeting will set the final terms for the funding. That night, it transpires that the council has a great deal more confidence in Evelyn than she has in them. It also turns out that opposition to the centre does not come from other African Caribbean associations. Instead it comes from somewhere rather unexpected.

> After I spoke to Councillor Marsden he said to the meeting: "There is one more condition. Mrs Wallace [Evelyn] must be the chair of the centre's committee." I think he said that because they knew me.
>
> Oh Lord! Mr Stennett went berserk. The way Mr Stennett went on I thought: 'Forget it. I don't have to do it.'

At the meeting, Evelyn did not say what she thought of Mr Stennett's objections to her being chair of the management committee. The meeting ended without agreement on this issue. Evelyn knows that if Councillor Marsden's conditions are not accepted there is a real possibility that the council will not fund the centre.

> At the time I was acting chair for the Afro-Caribbean Federation of Hairdressers. I thought to myself: 'I have other things to be doing. I have to travel and everything—let them do it.'

Evelyn approaches Mr Stennett and tells him news that makes him very pleased indeed.

> So I went to the bus station canteen where Mr Stennett worked. He was on duty. I waited for him and when he came in I told him: "As far as I'm concerned, you can have the chair. But if you can't manage, I'd like you to back down and let somebody else have it." He was happy then.

Just like that Mr Stennett was given the role of chair of the ACA.

> He called a meeting behind my back and they selected the people who they wanted on the board. My name was never mentioned. I said: "I don't care. I don't want it for myself—it's for the community. All I want to know is that there is a centre."

The centre is established in 1987 and Evelyn is elected to the management board in the same year. After some time, it comes to her attention that all is far from well.

> At that point I'll turn up at meetings and everything. I realize and people were telling me that money was going missing, which was also happening at other centres.
> They had a bar which they open upstairs and my husband say to me: "This bloke come in. He

took the till out, take it into a room and put
another till in. Money's gone."

I was going along the street one day and
this bloke stop me and he said: "Mrs Wallace,
I'm begging you, please save the centre." I said:
"What do you mean?" He said: "Well if you don't
take over as the treasurer, we won't have a centre
by the end of the year." So I thought about it.

When they had the AGM, they didn't wait
to have another meeting to select the officers.
They're doing it straight away and putting everybody back in. I put my hand up and said: "No!
I would like to run for the treasurer." I won by
one vote.

Evelyn is now the official treasurer for the African Caribbean
Association Centre and she is determined to clean everything
up.

Would you believe me, it took me six months to
get control of it. They remove every book. The
only thing I had to work from was the cheque
books because they couldn't take them. They had
books but you could see that they weren't kept
properly.

I went in one day and I opened one of the
accounts books. I could see where money was put
in there and somebody crossed it out and put less.
You go through the cheque books and cheques
would be written but not to anybody.

Continuing on with her quest to clean the centre up, Evelyn realizes she needs assistance and requests a finance officer.

> I thought we've got to get this right. I went to meetings and I waited for the grants officer from the council because everything I was trying to do they were blocking me. When she came I said to her: "You know, I'm put here as the treasurer but I'm finding it very hard to get control and I do not want my name to be put against any of the black things here to block my credit or anything. I need to have a finance officer."
>
> Oh Lord! They went berserk. But the grants officer said: "Oh yes, you can have a finance officer and anyone in here try to block you or do anything to get rid of you—let us know. We'll come in and we'll fix it."
>
> That's how I got a finance officer. I went back five years and the amount of money that was taken out of that centre—it wasn't funny. Even when the bar was closed on a Sunday, the barmaids use to serve drinks to people playing dominos and take the money. The things that they did was terrible.
>
> I tried to stop all of that and they hated me. I told them: "I love it because that means I'm doing a good job." Some of them even use go and fill their car with petrol then bring in the receipt. They claimed it was for travelling expenses, but travelling expenses doing what? You ain't working for the centre. All you do is come to meetings.

> You can have travelling expenses from home to
> the centre for meetings but that doesn't give you a
> tank full of petrol. So what I do? I put the receipt
> in an envelope and I gave it back to them.

Committed to making an honest organisation of the centre, Evelyn, finds herself in an awkward position. One can only imagine what members of the management board thought when they received a sealed envelope from the treasurer enclosing nothing other than their owed receipts instead of money. Before long, tensions between Mr Stennett and Evelyn increase.

> It was Mr Stennett who told me. He said:
> "Anything that's bad and any name that's bad
> that you can think of—they've called you." I just
> turned around and I said to him: "Look at me,
> am I the ogre? I come in and I can work with the
> devil. I go home, you go home. I don't have to be
> friends with you but I can still do my job and I
> will do my job. I'll leave the centre when I want
> to leave. I made it possible for it to be here and I
> will be here for as long as my body will allow me."

Whether Evelyn realised it at the time, Evelyn is now a Black community activist. Continually inspired by what she witnessed in America, Evelyn is committed to bring the Black community ideals of Atlanta to West Bromwich. This is also in tune with others around her who believe that Black people should be taking a great deal more responsibility for tackling disadvantage, discrimination and other issues working against their community.

In fact, on returning from America, the first initiative she worked on was not the West Indian centre but raising funds for sickle cell anaemia research.

Sickle cell anaemia is an inherited blood disorder. In the UK it is most prevalent within the African and African Caribbean population but it can also be found amongst people of Asian and Middle Eastern descent. Those suffering from the disorder are likely to experience tiredness, lethargy and breathlessness—particularly after physical exertion. Without treatment the disorder can result in tissue or organ damage and episodes of severe pain lasting from a few minutes up to several months.

This bloke Evans in the West Midland here, he had sickle cell and he got blinded from it.

They knew nothing about sickle cell. So I got in contact with JC [Douglas] from Sofn'Free and ask him if he would sponsor products and pay for the place for us to do a 'Curl-a-thon' with hairdressers from London, the Midlands—all over. It was in the dead of winter but the salon owners and their workers agreed to do it. JC said yes. The African Caribbean Hairdressing Council gave us all the things to set up and work.

We held the 'Curl-a-thon' at a building near the reservoir in Edgbaston. When we went there they said they could supply hot water for all our needs but they could not. After the first lot, everybody's hair had to be washed in cold water.

We did a pile of hair at £10 a head. I came

third in the 'Curl-a-thon'. There were so many hairdressers there and it depends how many workers you have working with you. I still have my little trophy.

It was primarily money raising for research. All the money we made went to a research centre in Atlanta to learn about sickle cell. That's another thing I'm ever so proud of.

Evelyn's passion for sickle cell anaemia awareness did not end there.

Sybil French, she was a councillor in Birmingham. She got a piece of land to build a place for sickle cell, I think it was in Smethwick. Then there were arguments about the money. That bloke Evans wanted the money. Because she didn't give him what he wanted, it was a big thing on radio and everything. The land is still there growing up in grass. It's sad, ain't it.

In 1988 a branch of OSCAR (Organisation for Sickle Cell Anaemia Research) is established in the area. Ten years later—with the support of the council and the NHS—a purpose-built sickle cell centre is opened. Though Evelyn later hears about the internal arguments and frequent change of managers, she continues to take an interest.

The bloke who's now the chair, he's very strict. He was a soldier and he had a coach business in

Oldbury.

At one point I went there and I noticed the workers weren't even talking to him because he's so strict. It was very bad. I thought it was because they can't get their own way. They wouldn't sit with him but they wouldn't talk.

I thought this is terrible because he'd just put a new structure in. Once you're trying to get things right, everybody turn against you. So you have to be strong. The centre is still going and he's still there.

What I would love to see is all the branches of OSCAR in the West Midlands coming together and just working together. But everybody is working by themselves. It's not good. It's a struggle.

Nor is this all in Evelyn's story of local community activism. On her return from Atlanta, Evelyn joins an informal network of Black and Asian women interested in tackling barriers to ethnic minority women starting their own business.

I got involved with setting up the Women's Enterprise Development Agency. We got finance from the council. I even launched it myself at Mitchell and Butlers—the beer company—at their place in Cape Hill, Smethwick.

The project came into being in 1989 as a Company Limited by Guarantee and Evelyn is a member of the Board of Directors.

The agency got off the ground but you couldn't find any Black person capable enough to run it. Everyone you get to manage it, they just couldn't do the work. Everybody was saying how good they are and what they can do. A lot of them say they go to university and have a degree. Bloody waste of paper, I don't know how they get it. You had to take them and train them to run the agency. My Lord, everything went pear-shaped.

I helped to get the agency to assist Black women but three-quarters of the time they weren't turning up.

This went on for nearly ten years. In 1998 a member of the Board of Directors is appointed to manage the agency.

In the end we got someone capable of running it—an Indian woman. Some of the Black clients pulled out. The odd one would go in but I doubt if any of them turn up there at all.

I stayed on the committee for so long. Then when I realise that hardly any Black women was getting anything from it, I just came off the committee. You try to help your own but they let you down.

It's still going.

Probably also influenced by her trip to Atlanta and the example of the Bronner Brothers, a known African American hair care company with strong ties to African American churches, Evelyn decides she might be in a position to help a local church with their community outreach.

> I got involved with the Shiloh Church. It's a Black church and they wanted to set up a luncheon club for pensioners. Because I can get things done, everybody is coming to me. They had a sewing club going there as well.
>
> I went to social services and we got the money to have a luncheon club. They said to me that they'll give me the money but I must not hand it over to the church because they have given them money in the past and the church could not tell them what they've done with it. So I cannot hand that money over—I am responsible for it. I went to the church and I set up the luncheon club.

At that time, the local authorities were not keen on funding church projects. Funding a project controlled by one church or religion would leave them open to accusations of bias if they did not fund other similar cross-faith projects.

What happens next may well have reminded Evelyn of her experience at the West Indian centre.

> They're all church people—say they're Christians. But if you say to them: "Can you set the table?" No, they can't. Even the very pastor wanted pay. I said: "No I can't pay you. The money goes into the luncheon club." They carried on, and on, and on.

The council was giving out prizes to voluntary projects. I petitioned them and they agreed that one should go to the luncheon club. Nobody from the Shiloh was going to turn up. I went up to the church and I said: "What happen? Ain't anybody coming to collect the prize?" They said: "Yes, just as long as you're not taking it."

Then, because they couldn't get control of the money, they started to say that I am making money from the luncheon club. I thought to myself: 'No I'm not getting any money from it. Sometimes I put money in. I take my car, I go out and I do the shopping and everything.'

When they start to bad-mouth me in that sort of way, I thought: 'No! Shiloh wasn't my church. I didn't even go there to worship.' So what I did—I just close it. The rest of the money I had, I gave it back to social services.

Evelyn's business approach to running voluntary and community organisations would seem to be at odds with many of those around her. Nevertheless—for whatever reason—she perseveres.

Then I got involved with the African Caribbean Enterprise Agency. The function of the agency was to help young Black people that want to go into business. You take them in—interview them, train them—and help them to set up in business. We try and get grants to help them. Then you follow them for a period until they settle in.

> You also help people to write CVs for a job,
> all those sort of things. If they went for interview,
> they came back and tell you what they fail on.
> Then you can sort of take them and tutor them
> up for when they go on their next interview. That
> was what the agency was suppose to do.

The first agency is established in 1994 near the train station in Smethwick and securing funding has not been easy. Both the government and the local authority are not convinced there's a genuine need for such an agency. An independent management consultancy firm is appointed to research and report on the proposal.

> I forget what his name is. He was the one who
> actually help us to get one of these council
> workers. He was the one who try and help us to
> get the whole thing through.
> The government got Tony Sealy to look into
> it and say whether it is needed or not. According
> to him, it wasn't needed. So we go back into the
> council offices and sat down to work it out.
> It goes back to London for a decision. They
> send a person from London and we had to go to
> Edgbaston to meet her to tell her in depth why it's
> needed and why the money had to be given. It so
> happens we got it.

Though Evelyn has managed to secure funding, issues begin arising.

The bad thing that happened was most of the committee members were academics. You cannot work just with academics. You need ordinary people. The whole thing—apart from myself and another person—was academics. It wasn't going to work. I'm telling them it ain't working—they're not listening.

We had this bloke from London. He came in as manager and he would prepare papers. He said he's done this, he's done that and he's capable. Nothing was happening. Oh my God, we then realise he was running a business from there for himself. After the agency got money to buy space for a Caribbean bakery to get Caribbean people into work—he bought the property in his name. He then got the agency to rent it from him.

In the end we held a meeting and I said it has to close and re-open. Hmmm! They all agree that it's got to close but who's going to tell the bloke? Nobody wanted to tell him. I had to do it myself because nobody else was going to do it. They chickened out. They didn't want to tell him that he's lost his job because he can't do the job.

In the end the manager lost his job when the agency was closed and transferred to a town centre location. Curiously, the ex-manager is still a member of the Management Committee.

He became the chair. Then he brought in this African bloke to run it and everybody who work in it was African. No other nationality don't get a break in there. If you go in there to get help to set up a business, you ain't getting it—but the Africans get it. So I just drop out of it completely.

Despite her involvement in a succession of local community initiatives, Evelyn is still very much focused on her hairdressing salon. Recalling the difficulties she experienced in gaining access to a recognised hairdressing qualification courses, she decides to do something about it.

> I was the one who set up the Black hairdressing exam in Handsworth College. I actually started it at the Winson Green Afro-Caribbean Centre—right by the prison. Then I moved it to Handsworth College which is now Birmingham College. If you're going to teach somebody something, you don't teach and give them a certificate which doesn't mean anything. You needed to be official and that's how it started. It's still there.

Evelyn's first trip back to visit family in Jamaica was in 1980. She did not go to see her father Bolas Spence because he did not put a stop to his wife and their children picking on her as a child because of her light skin tone. However, he came to see her twice during her visit. Though Bolas told her how much he loved her, Evelyn could not bring herself to forgive him. When he died, she did not miss him. In her words: "To me he was just another man that died."

The feelings she should have had for her father were, as

Evelyn has explained, transferred to Harold Ellis, her stepfather. He was the one who provided a shoulder to lean on when she was young. When she went to see him on her first visit he was ill and living in a dilapidated house owned by a member of his family. She bought a plot of land and made arrangements to send money from England to build him a small two-room house. Harold recovers, moves into the house and marries again. Later on, his health again deteriorates.

> He had lung cancer. I had to pay his nephew to look after him. When I realised how bad it was I sent money for him to be taken to the University Hospital. They told me how bad it was, about his age, and how much the operation would cost.
>
> I thought: 'At his age, I'm not putting him through that because he wouldn't survive it.' I made sure he had his medication and he was not hungry. I even sent medication from here.
>
> I remembered when he was really, really ill. In a letter he wrote to me he said: "Evelyn, God bless the day when I knew you." I wrote back and said: "God bless the day when you did not ill-treat me." If he did, I would not have done what I did. Luckily he behaved like that because in the end I had to take care of him—not his two children or my sisters.
>
> When my stepfather died, that affected me. Luke called and told me. I said: "OK, get the undertaker to come and take his body." I did not send them the money. I paid it straight to the

undertaker.

He had a beautiful funeral—a casket and a headstone. He had a lovely send off. People called and told me. I sent out money for my own wreath and everything. They took photos and sent them to me. Luke took photographs from beginning to end and send them all to me—so I had proof. I think I've done my best.

The next time I went out I went to see his grave.

By this time Evelyn's mother Winifred had also died. Apart from mentioning that she died 'thirty odd years ago', Evelyn makes no reference either to the cause of her death or her funeral.

In fact, after her stepfather's death, Evelyn returns to her home island several times.

I have been going to Jamaica quite regularly because I have sisters and brothers there and quite a lot of nephews and nieces and cousins—so I visit. When I go out I try to see them. I keep in contact with Gloria and Errol mostly.

When I'm coming out, they know that I'm coming, so the rest of the family is rounded up. I can't keep contact with all of them because if I do it's a very expensive trip. When I'm going I take things. I send out barrels—everybody gets something. But I do not keep it up throughout the year. I keep with Gloria and I keep with Errol— he's the last one. We ring each other, talk to each other quite regular and if they're in difficulties I try and help them.

Gloria and Errol are the children of her father Bolas Spence who she did not like.

Every time I want to go on holiday—if I'm going without a friend—I'm always heading for Jamaica. There's a certain feeling for me when I get there. I come off the plane and it's like every burden— everything that's bothers me—is gone. I'm home. I know I can visit my mum's grave and my dad's grave. It makes me feel good—I'm home.

Every time I get there this Tom Jones song: 'The Green, Green Grass of Home' comes to mind. I go elsewhere and I feel OK but not like when I go home. It's a big difference. I've developed a lot of friends since going out there— people that I did not know.

I have thought of moving back to Jamaica. But when you're out there because you've been here for such a long time—I've spent most of my life here—you want to come home. To me, I've got two homes. Sometimes you're pulled to go to Jamaica and when you're there for a period, you want to come back home.

***

Even though Evelyn has done a great deal to take care of family members in Jamaica, she does not agree with the view that people in Jamaica take financial advantage of their family in England. Evelyn has her own explanation as to why some Jamaicans returning home from England feel financially imposed on by their family.

To me, my family and friends don't put pressure on me when I go out to Jamaica. Some of the people that goes out there exaggerate. Some of them when they go to Jamaica they put themselves up there. People then think they're very rich when they're not. Some of them even borrow the fare on their cards but they're still bragging how rich they are. That's their behaviour.

I had to pull up one lady once when I was on holiday in Discovery Bay. We went up to Brownstone at the market and she was there. Everybody knows that in the Caribbean and hot countries, they have their food out on the ground. Some of the things they spread towels and put it on the ground. The woman said: "What you doing with the food? It's not suppose to be on the ground." Those are the same people who use to do it. Then they go in the market—the meat section—and it's: "Oh! That is what I buy to feed my dog!" I've heard it. I pull them up.

Some of them are over the top and because of that they're not liked. Some will get robbed. Sometimes their families think they've got a lot of money and decide: "I'm going to get as much as I can."

So half of it is their own fault. Some of them there get their pension from over here and think they can get anything. They get robbed. They cause it on themselves.

I've heard people in Jamaica say: 'Why do they come out here and make themselves prisoner with an iron gate and security around their houses?' They make themselves prisoners in their own house. Windows and doors—everywhere is padlocked. A lot of them cause it on themselves.

Despite Evelyn's opinion on the subject of finances and family, she finds herself in a challenging situation with a member of her own family.

I had built a house there and put my stepfather in it. When he died I moved my stepdaughter in with her children. I wasn't charging her rent and I had to sell the house because she tried to take it over.

Lucky that I'd been kind to people. The bloke who used to care for my stepfather was his nephew. I use to pay him to do it because he wanted pay and I needed to know what's going on and that my stepfather was being cared for.

I always still send him a bit of money now and then. If I'm going out to Jamaica on holiday, I'll take him some clothes and things like that. He was the one who called me and tell me what was happening about my house.

I called my lawyer and she said: "Oh you just hit it on time. If she got her name on it you could do nothing at all because she wasn't paying any rent." She was my stepfather's daughter.

It's like a squatter's thing. A lot of people who live abroad have lost their houses because of that. They don't know that they should charge rent—it doesn't matter how small—they just leave their family in it. Then some can't even go on the doorstep when they go out there. Their family think: 'You're there in England. You've got a lot of money, I'm taking this.'

You have to be very alert and know what's going on. I did not sell the land, I sold the house to "Jamalco"—the mining company. They have to pass there to go to the mines. I ask them if they would be prepared to take it and they said yes. So they bought the house and they gave me a plot of land in a different area which I went and choose for myself.

Then I passed the land unto my stepdaughter's daughter. She wanted to buy a piece of land to build a house but it was so expensive she said she don't think she can manage. Where it is, it's like three and a half million Jamaican Dollars for a quarter of an acre. I just said to her: "You know what, I'll give it to you." I signed it over to her when I was there last year. I gave it to her. I also gave her a deposit to start the house because she's ever so good. She's lovely and she tries hard. She's made something of herself.

***

Almost all of what Evelyn did after opening her hairdressing salon in December 1978, she did alone. Following an injury at the factory where he worked, Evelyn's husband Reggie ends up in hospital, before becoming progressively ill. He has not worked since 1987.

> It started from the accident. Then he use to drink and smoke a lot, so his body is paying. He got prostrate. The right side of his heart is not working—he had two heart failures. His kidneys are gone. He's got a lot of complications. He depends on me a lot.

When Evelyn thought of moving back to Jamaica, she was not just thinking of herself.

> They have some absolutely beautiful nursing homes out there, especially built for returnees. Oh my God they're beautiful and they're set in such a beautiful area with gardens and everything. They look after them really, really well—especially in Mandeville where I'm from. That has always been a tourist area. It's cool, you've got to wear a cardigan there. It's one of the best districts in the middle of the island but when I mention it to Reggie he said no. He didn't want to go back.

Though Reggie didn't want to return back home, Evelyn did not want her husband to end up in a local retirement home in the West Midlands.

> I've been into some of them and I've seen what happens. Unless you go into a very expensive home, you're not cared for properly. People are just sitting there like zombies. They do not even take them outside—residents just sit there.

On Evelyn's next trip back to Jamaica, Evelyn takes steps to ensure that her husband will be well looked after in [England].

> He was in Castle Bromwich and that was a beautiful home—set beautiful. It was really nice and he was cared for very well. I left him a phone so I can speak with him. They did look after him and the setting was nice. He had a beautiful room where he could see outside and everything. I went and choose it and it cost a lot of money.

To Evelyn's disappointment, she finds that there is no longer room at Castle Bromwich and she has to find another temporary care home for Reggie.

> The ones that care specifically for African Caribbean people are no better than most of the others. Sometimes I think they're worse. I put him in this one when I went to Jamaica the last time. Why I did that? It was close. My daughter have

to pass there to go home and she's in there all day on a Tuesday doing hair. She can cook his meals, take it up, make sure he's looked after. That's why I put him in this one.

Reggie's health continues to deteriorate.

He has a hernia but they can't operate because of his heart. Sometimes it will pop out, so you have to push it back in. If you can't get it back in, you've got to take him straight into the hospital. Then he got gout. He can walk or stand for a few minutes, then he just flop.

He's been confined to his bed for a good few years now. I bought a chair, it's in his bedroom and he can lie on it as a bed. He's mainly upstairs. Sometimes he use to try and come downstairs on his belly. Of late—a couple of years now—he can't come down. If he comes down, he can't go back up. So he just remains upstairs.

The responsibility for looking after Reggie falls mostly on Evelyn. Reggie is not your average patient and Evelyn is not getting a great deal of help.

He can be really, really stubborn. Then he's not doing anything. Sometimes he's nasty as well and it's frustrating—it really gets to me. That gets to me because I have to see to him before I can see to myself.

When he's like that you cannot get him to do anything. I try not to argue with him because after he's sorry. You must wait until he's ready. But I thought to myself: 'I made a promise—a vow—and I'm going to see it through.' If it was the other way round, I would want him to be there for me. Sometimes I don't get a lot of sleep because I'm sleeping and listening. I'm in the other room from him and you have to leave the doors open.

He has a carer who comes in. I got him because he's retired too and they use to drink together and everything. They have a lot in common so it keeps his mind off his illness. That cost me quite a bit to do because I haven't had a social worker for some time.

Besides the people I pay, no one comes in to help. Sometimes my granddaughter would come in when I need to go out, but she can't do anything because she's very frail—she's only tiny. She can only give him something to eat and drink or sit and talk with him. She herself is ill—she's got lupus. No one else comes in to help.

I said to my children that my main concern was at nights when I'm on my own—things happen and I can't manage properly. Half the time, if I call you, you're not around. Garry's phone is turned off because he's doing night shift. I just have to try and cope on my own. That is when I need help and I haven't got any—so I just have to carry on. If you have a night-sitter, it's £16 an hour. It's very expensive.

You see, the thing is he's a very sharp person. He can be very abrupt and even rude. The way he talks to the kids is not as though they're grown up and they take offence. The kids, they'll come. They'll go upstairs—maybe five minutes—and they're down. They're not going back up until they're ready to go. It's: 'Hello Dad! Bye Dad!' The grandkids are the same. As soon as they come through the door they'll go up. If they don't and he knows they're here, he can be very abrupt and rude. You have to be careful talking to your kids because they take offence.

Evelyn closed her hairdressing salon in 2007 when she was seventy-five years old. She donates most of her leftover products to the Organisation for Sickle Cell Anaemia Research Centre to help them raise money. Looking after her husband is now a full-time job but she still finds time to continue as a board member of the West Indian centre. In the intervening years, almost everything there has changed rather radically.

I'm still there and the centre is still there now. Twenty-six years it's been there and I'm still the treasurer. When I walk in there and I say something, I mean it. I am not backing down. As I said to the staff: "I come in here and I'll treat you the workers with respect. I'm expecting it back. I have a demarcation line and I'll meet you halfway but do not cross it and I won't cross it.

The board has changed quite a lot—quite a few have left. We try to take in younger people. They come to meetings a few times, then they don't come. "What's in it for me?" That's what they're asking. The last one on the board, he hadn't come to a meeting now for how long. I saw him the other day and I said to him: "Let me tell you something. You use the centre—OK. You come in with groups as well. You are there to represent young people and you do not come to the meetings. I'm expecting you at the next one. I'm not letting you go." He says: "Alright Mrs Wallace, I'll try and do my best to come."

The first generation of those originating from the Caribbean saw an urgent need to organise and build community. They were motivated to press for change aimed at tackling discrimination and disadvantage. They established churches and centres for community, resources, advice and arts. They built alliances with other immigrant communities to campaign on a wide range of issues. This carries through to the second generation who are often more ambitious and adept at gaining access to funding. However, as Evelyn observes, by the first decade of the present century, that original sense of urgency has largely gone. The community initiatives that she was so passionate in setting up are slowly dying out. In her opinion, young people do not see the need for them anymore.

The West Indian centre is still going and Evelyn is still treasurer. So how is it doing?

At present the centre is struggling. We go out and bid for contracts. We had the 'Meals on Wheels' contract for African Caribbean pensioners and the council went and decided to have meals from this big firm. They give people microwave ovens so they can warm up their meals. It's not a local firm. We lost the contract.

We then went in for homecare and we're struggling to get contracts because the council is giving the work to these massive firms. At the moment we're struggling.

We do day care on Mondays and Wednesdays and we do meals at the centre on a Friday for sale. People can come in and order the meals and we'll do it. A lot of young people won't cook or can't cook—so they come in and buy meals.

The bar is struggling because we haven't got the amount of people coming in. A lot of the older people have died off and the supermarkets are selling beers and things at cheaper prices but the bar is still going.

Black people love to dance and socialise so they still go to the centre on a Saturday night. Drugs can't come in there because we have surveillance cameras and things like that. Naturally, if you want to go somewhere you feel safe, you go there.

At one point we were doing well when we were doing 'Steps to Work' and things like that. All those contracts have gone now, so we're looking at other things.

> We do Saturday School and West Bromwich
> Albion Football Club sponsor football for younger
> kids, so we do that as well on Saturday.

The Saturday School at the centre connects African Caribbean
parents wanting additional tutorship for their children.

> I think we are the only African Caribbean organ-
> isation in West Bromwich doing these sorts of
> things. The funny thing is the people in West
> Bromwich don't support us. They want to go free
> for everything. They think the government give
> us money to run it. They don't realise that the
> government only give us money for the manager
> and the caretaker. Most of the people who come
> to the centre are from Wolverhampton, Dudley,
> Handsworth and elsewhere. They keep the centre
> going. The people in West Bromwich want
> everything free.
>   One of the things we do is to look after local
> African Caribbean people when they're ill. But
> when they die, the family go to the Indian centre
> and pay one thousand odd to hold wakes. Our
> centre is across the road. The two centres are there
> and they'll go to the Indian centre. They can't
> cook there or anything but African Caribbean
> families will pay a thousand five hundred to have
> their 'afters' at the Indian centre and we're just
> across the road. We only charge three hundred
> and something and we also do the catering if

they want it. We're good enough to care for their parents but the centre is not good enough to have their 'afters'. It's very sad ain't it, but you struggle and carry on.

We're looking for different things at the moment. We've made some applications—about four. We're waiting now to see whether or not we'll get anything.

We have seventy-nine workers in the care section plus the other sections—we're big employers. Next year we'll have to start paying private insurance but I have a very good rapport with the bank and I can make some sort of arrangement. If we're going to be overdrawn, they'll sort us. At the moment we're struggling but we're OK.

I keep on tapping myself on my shoulder. It makes me feel proud because I'm the only founder member still there. Everybody else has gone. I must have done a good job and if I walk out, it wouldn't last.

Even the workers tell me say: 'Mrs Wallace, you're the only person we can come to if anything goes wrong and if you go, we're all coming.' If anything goes wrong I'm the only person they can speak to and they know it will be seen to. We have a very good rapport.

If I can't get down there, they'll come here and we'll sit here and decide what we have to do. If a meeting is needed, I'll call a meeting, thrash it out

and finalise the decision. As soon as that's final-
ised, to prevent anybody from changing it, the
decision is written down and put on file. Nobody
can change it.

One thing that has remained consistent within the centre after
all these years are the challenges that come with keeping control
of the centre's finances.

I've tried it—I know. In the finance office I
haven't got a Black person. I've got two whites
and one Asian. I had a Black finance manager
once. One month she took her monthly pay
twice. She was paid twice in one month and she
wrote the cheques. Three people are authorised to
sign cheques but only two signatures are required.
If you're not careful they can go behind your back
and get cheques signed. I had to make it know in
the office that any unauthorised expenditure will
come out of their wages because I'm on the other
end of the phone. Now nothing goes through
without me knowing about it.

The council has been really good because
they know how the money is spent. At one point
the woman who was chair of the management
board left. She left in anger and she wrote to the
council. I know that she did because the council
wouldn't send somebody in to check your books
if somebody hadn't made a complaint. She always
said anytime she leaves she'll make sure the centre

close. She did the letter. The council came in and they hold back our grants until we were clear. Our books were as good as theirs. So I'm rather proud.

Out of all the organisations I help to set up, it's only the Women's Agency and the West Indian centre that's left out of them. So we're still lucky.

***

Evelyn's daughter initially went into office work. She did not like it and later joined her mother at the salon where she trained as a hairdresser and remained until the salon closed in 2007.

Janice now does mobile. She didn't want to take over the shop because it pins her down. Doing mobile, she can choose the days when she want to work. She has most of my clients that use to be at the shop and she does a lot of the elderly ones who can't come out or wouldn't settle in another shop. At one point I use to do the nursing homes because it perks them up to have their hair done. I used to go in there or send someone to do it. She does hairdressing at two nursing homes now. I don't think she will ever stop. She owns her own house—a three-bedroom semi-detach—and her two children who have now grown up.

Garry went into this factory less than two years ago. There were other tool setters there before him but he's the one now that even have the keys to lock up—not the ones that was there before him.

He's very good at his job.

Growing up, Janice's children might also have had little doubt concerning their granny's views on earning a living—whatever the circumstances.

> One went to university then she worked for six months with the council. That job closed. She's tried and tried but she could not get a job. At the moment she's at the bloody Pizza Hut. She finished university about three years ago and she's now working at Pizza Hut—it's very hard. I said to her: "You can't get the job you train for but a job is a job. You're earning a living and you're not going to sit at home claiming benefit. You'll go out and earn it. You'll take any job until when you get the one that you want." She working at Pizza Hut and she's quite happy doing it.

This is the same granddaughter who would sometimes come in to keep an eye on Reggie when Evelyn had to go out.

> You cannot encourage them to sit at home because they cannot get the job they want and you're carrying them. They say: "Why should I go and find a job?" No, I'm not having it.
>
> Some parents say: "Oh, I don't want you to do what I did." What's so degrading in working? If you can do it, why can't your kid do it? So you're telling the child that the child is better than

you? No, that's one phrase I'll never use. A job is a job—you're earning your living. You're not living off anybody else's back. If you have to dig a hole—go and dig it. Do not tell me you're not working as slave labour. Don't you dare say that to me. From your child is small, you have to tell them that. You have to say no—this is it. I've set the example and I'm going to see that you do it.

My kids and grandkids know exactly where it stops because I don't stand for it. I've told them: "You do not go out and have any children believing that you're going to live off social. You have your kids when you can afford to carry them. If you choose to have them, you must be able to take care of them."

Jason—my grandson—has done well. He's in car sales and he has his own business. He was a baby when I bought this house.

In Evelyn's view neither of her sisters—Eloise and Louise—have made much of their lives.

Eloise is still here. When I sent for her, she came to live with me in Trinity Road and Eunice was born. Then she just keep running all over the place. She married twice and have another three children. She divorced her first husband, then she re-married and that one died. When her husband died she was so rude and out of order, I didn't speak to her for a while. But I always said: "Whatever happens, she's my sister. She's my mum's child and I'll be there for her."

Louise, she never leave Jamaica. She was married but her husband died and she had no children. When her husband died it was coming up one o'clock in the morning and the first person she called was me. I had to arrange the funeral, do everything. Then I did the probate for her. It cost her £90 instead of thousands. I'll always be there—it's family.

She is now pretty ill. I went out last year and had to make arrangements for her to be cared for because she is getting Alzheimer's. I set up a bank account in her and my name. I put in money every month to see that she's fine, see to the house, pay her light bills, buy her gas and food—make sure she's OK. I enjoy doing that. It's given me a lot of comfort doing that.

Reggie is not getting any better. Given Evelyn's age, members of the family are increasingly worried that the burden of looking after her husband may be damaging her health.

They were here recently and all their concern were around me. Garry said: "Mum you're wearing yourself out and I don't want you to get ill. Why don't you put him in a home?" I says: "No." On another occasion one of my grandsons said: "Nana I'm very concerned about you because you're the only one caring for him. Can we pull together to help pay for his care?" I said to him: "At the moment I'm not struggling and I don't want you to do it because you have to look after yourself and help your mum. I don't need you to do that. If I needed help, I'd ask for it." He said: "But Nana, we don't want you to get ill."

A few days later he came back and he said: "Nan promise me that if anything happened, the things you wanted to do and you haven't had time to do, you're going to do it. Don't stay in the house if he passes. Try and do whatever you have always wanted and I want you to shake on it. You've given up all your social life to take care of him."

I did think on it and I said to myself: 'If he had passed on before me and I feel that I wasn't going to be cared for as I wanted to, I'd go back to Jamaica.' I told my children: "You see how I care for all of you and I look after you. If when I need you and you're not there, I'll leave this country and you'll never hear from me again. I would not want to go into a home."

Reggie died in 2014.

***

Looking back on her life and the community she lived in since first arriving in the 1950's, Evelyn has a great deal to say. To begin with, she is not convinced that her community has done as well as it could have.

> We have a community that could have done
> better. When you look into it, we could have
> done better. You have to look at why we haven't
> done better. When we first came here things was
> very hard. We had no one to rely on apart from
> friends. We clung together to help each other out.

When discussing the impact of racial prejudice and discrimination against her community, Evelyn doesn't deem it as the most decisive factor.

> There was racism but it wasn't rife. They're call
> you names and things like that but some of the
> people had never seen Blacks before. Sometimes
> it's the Black who don't want to mix with them.
> Whites want to speak to them but they don't want
> to speak to whites. It's a two-way thing. What I
> find is a lot of people use racism as an excuse. I'm
> not saying it wasn't there but it was not just us.
> The Irish got it. Notices would be put up in the
> window: 'No Black—No Irish.' It wasn't just us,
> the Irish are white. So you find that the Irish and
> us got on better.

Evelyn is far more concerned with the reasons why members of her community did not take more steps to help themselves—in particular—women.

Some wanted to further their education. Some couldn't because of the demands of work, children and family. Some did it and it was hard. I did it under very hard circumstances. You have to be very, very strong and strong-willed. My other half didn't want me to do it. I did not get any help from him but I thought to myself: 'I can't let you make decisions for me. I'm a person. I'm an individual with my own brain. If I sit back and let you make decisions for me, then why have I got a brain? You're not doing anything to even help yourself.'

At that point a lot of the men did not help the women. They go to work, then they're at the pub. Their friends come first and the drink come first. That was another situation.

Some women couldn't do it. A lot of women, the blokes send for them and bring them here. When they go to work, some of them could not even open their pay packets—that money was taken over. You have to remember in those days women had no rights. It was hard. Some of them had not got the education to further themselves. They can do manual things but the reading is not good—some can't read.

As a woman—if you're very ambitious—the men try to hold you back. You have to be brave not to walk away. I think if I wasn't strong, I would have walked away. I didn't want to walk away because it's not good for my children or my grandchildren and it's not good for myself either. You don't have to argue and fight, just do what you have to do. If you're not prepared to do that, you won't make it to where you want to go. If you give up, you have a lower opinion of yourself. You have to be brave and speak out logically. My brain is mine and if I can't use it in the way that I can or should use, then something happens and my brain goes.

I am willing to follow if you're leading me to water to drink. If you're leading me to an empty trough, why should I follow you? You should follow me, then we rise together. But I realise this doesn't happen. It's if you're a woman—you can't lead me—I'm a man. Either one can lead. If I can't agree then forget it, I'm not coming. I'm glad that sort of thing had been instilled in me from I was small. I'd rather give up the whole thing than come in with you. If I don't believe it, why do it?

Evelyn's most significant concern is how children within her community are being brought up. This is an issue she has raised over and over again.

First generation African Caribbean parents did not have time to look after their kids because they always had to work. You find that a lot of the children were dragged from pillow to post because both parents worked.

There were a few women not working who

took in children. To earn money they take in X amount of kids because there are being paid to look after them. Some of the babies were not changed from they were brought in the morning till their parents come back to pick them up.

This is an important factor. That's where it went wrong. You're training your child to do certain things and telling them not to do this because it's wrong and that person is telling them to do something else. The children get mixed up—don't know which way to turn.

Don't forget small children they're like sponges. You have to teach them everything. They imitate you and it stays with them through their lives. That's the beginning of their future. If it's wrong, then it's hard to straighten it out because it follows through. They watch what you do. They're going to copy you. So you have a duty to make sure that your child is brought up right because they are passing it on to their own kids. Maybe it has to go to another generation before it starts straightening out.

EMMA

It is 1991. Emma and Mathew have been fostering children for seven years. Not many African Caribbean families are fostering at the time though African Caribbean children are over-represented in the care system. Their daughter Donna is now living in her flat with her baby son. Donna remains there for two years until a better offer comes her way.

> Then she was offered a brand new two-bedroom house with the same housing association. While she was there she had the 'Right to Buy'. She couldn't buy that property, it was a new property. The scheme that they had was that she would be given £10,000 in cash. Whatever the property cost, she would have to pay £10,000 less on the mortgage.
>
> We encouraged her, especially me. I said to her: "Donna, if you can afford to be paying hundreds of pounds per month in rent, you could be buying your own property." That's what she did. She went and looked at another property which took her 'Right to Buy' money as a deposit. So that's how she purchased her first house.

I have to hand it to Mathew. He said to Donna: "When are you going to take your mom to look at the house you're buying?" She wouldn't have told us until she'd moved in. Anyway she took me to see the property. I can't remember if we both went or I went with her on my own.

This is further away now from her two-bedroom flat. This is going out to Sutton Coalfield—Streetly. I'm thinking to myself: 'Way she gone so far fer?' That's what I'm thinking to myself: 'Why she didn't go to Great Barr where she was living before, easy for me to remember. How we going to find this place again.' This property was nearly new.

She didn't tell us this at the time but Owen encouraged her to buy the property between them. Now he had got another property—solo. So with her getting a property with him, he's building up his portfolio.

It is now over two years since Donna left the family home. Despite their support and encouragement, Emma and Mathew are still not reconciled with their daughter.

Shortly after Donna moves into her new home she finds out she is pregnant again.

She moves into her new house and is now pregnant with a second child for Owen. Not too long after, he actually moves in with her. From what we were informed, he'd never actually moved in with a woman before. So I think Donna now thought: 'Yes progress.' I expected them to be living together but he only come and go.

Donna had three kids for Owen. She didn't know then that he'd got a string of other children out there—similar ages to hers. But it all came out. Just to run the story forward a little bit, much was revealed when his eldest son died and all these other children attended the funeral. With her three, there were about eight or nine of them with different mothers. Thank God something good came out of the funeral.

It seems unlikely that Donna would not have known of at least some of Owen's children until the funeral. Nevertheless, she sticks with him until one day Owen pushes her too far.

She was part of this entanglement for a number of years. The light bulb must have come on when he decided he wanted to move another woman in with her. Another woman—probably with a child—into the house that she and he had bought. He made her life hell. She didn't want anything more to do with him.

She, by God's grace, managed to get the house she's living in now. That was a gift from God because it had been advertised for maybe about twelve months and they drop the price on the property to get a quick sale. She bought it. The house she bought belonged to the son of one her neighbours from the first house where she lived in Great Barr.

Around this time Emma and Mathew decide to take a holiday.

No longer fostering with Sandwell Council and having been approved to foster children by the London Borough of Southwark, before the first child arrives Emma and Mathew decide to go on holiday.

> Both of us went back to Jamaica for the first time together in 1991. Without a doubt, it was a journey of discovery. It was a holiday where we discovered a number of things.
>
> We went to visit my mom's cousin Renie. We went to visit the area where she was staying for a couple of days. She told us that when our parents were courting, our mom would tell her parents that she was going to visit. Me and I would be here talking to myself as if your mom was here. She shared this with us though my mom and dad was still alive at the time. She said: "Yes, when your mom and Johnny wah go out—go go on a breeze—ah me them got as excuse and me sit down there ah talk to me self at de back ah de house like me damn fool."
>
> So that was their courting. What I also didn't know and only knew through cousin Renie was that my mom and her mom, they were like 'Chalk and Cheese'. They were always arguing—they were fighting all the time.

I'm so much like my grandmother and I realise now that would have suited my mother well. As an adult, she and I would have the same relationship. But she couldn't get me to be arguing with her or anything because we weren't communicating. I definitely wasn't playing up to her scenario.

Millie—Emma's mother—never went back on a visit to Jamaica.

Dad did in 1991 and 1993. He and my sister Emily went in 1993. They never said what it was about but from what I understanding it was over some land business. I was not interested because I live in England. Even if I had a piece of paper right now to say that this land belong to me, I still wouldn't be interested because I don't need it. I don't need that headache. I don't need that strain or stress.

In 1993, shortly after her father's return from his second trip to Jamaica there is a tragic loss in the family.

He was here for thirty odd years before he went back to Jamaica. He died within six days of being back from his last trip to the Caribbean. He was in his eighties and he would have been a hundred this year in October 2013.

Millie—her mother—did not survive her father for that long. She dies in 1995.

Mom was seventy-nine. That's eighteen years ago, so she would have been ninety-seven now.

I love my parents. They're dead and gone. Even before they passed they knew I loved them—they knew that. I reach a stage with me dad where he would be asking me: 'Yer not going to give me a kiss?'

Since my parents passed away, in some ways—within the family—what we've been told is something completely different to what we actually see now. Are you with me? They were like the matriarchs or patriarchs in our community and in the family. They were here first and they sent for all these other people and what have you. So people had a high regard for them and they would listen to whatever they said which was not always the truth.

Emma may well be referring to her early life. In particular, how it came about that the little girl she thought of as a cousin in Jamaica turned out to be her half-sister, the child of her father and her grandmother's sister.

Around the time of the death of Emma's parents, Emma and Mathew are responsible for providing care to a boy named Armstrong. He is placed with them by the London Borough of Southwark and he has severe medical issues.

Emma recounts what was happening with her two sons—Samuel and Ethan—at the time.

They had opportunities but it was up to each one.

In actual fact Mathew started teaching Samuel to drive when he was thirteen years old. He was a very good driver, both he and Donna could drive before I could. Dad saw his leaning and was prepared to get him a van to set him up in business.

However, according to Mathew there were some aspects of his son's behaviour that bothered him. Behaviour similar to Owen's—the father of Donna's children.

I was saying to my wife, if Samuel bring a young lady home come to introduce to us, I would say to that young lady: "You be careful. He's got the sweetest charm in the world. He can charm the birds off a tree. He's got the gift of the gab." But he's only got the gift of the gab. He's got nothing to back it up—you know what I'm saying. He could talk anybody into getting anything off them.

Even girlfriends, he didn't even go out to look for girlfriends. He would wait for his sister to get friends and he'd just poach them. He's that type of young man. So if he bring a girl to introduce to me, I would say: "Young lady don't get involve. Don't get involve." One of the things I am is I try to be as honest as possible with whoever I deal with. That means I expect the same honesty from that individual. I would tell them: "He's my son and I love him to bits—but be careful, be careful.

So when it doesn't work out don't come back to
me and say you was not told because I'm telling
you now."

He's my son and if he comes in here now, he'd
be smiling and he'd be charming.

Apparently Samuel's younger brother Ethan is not as adept at
charming the 'birds' out of the trees. This is a point of concern
for his mother.

Ethan has not been able to establish a relationship where his girlfriends could even be invited
home to see Mom. He's never brought a woman
home. Each one that we've know of, it's always
somebody who's in trouble. Somebody who he's
rescued. He's like a guardian angel.

Mathew provides further explanation of what his wife means
by likening their son to a 'guardian angel' in relation to his
girlfriends.

There was this Indian girl and she came from
Leicester with a baby. She was in trouble. He's not
somebody who pick up strays but if you was in
trouble, Ethan would be the one to help you. So
all the women them that we know of, it's somebody who have got problems with relationships
or have difficulty. He never find a woman and
bring them home say: "Mom, Dad—this is me
girlfriend.'"They were always in trouble.

Emma and Mathew also do not understand their youngest son's apathy in developing a career for himself.

> Funny enough, we were talking about this only yesterday. The potential Ethan always had! From he was born—from he was dot—that potential was always there. With all our encouragement he's never harnessed it. He just didn't seem to have the ambition or the drive to have done anything really worthwhile with his life.

As the two brothers are growing up, both parents worry about the relationship between them.

> He Ethan adores Samuel—he adores Samuel. When you adore somebody, the person knows that they can actually affect your way of thinking towards them. Samuel could lead Ethan by a little piece of string.

As a teenager, Samuel has a minor brush with the law for which he is cautioned by the police—nothing serious.

> There was no indication of unlawful behaviour before. We know that Samuel was hotheaded— we knew that. To our knowledge they never got into trouble until seventeen or eighteen years ago.

This would be around 1995. Samuel is twenty-eight and Ethan is twenty-two.

By this time Samuel was living in Stoke-on-Trent. He lived up there with his girlfriend Julie in her parents' home—lucky fella!

The parents' home got broken into. Julie's dad, he was a cameraman. He collected antique cameras as well. Anyway these guys broke into the property. Samuel found out who these guys were and he mentioned it when he came down here, saying: "He's going to go and sort them out. They shouldn't be left to walk the face of the earth, blah, blah, blah." Very ho headed. It was in this living room and I said to Samuel: "Dear God, just leave it." He didn't. Him and his brother, they use to do bouncers in clubs. He got his brother to go up to Stoke-on-Trent with him.

Now the night that Ethan left here, I was sitting in the back room by that window in the dining room. This sensation came over me. I couldn't breathe. I felt nauseated, I felt sick. It just came on me. I say to Mathew: "Open the window I'm feeling stifled." That was the Thursday evening.

Ethan was dressed in black when he left here. We thought he was going on a job in a night club or something. It was my birthday that day or the day after. That was the Thursday or the Friday—I can't remember exactly. Anyway, Ethan didn't come back on the Friday, didn't see him on the Friday. I am expecting them both because I was having a party for my birthday. Neither of them showed up.

When Samuel's girlfriend rang me, my heart just sank. She says: "Mrs. Thompson, Samuel and Ethan, they've been arrested. They've been locked up." I says: "What for?" She said: "Assault."

We were having a party for my birthday and we're going to be expecting guests. My heart sank. I just could not believe it. I thought: 'My God! That was the sensation I was feeling just before it happened.'

The thieves were police informers but Samuel didn't know. I did say to him: "Leave it alone." They went to the guys' house. It was a high crime area—that's the terminology the judge used in the court. They went to where the fellas lived. They took a replica gun, don't know where they got it from. They took it to frighten the guys. Maybe if the parents were there, things might have been different—I don't know—but their parents weren't home. The guys were both police informers, known to the police. So what they'd done as thieves, it didn't matter. The police, they even managed to get back some of the stuff.

The fact that they used a 'mock' gun to ruffle these guys up, that's why they got sent down. Ethan got twelve months and Samuel got eighteen months.

It was a very lonely, lonely, deep time for my life. We were fostering. Mathew went up to Stoke-on-Trent on his own the day that they were sentenced at the court. I felt thankful that it wasn't a local thing with the embarrassment and everything.

Neither parent saw this coming and Mathew concedes that they did not know a great deal about what was going on in the lives of their two sons at the time.

> In Jamaica they say: "Show me your friends and I'll tell you who you are." The friends that they mixed with in the area that they move into change their outlook or influence their outlook. When they come home—in West Bromwich or in this area—a lot of people knows them. So the behaviour in West Bromwich would be different from the behaviour in Stoke. Well, us as their parents cannot say about their behaviour in Stoke because we don't know.

For most of the next year or so, Emma and Mathew settle down to make sure they can make it to their sons' prison visits.

> At the beginning they were in the same prison— Shrewsbury Jail. Ethan remained there, he did his twelve months there. We would go to church then we'd be having something to eat—stopping at a KFC or somewhere on the motorway—driving to go and visit them in prison. We very rarely had a normal Sunday dinner.
>
> It felt degrading because you were treated as if you were doing time. Armstrong missed them.

We discovered that it was a good thing to take Armstrong with us. He didn't really know where he was going but he was glad to see them and vice versa.

Both of them during their time 'inside' had glowing references from the governor because of who they were brought up to be. They showed it there.

When their sons are released from prison, understandably Emma and Mathew want to know how they intend to proceed with their lives going forward.

You'd think that they would both have learnt something. They didn't go back inside. They never get locked up again to our knowledge. But the way they were talking about what they were going to do with their lives when they came out ain't adding up.

Emma and Evelyn, it turns out, do not live that far from each other. In fact, they know each other as both are members of the same African Caribbean Association.

It was the West Bromwich West Indian Centre. The centre was first opened in 1986 or 1987. I was behind the scenes before the centre was opened because the original chairperson—Mr Stennett—he came here one day out of the blue to meet with my husband and myself.

He asked us if we could come and join the steering group. We were the only people he knew who were foster carers. He still speaks fondly about us.

In order for the centre to come about the council gave us a building. It was four Black organisations coming together in partnership. That's how we got the building.

Very soon two of the organisations became defunct. So in essence, the only representative of those four groups that is left on the board is Mrs Wallace, who's is the treasurer. Mrs Wallace and my mom came here around the same time. She's one of the founder members who did the original constitution for the centre. It was a model from the Martin Luther King Centre in America. She's taught me a lot. My mom use to volunteer at the centre. It's part of my DNA in a sense.

Mrs Wallace is a very strong lady and she's had to be strong to do what she does. When you continually try to bring about better ways of doing things and there's a failure to even see the good practise you're trying to bring in—it is undermined. That has repeatedly happened.

I was the assistant secretary.

By 2003 Emma has been the assistant secretary for eight years.

One day the acting chair just came in, brought a letter and said she's stepping down. That was it.

The person who was acting chair, she had the role not really for that long. Things were rather dire at the time. This was like a bombshell that came on us.

Our board consisted of fourteen people. The following day we convened a meeting. There was myself as assistant secretary, the secretary, the treasurer, one of the trustees, our accountant and our auditor—six people all together. The secretary—Mr Macdonald—chaired the meeting and he said we can't operate this charity without a chair. He looked at me and he says: "Mrs Thompson, the AGM is nearly three months away. Could you assume the role of acting chair until the AGM." I said: "Mr Macdonald, I haven't had time to pray." The accountant says to the auditor: "Well, I think we'd all better pray."

God is so good. That's when I first knew that these two men were Christians. I didn't know before. I know that one went to church—the auditor. He drives lorries over to Romania in his spare time—taking things. That's just an act of charity at his own expense.

Emma accepts the role of acting chair and goes on to be the elected as chair for the next ten years. From the very beginning things are not exactly easy.

We needed a financial injection from different directions to help see us to the end of the financial year. The council gave us £35,000.

There is a gentleman whose funeral my husband is going to on Friday—he's a former member of the centre committee and he basically couldn't tolerate women in charge. Some men have difficulty with that. He would do some sneaky things to undermine women committee members. I said to him once: "You only want to destroy. Why don't you just tell me to step aside if you think you can do a better job."

He had to step down, he and somebody else. As an individual, I would have taken him to court for what he said. What he said—as a former chair—was actually libellous in the presence of other people.

There were lots of things that you have to be able to deal with—see through and work through. At the same time you've got to have a balance when you come home. When I was blinking well dealing with this sort of thing, I can't shut off because I've come home from a meeting—I've got to unload. Thank God for my husband, I'd unload all this onto him.

My husband was not a member of the board but he has always supported me. With all the women that have been involved there over the years, the husbands have been supportive.

Mrs Wallace has been treasurer now for maybe about seventeen or eighteen years—probably longer than that. They only had one other treasurer before her and I was the fourth chair.

While all this is going on, Emma and Mathew are fostering children from Southwark. Armstrong came in 1993 and Stephanie followed in 1998.

> We tried to have an understanding of each parent because the children came with their own difficulties. We didn't meet all the parents—most them we did. We never met Armstrong's or Stephanie's parents.
>
> She was the last person we had. She'd been in care from she was about four. She came to us when she was about seven and she left and returned to London at fourteen—eight years ago in 2005. So she was with us long term.
>
> The only person that we had met or knew—seen a couple of times—was her older brother who incidentally is white. Yet his name came to us first. She was amongst a family—a sibling group of eight or nine children. She wasn't the youngest but she was the only Black one. None of the others went into care but social services had got their eyes on them anyway. She went into care and had been in several foster homes before she came to us.
>
> First it was recommended that we see her brother. His name came to us about two years before her name came. With the difficulties he was already presenting, they wanted to move him

from the area. If we'd said yes and agreed to it, fair dos because Black children were still being placed with white families. The excuses were there weren't enough Black foster carers. You can't argue with that if the authorities say well they aren't enough. But we knew for a fact there were periods when there were Black carers. With Southwark and Sandwell we were approved to have three children.

I've never fostered any white children. Mixed race yes—Siarah and Stephanie. Siarah's parents was Chinese and white. Because of that, they classed her as Black. That's the reason why we had Siarah.

Armstrong's been here obviously the longest because he's been here the last twenty years. He's twenty-five and he's a man.

Armstrong was the first child Emma and Mathew took in from Southwark, he arrived when he was just five years old. He has a mental disability. Now, he is in his mid-twenties and is still being looked after by the couple. He is as much a part of their family as their own children.

We do all the championing for him but we have got an independent advocate for him. She should have step down when Armstrong became twenty-five.

By the age of twenty-five—if a person's been looked after and if they'd gone to university or college—all that would have finished. They're grown up and living independently. But Armstrong lacks capacity. He will never be able to live independently.

We have a spare bedroom and when Armstrong's back-up carer comes, she's got somewhere to sleep. Our other support back-ups is Ethan and our granddaughter. They can stay here with him or he can go to our daughter's home.

Emma and Mathew try to keep in touch with the children they have fostered and where possible their parents. Jacob, is the first child they fostered. His mother, Helen, lived in the area. Initially Jacob's mother wanted Jacob to go for adoption but the social services kept telling her that she could cope. Emma and Mathew keep in contact with her.

Mathew hadn't been [to visit Helen] for a week or so and the weather got really cold. He went to visit her and noticed she hadn't had any curtains at the window—it was just iced over. He came back and told me and I got some stuff down. So we started visiting her more often. We had a good relationship, we left an open door and she used it for her advantage. In the finish I think she felt quite self-sufficient. She even moved closer to us which we thought was good. We thought she could even help us in some way with Armstrong. It didn't really make any difference. In fact, I think the first time we ask her to support us with

Armstrong—it was only for an evening, we'd got a meeting—she says: "Oh, they coming to fit my carpet." In the night this was, you know. We never asked her again. That was the first and only time. But since then—although she doesn't live too far away—we don't see each other that much. She'll make much of us, but it was always us that was making the effort.

Emma, very recently ran into Calvin and explains what this interaction was like. Calvin was the child who accused Mathew of trying to strangle him in the early days of their fostering journey.

I saw him less than twelve months ago. I started meeting him for different reasons and I ask him: "How you're getting on Cal?" He says: "Oh I'm alright, I'm alright." But I don't think he was. He wouldn't settle in a job because he'd got so many different issues which I don't think he'll ever get dealt with. I don't think he ended up in prison or anything like that because the things he did was so petty. The things he did was like petty.

Emma goes on to say more about her daughter, Donna.

I told you about Donna. She's so much a combination of both me and her dad. She's headstrong. We're both headstrong in our own ways, aren't we babe? I'm very assertive, she's very assertive. She

don't take any passengers, you know. We taught
her well plus what she's learnt at college and uni.
Since she left college she has worked for two
authorities.

After leaving Owen, Donna decides to move on with her life.
In 2008, at the age of thirty-nine, Donna gets married. Unlike
Owen, the new man in her life is someone Emma and Mathew
know.

Donna had known of him when they were
growing up. His eldest aunt was one of Donna's
best friend and we already had a good relationship
with members of his family before he came on
the scene. We met him when we went to one of
his family's weddings. Donna simply said: "This
is Nathan." By that time the relationship had
already started.

They were both the same age but she had three
children from a previous relationship—whose
father is still around. He had one child. His son
would be about thirteen or fourteen now.

He was of Jamaican heritage and worked in
motor insurance. He wooed her and he wooed
her and he wooed her—flowers and turning up at
work for her and at her home.

Mathew is confident that he knows the reasons why his daughter
succumbed to Nathan's charm.

I'm a man and men can be very devious, very devious. If a woman had a relationship where she wasn't treated special—flowers and chocolates, the theatre and movies—you could find these things out before you get involved. So when you start, you flourish with them. It's all a mental thing with the woman saying: "Wow! This is good—this is good." You work your way in.

Given their daughter's experience with Owen it is natural that Emma and Mathew were cautious about Nathan. For one, they saw very little of him but there is also another glaring concern that makes them feel particularly uncomfortable about their daughter's new relationship.

She's got everything—a good job. She's got her own home not many years left on her mortgage. She's got a car and was learning to drive. He's got nothing. I know love covers everything but it doesn't pay the mortgage.

Nevertheless, when Donna and Nathan announce that they are going to get married, her parents are happy and supportive. Excited as they are, Emma and Mathew advise Donna on what type of wedding they think she should have.

When they came and told us, we both said to them: "If you plan to get married consider going abroad. Why not do it on a cruise ship. Marriage on a cruise ship would be marvelous and we could

all have a holiday at the same time. But give us at
least two years notice."

Donna being 'assertive' like her mother pushes against the
wishes of her parents. Instead Donna chooses to have her
wedding in West Bromwich and much sooner than her parents
have suggested.

Donna says: "No because I want our friends to be
there." They told us the December and they were
going to get married in May of the following year.
It seems like it was five minutes.

His mother made the wedding cakes. His
mother said: "My mother buy my wedding dress
so I will buy her wedding dress." I never ques-
tioned how much the wedding dress cost and I
never asked them how much they spent on the
wedding. I know how much I spent. We didn't
sit down together and vote for this wedding. She
spent and I spent. We did that because she was
our daughter.

Mathew remembers his daughter's wedding day clearly. At the
time of Donna's special day he is unwell and recovering from
an accident.

Anyway on the day I get up and—in my
opinion—make a great speech about myself and
my daughter and how this guy going take my
rose away from my garden. My wife get up and

she says: "The Princess has left the house but the Queen is still in the house."

I stood there and I heard my daughter's husband say: "This here family ah boasty sah." I remember him saying that this here family boasty.

Needless to say Mathew never took kindly to his family being called "boasty" by Nathan. The remark leaves a bitter taste in Mathew's mouth long after it was said particularly because it was the term that Millie, Emma's mother also used to describe Mathew.

Mathew go on to explain why this word was incorrectly used to describe him.

> It was pride. We put all our energy into our children. There is nothing we have for ourselves that we haven't worked for. We don't come from a background where our families are rich. Our families didn't leave anything to us. They could just both feed you and clothe you. There is nothing to leave for anyone to have.

With the wedding out of the way, Emma is of the belief that her daughter's marriage is going well.

> We had our reservations. I would ask: "Where is Nathan?" It was excuse after excuse. She would say: "He's is at the gym. He's been at work all day and he's at the gym." He's as thin as a rake.
>
> There were family events with his side of the

family and he would be absent. We had to give her some space, after all she's now a married woman. But I was already seeing that something wasn't right. It reached a stage where she was running out of excuses.

Donna's marriage to Nathan last less than eighteen months. It is only then that her parents finds out what is going on with their daughter.

It was no fault of her own. On hindsight we probably should have said something. But sometimes by saying something, you drive them even more together. We very rarely saw him. I can hardly recall him coming into this house. If he did, it was no further than the front room. That was his choice.

He was not emotionally stable and I picked up on his emotional imbalance. I was frightened to say anything in case it would have offended her. He was uncomfortable when I was around— didn't want to face me. He actually said to her: "Your mom don't like me." She told him that it's not that I didn't like him.

I never would ever feel that way or even show it. They were incompatible. Unfortunately, her vision of what marriage should be didn't tally with her husband because he wasn't really prepared for that sort of responsibility. He was after all the material things which she'd got. I think he wanted the things that marriage would bring because she'd already got a home and a car.

He would drive her car all over the place and then she found out that he hadn't even got a licence. He could have crash the car and her insurance would have been null and void. He's got no sense of responsibility. She got everything and he didn't even believe in having a driving licence.

Whatever his issues are, we believe his family knows some of his past history which has never been disclosed to us. He was warned by his aunties. The eldest—Patricia—warned him not to mess Donna up.

Emma laments over their daughter fighting to make her marriage work.

Donna was prepared for them to work through whatever the problems were. They've had offers of Christian counseling within and outside of their church. Well Donna took full use of it. He rejected it, he didn't want it. Even though they had marriage classes with the minister who conducted their marriage, he wasn't prepared for that sort of relationship.

My daughter even made an arrangement with the mother of his child so that Clayton could spend time with them.

Donna and Nathan separate in 2011. Donna is forty-two at the time.

> We went to Jamaica as a family two years ago this October. It would have been twenty years since my husband's dad died. We went out there— Mathew, myself, his sister Gloria, our daughter and her three children.
>
> When we came back from Jamaica, Nathan had left the family home. She didn't tell us this but Christmas was now approaching and she couldn't keep it secret any longer.
>
> Just before Christmas last year he text her to say that he is about to start an adulterous relationship. That is suppose to have messed her head up but she survived that. He'd been gone over twelve months. They've been separated now nearly two years.
>
> She's had a raw deal in her life with the men that she choose. Her idea of trusting men is not good.

In hindsight, Emma thinks that Donna was in a low place when her relationship with Nathan began. She notes that Donna got with Nathan very shortly after she split up with her first husband, Owen.

Emma then recalls the time when Owen physically attacked Donna and Donna got him arrested. Importantly, Emma states that Nathan was aware of this and the impact it had on Donna at the time. Emma is convinced that Nathan used this to his benefit, taking advantage of Donna's vulnerability.

Owen tried to kill her in an open public place where there was cameras. Nathan, this gentleman who she married, knew all about that—how she'd been treated. He was there with us in court hearing parts of her life story, the way that things had been. He wooed her. My husband said about his 'sweet mouth'. He courted her and he wooed her when she was very vulnerable. That's what he was doing, he'd got a plan.

***

By 2013 Samuel is forty-five and Ethan is forty. It has been sixteen years since they were released from prison when they promised Emma and Mathew that their lives would change. Samuel is now father to three children—two daughters and a son. But his parents only got to see two of them Taylor and Pat. Samuel is yet to settle into regular employment and often looks to his parents for financial support.

Samuel's not working. He has repeatedly borrowed from us—indirectly. Comes with the intention that he's borrowing and never returns it.

The last straw was about twelve months ago, Babe? We've only seen him once since last September—that's ten months ago—and it was before then.

Emma remembers when one day Samuel visits her and asks if she can assist him with some of his expenses for his son Taylor.

> What he came here with was so straightforward. He's got two daughters and a son but we only see two of his children—Taylor and Pat. Taylor's into go-karting. I would say he's probably semi-professional now. I believe that Samuel is trying to live his dreams through Taylor. He had got a go-kart and was going to sell it to get this better one. Somebody was going to be sponsoring him for this new one.
>
> Samuel's proposition was that he needed money to get doing some things for Taylor. When he sold the go-kart he would reimburse us. So that's what he came to me with and I spoke to his dad who was sceptical.

Mathew remembers another day Samuel came to ask for another 'loan'.

> I wasn't here. When I came in, he was sitting in the front room where you're sitting. I knew, I knew he was up to something. I blame myself in a sense because what I should have done, I should have just walk through here to the back and get in the car. I knew he was up to something. I was in the kitchen and he came in. He's looking through the window and he pats me on the shoulder. He says: "Oh Dada. I come to see you and Mom but you

wasn't here. I've spoken to Mom so I'm talking to you." He told me what he wanted. His mother and I went upstairs and had a natter about it. We decided to lend him what he wanted.

The simple reason why is, I don't tell lies. I'd rather say no than tell lies. I couldn't say I haven't got it because we had it and he's me son, you see. Your son has that little more draw on you than the person outside. So we take his word for it. He and his motber went up to the high street. She went to the Bank and gave him the money.

Emma continues.

We saw him once after that. Some of his cousins were coming down and we'd never met all these nephews and nieces together. We heard about them but we only knew one because the nephews and nieces they'd now got children of their own and we only knew them when they were younger. We hadn't seen them for a long time. We needed to see these children, so they came down. We made a nice meal for them.

By Mathew's account, this day was a significant event.

We organise for them to come down. They put it on Facebook. Samuel saw it on Facebook that they was coming down. So he went and fetched his kids didn't he. We had a bit of a get together.

It was a good evening. We planned it. Also we got an envelope for all the mothers to say this is a gift for you. One young lady was saying: "No, I can't accept this." We said: "It's a gift from us to you. Just take it and you can do what you want for the children."

It was my birthday in October that year. Samuel rang and said: "Dad I'm coming down to see you." I said: "Sam, if you're coming down and you're coming down empty handed—don't." I know him—I know him. We haven't seen him since.

I'm telling you, I'm not short of anything—anything. If I want something today and it's in Birmingham, I can get up now, go to Birmingham and get it. It's got to be in my price range. You've got to set a limitation on whatever you do and within my limitation I'm not short—so my children and grandchildren shouldn't be short. But their parents have also got a responsibility to us and they should bring their grandchildren and say: "This is your Nan and this is your granddad." That's how a relationship is built.

All this happens in 2012. A year later Emma believes her eldest son's prospects might have improved, though she is not sure.

Samuel is self-sufficient. He's come to a point where he is self-sufficient. He doesn't make contact with his younger brother because over the years he's actually carried him down financially—badly.

We understand Samuel's got an Internet business—so we've heard. I rang him the other week and sent him a text because somebody was after him. I told him who it was. He didn't even respond to say 'thank you'.

Emma is notably less confident about how her younger son Ethan's life is going.

He's not working at the moment. He hasn't done for two years. The woman he's been living with for five years, up until this day we haven't seen her. She doesn't live two miles from here. He is sharing his life with her. She's going nowhere and he's going nowhere fast.

We've tried to get him to lift his game. His sister's tried, his brother's tried and others in the family who care about him have tried. It's like he's got tunnel vision. He'll say he can't understand the woman he's living with and yet he stays in the relationship. So I don't know, I don't know. He's forty.

Mathew is also concerned about his forty-year old son and feels he is still too dependent on his parents.

You see the thing we got to take into context is that he's got Mom and Dad. Even though he's forty, he's got his own key to this house. So if anything doesn't go well with him, he knows he can come home. He knows his food on the table. In this house he knows where things is more than I do.

If we were going out tonight, he'd stop with Armstrong because he's one of our back-up carers. If we were going on holiday, he'd support our back-up carers. He practically lives here because his mail comes here.

You see you got to look at these things when you talk about it. When I was younger, if I had an opportunity like that—got me own front door key, can go in every cupboard—what would I do? He even knows where I've got my few cans of beer. So there's nothing for him to push himself. If he come and he say: "Dad I want a new suit, I want some shirts?" I says: "Go in the wardrobe, see what you want and take it."

Emma chooses to emphasize another aspect of her younger son's character.

Just to say, all the three children are so different. Ethan would give you whatever he's got, he'll give you to his last. Yes he comes to Mom and Dad. We were talking about that this morning. When he was at home we encourage him to save and when we were married twenty-five years, he gave us £500 towards an anniversary holiday. That is the way Ethan is.

When he was working, he looked after us. When he got a job he looked after us because he's got no children. So regardless of who him have relationship with—Mom and Dad still come first in his life. Even though he's not living here, he'd phone every day just to see if we are at home.

Mathew does not dispute this account and goes on to expand on his and Emma's relationship with Donna.

I've got a different relationship with my daughter than her mom. One of the things she says is: "Dad, I know you two. If Mom says no, you will always says yes. If you says no, Mom will say yes." So she knows us.

She keeps in contact more than Samuel. She nearly always ring me in the week and sometime she speaks to her mom. If she's already spoken to her mom that week, she will ask to speak to me.

The simple reason is she's got three children. They're not always in the best of health and Mom and Dad are nearly always at home. If she rings up and says one of her kids is not feeling well, can she bring them over—it's yes. There's a guarantee babysitter. They're not babies anyway but there's a guarantee. If they're not well, we'll make space for them because she has not got enough resources to pay someone else to do that. We can do it all and it's expected as well.

What disappoints me is that it takes two to

make a child and that means the father and his parents should also have a part to play. But she never use Owen's parents as a resource.

When speaking about their children's relationships with the wider family and local community Emma commends her daughter and to some extent her youngest son.

Donna, she's got that down to a fine art. She's been sitting on the management board of the West Indian Centre for nearly three years. She is a second generation young person but she is very interested in who her relatives are and she makes every effort to keep that link, that connection.

If there's a death in the community because she is community minded and goes to places where we go, people know her and know Ethan. They can't miss Ethan because he looks so much like a miniature of Mathew.

But Samuel, there is nothing happen in our community that he's got any time for—never has. That's the way my dad use to be as well, he didn't mix. Mom did and when Dad was seen with Mom within the African Caribbean community, it would be because Mom was driving him. That's why he'd be there.

Samuel, he's just so indifferent. I actually asked him more than once. I says: "I'm sure you're ashamed of your background and your heritage." He replied: "What Mom?" I says: "Yea, you got to be. I'm sure if your parents were of a different colour, you'd probably be more akin to them." He said: "That's a racist thing to say!" Well I don't have that conversation with him now. He knows where I'm coming from.

It is 2013 and Emma has been chair of the West Indian Centre for a total of ten years. She is sixty-two years old.

Don't get me wrong, I was passionate and I'm still passionate about what I did. But that responsibility now is somebody else's. I can focus on what I believe to be more important. Let somebody else have this role.

New people coming through to take these roles? It's not there, it really isn't there. I can't see it. They did this presentation for me three weeks ago today. What I said in my speech to all the people who were there—it was mostly seniors— was that although I'm stepping away, I'm praying for a transfusion of young blood who would be passionate in all the aims and objectives that this organisation has got. We've had young people join the board. There's so many people that will come forward but it's always what can they get out of it.

I would say it is very true that there is less a sense of community amongst people who are African Caribbean. I think the more we have acquired over the years, is the more selfish we become. When we first came here, it was still like a village mentality. But whether it's first generation or second generation, as the children have grown up and gone to university they tend not to return back to where they live for whatever reason.

Some have though. Our CEO at the centre is a testimony to that so happening. He went to uni down in London. He came back and he was working with the PCT—the health authority—before he became the CEO here. He's not just the face that people see and speak with. It's not a nine-to-five job, it's a way of life for him. I believe you need to have that mentality and heart for your community to want to do it and do it well.

One reason why Emma decides to step down as chair of the centre is that the role takes up a great deal of her time and her energy. She thinks she has done more than her bit in this respect. There is also another aspect of her life that she wants to devote more attention too—her faith.

Before I got involved with the centre, we'd been Christians for twenty-three years at West Bromwich Baptist. Both of us were baptised there twenty-two and a half years ago. So most of the things that I've have been involved in doing has been with the church and the centre.

The church for me is more than a place of worship. We're not just about the church being there for Sundays. I've been church secretary—the church administrator—for ten years. That is a huge responsibility and it actually goes beyond this. I'm a lay preacher within the church. I decided to become a lay preacher because that's what I feel the Lord calling me to do. Remember I said before: 'One door has to shut before the other door of opportunity will open.' I will be preaching on a Sunday morning for the first time ever in three weeks' time. Until now, it's always been on a Sunday evening.

As Emma says, her church is not there just for Sunday worship. Her church is very active in the local community and this is something that Emma is very proud of.

We had two children's projects. One was called 'The Base' for children of primary age. That folded at the end of 2010 because of lack of funding. Now the person who managed that part-time, he also had a part-time role mentoring youths at the West Indian Centre. So I knew he was doing similar work.

We also have a 'Kids Club' which is not funded by anyone. It's what we put on with a Christian perspective and there's over thirty children that come in on a Friday night. My husband helps to run that. This is for the community but there's an ethos of Christianity with the youth leaders.

Then we have a project which is local-authority-funded call 'You Choose'. It was set up primarily for the young people who were no longer in education or training, or on the verge of exclusion from school. That runs two days a week—Tuesdays and Thursdays—on church premises. My husband is one of the trustees. We recently advertised for a youth worker because the previous manager—he was nearly sixty-seven—stepped down. He'd got health issues.

The church is widely used. The Guides and Brownies, they meet on a Thursday evening. One of the local residents associations have their twice monthly meetings in the building. They put on Community Fun Days and we give them the facilities to do that.

There's another church that have their Sunday afternoon meetings in our church. It turned out last week they'd actually had a convention there but they didn't tell me that it was a convention. They ask somebody else if the building was going to be unoccupied. That caused a bit of a friction because the neighbours have been complaining. If we did know that it was going to be a convention, we would have said no because the length of time involved and the noise of this African church which was really loud.

Anyway, our church is used seven days a week.

Emma's roles as church secretary and chair of the West Indian Centre could be seen as similar, even complimentary.

> I've been in a unique place for a number of years. I now want to go into the Ministry. I've already started to study and I realise that some of my energy was being sapped by my role at the community centre.

In fact, for all its activities in the community, Emma's church is doing no better than the West Indian Centre. Both were established by and around the first generation of African Caribbeans. Both organisations are in decline. Though she concedes that few young people were coming forward to join the management board of the centre, she tries to be a little more positive about the future prospects of her church.

> Forty-one is what's on the membership register. But if all the other people who'd would probably call the church theirs and aren't on the register, it's about seventy-six.
>
> I would say membership is more or less static. It's fell the last two years because we've lost four people. Four people have died. It is an aging congregation. When I and my husband became members—twenty-two years ago—there was only a couple of people younger than me. Yes there are younger people than me there now but there's quite a number that's in their late seventies and eighties. That cuts down on what the church can physically do.
>
> I've been church secretary for the last ten years. The lady before me was church secretary for

twenty-two years. The person before her was church secretary for about ten, maybe twelve years, she is one of the elders now and she lost her husband in April this year—2013. He was the eldest elder, so there is only one other elder and myself.

Don't forget we lost our minister. He moved away to Maidstone in Kent. He came back to preach last Sunday morning because he was down for the weekend at a wedding on the Saturday, so we booked him in to preach on the Sunday. That was good.

It's an aging congregation and we called in a young minister just this last month to help attract the young. He came and preached all day Sunday—morning and evening. Then on the 2nd of July we had a special church meeting where it was a unanimous call for him.

My husband and others had been cleaning up the Vicarage when the previous minister moved out. We were so fortunate. Before I'd got a chance to actually advertise the vacancy, we had a tenant.

While Emma is still serving as chair of the West Indian Centre and church secretary, she and Mathew attend one of the main annual events of their church.

My husband and I went to the Baptist Assembly in Brighton more than seven years ago. That's where I met Pastor Les Isaacs—a Black man from

Antigua—for the first time. He was so concerned with all the 'Black-on-Black' killings, assaults and what have you. He asked: "What is the church doing about this?"

He went to Jamaica to see the policemen as well as ministers in Kingston and asked them how was the church dealing with crime in Jamaica. That's where this idea came up that the church needed to be on the streets. Not out there preaching. The very action should be 'Christ-like', it would be the Gospel in action. That's how the street pastors came about ten or eleven years ago.

When I heard about him and it, street pastors had been going for a few years in parts of Birmingham and London. That was in the early days and I didn't realise then how much my church was actually against it because of the word 'pastor'.

Ministers are in the church, ministers aren't on the streets. That's what the role is, on the streets. A phrase that Les Isaacs uses is that: "Some Christians are too heavenly-minded and not earthly-good." If you are a street pastor you can be heavenly-minded and earthly-good as well.

I felt that this was something the Lord called me into at the assembly convention down in Brighton. I went forward to pray after the seminar on street pastors. That was where the seed was birth in me, but I didn't do anything about it. I was waiting to see if anything was happening in this area—not in Birmingham but in West Bromwich.

Now to get a street pastors project to come together in an official capacity, you need to have a steering group which should have representation of ministers or officers in a church. You need to have at least four churches partnering with the support of the local authority and the police to set the street pastors up. It's called working in Trinity—that's the church, the police and the local authority. Of course, the ambulance service and other agencies also give support.

Our minister said that they were going to have a meeting over at a local church in West Bromwich on street pastoring. It didn't happen. It happened the following year and I went along. I was the only one that went from my church. There were people there from two or three other churches. The people there were Black, white and Asian.

They formed a steering group. I didn't want to be on another steering group, I already had an arm full of them. We officially launched on the 12th April 2010—this is in West Bromwich. We're all volunteers. We grew from very humble beginnings, there was just seven of us. We barely had a team but we've grown. There are about nineteen of us now. There's about five thousand street pastors now all over Great Britain.

You had to go and do a lot of training. The

biggest training you have to do—which lasts a day—is what your roles and responsibilities are as a street pastor. I have been doing this for three years.

When we go out, we have to sign-in first with the police so they know we're out there. They don't need to have the names but they need to know how many of you there are and what time you begin. We're based at my church at the moment. We use to be at another church but they're having some building work done. We patrol the town centre.

In the winter months we know there's places where some people will be sleeping rough. We give them blankets, we give them water. Those who look as if they're the worse for drink and need a bit of sobering up, we even take them back to the church and give them a hot drink, if that's what they need. We try not to give them money. If they're hungry, we will buy them food from shops that are open. The girls that have been wearing high-heel shoes—their feet can get cut on glass or anything—so we give them flips flops.

Though the street pastor initiative is about helping those at risk in the city centre, Emma sees it as part of her Christianity and contributing to helping her community.

Initially, I would go out every two weeks. Now I go out at least once a month. We have two teams.

They go out from ten o'clock in the night until two in the morning—Friday and Saturday nights. There's no fear in me because there are prayer pastors—people who are behind the scene—praying. Ideally they should be in the church but there is only one minister that stays in the church.

We are very well received. Everywhere the street pastors have operated, the crime rate has gone down. We bring a 'peaceful presence' to the streets. You meet more people on the liquor than anything else, but you know that.

You don't work on your own. Even if it's one person that's speaking to an individual, the partner's there—or whoever is patrolling—on the other side of the road. You stop and just observe from a distance because they may need your help. There's things from our training like just taking your hat off to indicate that you need some assistance. This is something I know I would not do if my husband didn't give me full support. How does he support me? He cares for Armstrong. He wouldn't go to bed until I return home.

When I go out on a Friday night I sometimes see some of my relatives, grand-nieces and -nephews. I say: 'Huh! Hope you're enjoying yourself.' One cousin I met—she's about forty-six—I said: "Jackie don't you think it's time you start wearing longer skirts?" She said: "Oh! I didn't expect to see you." I says: "That's why I'm out here. I'm making sure you're safe." She says:

"Oh I am glad."

Then I saw this young man I knew. He says: "Mrs Thompson what you're doing out here—it's dangerous." I says: "Is it dangerous? I'm glad you recognise it's dangerous. That's why I'm out here to make sure you lot are safe."

Though she is concerned that volunteering within the African Caribbean community is dying out, Emma continues to be very positive, and passionate about what she does in her church.

Mathew and her have been married for forty-three years and she's still very positive about that as well.

We're more in love now than we ever were.

IVY

It is 1993 and Ivy is sixty, living on her own in a council flat in Barkingside. Her three children are in their twenties and have left home. Her husband is now in Jamaica.

Ivy is now working as a security officer at Kensington Palace.

> I can't remember exactly when I started. When I
> first started and didn't actually know what to do,
> there was this lady who liked me. She took me in
> her arms—showed me this and that, what to do
> and everything. She kind of trained me up.

Very early on however, things with Ivy's colleague take a strange and dark turn.

> Then all of a sudden she turned against me and
> I didn't know why. We had an argument. I don't
> argue but we had an argument. I went in one day
> and she was there in the staff room with the door
> closed. I went in and I closed the door. She got
> up and said: "No, no, no. I won't have it!" It was
> kind of a shock. So I said: "Have what?" She said:
> "Open the door." I said: "But you was in here

with the door shut. Why do you want the door open?" She said: "I'm not staying in here with you with the door closed." I said: "What? You smell me? I have a shower every morning, so if you're smelling anything it's yourself, not me."

She started going off saying you people come in here and this and that. I said: "Listen, I don't argue, I don't quarrel and I don't fight. But if you bother me, I'll just catch you by your hair and duck your head in the toilet. So leave me alone." I think she got scared when she heard that. I don't know what happen to make her change.

I was the only Black person working there, so everybody makes much of me. I was like an idol. I am welcomed in the family. All of a sudden she changes and that was it. She never spoke to me again until she left there. I was still there.

Ivy recalls another run-in she had with a separate colleague.

I had another run-in with one of the supervisors who told me: "You're not suppose to leave the position you're working in unless somebody comes to relieve you." This was a Sunday. People were in the garden and they were not allowed to be in the garden. So I used my two-way radio to call for somebody to go there and get them out.

Then the supervisor came down and started cursing and swearing at me, that I should go and get them out of there. The room was full of people on a Sunday evening. I said: "But you told me I'm not suppose to leave where I'm working unless somebody come to relieve me. There was no one to relieve me so I called on the radio for someone to look after it." He swear and he cussed. I was so ashamed, I burst into tears and I went downstairs. I didn't say anything to him that evening because when I'm like that I can be rude. I never fear people anyway, I could stand up to anybody. I didn't say anything to him that evening and I went home.

The following day I went to work. I went to his office and I told him: "You spoke out of turn to me yesterday. Ever since I'm here, I respect you and I show respect to everybody. Because of that I expect people to respect me as well." So he said: "What do you want me to do? Do you want to take me upstairs?" I said: "No need for that. I just want us to understand each other. You treat me the way I treat you."

That was it. We became the best of friends. Once I wanted a day off and I said to him: "I'm having Monday off, I won't be here." He said: "You'll have to take it as holiday." I said: "No it's not holiday. I'm going out." He said: "Sick leave?" I said: "No I'm not sick, I'm going out. I have business to do and I have to get time off." He said: "Well you will lose pay for it." I said: "I don't mind. I'm not going to lie to say I'm sick or anything else to get pay." If he say I can't have

it, I'm going take my day off and I'll get my pay.
I don't know what he writes there but I've never
lost a day's pay.

I was there until I retired.

**

When Ivy's mother, Estell, first came to England sometime in
1977, Ivy was anxious to stop her putting pressure on Ivy's three
children to succeed at school. Ivy remembered that Estell would
punish her for not completing her schoolwork when she was
young. It did not work for her and at the time, she was certain
that it would not work for her children. On reflection she's not
entirely sure.

> I think I let them go too far, not insisting on too
> much study. They had the brains to—especially
> Charles. He went away to do computer training
> in Bristol or somewhere. Then he would go away
> to work in Germany, Ireland, Holland—all over.
> He was doing very well for himself.
>
> Then he went on to be a chef which is what he's
> doing now. He's like that big! I don't know why
> he changed profession. I teach them to cook when
> they were younger. I wasn't very well myself and
> I teach them at an early age—six and seven—to
> cook, wash, clean up the place and do everything.
>
> Charles was lazy, didn't want to do much. So
> I reckon he just loved cooking and wanted to
> change. I did never ask him really. He used to

love cooking. All of a sudden he just went into it. Went to night school, did a course in cooking and then started working in hotels and restaurants.

He is an accomplished cook. On my eightieth birthday he came and he help me to cook. There would not have been a birthday dinner if they didn't let me cook. I did all the chicken and the curry. He does the salad and all that. It's funny— even my kids, if they come for dinner and eat and they want to wash my dishes—I chase them out my kitchen. Nobody goes in my kitchen to do anything. I used to tell them: 'Get out of my kitchen'.

Then I broke a bone in my foot and I wasn't able to walk. I was in cask from my toe up to my knee and Charlie would come and cook. He was here for days, then when he left, Daniel came and took over. Simone couldn't because she had Darrell. At Christmas, Daniel was in my kitchen and he was going like: "Santa Claus: Ho! Ho! Ho! Mom guess what? I'm in your kitchen and there's nothing you can do about it."

Charlie has two children. He is happy with his two girls and don't want any more kids.

Despite having a mental breakdown in her late teens, Ivy thinks her first child, Simone did relatively well. However, once Simone reaches thirty, things change for her.

Then she went and got herself pregnant and had

a disabled child who is severely autistic. He's sixteen and he doesn't eat food. Everything has to be liquidised and he's fed with a syringe. He doesn't speak and still wears nappies, so he goes to a special school at the moment and she has a full-time job in her hands looking after him. She doesn't work. She does voluntary work with the police at the moment. She does two days a week with the police. She got an award last year for her voluntary work.

Charlie lives in Leytonstone and Simone lives in Forest Gate—just close by. Leytonstone borders with Forest Gate. It's just a walk from one of them to the other.

Ivy's other son, Daniel, who was good as fixing things as a child, is now living in Godstone, Surrey.

He's got a house there and he has four children— two boys with his first wife and two girls with his second wife.

I've got seven grandchildren—four girls and three boys.

When it comes to keeping in contact with her family in Jamaica, however, Ivy is not moved to do so.

I am not aware of any of my family left in Jamaica. My father's family is a big family that lives in Evergreen District but I don't know them. The older ones that I should know, they've all died off. The ones that comes after, I don't know.

I don't think Jamaica is home for me because my grandmother died, my father died, and my Aunty died. All the older aunties and uncles that I knew when I was growing up, they all died out. Even my mother's nephews and nieces, I don't know them. They all moved out to different places and I don't know them. So I can't really call it home.

I don't go back often. The last time I went back was in 1970 to see my mum. I should have gone back this year—on the 18th of May 2013. My friend was getting married and he invited me. That's the family where we had the flat in Chadwell Heath but I couldn't travel. I'm having ear problems and I didn't want to go in a plane. The doctor said it would make my ear worse.

Ivy's husband, Wesley, is still in Jamaica and they keep in touch.

Wesley is still in Jamaica but he's in St. Ann's, not in Manchester where I come from. He knows my family in Evergreen. He goes there to visit them and goes to church down there all the time. He'll phone or write and tell me about this one and that one, but I don't really know them.

Surprisingly, one of the few people Ivy chooses to keep in contact with and support before he dies was her father, Jamsey.

The man who sexually assaulted her in her youth.

> When I was working, I sent money to my dad and he built a two-bedroom house there. I owned that house. I've never seen it and I don't want to see it. I just don't feel comfortable there.
>
> The house is still there. I don't know if anyone is living in it. I suppose people would live in it. If they haven't got anywhere to live and there's a house there, they would go live in it. But nobody I know goes there. My brother went down there when my Daddy died. My dad was living in it. Once he built it, he went to live in it and then he died. My brother went down there and buried my dad then lock up the house and left. But we don't think it's a lock-up. This is years ago.

Ivy decides to forgive her father for what he did to her.

> I also forgive my dad because I think he's an idiot. He died before I could tell him I forgive him.

Though they are writing to each other, Ivy's relationship with Wesley in Jamaica does not improve.

> When my husband left and I realise I'm going to be on my own, I vowed that I am going to make it—I have to make it. I'm not going to walk the street and I'm not going to beg anybody anything. With that determination in me, I just get on with

my life.

I never think of divorcing him. I'm still officially married to him but it's just in name.

At this time Ivy still does not know why Wesley left the family home.

Twenty odd years we've been separated and I didn't know the reason why. Maybe just a few years ago I found out.

He came here in my spare room after my mother died. He came up on holiday, this was about three years ago. He's got a bad knee and he couldn't go up any stairs. I live on one floor. He's got many, many relatives around here in London that he used to stay with. But when he got bad knees—arthritis and that—he can't go up and downstairs. So he asked if he could come and stay in my spare room. I said: "Ok, you can."

We were talking one day and I said to him: "Why did you leave? We never had an argument, we never quarreled." If anything doesn't please him, he would sulk. Then I would say I'm sorry—not even know what I'm 'sorrying' about—just to have peace and quiet in my life. That went on for a long time.

So I said: "Why did you leave?" He said that: "Teresa's husband use to tidy the place on a Saturday—vacuum and clean the place and that they expect him to do the same." I said: "Did they say that to you?" He said: "No." So I said: "Why did you think that?" He said: "Because Teresa's husband was doing it and he was doing it every week." I said: "...and that makes you feel guilty?" He said: "Well I suppose." I said: "Why didn't you say that? Why did you just get up and leave?" He didn't want to say anything to that. So a silly reason for him to leave—leaving his wife behind. But that was it.

As a teenager in Jamaica, Ivy found the will to defy the advances of her father through the church. Though in a different denomination, Ivy's commitment to her faith continues.

My husband was a Pentecostal and eventually when we got married I changed to the Pentecostal church. When I came here I went to church regularly from the beginning because my friend, she went to church—both wife and husband go to church.

I became a Sunday School teacher. This was from before I left Jamaica. When I came up here and they knew I used to teach children, they gave me a class to teach and it was the worst class. Nobody wanted to teach those kids and I got them.

One little boy he was so bad—he bit me. I bit him back and he said he was going to tell his mum that I bite him. So I said: "Yeah? Go tell your mum! I'll tell her why I had to because you bit me first and I had to show you that it hurts." He said to me: "Please don't tell my mum." I realised that he was only being bad on the outside and not on the inside—so I had that over him. Every time he start to do something I would say: "I'll just tell your mummy after Sunday School." He would beg me not to. I got to do that with all the other kids and they became the best Sunday School class in the church.

I still go to church now. There's a care team in the church and I'm part of that team that take care of people. There are some young teenagers having kids. We're there to support them. We phone them and talk to them, visit them and take them out for a meal—anything we can do to help.

There is somebody looking after the older people. They meet up once a month and we all get together for fellowship. We eat, talk, give testimonies, share experiences and encourage each other.

My church is getting stronger. I think they have over three hundred people. I don't know everybody that's there because it's so big. It's got different sections: one on the right, one on the left, one in the middle, then there's upstairs. On a Sunday, upstairs and downstairs, its choc-o-block. I don't know if I will ever get to know everybody there but most of them know me.

Ivy also takes an active interest in her local community.

I was doing voluntary work at Age Concern at their kitchen. I used to go in on a Wednesday to the canteen. They cook for older people and I use to go there and the cook always tells me she goes to a church in Forest Gate. The first time I went there and she saw people were coming hugging and kissing me, she came to me and she said: "Are you royalty?" I said: "No! I know these people." Some of them used to go to my church then left to go to different places—so they were happy to see me. I've looked after some of their kids from they were babies.

I also use to do voluntary work with 'Victims of Crime'. Even when I was at work I would come home in the evenings and go visiting. On my days off I would go and work for them. I did that for fifteen years.

When my Mother took sick I had to give it up. My Mother needed full-time care and I couldn't leave her to go visit other people. Now I just do one day a week.

Because people haven't jobs now, they go volunteering. It looks nice on their CV. People like to work and get money—being paid—for what they're doing. I love to work with people but not for money. I give my service to anybody who needs it, like mothers who want to leave their children and go on holiday. I go and stay with the kids, see them in and out of school and all that.

I'm still doing things like that even now. I like

to be of service to people. I had a hard time when I wasn't able to move about and people coming to do something for me. I didn't want them to come and do anything.

Reflecting back on her life, Ivy regrets not being able to achieve the goals she had in mind when first coming to England.

I tried doing the thing that I wanted to do but I never accomplished it. I never see it out to the end. I wanted to do dressmaking and dress designing but I couldn't be bothered because the teacher didn't know enough to teach me—so I didn't go back.

When I came here I wanted to do so much. I always wanted to be somebody. Not somebody big and famous but somebody caring for people who doesn't have anybody to care for them—like kids on the street. I wanted to have a big house and collect all the stray kids and look after them. I wanted to open a home for children on the street.

I haven't reached there and I don't think I will.

IRENE

In 1996 Irene goes off on her Christian mission trip to The Gambia. This was instead of her annual holiday with one of her friends. Convinced it was God calling her to do missionary work, she returned to The Gambia two years later. She is now on the lookout for further opportunities to do similar work.

Next I went to Grenada with the New Testament Church of God—not my church—after they had the hurricane. I think it was Hurricane Ivan in 2004. My lifestyle was quite good and I think this was again the Lord saying: 'You need to get you down to earth, get a bit more reality in your life.'

My friend, Phyllis, who's from the New Testament Church of God, said: "Irene we've got a group in London who are going to Grenada. Would that fit in with you?" I said: "Yeah, give me the contact." The group was led by Les Isaacs—I think he got an OBE last year. He got the vision about going out to Grenada. My Pastor had to do a reference and I went to meet the group. About twenty of us went. We were all from different churches—different people who wanted to do something.

"We brought a container full of stuff. In each area we went to we would distribute clothes, shoes, soap and other things from church halls. It was like a big fashion store in the church. We were preaching and teaching as well—we would have mission meetings with loudspeakers outside the church. I spoke at some of those. We were there to help and to preach the name of Jesus to say the Lord can change your life if you give your heart to him.

I always feel I'd like to leave a mark. When I go, I'd like to think they know Irene was here. I like to feel I've done something. It's this thing about wondering if I've done my best. If I can help somebody as I go along then my living will not be in vain. That's my mentality. I've got to do something to leave a mark.

Though God is a key driving force in her charity and missionary work—her motivation is also because of another reason.

I haven't got any children and I didn't want to adopt. I didn't want to do any of that but I feel I want to give some of my skills and some of my knowledge to help build a better society.

Dating back to her first post at Selly Oak Hospital, Irene considered what she regarded as an exceptionally long delay in her eventual promotion to senior pharmacist as evidence of racism within the NHS. She later found out that she was one of the first students in her college group—most of whom were white—to be promoted to a senior post. Nevertheless, based on the experience of the Black staff around her, she is concerned that racism still persists within the NHS.

I was a trade union shop steward at work. It started off when I was at the Queen Elizabeth Hospital in Birmingham. I was quite an active union steward for the pharmacy but some of the nurses on the wards would come to see me as well if they had problems they wanted sorting out. From that, I joined the Unison Black Members' Group. At one stage I was chair for the local Birmingham Black Members Group, then I was appointed to the Unison National Black Members Board.

This was a political time in my life. It was mainly about discrimination at work because of the colour of people's skin. Some nurses would be working for ages and not get to the higher ranks. Even when they were qualified for the job, their face didn't fit. They had the ability but the colour of their skin wasn't right. It was about fighting cases like that, trying to push forward on some of those issues. Immigration was also a big issue back then—asylum seekers, people coming in and being abused.

It wasn't easy to change views in Unison. At one stage people didn't want us to have a Black Members Group. They said: "Why do you need it?" We said: "Why do you have a Gay Group? Why do you have a Women's Group?" So we had to fight to get a Black Members Group because of people saying: "We're all one in Unison. Why do you need a Black Members Group?" We said it was because we need to talk about the issues for Black members just like we do for women and gay members.

Her commitment to these external organisations result in time being taken away from her paid job. It is not long before questions are being asked.

I would have to go to a lot of meetings in London. We use to have local group meetings in Birmingham and then once a year we'd have a National Black Members Group in different parts of England.

They had to give me time off at work and after a while my boss at the pharmacy was saying: "This is getting a little bit too much." So I started to cut down.

I do keep up-to-date with what's going on. I think a Black woman is quite high up in Unison now—on the executive board. There were no Black people on the executive board when I was active which was quite interesting. This is a big union and not one Black person. I think last year—or maybe this year—one Black person has made the executive board which is a big thing.

There were times when I went to Black Unison board members' meetings when I felt: 'Oh, I think we're moving.' But sometimes I feel that we were doing twenty steps forward and then—after a while—it was thirty steps backward.

One of the good things about Unison is their partnership with Vauxhall—I use to get quite a discount on my car. There were some good bits about the union but with me being a manager, Unison has not been that much of a friend to me. I've seen the other side of the union, for instance when they were acting for people at stage-three sickness, which is just before dismissal. So it's like them acting for one member against another who was a union steward.

After a while—with church and everything—I was just juggling too many things. Work was also saying I need to cut down.

For Irene, however, her church is very important.

My church is Shiloh Apostolic Church. It's an all-Black Evangelist church, mostly African Caribbean, no Africans as yet. There are a lot of African churches in Birmingham. We did have some white Sunday School children come in which really pleased me because I don't really like belonging to an all-Black church. I like a multi-racial church. That's my vision of heaven—multi-racial.

I've been in that church twenty-eight years now. It's doing alright. Church funds are good. We believe in tithes but we're not a church that talk a lot about money—people just give. We own our church building and we're trying to register as a charity. At church we're very businesslike on the management committee. I'm on the management committee. We have to be quorate, take minutes and everything. All those principles I've pushed for based on my experience of committee structures and procedures on Unison's National Black Members Board.

The congregation is about a hundred who would attend. Membership might be about seventy, eighty. It's pretty static—some come, some leave. The congregation is aging but we have a good structure of young people. To me, any church that's not got young people, they're going down. We've got about twenty-five young people which is good because you have to pass the baton on. However, our congregation is aging, we are aware that less income is coming in. Financially we're managing OK but we're looking at strategies to meet that at the moment. We've got a very large area which we're going to rent out to the community. It's a big hall and we're just doing that up. There's a lot of potential.

Church for Irene is all day Sunday. It is also evenings in the week. Irene, in addition to being a member of the Management

Committee also has other roles.

> I did twenty-five years as the youth president and before that I was doing youth and community work. I love working with young people. Not having any children of my own, I like to feel I'm sharing what gifts I have but I was getting a bit too old.
>
> I then became the Ladies' President. I'm an ordained Evangelist and I'm vice-chair for the management committee for the church—Pastor is the chair.
>
> I did belong to the Council of Black-Led Churches as well for a while. I just couldn't juggle that either. They would have Prayer Breakfast with different speakers on different themes and subjects. They'd do like a West Indian breakfast which was held at different churches. That was just my own interest, that wasn't my church. I went to a group and it was like a leadership group of all the Black leaders meeting together. I always believe—I said this at church as well—I don't believe heaven is going to be just for Black people and I am a very multi-racial person and even inter-denominational. Although it was a Council of Black-Led Churches, we had white ministers from Birmingham Pentecostals that was coming as well.

Despite realising and being told that she is massively

overcommitted, Irene sees no need to give up her missionary
work.

> Now and again I think I heard the Lord saying:
> 'It's time to go on mission again.' I didn't know
> where to go. I kept getting different leaflets
> through the post and this one—which was about
> working with young disadvantaged children in
> the Ukraine—really grab me. It was from the
> Mercy Project.
>
> I didn't know anything about the Ukraine so
> I sent off the leaflet to ask them a little bit more
> about it. I don't know if this happen to you—
> when you start something, everything starts to
> happen around it. I'd read in *The Voice* newspaper
> about this Black model who was African. She was
> in living in London but she was talking about her
> past, her time in the Ukraine and all the racists.
> She left. Then I heard them talking about the
> Ukraine on TV, how racist it was. I'm thinking:
> 'Gosh God! You've got a funny sense of humour.
> These people don't like Black people. You certainly
> don't want me to go to the Ukraine, do you?' He
> did. That's where he wanted me to go.

Convinced it's the Lord's will, Ivy gets in touch with the Mercy
Project.

> To cut a long story short they sent me all the
> details. The Mercy Project was a Christian group

attached to an Evangelical church in Chester—a bit like a healing church. I had to go all the way to Chester to meet up with the rest of the group. Before I met them, they said they'd never had anybody from outside Chester who had actually gone on a mission trip with them. I was not in their little circle and that was challenging for them. They thought it was fascinating how I decided that I wanted to go and they asked for a reference from my pastor. That always happens.

I told my church about it and they said they would pray as well. My pastor gave me a reference. I paid with my own funds but—you know—I always say: "If God gives you a vision—God will provide." So I never have a problem with that.

I had to fill out an application form and say why I wanted to go. Part of that was the reference from my pastor. I stressed that I'd done mission trips before and that I'd done a great deal of work with disadvantaged children.

Once they decided and before we went to the Ukraine, I went to three meetings in Chester for us to plan how we're going to work. I think the mission was for up to two or weeks and—of course—you have to 'gel' as well. It was people coming from America—doctors and all different professions coming together to work on the project. Altogether there was fifteen of us went. There were eight women and the rest were men.

They were middle-class white people. I was

the only Black person but I'm use to that in pharmacy—so that was nothing new. You know, they were just as apprehensive as I was because although we'd met, we now had to live together. They were easy with me—no problem. I got pictures of the group I can show you.

Irene remembers her time in Ukraine clearly.

The children in Ukraine who've got Down's syndrome or things like that, the government don't look after them or provide for them. They don't go to school. As you know, it's a very poor country. It's alright reading about these things but when you're there in Ukraine and see what the country is like—it's different.

There were two women over there who are part of the Mercy Project centre. They run the centre and when we're not there it's like a school.

They have a team of people there—some of them are the mothers who cooked for us. You would get like a heavy breakfast—cabbage. You have to put all that aside and get use to the food, it's very different. You can't go with all your: 'Oh I don't eat this and I don't eat that.'

The Mercy Project is in England and America as well. They have winter and summer camps. Although it's called a camp, it's more like a hostel with limited facilities. For the women we had three single beds in each room and then the men had their beds in other rooms. Luckily I was with the older women because you have some younger girls as well who stay up till late playing and stuff. There's one shower, so we have to have a rota for the fifteen of us to share the shower.

The children come in from outside each day—they're bussed in. During the day there's about fifty-odd of us sharing two toilets. It's really is very, very basic. There are no inhibitions—you just get on with it. It was great!

We have a structured programme—from ten o'clock till five o'clock every day for ten days. We would do football and different things with the kids. I was good at Drama at school so that's the area I got to take. I had to meet with the group for us to plan some of what we were going to do before we went to the Ukraine. I got some tapes—and I did try to do a bit of Ukrainian before I went—but we had interpreters. After activities we would go on visits to different places, like museums. They were so grateful to us.

Of course, the children all looked at my skin and made sure it didn't rub off because they're not use to seeing Black people. That worried me a bit. There was a young boy—Andre—who couldn't speak very well. Some of our people who had been before knew him. Apparently he was always around and didn't settle or sit down in class—all he wanted to do is play football. This boy attached himself to me, he tagged on to me. Though he didn't like being in class for that whole week we would do masks, face paints, all sort of different things. Andre made bangles and different things. We went kayaking. We went to the beach.

I got on with some of the other mothers as well. I'd never met these people but we got on. They'd take us out in the evenings after work for food and to do different things. It was good.

At the end of our mission they had a big dinner for us and Andre's mother cried. She said: "Irene, God sent you here. All the years we've been coming to this project my son has never settled down. All he wants to do is to play football. You got him to work. Nobody could get him to do anything else but football. The things he was making and coming home saying 'Momma, Momma!' How did you do it?" She started crying, then we all started crying. Well I thought: 'Thank you God.' She was so grateful, she bought me a present. It was nice but I knew what it meant: that was God. When I came back I said to the church: "If it was for that one boy—fantastic."

The project is about fun, games and learning activities for disadvantaged children but it's also about preaching the Gospel of Jesus Christ. They give you some paperwork beforehand and Bible stories for you to do.

When I came back I went to work straight away and my boss says to me: "Irene you haven't got any energy. You should have taken some time off when you came back." I said: "I didn't realise how much it took out of me. I think you're right."

Irene's mission to the Ukraine was in August 2011. Despite the Spartan living conditions she describes at the Mercy Camp and the barriers of language and race, Irene goes back a year later.

The first year I didn't know what to expect. In the second year it was the same group. They actually wrote me a letter, rang me and said: "We would like you to come because you got on so well. Are you able to come? We would like you to come again."

I'd say the first year was better—it was like stepping out on water. The first year I was on the outside, just assisting people because I'd never been before. The second year I knew what to expect but knowing my skills they said can you organise this, can you do that? They got me to do much more. I was doing more teaching and various things which took a lot of energy.

Each day I had to do a session where—with an interpreter—I had to talk to the kids and give them a sketch of whatever our programme was for the day. I had to organise that with team members and delegate work as well. That was a little bit more taxing. I was able to do it, so that was good.

Irene recalls her experience being the only Black person in the camp.

The only incident involving the colour of my skin occurred in the first year. The second year I was the only Black person there again. I'd seen the kids the first year. In the second year there were so many more kids—about sixty.

We didn't have lunch at the project—we went down to a village hall to have soup, bread and goulash or whatever it was. We'd walk down from the centre to the village hall just down the road. The children would go to their favourites, so I had all these kids holding my hand. I felt so good. The first year it was the colour of my skin—they weren't sure. The second year they got over that— it was just genuine love: "Ira, Ira!" That's what they called me. "Can I walk with you Ira?" That was so good.

Andre, he didn't go round with me so much the second time. I did try my best but you get a certain age group. We worked all that out in England, what age group you're going to be doing. My age group had changed but he still followed me around. We went to his mom's house—she invited all of us.

The benefit to the kids is that they come into the camp for whatever period and then they learn from different people. It's through the Gospel but they actually make stuff that they can take home. They make bangles and loads of other things that they can take home. The parents come in and help with the group, especially those that can speak a bit of English. We sing songs, some in Russian and some in English. It's challenging their skills—especially when we sing in English.

These are the kids who are thought to be 'nobodies' in the Ukraine. They have got no time for them. If they're got a disability the government doesn't look after them at all. It lets them stay home and their parents look after them.

We did get to see more of the Ukraine outside of camp in the evenings. They took us out on the bus to museums and different places. We went to the river and had a picnic there. Someone invited us to their house which was quite far away. They use to adopt children and they'd got a farm. When we were finished for the day they made us a meal.

The weather—like Jamaica—it's boiling hot. Thirty-eight, even forty degrees when you go in August so there was a lot of barbecues to sort of wind down a bit. Then on the last night we have a big cook-up. The parents cook dinner and all the kids put on a show of what they've learnt. They buy us presents as a surprise. They sing, act, mime, dance—they put on a special show for us. That's quite hard—they're crying and we're crying.

I didn't go this year in 2013. All being well—God willing—I will go back next year. I never pick the places to go on mission myself. I always say: "If it's the Lord's will, everything just fits into place." It wasn't cheap to go to the Ukraine—it's £750 inclusive. To get their fares some of the people in Chester do sponsored walks and different things. My church did gave me £100 towards it. I didn't ask for what they gave me. I was on a good salary—I don't have to depend on the church. Whatever money my church gave me, I gave some to the Mercy Centre because I could see the work they were doing.

I haven't maintained telephone contacts with the people I went to the Ukraine with. I still get letters from them. I warned them last year that I was planning to go on a school reunion this year and I wouldn't be there. So, of course, they didn't send me any information about coming to Chester.

As might be expected Irene's school reunion is with her tight circle of friends. They take their girls trip to Jamacia in 2013.

It was at a hotel in Ocho Rios, Jamaica. There were about ten of us who all went to Handsworth Wood Girls School and were in the same form. We were going back to our school days. People came from America, Canada, England and other countries. All of us were in professional occupations, celebrating our sixtieth birthdays.

Though their schooldays are now nearly four and a half decades behind them, remarkably small teenage niggles persist.

Some of the group were in different forms at

school. Two of them were actually fifty-niners—
they sneaked in. I don't remember them. I
remember their faces because I was a prefect but
they were fifty-niners—the rest of us were sixty.
This one 'girl'—she was a fifty-niner—said to me:
"Irene, I remember you. I remember you never
like chips at school and you use to give me all your
chips. I just want to say thank you very much." I
said: "I don't remember giving you any chips!"

Fortunately, it is the sense of celebration that dominates the
reunion. They are all women, all born in Jamaica, all in professional occupations celebrating life in a hotel resort in Jamaica.

It was very emotional, very beautiful, very
touching. We had a bookmark made and T-shirts.
Somebody made a cake with the school colours
and put all our professions on it. We gave gifts
out to each other.

It was very organised. We wrote profiles about
how our lives had gone, so we ended up having
to give a little talk about ourselves. Some had got
married, some divorced, some were grandparents.

In all the profiles that was read out at our
reunion in Jamaica, nobody had left school
knowing what they wanted to do. I said I was
unsure of my career path. All of us more or less
said that we were unsure. None of us could be
specific. We all went on to further education and
then decided yes, this is what I want to do. It's

fantastic when we all talked about it. The teachers at school were always telling us the sky's the limit. We've all done very well. It just shows what happens when you get that sort of motivation. One of the girls said to me: "Irene, I thought you'd have been a lawyer. You were always talking and doing debates." Some people when they presented their profiles said they've done a couple of things and have changed professions. It was quite interesting. It felt like I was still at work because we had to do a presentation of our profiles.

Whilst this gathering is for a specified event, it allows the women to see what is happening with their home country of Jamaica.

We all stayed at the 'Club Rio' hotel in Ocho Rios. This was all-inclusive. You're talking about a massive hotel—eight hundred odd rooms with about ten restaurants—beautiful. You can eat as much as you like—ackee and salt fish. I put weight on with the amount of food you could eat. I thought: 'Yes, this is the right place to have our reunion.' I booked my hotel room at a travel agent in Perry Barr which is just a walk down from here. The person taking the booking was a Black girl and she said to me: "I'll get you a nice room with a sea view."

You know why I was proud of it? The hotel is Spanish-owned but all the people who work there are Jamaicans. There were Jamaicans at the front desk and even at a high managerial level. You know sometimes Jamaicans can have a nah, nah, nah attitude problem. One of the days I saw somebody complaining about a dirty glass and I heard the waitress answer back: "OK madam, I'll change it for you." That impressed me. Because of their behaviour, staff at the hotel ended up with loads of tips.

I called one of them over and I said: "Where have you been trained?" She said: "They train us in Discovery Bay." I said: "I've seen how staff here behave—not just you but others. I'm impressed, I've seen no attitude. I really expected to see attitude." She said: "Oh no ma'am, the customer is always right." I said: "You're doing Jamaica proud." I said to my friend Phyllis: "I'm proud of the Spanish here because in the Asian restaurants they only have their own. They all sell Black food but you never see a Black person employed in there restaurants. It's all their family."

When I came back I popped into the travel agent in Perry Barr to thank the girl who booked my room. I showed her pictures of our reunion. She said: "That's my cousin! That's Mavis my cousin." I said: "Yes, her name is Mavis. We went to school together." Then I showed her a picture of all of us on the balcony of a house. She screamed out: "That's my mother's house! You were at my house. That's my parents' house." I explained that because of the hotel's health and safety policy we couldn't have a cake with lighted candles in our rooms and Mavis said: "My cousin live just ten minutes away—we'll go there." Looking at the photo of us at the house, the girl at the travel agent's said: "That's my mum!" She got on the phone and she rang her mum in Jamaica: "Irene has just told me she came to your house."

I just went in to thank her and show her some photographs. I didn't realise that she knew all these people. Small world."

***

Upon Irene's arrival to the UK from her school reunion in Jamaica, she finds that nothing about her job is getting any easier.

I was at High Croft in Erdington. They built a brand new Queen Elizabeth Hospital and dismantled our unit, so they built a new pharmacy in Erdington. I've been there for five years—from 2008.

High Croft was my biggest challenge because I never had that amount of staff to deal with. It's a big pharmacy and pharmacy was changing again. To maintain the money we got from government we had to outsource—go 'private' on some of our functions. So we've now got two pharmacies in one big complex: inpatients and outpatients. The outpatients is kind of private. If we worked like a chemist, we'd get a lot of money back from the government. This is all new strategy. It was just too much. You had to do staff rotas for 'in' and rotas for 'out' patients.

Irene finds the difficulties within her job continue the longer she stays.

It's a totally new way of working in pharmacy. In hospital we're not use to working like that. It's really quite challenging. If staff were sick and got to a stage three—which meant possible dismissal—HR and everybody got involved.

Four months ago somebody could have got the sack. In the old days—when I was at the QE—I could use my discretion. Staff would come into my office to talk. When I'm dealing with them I know their background—I'd know if they've got a partner who's alcoholic or a bereavement. I'd know the reason for their absence and could use my discretion as a manager not to write it down as stage one or stage two sick leave. I would manage with compassion. It's very difficult now. You can't use your manager's discretion because HR—'Big Brother'—is watching every move you make.

I was going to stay till I was sixty-three—that was my initial plan. Then I thought about all the changes. I didn't even realise it but when I sat down and began to work it out, I'd done forty years. I decided to retire. High Croft was my final posting. I finished as dispensary manager. That's where I retired from.

MELISSA

Melissa has just moved into her own house in Godgold Road following the recent death of her husband Dennis. It is 1997. She was forty-four when they married in October 1992, he was sixty-two.

Melissa's daughter Cantrice's attachment to her now dead stepfather continues long after his death.

Even Sunday gone, Cantrice came here to pick up some things I had for her in the fridge. I was saying something to her. She says: "Ooh my 'dad' use to be so lovely. I can still remember when we use to go down to York Road when Dennis come back from Norway."

There's a place down off Baker Street—York Road—they're holiday rental flats. He would rent one and if he stay for three weeks, him, myself and Cantrice would stay there. Oh, Cantrice use to love it—she use to love it. They are very lavish flats. So this is what Cantrice is remembering. She said: "Oh, did you remember when we use to go down to that place at Baker Street and stay in those flats? I remember that Christmas when

we had Christmas pudding and all the trimmings
and everything."

Melissa continues to make it clear she does not want to talk
about her *other* daughter Jean. She does, however, describe her.

> She's a little outlandish. Very often when people
> don't listen, you just leave them to their own
> devices. Now she's realising that she's kind of
> damaged herself a lot.
>
> There are bad seeds which I want to forget.
> God's making changes and because of that I'm not
> going to dwell on that bit. But she's now come
> round to the fact that there's a God and she's
> making amends but her health is damaged. There
> you are, that's part of it. When people think that
> they know more than you, you leave them to their
> devices. If you advise someone and they don't take
> your advice—what can you do? She went down a
> road that I would never want to see a woman go
> down again. But God is good, God is great.

Jean would be around twenty-three or twenty-four in 1997 and
Cantrice is fourteen.

It appears that Melissa is not getting on with Jean. She is
a great deal more positive about how her daughter Cantrice is
turning out.

> For one reason or another she did very well in
> school. She went to university and got 2:1 in

Law. She started working with a law firm to get experience. Then she was to go and do her Legal Practise at Westminster University. When she made all the enquiries it was about twelve thousand a year in fees. To be honest, I didn't have the twelve thousand and she didn't. So I said: "You know something, you've got one loan already from the other university which you're paying for, why go and take another one? The LPC [Law Practise Council] wouldn't give you a loan. You know Accounting goes very well with Law, go and do Accounting."

She did Accounting for a year and got her ACCA [Association of Chartered Certified Accountants]. Now she's working as an accountant with a background of the Law. She's doing very well. She lives in Woolwich. She's got a two-bedroom flat—one of those modern flats. When I want a glass of water I have to ask: "Where's your fridge?" She says: "It's there." I'm looking and I can't see no fridge because everything is built-in.

After some time, Melissa uncovers an issue with the property she bought in Jamaica when she was there for her mother's illness. Whilst there, advised by her close friend Carl Millet—and with a loan from Lloyds Banks in England—Melissa decided to buy a property in Ironsure. The owner of the property was a Chinese man moving to America.

The house is beautiful, equipped with a swimming pool and a maid's quarter. Like the previous owner, Melissa intended to rent the property out to people on holiday from England, America and Canada. She gives the responsibility of managing the property in the hands of a local estate agent, Mr Daly. To Melissa's dismay, she discovers that Mr Daly is unreliable and dishonest.

He took my money and told me it was an American who rented the house and went away without paying. One day I rang the Chinese man who I had bought the property from now living in America. When he went to America he was working in a hotel because I was paying him his money from here. He was a manager at the hotel there. He says: "Look Melissa, I paid Mr Daly in advance in US dollars."

Mr Daly eventually got himself a hotel—the Woodford Court Hotel. I thought: 'Oh, my money help him to get that hotel.'

But I've got another cousin and I left her husband to sort it out for me. I thought: 'Alright let me ask my cousin and her husband Floyd to manage the property.' Floyd used to work for Jamaica public Works—a very brilliant guy he was. I remember when I was going to school in Jamaica, he was my classmate. We grew up together and I thought let him and my cousin run the place for me.

When I did bookings here I use to keep a diary. I still have it, I haven't thrown it out. Most of the time I send the money to Jamaica so that the people are being treated properly. I wanted the staff to be paid, the place to be cleaned and in shipshape.

My dear, I open an account with him when I was handing over the place to him. That was when I came back from Nigeria in 1980. I open the account in 1980 at Workers Bank—now called RBTI—with £100 sterling.

In 2006 I went out to Jamaica. It was the same £100 in the bank account. Floyd was getting people in every week. He would also rent the place out for weddings.

The same year, Melissa finds out some life changing news regarding her health.

When I went out to Jamaica in 2006, I had a brain tumor. I had an operation in England to remove the tumor. I went to Jamaica to recuperate.

Floyd had the house from 1980—managing it. When I saw my house in 2006, I burst into tears. When you go round to where the swimming pool is, the tiles are lifting up. I had a car poach at the front of the house, it was made of wood and all the posts are falling down. Sometimes Floyd would receive a thousand US dollars a week rental for the house. You know what Floyd did?

When I went out there 2006, Floyd was building another two storey's onto his own house. My house was falling apart and that was where the money was made. He had a son who's in America—he got a PhD. His school fees was paid for in US dollars. That's where the dollars came from to pay for Bruce's education. Not even another penny was there in my account in 2006, yet my place was falling down.

Melissa tired of being ripped off, decides to take decisive action.

I thought: 'Alright, this is it! I'm not arguing and I'm not quarrelling.' I came back to England and I put the house up for sale. I saw a guy here who I know. He says: "Are you selling the house in Jamaica?" Me say: "You seriously want it?' He say: "Yeah man." He'd stayed there before.

The guy bought the house. He says: "Look what I will do, I will make sure that I give you your money. How much do you want for it?" I told him. He said: "Alright, I'll get someone to check it out for me." When he came back he says: "I will pay you part of the money in Jamaica and the rest of it in England because you don't want all of it in Jamaica darling." I said: "I want you and I to go to the solicitor to draw up the agreement." He did. He paid me the money in Jamaica. It came from a bank where he had borrowed it. The bank paid the solicitor in Jamaica. Not knowing that it was the guy who was here that was holding it back, it took a long time for all the legal documents to go through. Why he was holding it back was because he was to pay his solicitor in Jamaica. He didn't pay his solicitor in Jamaica.

He was out there one day when I rang my solicitor in Jamaica. The woman says: "Mrs Paquette I'm going to be honest. I don't know what's causing the hold-up but here's the number of the bank." I rang the manager of the bank loaning the money and she and I started talking. She says: "Look, I'm going to tell you something but don't tell anybody that I tell you. You know the solicitor that Mr Salter is using? The solicitor says that Mr Salter hasn't paid her the legal fees and that's why she's not doing anything until that money is paid. That's what's holding it up because the money is here waiting for you."

I rang the guy who was on holiday in Jamaica. I said: "Why haven't you paid your solicitor?' He says: "Oh you know, I've gone short. I didn't want to tell you. I'm going to ask the bank if they can release the money to your solicitor. If they do that, can you lend me £3,000 out of your money so that I can pay my solicitor here so that it can go ahead." I thought: 'It's better I do that than still waiting.' So I says to the guy: "Alright do that, I'll lend you the £3,000 on top of the £48,000 you have got to pay me." He say: "I've asked for a second mortgage on my house, so I can just use that money to pay you the £48,000."

Me ah fool man, not knowing that the man is a scammer. He has got £51,000 for me.

Melissa has found herself yet again being scammed in the name of her property in Jamaica.

When I went to Jamaica in 2009 a guy I know very well drove me up to the house one day. I saw Mr Salter coming out of the house. He was on holiday in a beach buggy with another man living across the road. They were doing scamming in Jamaica, the two of them. He had a girlfriend in the beach buggy. Someone had told me it was a woman who was working for him there. He became friendly with her and she was pregnant.

So I said to him: "You're not giving me the money for my house. You bought my house and you have the rest of the money left and you're not paying me my money. I want my money. You're telling everybody it's your house. Have you told them that you owe me £51,000 which you haven't paid?" The man in the buggy, his friend, look at him like this and the girl looked at him like that. I said: "Yes he didn't tell you that he owe me £51,000. He's the one who cause my illness because of the stress he put me under." He said: "I'll pay your money. I'll pay you your money!" I said: "Here's the paper what you've signed."

What I'm going to say now should be off the record. The guy I was with says: "Do you want me to kill him for you?" I says: "No. I don't want your hands have blood on it because of that man. Leave him."

When Melissa arrives in England, she gets legal advice on the best method to get the money she is owed.

> When I came back to England the solicitor here looked into it. He said: "Melissa, I'm going to tell you the truth. Just leave it and hope one day he may come into money and he just drop a cheque through your door. For us to start running after that £51,000 by the time we get a solicitor in Jamaica to sort it and for you to pay me and the solicitors there, the £51,000 would be finished. Just leave it." So that's how it is.
>
> Until this day I've not seen my £51,000. Until this day I have not received a penny. He has the deed to the property but you know, I believe strongly in God. He may do things to me and think he get away with it but he doesn't know round the corner what will happen to him. I just leave him to God.

Melissa also speaks on Floyd, who also took advantage of her and used her rental money for her property to pay for his son's tuition.

> My cousin's husband Floyd don't even talk to me now. Floyd came to England on holiday in 2012. He stayed at one of my cousin's in Lewisham. He never even rang me. So I just leave it. That's life!

***

Melissa delves more into the life threatening operation that was behind her trip to Jamaica. Melissa recalls this episode of her life in precise and painstaking detail.

> I became ill with a brain tumor in 2005. It was a brain tumor on my pituitary gland and it's due to my diabetic clinic that it was discovered. Every three months I visit the dialysis centre—the Shrewsbury Clinic in Eastham. That is where I get my blood pressure and my cholesterol checked. These tests can tell you a lot of things. My blood sugar level was always very high. It never seem to go down, no matter how many injections I take because I am on insulin.
>
> My GP is a Nigerian doctor born in England. One day I went to see him and when he looked at my blood pressure he phoned the Newham General Hospital and he said: "Emergency! I'm sending her in." But I use to live with that blood pressure that he was afraid of. It was two hundred and fifty over one hundred and twenty.

Melissa does not agree with her doctor's decision.

> I didn't go. He made all the arrangements for me to go into hospital but I didn't go because I've been living with that.
>
> Now that type of high blood pressure is because the kidneys are damaged and the blood pressure is out of control. So no matter what medication

they give for the blood pressure it wouldn't bring it down.

Blood pressure is high for most Black people. The medication that controls white people's blood pressure doesn't control the Black ones. They did research in America and they found that it's the same problem they're having with their Black people but they will combine different medications. Sometimes the combination of different drugs that they give you to take to bring it down is damaging our organs. Alright as you know, all medication has side effects. The side effects are not good. Some of what we call beta blockers, those are for blood pressure. If you read some of the leaflets in the medication packs they'll tell you if you've got that you're not to take it, or if you're got something else you're not to take this one with that one. But the GPs sometimes prescribe two or three of these medications together.

A layman who doesn't have any experience of the medical field will take it and say: "Oh I can't miss my medicine." Now if I was taking all the medications they gave me, I would have been dead already but I know the dangers with certain types of medication. I will give you a good example. You go to the GP and you say you're having severe pain—maybe arthritis setting in—they will give you tramadol. This is a dangerous drug. You can become addicted to tramadol, you can have hallucinations—but that's the quickest thing the

GP can write. Five minutes and you're out of his surgery. If you do not know the medical jargon, you will take it and live on it. It damages your kidneys, your heart, even the brain. Sometimes you're being given pills to control pills. You see the contradiction?

Melissa then meets Dr William Drake for whom she develops a great deal of respect.

As I told you the diabetic clinic found out about the brain tumor in 2005. There was a young Chinese girl, she was a doctor doing training at Bart's. In Bart's NHS Trust you've got different departments. There is a department for endocrine which is about how hormones affects the body. There was a doctor there who later became a professor. His name is William Drake. This girl was training as an endocrinologist under William Drake who is a white guy. I would say he's about forty-nine now.

When I went to the diabetic clinic at Shrewsbury Road, this young medical doctor— the Chinese girl—says: "I can't understand why your blood pressure is so high Mrs Paquette, even though you're taking all this medication? I think something is not quite right. I am going to get you to do a test. I'm going to give you a prescription for seven tablets. Take two now when you get it. Take two the next day until you get to the end of the fourth day when you take one. When you finish taking the tablets go and do a blood test."

I did the test and the following day she rang me. She says: "I thought as much. I thought that something wasn't right. Now I've proven something is causing pressure in your brain. I'll tell you what I'm going to do. I'm going to refer you unto another colleague of mine who is in Newham. I'm going to send you to do a brain scan." They did the brain scan. That was within eight or ten days of me going to Shrewsbury Clinic to do the blood test.

The Friday I was working at the care company I was employed with. A call came through and I picked it up—funnily enough I was answering the phone that day. It was another young Chinese doctor but he was male. He said: "Mrs Paquette, I'm sorry to tell you we've found a shadow on your brain. Can you come to see me now, I'm at Newham General."

My boss was sitting across the table looking at me. It was that woman from Barbados. She said: "Mel is there something wrong?" I said: "It's alright." She came over and she held me. She said: "Mel something isn't right. What is it?" I said: "Don't worry. They said they've seen a shadow on my brain but don't worry. My doctor ask if I can come down. Can I leave?" She said: "Yes, yes, yes."

Whilst Melissa is waiting to be seen by the doctor, a patient next to her appears to begin to have a seizure. Melissa's nursing experience comes in handy and she is able to effectively deescalate the situation.

While I was sitting waiting at the hospital to see the doctor, a man who was also waiting—I don't know whether he was also a patient—had a convulsion. He was on the floor flapping about. Everybody was looking at him and doing nothing. I just calmly went over, put him in the left lateral position and held him like that. I kept calling to him although I didn't know his name. He came round a little and I said: "What's your name?" He told me, so I started calling his name and massaging his ear. He came round.

That consultant that I was to see, he was frighten because he didn't know what to do. Another nursing sister came running—she didn't know what to do. I said: "It's alright!" She was worried that he was going to bite his tongue and that something should be put in his mouth. I said: "Don't put nothing in his mouth. Just leave him there, he will come around." Usually when they have a convulsion you find that they pass water—they pee themselves or they will poo themselves. He peed himself and after he came around I ask them to check him out and give him something to wear.

When I went in to see this Chinese doctor, he says: "Oh my God, you handled that like a professional." I said: "It use to be a part of my job." He says: "You're a nurse?" I said: "Hmmm... it depends. I'm an ex-nurse. I am a psychiatric nurse. I use to see a lot of this." In general nursing you don't see all these things, so they don't know how to handle it.

This is why you find today they're having problems in the general hospitals when older people go in with dementia—they don't recognise it. General nurses need to know or have awareness of epilepsy and awareness of dementia. This is why they're treating the people them that way because they think they're being aggressive. It's not aggression—it's part of the condition—especially with dementia in the second stage when they'll bite you, pinch you, scratch you. When it gets to the third stage you're sitting there and they don't even know you're their child. You give them something to drink, unless you feed them they don't know that a cup of tea is there. They will say to you: "Oooh, I'm so thirsty. I've not had a cup of tea since yesterday." You've just given them one but they forget because they have what you call short-term memory and it is so blown that they can't even remember their names to tell you who they are. That's the experience that is lacking in hospitals. This is why you find so many of them are dying.

Melissa continues to describe the moment she found out she

had a brain tumor.

> Anyway I'm talking about my brain tumor. To cut
> the story short, the consultant said to me: "Mrs
> Paquette, we have seen a shadow on your brain.
> The shadow is very big and it's on your pituitary
> gland. I'm sorry to tell you it's about the size of
> your thumb."
>
> He says: "I'll tell you what. Today's Friday, my
> colleague is going down to Bart's and I've spoken
> to someone at Bart's about you. My colleague is
> taking your case file down to this person in Bart's.
> They're going to have a meeting on you and you
> will hear from them over the weekend. Someone
> will phone you from there." I didn't worry too
> much. I thought: 'Well, whatever will be, will
> be.' I don't think I did tell Cantrice or Jean what
> was happening. I just thought: 'Let me see what's
> going to happen.'

Melissa then gets a call from the doctor William Drake calling
her into hospital.

> By six or seven o'clock that Friday evening
> someone rang me from Bart's and says: "I'm Dr
> William Drake. Can you come in tonight? Bring
> a few things with you when you're coming, like
> toiletry."
>
> I packed a bag and went over. When I went,
> I met this nice man. He was so nice that even

now I call William my son. He says to me: "I'm going to ask them to give you a special room. It has a shower and a toilet. It's like a suite. We need to collect some blood. We're going to do some further tests."

When he had collected the blood samples he came in and had a conversation with me about my history. We started talking and somehow I think we just bonded with each other. Trust me, I've never seen any doctor since I've been going into hospitals so good like William. He says: "I'll tell you what. After all the tests and everything, I was trying to see if we could get you into a theatre at Bart's on Monday but the theatres at Bart's are full. I'm going to arrange for you to go to Royal London. There is a surgeon there by the name of Seeben. He wears leather trousers and he rides a motorbike but he's fantastic."

Monday morning an ambulance picked me up from Bart's and took me over to Royal London. While I was in the ward they prepared me at about 12:30 and said they would come for me between 1:00 and 1:30. They push me down to the anesthetic room at about 2:30. I know that because there was a clock above me when I got there. I looked at the clock and it says 2:30.

But it's not that. While they were pushing me in, that ten minutes space that I had before the anesthetist came over, I thought: 'Oh God! This is the end of my life. It was as if I was being pushed into a wall and there's no way out. There's no way of escaping.'

So I prayed and I said: 'God, my life is in your hands. There's nothing I can do about it. I need whatever it is in my head to be removed. I leave it in your hands. If you want to make me well you will give the surgeon, the nurses and the anesthetist the ability to see that I have this operation and come back out safely.'

The anesthetist came over to me and he says: "I'm going to ask you to count to ten." I started counting and it was as if I was going through a l-o-n-g black tunnel. There was no light in the tunnel until I couldn't remember anymore. Well I assumed that I was still waiting for surgery. When I woke up my bed was still right back under the same clock and it was saying 5:30. I said: "You tell me all this time you lot kept me here from 2:30 to 5:30?" They said: "You're out of surgery." I said: "Pardon me?" They said: "You are out of surgery." I said: "Aaahe God—thank you God. Aaahe God—thank you God."

They had a tube in my nose. The nurse said: "Calm down, calm down Melissa, calm down. We don't want to excite you and cause the fluid to start running out of your nostrils. If you see any white clear fluid like water, inform us straight away because that's the brain fluid." They push me up to the ward that I came from and they said: "You're not to move out of bed. If you want anything, call the nurses."

I wanted to pee badly. Because of my size I wanted to pee. I call the nurse and said: "Can you bring me a commode?" She says: "No, you're not to have a commode. You have got to have a bedpan." I says: "Can you see my size? Can you see me using a bedpan on a hospital bed?" She says: "It's not our instruction, it's the surgeon's instruction. You're not to get out of bed." I says: "Look, I'll take the responsibility. Bring me a commode and put it by the side of my bed there." She says: "I have to ask the charge nurse." I said: "Go and tell him that I said it's my responsibility." The charge nurse came and said: "You're not to get out of bed." I said: "I'm taking it on my responsibility, put it in your notes." He said: "Well if that what you want." They brought a commode, put it at the side of the bed and I peed. I says: "Right, can you take it back for me now and bring me some tissues?" They brought me tissues and I went back up on my bed.

Mr Seeben who did the surgery came up to see me at seven o'clock. He said: "What is this I am hearing? I have been told that you came out of bed and nothing happen to you. You're not having any flu?" I said: "No!"

I have the operation on the Monday. The Tuesday morning I was out of bed, washing and showering myself—going to the toilet. Mr Seeben said: "I can't believe it." When he came up to do the ward visit the morning, he says: "I can't believe it. You are healing so fast. Wednesday morning I will send you back to Bart's."

I went back to Bart's Wednesday morning. The minute I was back in my room, my 'son' William came. He says: "We're going to take some blood now." There was a new wing on the first floor of Bart's—Edward Ward. He's on the entire first floor—even his lab. You don't have to go to the other section where you do your blood, because they do it there.

Usually when you do tumors they're like little peas. He says to me: "It was a big one. I cannot understand why yours was so massive—it's like your thumb." He brought it over to me and I saw it. He says: "Can I ask your permission to keep it because I would like to teach the students about this?" I said: "Yes." He puts it into a bottle with saline. He says to me: "Some people lose weight when they remove a tumor and some put on weight. I don't know what the outcome is going to be yet with you but you will be doing a quarterly visit to check for any changes."

Now what you don't know is sometimes when you're short of certain enzymes, certain hormones, it can cause havoc. You don't know what's happening with your body but thank God that was alright.

After the operation, Melissa receives a phone call from her

doctor, William who asks her if she can come in to see his students. Melissa's respect and admiration for her 'son' William meant she would always help him if needed.

Now I was telling you about William and him keeping my tumor. One day after I was discharged, a phone call came through. It was his secretary saying William wants to speak to me. He says: "Mrs Paquette would it be possible for us to have you one day? I've got seventeen students and I've been telling them about you and the size of your tumor. They've seen it and they just can't believe it. Would you be able to come and give them your history?" I said: "Yes, I wouldn't mind." He says: "When you come I will pay for your transport." I say: "Mr Drake you don't have to do that. I am grateful for what you've done." He says: "Look, I've got funding for this." I says: "No, I will come. I am grateful for what you and your staff have done."

Anyway I went. He introduced the students to me. He says to them: "I'll tell you now, be extra careful because she's very smart." Then he says to me: "I'm leaving them in your hands. You tell them as much of your history as you can. They've read your notes but you tell them again." Now he thought I may possibly have had the tumor from childhood. There was a time when I think I may have been two years old and my mother and my grandmother Doule told me that I was very ill. I was already walking then as a child and the illness was so bad that I wasn't able to walk. After the illness—whatever it was—I had to learn to walk again. I don't know if that had anything to do with it—I don't know.

I started talking to the students and they're asking me different questions. I started to tell them my history from my youth. There were two of the students that I thought: 'They're not going to pass!' The others were asking me questions but they were kind of bored, if you know what I mean. When the session was finished, William came back into the room and he says to me: "How did you find them?" I says: "Two of them won't pass. I don't know their names but I'll tell you what clothes they're wearing." About two week after William rang me. He says: "I don't understand. Do you know those two lads you told me about? They've not passed."

∗∗∗

Given what happened with Melissa's villa, her return to Jamaica in 2006 did little to help with her recovery from her brain tumor operation. She was already suffering from high blood pressure and if anything her 'holiday' only made matters worse.

As I told you I sold my house in Jamaica in 2006. When I realised that the guy was not paying me my £51,000, my kidney's started playing up and I started having serious pains.

Unfortunately for Melissa this isn't the only health problem she is suffering from at the time.

I was doing yearly checkups with William. If he's too busy I'll see his registrar but when the check-up finish my notes are taken directly to him. William is always there. This is why I call him my 'son'.

One day in 2006, his secretary rang me and says: "Mr Drake would like to speak to you. Do you think you could book an appointment to come down to see him?" I went. He says to me: "You know, of all the patients that pass through my hands over the years, when I finish with them I forget their names. But something is bothering me about you. Your eyes have been affected because I know you've been going for repeated laser treatment—about twenty—at Moorfields Eye Hospital and I think they're given you too much."

The tumor that I had was pressing on the optic chiasm. Whether you call it muscle or gristle or what in the back of the eye—the tumor was pressing on it so much that I would lose my sight. When they operated they took the tumor out but it leaves a stamp on my brain which could not be cut out without damage. He was not happy because the stamp is causing pressure on the chiasm—stretching it. If the chiasm stretches, eventually it will break and I will lose my sight.

By then I was having such difficulty with my sight while at Moorfields. It's a big eye hospital in London—one of the best teaching hospitals in the world for eyes. When they were giving me laser treatment they damaged my cornea. There was a time when there was so much fluid in my eyes because I was having what you call optic edema and laser treatment was intended to mop up the fluid in the hope that I would be able to see— but the laser treatment was too heavy. Instead of actually mopping up the edema in my eyes, it was making me blind—scarring my eyes too much.

Dr William Drake is deeply concerned for Melissa and offers a suggestion that may help. However, William lets Melissa know there is no guarantee that what he is suggesting will work.

Mr Drake says: "I don't want you to lose your sight. There are many people who pass through my hands and I don't bother with them but you're bothering me because I don't want you to lose your sight. What I'm going to do? I've already done it but I'm just asking for your approval. I have sent your notes to a professor of radiology. It's a chance—it works or it doesn't work. If you don't try, you won't ever know." I says: "Mr Drake, I'm going to France on holiday for a week. While I'm on holiday I'll think about it. When I get back I'll phone you."

I went to Lourdes in France for a week with a friend of mine. When I came back I rang William and says: "I'm all for it." Within the same day the professor's secretary phoned: "Mrs Paquette do you think you can come down tomorrow to see us?" I went down and saw him. He says: "I know everything about you. The only thing I want was to see who you are. William told me everything about you. He told me that he is your 'son'. This is what we're going to do. You're going to go to the nurse now. They will take you downstairs to see someone. They're going to take a mask of your face." They took three or four plaster of paris masks of my face. The nurse explained to me: "If they are alright, I don't have to tell you come back. But if they're out of sequence, we will call you back." I was still working with Wanstead Care. The following day they phoned and asked me to come down—that was 2006. I went down and saw the professor again. He said: "Everything is alright. You don't have to do the mask again. You will hear from us."

They phoned the following day. Within five days of me seeing the professor in the radiology department I went back to see them. The nurses took me downstairs to try on the mask, it was perfectly fine. She says to me: "Next we're going to the treatment room." I said: "Pardon me! I wasn't told I was going to get treatment today."

Now the mask that they took, it covers my face and is screwed to a couch holding my neck and head steadfast. She explained to me why it's like that. It was because the radium would be to my temples hitting directly at points indicated in the x-rays. That was the first bout of treatment lasting for eight weeks. Every Monday to Friday I must be at St. Bart's to get that treatment.

Melissa recalls how physically taxing the radiotherapy was.

Now you must have heard. People with cancer when they have radiotherapy, they tell you how it drains them. I was d-r-a-i-n-e-d. I didn't have money, my husband had died. I need to pay the mortgage and I had to support my daughter who was going to university then. Yet each day I would leave home at eight o'clock to go to work. I was still doing the on-calls although I was ill. I work from eight till twelve and then I leave to get to Bart's by buses for one-thirty to get my treatment.

I remember one day I was coming back from Bart's. I had left my car at the work compound and the evening I was coming back I was so ill—I was walking and staggering like a drunkard. Just as I reach in the street where my work was, I saw a Black man and a Black woman walking by. The woman came over to me and says: "Are you alright?" I tell her I'm feeling so ill and where I'm coming from. She says: "Where do you live?" I says: "I work over there. My car is in the compound." I think she and her husband were from St. Lucia. They held me and walk me over to the car park. I open my car door and they put me in. I sat there for a good hour before I moved and came home. The following morning, work again. I leave at twelve o'clock to go for treatment and I did that for eight consecutive weeks.

Then at last, some encouraging news.

On the last occasion I saw the professor, he says: "I think we've got it. I'm going to tell William that I think we've caught it." He gave William my medical report. I saw William about a month after the treatment ended. I can now see without glasses, I can read without glasses. In the past I couldn't drive at night because I was going on the pavement. I can do anything now. Also, since the radiotherapy, I no longer have laser treatment any more. Each time I go to Moorfields to see them they say: "Oh, your eyes are perfect, perfect." That fluid that use to accumulate in my eyes—that they were so worried about—is not there. God is good, God is great. I am seeing today.

To top it off now. After the radiotherapy—when I started seeing well and I felt a bit better—I went and bought two bottles of champagne and two 'Thank You' cards. One for William and one for the professor of radiology. I went up the day to see William. He was doing a clinic. I said: "I'm sorry. I know it's not my clinic day." I had a gift bag and I said: "This is for you. Thank you very much for your care." On the 'Thank You' card I wrote: 'Just to say, thank you for your TLC.' Medical TLC, of course. That evening my telephone rang—it was William. He says: "Mrs Paquette, I have never, ever seen anything like it." I said: "What?" He says: "Oh I can't believe it, what you've done for me." I said: "What I have done for you? It's to say thank you and that I have adopted you as my son."

Though Melissa appears to be conquering the worst of her health issues, more seem to arise.

I then became ill with the blood pressure—it wouldn't go down. My feet started swelling. Swell, swell, swell like jackfruit. I couldn't walk. That was in 2007. There were times when I couldn't even breathe, so they use to send me to London Chest Hospital. London Chest is another Trust of Royal London as Bart's Hospital.

One day I was in the ward because I would be admitted maybe for ten days or so. A friend of mine who goes to my church, she is also a ward sister at that hospital. She bumped into me. She says: "What you doing here?" I told her what happen with my feet—I couldn't walk. We would sit down and talk. That time Cantrice was at university still, so I tell her don't come down. We would talk on the phone. She use to cry as she didn't know what was going to happen to me. I said: "God will take care of me. Nothing will happen to me."

The doctor who I was seeing—Dr Lloyd Owen—he was a professor as well. When I went in there, him and I was talking and I was telling him about my tumor. He said: "Yes I noticed and it's William." I said: "Yes, my son." Whenever Lloyd Owen come on the ward to do visits, he says: "I have to go and see my mother."

When I was there they use to give me a sleep pack because they reckon that I snored and it affected my heart. I've not got a heart problem but it could lead to it because there isn't enough oxygen coming into my blood and I have sleep disturbance. So they give me this machine—it has a mask to help you breathe. It kills the snoring and it also makes you sleep because it oxygenate your blood while you sleep.

Anyway they decided that all they can do is take off the fluid each time. After the fluid was removed and the leg goes down, they send me back home."

Melissa returns to Jamaica in 2009 partly as a holiday to visit family and partly because she believes a break from work may help with her blood pressure problem. The visit also serves as a treat for both her and her daughter. Interestingly, Melissa doesn't reveal which daughter she goes away with, at first.

> I stayed at a hotel named the Oriana. It was owned by very strong Black woman—strong in body, strong in mind. She is the only Black person who give the white companies a run for their money in the hotel business. All the white hotels are big and lavish but she stands firm. She had one part which was about eight rooms, then she started adding and adding. Now she's got thirty-six to forty rooms.
>
> She have staff who cleans the place, make the beds, do the washing, cooking and provide security. While I was there Mrs Gloria's staff go on strike, gang up on her because they wanted more money. She go round and do everything. She clean the floor, she wash, make the beds, do the reception and the cooking—she'll do everything. Sometimes when you see her out in the yard in the morning—when the boys them to wash the yard are peeing about—she roll up her trousers man and she take the heavy broom and in no time at all, she's finished.

Melissa has a great deal of respect for Mrs Gloria, the owner of Oriana hotel and speaks of her very highly.

> She's a strong Black woman—her husband died. I admire her as a Black woman because this tells us if you give up, you're finished. She made her

money out of ganja. Yeah, her husband made his money out of ganja. When he died, she took the money and opened the hotel.

Oriana hotel is very close to the airport. Her place is not top, top class. I would call it five star but you can walk from her hotel to the airport in fifteen minutes. I didn't know her before I stayed at her hotel. She's a lady who mind her own business. She's a nice lady but I've got to tell you something and I'm sure it is that. You never see Gloria and she's not wearing white.

Whilst in Jamaica, Melissa meets up with her old friend Carl Millet.

I think I told you I had a solicitor friend in Jamaica who use to be a Minister of State—Carl Millet. Carl came to see me at the Oriana. We were laughing and talking when Carl says: "Humm... this woman Gloria is always in a white suit." Me say: "You should know why she's wearing white, shouldn't you." He say: "Why? Me nah know." Me say: "Yeah man, you know. Nobody no tell me but I swear to Almighty God it's her Obeah man [witch doctor] who tell her fe always wear white."

There was a lady who rented a part of the premises not connected to the hotel—it's in a little side part on the grounds. It use to be a shop and they use to sell tourist gifts but it wasn't going great so she rented it out. This friend of mine started doing a coffee shop there. I went to see that friend one day—Carl and myself—and we were all talking. She was telling us that Miss Gloria is giving her a hard time, want her to leave the place. She was saying: "When Miss Gloria go ah Obeah man!" I said: "How you know she go ah Obeah man?" She said: "You nah see the white clothes she's wearing. She never wear anything other than white." So that's her thing with the Obeah man—wear the white suit—you're in authority. That's what she wears. But you know— whatever she does—she treats her customers very well. She has their respect.

Melissa has never been one to believe or indulge in 'obeah', this was clear from her time in Sierra Leone. Nevertheless, though she is firmly grounded in professional medicine, she cannot resist wondering about 'traditional cures'.

I was ill with kidney problems when went back to Jamaica in 2009 and I thought I would go see if I could find natural herbs to help me with my kidneys. While I was visiting, there was a programme on the telly about this Indian man in Kingston—name Emanuel—who's a herbalist. The reporter even claimed that someone had cancer and after Emanuel gave them this herb to drink, the cancer dry up and came out like carti- lage out of the person's bum. When the person went to hospital and they were doing tests, they found he was cured of it.

So I thought I'd go see if I could find anything. I did find this Indian man. Funnily enough—you're not going to believe it—he's from St. Lucia but he lives in Jamaica. He married a Jamaican there. He's got a beard and the beard reaching down to here. Everybody called him 'Prof'.

So Melissa goes off in search of 'Prof'.

How did I find him? One day I went to the beach. I couldn't go in the water but you've got some Rasta boys there—they would sell things like fruit or coconut. I go over there for some coconut water, I would drink two or three. I just want them to have some money. I was talking to one of them one day and he tell me that he's from where I come from. I started asking about certain families. He said yeh man, I know so and so and so and so. I says: "You know Springfield School? That's where I use to go."

While I was there talking, there's a hotel over the other side and it was this Black man who have this hotel. It is one of those hotel which was traditional English—very English. This man came out, he was wearing white shorts. He says to me: "Man, you're not well." I said: "No I'm not well—it's my kidneys." He says: "Look you know something? I'm going to get in touch with this herbalist doctor. He's good. Man when I tell you he's good—he's good."

So he got in touch with this man. He says: "Can you come back down here tomorrow? The man is going to come the evening." I came back and I met this Indian man with his beard all the way down to here. I think he had a band round his head as well. We went over to the hotel, sat there and we're talking. The hotelier said: "I'm leaving this lady in your hands. I'm the one who introduced you to her, so take care of her."

After I met this Indian man he came up to my hotel at the Oriana and take me in his car—he has a driver—down to where he says he makes his medicine. He was in a trailer, said that's his office. I can remember he's got a drum pan outside always burning with fire and smoke coming out. I says: "Why you've got this?" He says: "You know, us Rastafarians we believe in..." I said: "Alright." I never argued it any further. He would bring herbs. There's one he had, it wasn't slimy—it was slippery, shiny. He said it's down in the sea bed they got it from. They dry it and he puts that in his medicine.

Anyway people use to come and sit there in his trailer because there are chairs like doctor's surgery. People would come, sit and wait for him. Whether he was doing that for me, I don't know. He says: "Look, I'm going to give you this medicine, I'll bring them up."

He drove up one evening with about eight

bottles of something. One I know was cinnamon. He boil the cinnamon and he put something else in it. He have one and he said: "This one is for your bowels." I don't know what it was but when you drink that thing—heh! You would think that your entire body is coming out. He said to me: "Drink it last thing before you go to bed at night." Heh! I'm out of bed all night at the hotel—flush, flush, flush, sometimes it can't go down. But it made me feel so good. I stop taking my medication prescribed by the clinic in London. My feet which were swollen up like jackfruit then, went right down. Nobody could believe it. I was losing fluid and I thought this is fantastic.

Now he says to me: "I will give you ten bottles of this thing to take home. While you're here I'll give you this to take. When you finish just phone me and I'll bring another lot to you." He brought me two lots of ten different herbal medicines to take and I took them.

Then he says to me: "You want to stop eating rice and all them things. You want to eat 'life food'." I said: "What is live food?" He said: "Raw food." So me say: "What kind of raw food?" He says: "Yam and all dem things, they are pig food man—nah eat all those things. Go and eat vegetables like lettuce, cucumber, carrot—all those things—but don't cook them, eat them raw. I'll tell you what, I'm going to take you to a Rasta restaurant."

He took me to this guy. He says: "I'm going to order something for you. Taste it and tell me if you like it." It was only salad but the salad was nice. I said: "What! If I realise that salad could be that nice!" He used balsamic vinegar. Since then I make sure I don't run out of balsamic vinegar. He used garlic, olive oil and boy when he finish with that salad dressing and you put it on that salad—lettuce, cucumber and grated beetroot! I use to order it every day—morning and evening—that's my meal. I said I want a vegetable drink, so he will do cucumber and carrot—not sweetening it with condensed milk—natural. Every day he will give his driver a disposable cup of juice and my lunch and they will bring it to me. I was in Jamaica for three weeks. I lost over a stone and a half. I felt soo good.

Now when I'm ready to come back to England, the Indian man was to bring my medicine. He said he would be there at such and such time. He never come. I had said to him: "How much do I owe you for what you've done?" He says: "Well that is five hundred thousand Jamaican Dollars." At the rate then, that worked out at £500. He says: "Leave it man. When you go over you can send it to me. What I'm going to do, I'm going to post over your drinks to you because it would too heavy for you to put in your suitcase and they may stop you with it. So I'll post it over for you."

I came back to England. The same week I

came over I go and draw his money. I phoned and told him I'm sending it by Western Union. Now he told me what his name was. But about an hour after I phone and tell him I've sent the money, he phoned back and says: "Oh, I should have told you to send it in my other bank account. Look send it in this name." I said: "But I've already sent it." He says: "Please!"

I had to go back to Western Union. I have to show them my passport and my ID. They see the passport, they see I'm genuine and they sent the money in the name he gave me. So each time now I'm phoning him: "Where's the medicine?" You know after the terrorist attack on that plane, they had said that no liquid can come. He said: "Oh, I can't send it. They said no liquid." I thought: 'Oh Lord, Jesus! I given all that money now and I'm not been given my medicine.'

Despite his explanation Melissa is still suspicious of the Medicine Man. Her daughter who accompanied her on holiday to Jamaica in 2009 went back a year later and was able to find out more about him.

So that daughter went home on holiday in 2010. When she came back she says to me: "Mum you know the lady friend that is next to Oriana—your friend and Carl's friend? I went up there talking to her and she was telling me about this Indian man." She showed me a photo of the man and that's the man who gave me the medicine. She said: "The police are searching for him—he's a con. He run away and they're looking for him to arrest. That lady's cousin—who is a solicitor—had taken him to court because he's taken so many people's money." That's the same thing he did to me.

I telephoned the woman and she said to me: "Melissa have you got the receipt that he gave you for the £500 you sent by Western Union? Send it to me. I'll get my cousin to take that up as well." I say: "You know something, it's one of those things—it's my fault. I am the one who make myself gullible—forget it."

Though the Jamaican Medicine Man 'Prof' turned out to be a con, his philosophy and approach to herbal medicine has a lasting impression on Melissa.

"He gave me a drink which he call a herbal punch. It's made up of pumpkin seeds. He just take out the inner part of the pumpkin—the wet bit with the seeds—put it in the liquidizer with some honey, some cashew nuts, some peanuts and something else—I can't remember what it was. Well it wasn't him, it was his wife. His wife is the herbalist. She liquidised that thing, put in the freezer—it's cold. The thing nice, it nice, it nice. When I say nice—it's nice. He brought me about three bottles of that while I was in the hotel. As

I said to you, he was a con—but I'm yet to make that drink and I need to make it because it's good. When I tell you it's fantastic—it's fantastic.

Right this minute as I am today on 25ᵗʰ July, 2013, I'm seriously thinking whether I am to go and open a healthy eating bar. Start making those drinks, start making the food what that man called 'life food' here in England. But because I have to go to dialysis three days a week, who will I have to take over the other three days when I'm not there.

Cantrice, my youngest daughter, works—she is now pregnant. That is her first child and my first grandchild by the grace of God. She would be the most likely one to help with the healthy eating bar but I can't ask her.

Pointing to a photograph of her eldest daughter—Jean.

That one is useless. I can't say to her go there. Forget it! She's not dependable. She's changed a lot but she's bloody lazy—'lazyvitis' is in her. She should thank God it's this country she's in and they provide money for you to eat but that's another thing.

The trip to Jamaica has a lingering effect on Melissa. Interestingly, Melissa eventually goes on to reveal which of her daughters she took the trip with.

I didn't go to see that relative who cheated me out of the rent for my house. I was there with that daughter. Yes, I did go with Jean in 2009.

Melissa reminiscences about an interesting encounter she has with another one of her cousins whilst on her holiday in Jamaica. Her cousin is called Gina, she lives in Canada but is visiting Jamaica at the same time as Melissa and Jean. Gina's building a house of her own in Jamaica and invites Melissa and Jean to visit and stay over.

I had a cousin who live in Canada. She was building a house in Jamaica that wasn't finished. I went to see her because she's like my sister—we grew up like sisters. My cousin in Canada, she kept phoning me. She says: "Oh, I'm building a house in Jamaica."

She had a piece of land on a hill near Montego Airport. It was her mother's land and her mother died and left it to her. She decided to sell it and was looking for a buyer at the very time when I was selling the villa with the swimming pool to this man. I even introduced them and he wanted to buy her land. As God so have it, things was dragging along and he didn't phone her. We didn't know he was a swindler at the time. Anyway someone came and bought the land and she use the money to buy another bit of land in St. Elizabeth Parish. She then decided she was going to build a house.

She and her daughter would go out each time. Her daughter lives in Canada with her. She kept saying: "Oh, I've built the house now you know. We've only got one or two rooms left to do. Jenifer and I usually stay there when we go, so if you're coming out you can stay with me." So I says: "Alright." She and her family use to stay at my villa in Montego Bay and she would give me £400 or so to help with expenses. So when I was going over there I told her that I would give £400 just for me and Jean to stay.

Anyway I was at the Oriana Hotel. Then it was going to be Christmas week so I said to Jean: "Come on, let's go up to St. Elizabeth to stay with Aunty Gina and we'll spend Christmas with her." Aunty Gina said: "Alright, we'll come down to collect you." She came down with a boyfriend she has who drove the car. I think her son and his girlfriend came as well. They rented a car and they drove us up.

Melissa has not had a great deal of luck with her relatives so far. She is expecting this to be better. However, upon her arrival she is astonished by the state of Gina's house.

When I went up, I see this half-finished house— no windows in the entire house. I says to Jean: "How Gina tell me that she finish the house and it don't even have windows." I thought: 'This is funny!'

Gina says: "Oh you've got to be careful when you're coming up on the veranda because there's no steps. I've put a stone to step on." Me now, with my feet swollen like this. Can you imagine me with my big body trying to get up. So there she is down there pushing me up by my bottom and Jean pulling me up. I say: "Eh, Eh! What is this?"

When I went in she says: "Oh, you and Jean can stay in this room." There are no windows. I say: "It's getting a little bit dark. Where's the light? Turn on the light." She said: "Oh, it's only the main light I have in this living room."

I say: "What! You tell me that you finish the place. What is this Gina?" She say: "Oh, just bear with me a bit. I'll get Mr Powell to come tomorrow morning. He'll do up all the things for me and it will be alright." Me say: "But you have no flooring." When you render a place it rough and when it dry the dust is flaking off. That's how it is on the floor. If you walk, the dust come up in your nostril. I said: "Raatid!" I started coughing and coughing.

So me say: "Jean, what is this?" She say: "Ah you gone make an arrangement with Aunty Gina." Me say: "But Gina tell me that she finish the house." When you have to go to the toilet, the toilet no have no door on it. She put a sheet over it. Me say: "Me no live them kind of life here." So she come in the room the night with two sheets—one at each side of the window. She come with some bedclothes which she got from the basement. They're all smelling of mildew. Jean said: "Aunty Gina, them things are wet. Can't you smell the wetness in them?"

I never slept the night. I kept coughing and coughing all night. I kept worrying: 'Lord Jesus, what happen if thief come through the window because there's no way of keeping them out—there's is no glass.'

The next day Melissa finds out there's virtually nothing to cook on and decides the take matters into her own hands.

Anyway Jean and I woke up the morning, I said: "We want a cup of tea." Gina said she going to put on the water to make us a cup of tea. When we go in the kitchen me see a little two ring burner. I say: "Where's your stove?" She say: "'Ah this me and Jenifer use when we come here." Me say: "You mean to tell us we've to come and spend Christmas with you and you don't even have a proper burner where you can cook for four people. The pan what you have can only cook like two eggs."

I had to ask Cantrice to go and draw some money—£800—from my account in England and send in down by Western Union. The equivalent I got for it, I think was sixty-eight thousand Jamaican Dollars.

I said to Gina: "I want to go to town to Western Union." So she know is money I'm going to get. I said: "By the way—with that stove that you don't have—where is a place you can buy a stove here?" She says: "Oh there's a place up here where they have stoves—the four-burners." I says: "Alright, wait for me."

Her and the man who drove the car waited and I went to Western Union, drew the money and I came out. I says: "Alright I'll tell you what you do. Let's go up to the place and buy a stove." We went up there. The four-burner stove cost six thousand dollars, it's got a hose that attach unto it and you've got the Calor Gas drum.

Gina turn around and said to me: "Oh by the way, the additional bit we have to pay separately for it." I said: "Pardon me! Pay what separately? They're selling the additional bit with the stove for six thousand dollars." She said: "No, no—it's eight thousand dollars. You have to pay extra for the bit." This got Jean's back up and she started quarrelling: "Boy, you think say we fool?" But I gave her the extra two thousand dollars.

When we go back to the house she started cooking. She said: "Oh Melissa, what you want?" I said: "I want nothing." Jean say: "I want nothing." The morning we woke up she cook breakfast and put it on the table. I ignore it. Jean ignore it. Jean go in the bathroom and started showering. Cold water, of course. Gina shout out to Jean: "Nah use off all me water. You know say me have to pay for it." Jean come out, she say: "Yeah, when you tell me mom say the house finish..." Jean start to cuss. Me say: "Jean shush. It's not the mouth, it's the action. I'll show you what I intend to do." Jean say: "Me want to go back to the hotel."

So when Gina's boyfriend came in now, I says: "Oh by the way, could you drop me down the bottom of the road please? I need to get a taxi to take me to Montego Bay." He say: "What you want to go to Montego Bay for?" I says: "I'm not staying here. Don't you see that the house is not finish. Don't you see I'm coughing like nothing. If anything, I want to be where the hospital is. Drop me back." Gina said: "Alright, alright. If that's what you're telling him, I'll go with you and him."

We got in the car and they drove us down to the hotel. I said to the man: "Here's your petrol money." I said to her: "Gina, I told you I would have stayed with you for the rest of the three weeks. I would have given you £400. I only stayed with you for two days—I would say a thousand dollars a day for me and Jean. I'll give you two thousand dollars plus you've got the two thousand dollars that you say for the stove parts. You think I'm a damn fool? You told me that you have to pay for the extra parts but you didn't pay for it because it was in with the stove. It's alright—it's my mistake, don't worry."

From that, she used to phone me regularly.

Sometimes I'll pick up the phone and I hear it's her, I just put it down—pretend as if I'm not around. This is what I'm saying to you: "People where money is concerned—heh!"

***

Going back to 2005. Melissa has just had her brain tumor operation and is now having trouble with her eyesight and high blood pressure. Though she is still working at Wanstead Care she decides to pursue a longstanding aspiration of hers. She starts her own business.

I opened my Afro-Caribbean restaurant in 2005—me and my nephew Damien. It was down in Forest Gate. My nephew was in Birmingham and he was getting a little bit naughty with his friends them. My aunt—it's my second cousin but she's elderly—phone me and tell me that he's with some friends which she doesn't like and something happen between him and his friends. The friends want him to go out to sell drugs. He doesn't want to go, so this guy pull a gun on him.

His two brothers and a sister was in Brixton. He went over there to see them. I think he was with them for about a month. He took his passport with him because he had just come from Jamaica and his sister stole his passport. What she did with it I don't know because she's now in America with her father.

One day he rang me. He says: "Aunty Melissa, I'm doing some painting with somebody and I'm in Forest Gate. Isn't that where you said you live?" I said: "No, I'm in Stratford." He said: "Yes, yes. Stratford is near." I said: "Alright, come and see me." He came over and he told me about his passport. I said: "I don't want to hear anything because it's a month since you've come down to London. You've never once come over here to see where I am and you know where I was because you've come here once already. What you're telling me—it's your problem." He said: "Oh my sister took my passport." I said: "That's your problem." Anyway he says: "Aunty Melissa, I don't have anywhere to stay." I says: "Well, if you don't have anywhere to stay!" He says: "I'm staying with this man that I'm doing the painting with." I says: "Who is it?" He says: "Oh it's just a friend." I says: "You can come and stay here. Cantrice is at university and there are two empty rooms." So that is how he came over.

When he came over I kept racking my brains. What to do? What to do to help him because he was still young. He's only twenty-nine now. What to do, what to do? I saw an advert in a Caribbean paper—I think it was *The Voice*—where this restaurant was for sale. I thought where am I going to get the money from to buy this thing. I rang the guy who said yes he's selling it for £25,000. Where am I going to get money from? I haven't even got twenty-five pennies.

Melissa, with no money commits to the idea of buying the restaurant that is for sale. Next, she has to figure out how she will find the money to make the purchase.

Anyway it was a Saturday morning. The Friday evening, I phoned the guy and the Saturday morning when I woke up, I thought: 'I'm going to phone my bank—Lloyds TSB.' I rang them and I says: "Look, I want some money to borrow." Didn't tell them what I want the money for. They said: "Yes Mrs Paquette, you can get a personal loan." I took out a personal loan. I didn't tell them that I wanted the money was to buy the restaurant because they're going to ask me if I've got all the knowhow. They said: "Yes, we can put the money in your account." To be precise it was not even twenty-five thousand they gave me—it was £30,000. They put it into my account that same Saturday and I went and I bought the place.

The restaurant was called 'Taste of the Caribbean'—it was very popular. I was still on call doing my care work. I usually wake up about four o'clock in the morning to go to buy fruit, meat, fish and things at the market. Damien live here and him and I would go to the market. When we finish he would unload it from my car and then he stayed in the restaurant for the rest of the day with them just to watch what's going on. It was

me, Damien, Miss Bonnie—who was the cook—
and Lorna who use to run the restaurant before I
bought it. I just kept them on as staff because they
know the customers.

Then if Miss Bonnie is off sick—or whatever
it is—and if I'm not available to cook, Damien
would do it. It was from there he learnt his
cooking skills. He's now working as an assistant
chef and it's all through my restaurant he got the
job.

Things are looking up for Melissa. Her restaurant is doing
rather well, her nephew Damien is out of trouble and working
efficiently within the restaurant. She is happy.

Rudi, the previous owner of Melissa's restaurant, still lives
in the flat above. Melissa knows little about him but that is
about to change.

Anyway one day I went to the restaurant. The
police had cordoned off the entire street. I asked
them: "What is going on?" When I went there I
saw the borough councillor, two policemen and
the local newspaper. I said: "What are you all
doing here?" The policeman said: "You can't go
in madam." I said: "Of course I'm going in. That's
my property." He said: "What's your name?" I
said: "You already know my name. If you close
off here and you close off there—you would
have already known my name." He said: "What's
your date of birth?" I said: "You've got all that

information."

Little did I know there was a drugs den upstairs. Hehh, my dear—hehhh! At the side of the restaurant there's a door to go upstairs. I never knew that the guy who I bought the place from was a druggie. He look clean but underneath he was a druggie. So all the Jamaicans them that come—the 'Yardies'—that's where they go. They do gambling upstairs, they do everything. It's not my part. The part that I bought was downstairs. Upstairs have nothing to do with me—that's another flat altogether.

The fact that the restaurant downstairs and the flat upstairs are owned by different people is a distinction lost on the police.

I went in the restaurant and I saw Damien. He said: "Aunty Melissa dem come and search the place—dem search the place. Dem say gun— somebody got shot here." So me look pon the police. Me say: "Oui! Let me tell you something now. Hear this and hear it clear. You see me? I work. I don't live off handouts and I don't live off drugs. You see this? It cost me £30,000. Go down ah Lloyds TSB ah Stratford and ask them. That's where the money come from. Back off!"

What happens next could well be mistaken for comedic opera.

The following day they remove the cordon things

dem. It was in the newspaper and all. I just smile.

Around lunchtime Damien was cleaning up outside because we sweep the pavement outside and wash it down every day. Me see two blonde girls came in. They ask for curry goat and rice and peas. So Lorna serve them curry goat and rice and peas. I says: "Hello cops, you hungry?" They look at me. I says: "You two are coppers." They says: "No, we're not coppers." I says: "You two are coppers. You think you're going to catch us out? I don't take drugs because I'm very much against it. You're are from Forest Gate Police Station. You must have picked up my daughter Jean soo many times and you expect me to be involved in it." The police them even took Jean down to the station and ask her about me. Jean said: "No, you don't know her. She's my mother. My mother don't touch drugs. My mother don't involve with drugs—whether pot, whether cocaine, whether heroine, whether crack. Not my mother."

A few days later I saw two police guys came in—plainclothes. They said: "Oh, can we have some jerk chicken?" I say: "Are you sure? Let me tell you jerk chicken is not fry chicken. It's very spicy, it's very hot." I sold them the jerk chicken. They started talking, talking, talking. One said: "Where are you from?" I said: "You don't have to ask me where I'm from. You know where I'm from." They says: "Yes, but whereabouts?" I said: "If you're asking me where I'm from, you know

I'm from Jamaica." They says: "Yeh, yeh—we know." I says: "Yes because you're cops. You know everything about me." So they said: "By the way, we want to ask you something. There's a guy name Rudi who use to work here. Does Rudi have a gun?" I says: "What the backside you're asking me for? How am I to know? I don't involve with them. I am down here, they are up there. But I'm going tell you something. Of all the guys them who goes up there—not Rudi."

Up until then Melissa had only bumped into Rudi on the odd occassion.

Sometimes Rudi would come in the daytime. He would take the broom and sweep up when Damien is not around. He would take out the bin—do him stuff. Once he says me: "You know something Miss Melissa, me have to survive fe send a little money home for my mother so that me mother can eat and that me can eat. But I would never, never have the rudeness to come into you shop and sell drugs." That's what me respect about him.

Despite Rudi's assurances, there is no way he can control his friends. Though Melissa takes steps to ensure that no drugs are being sold from her restaurant, the police are not convinced.

Me going tell you how foolish they are. Two

brothers, they come in one time and they started selling their stuff. I said to them: "Me no mind unno come and spend unno money to buy food but unno nah go sit down in here. Go long out." One day, me don't know what happen but one of the brothers—the shorter one Dean—the police dem chase him. Dean go run come straight in the shop. The police dem run behind him. Me just grab him and me chuck him out. Me say: "See them ah wait for you out there!"

Sometimes Melissa would also try to convince those she thought were criminals to change their ways.

My dear, dem boys they used to have shooters. I would say to them: "Boys, why unno behave so? Me know you try to survive but you don't be a bad man. You know say the Chinese, the Indians, even the MP's them are in ah this stuff—but nobody no know. Why unno have to go bling, bling and show off unno self? Behave unno self." You know say those two brothers, the police deported dem back to Jamaica. When Immigration found out they were out of the country, the police dem at Forest Gate had to bring them back from Jamaica because their permission to stay in England had come through the day before they were deported.

Another time one of dem came in and said: "Oh me going home, me going home. I apply to stay in England but Immigration say me have fe go home to apply for it—so me ah go." This night he's walking up and down the road outside—up and down the road. He come in and he say: "Miss Melissa, me want pattie." Me give him the pattie and him sat on the chair. Me hear him on the phone. Me say: "Come out! Come out!" He says: "Oh Miss Melissa me tired, me ah walk all night." Me say: "No, you nah a do no dealing in me shop. Come out." He's a tall boy. Me just go up to him and hold him ah him front and push him out. Me say: "Stay out!"

Despite the problems associated with those in the flat upstairs, the Taste of Paradise is still doing well. It is even being patronised by local authority staff.

I use to have some people that work in the borough council. They have one department—I think it was Finance Department. This guy use to come and buy sometimes up to £100 worth of food for the day. He would come in five days a week.

But there was a camera across the road and every time he comes—him and me not knowing that they have a concealed camera there—he would get a ticket. The guy says: "Look, I'm paying money every time I come here." I thought: 'Boy, it's like the council wants me to close this place.' Even when my car park outside and we're taking out goods—they would give me ticket.

This went on until the council say I owe £1,500 for tickets. When I try to do something about it, they say it's two yellow lines right in front of your restaurant. So I thought: 'This is it, you're trying to help yourself and they're trying to pull you down.' I applied for an unloading parking space in front of the restaurant. It was refused.

When I again became seriously ill in 2007, I would leave my nephew Damien, Miss Bonnie and Lorna in charge. Where sometimes I use to make £500 a day, when I come in I'd be lucky if I find £90 in the till. I thought: 'I am losing my money.' I even use my credit card to buy supplies for the restaurant until I thought: 'Wait a minute Melissa—you're a damn fool. You're just giving Lorna, Damien and Miss Bonnie this money. It's money in their pocket and you're not getting nothing. You're sick, still working and doing the restaurant. Every penny you get—your salary—you plunge it in.' I thought: 'That's it!'

Before Melissa can decide exactly what is to be done, events take a hand.

One day I went to do a risk assessment for Wanstead Care at a service user house in Greenwich and my mobile rang. I picked it up. It was the previous owner of the restaurant—Rudi. He says: "There's been a fire in the night." I think it was him who did it because he wanted me to sell to him. I had eight years lease left and he wanted to buy back from me for something like a thousand pounds. I thought: 'No way! It was a way of him getting me out.'

When I finished what I was doing—the risk assessment—I drove down there and I looked at the shop. The front door was kicked in—the blackness. I looked in and I just walked out. Not even a spoon did I take from there—not even a spoon. Funnily enough, I couldn't afford to pay the insurance because it was getting that bad. By the time—as I told you—I was using my own salary to pay the bills. So I thought: 'Let's call it a day'. That was how the shop end.

***

Like Evelyn, Irene and Ivy, church is a significant part of Melissa's life. She has been attending an Anglican church in Stratford for many years. Though she has no official role in the church, she is by no means an inactive member of the congregation.

In 2011 they brought in a Reverend who was a lady—a very nice white lady. She has a dog and she wasn't married. After she settled in 'we' started suspecting something.

One day we had a get-together. I think it was a lunch and we were talking. There was a discussion where they said a law is going to be passed about homosexuals being married in church and

I said: "Never under your Nelly!" The Reverend said: "So what if they do marry in church?" We started debating it again and I said: "I don't believe in homosexuals and I don't believe in lesbians. If God did believe in it, he would not have destroyed Sodom."

Melissa's church congregation were discussing the Same Sex Marriage Bill later voted into law by Parliament in July 2013 following the consultation in which the Church of England played a leading role.

Anyway we were there talking and I thought: 'What I'm suspecting? Could it be true?' The only way I'm going to find out if it is true, you God going to tell me. The following Sunday we were at church and she went on the pulpit giving her sermon. She says: "Homosexuals are people too— we should love them." I thought: 'Is this woman trying to tell me something?'

Though the Reverend has done little more than indicate her support for the proposed legislation, Melissa's suspicions goes into overdrive.

She would go away to see her father who she said was sick. Her father is sick all the time. She'd go away and stay the weekend. I think she was having more holidays than she was signed up for because she is supposed to have four weeks a year. But she was going away more often. I thought: 'She's a lesbian. God please forgive me if I'm wrong.'

Pearla was a warden at the church and one of my friends—she's a Barbadian. I said to her: "I think the Reverend has got a lover and the lover is not a man. I don't like what is happening. I am worshipping under a church that's under the umbrella of homosexuality and lesbianism. The Anglican Church is quarrelling and the African Anglicans want to break away because of this. They are practising it and I don't want to dwell under that. There's no spiritualness in this church. If I'm worshipping God, I want spiritualness. When I go there—there's none. All they do is socialising. Socialising is not spiritualness."

Whether it's because of her suspicions about her Reverend or the position of the Anglican Church on same sex marriage, Melissa begins looking for a new place to worship.

I had a builder—Donald—come here to my house to do the bathroom, put in some tiles. He's a Jamaican man—a very nice man. When he finished, he left his card here. One day I was tidying up and I saw this card and it says ARC. The card was for a church at Seebut Road. I wondered where the card came from. I can't remember having it but it was Donald who left it here. So I look on it and I saw this number.

I rang the number and this man answered.

I said: "Are you a church?" He said: "'es, we are a church at Forest Gate." I said: "What is your name?" He said: "I'm Pastor P. They call me Pastor P but I'm Pastor Nimbard." I thought: 'Nimbard? That rings a bell.' I said: "Do you remember a fat woman, use to have a restaurant down Forest Gate off Romford Road name Taste of the Caribbean?" He stop for a minute. He said: "Yes, I use to come there to buy food." I said: "One day you and I was talking. Are you telling me you're Nimbard from Jamaica and I looked at you and I said you're from St. Elizabeth because that's a German name." He said yes. There's a part in St. Elizabeth named German Town—those are the names you find there. I says: "Oh, that's who you are! I know who you are now. How radical is your church?" He say: "Radical!' I says: "You mean Jamaican radical? Raw!" He said: "Raw—Jamaica radical—spiritual."

So I says: "I go to another church you know, but I don't like what's happening. I am in an Anglican church. I was married there, my daughter did conformation there, my husband was church there when he died. But there's something not quite right. I'm going to be very frank with you. I think the Reverend we have is a lesbian and I don't want to be there any longer. I'm looking for a church to go. What do you think of lesbians and homosexuals?" He says: "You know it's against God's laws." I says: "Thank you!"

Having been reassured that the ARC is 'raw', 'radical' and has the same views on homosexuality as Melissa, she commits to her new church.

> We have a lot of youths from the age of thirteen
> to about thirty. I've never seen so many youths
> in one church and they're from all sections of the
> Black world. Some are from Nigeria, some are
> from Ghana, some are from Sierra Leone, some
> are from Jamaica, some are from St. Lucia, some
> are from Grenada, some are from Montserrat.
> We've got a variety. We've got whites, we've got
> Indians, we've got Filipinos. I would say the
> congregation is about two thousand.

Melissa becomes very involved in her church and takes great interest in its development.

> The church building is too small. We're trying
> to modernise and extend it. We have so many
> youths. They're coming in, they're pregnant, they
> have young children. At this minute we don't but
> we're trying to make accommodation for the chil-
> dren. We have a little room where they go in and
> play but we need somewhere separate from there
> so mothers can have a place to change and feed
> babies. We need a disabled toilet.
>
> Pastor P's father is disabled as well. We need
> a wheelchair entrance to the church. We've got
> a portable ramp. I said to Pastor P: "Me! Me

standing on that! You're joking! We need a proper
ramp."

Sometimes our church is so full that when
visitors come we have no space for them. We have
an upstairs and they go there. But sometimes
people want to stay down because they can't go
up the stairs. We need more space, more seats so
that they can sit downstairs. We're trying to raise
funds towards that.

Melissa's knack for gaining access to exalted political circles has
not deserted her. She becomes close with the Deputy Mayor of
London at the time, Ray Lewis.

Anyway, that same church use to be Ray's church.
Who is Ray? Deputy London Mayor. Hummh!

Melissa explains the nature of her relationship with Ray Lewis
who she sees as her 'son'.

Ray—like how you sit there now—use to come
here and sit. Yes Ray and I, he used to be like my
son. I use to tell him about things in Africa—what's
what. I said: "You are so good with the youth in
church, they will follow you to Timbuktu." Now
I know where Timbuktu is—it's in Mali, right? I
said: "They will do anything you ask them to do."
So he decided to open the after school club.

There was a white lady by the name of Abby
who use to go to the church as well. Abby was a

teacher. She married a guy from St. Lucia and she had some 'half-caste' children, but because she have the children she wasn't able to work. So Ray discussed with her for them to do the after school club. We use to have a hall in the church but Ray had rented it out to a nursery teacher who use to have a nursery in there. There was not enough space there anyway so Ray went to a church in Stratford—it's a Methodist church—and asked if he could rent the hall. That church use to rent out their halls if you're having conferences or meetings. So he rented it from them permanently and started the after school club.

Ray was making quite a lot of money from the after school club. He didn't realise that money would come in so fast and he's getting to know the borough councillors—the this and the that. Anyway, I said to Ray: "You see how good you are with children."

Then he moved from the Methodist church and he went somewhere else—to a community hall—and he set up the after school club there. The parents of the children were so happy. I said to him one day when he came here: "Ray those children. You must treat those children as if you are their father. That is the mentor that they need. Be their mentor—a father to them."

Ray is father to three girls, no boys. Of course he took my silly advice and the children started getting very good grades in their school. The teachers were thinking something is happening—these kids are getting good grades. So because he knows the councillors, Cameron, the Prime Minister, even went to his school. Then Boris Johnson came to visit Newham—though Newham is a Labour Party Borough—and he met Boris Johnson. Boris Johnson as you know was the mayor—still is.

Ray Lewis then gets into some trouble but Melissa chooses not to divulge the details. She remembers after this, Ray takes a trip to Grenada where he finds himself, once again in some trouble.

Short story. Ray did some little naughty things— some little naughty things. I'm not going to say what they are. He went away to Grenada and did some naughty things with a bank manager there as well—have to run back here.

Melissa recalls the day Ray comes back to London from Grenada, where she confronts him about his wrongdoing and warns him about the repercussions of his actions. Despite his shortcomings, Melissa still loves Ray, he is after all like her 'son'.

One day I was at home, heard the doorbell ring, open the door and it was Ray. I says: "What you doing here? I hear that you were in Grenada. Well I know you were in Grenada because we had a party for you at your house the night before you left." He said: "Oh, you know, there's lots of things they're saying about me." I says: "You tell me. Did you do them?" He says: "No! No!" I says: "You did cause I tell you why. Molly—who the thing happened to—told me you did what you did and it wasn't right. I told you that whatever you do to anyone, if it doesn't affect you, it will affect your children. You've done wrong. Molly got her pension of £30,000. You told Molly that you would invest it. You bought—was it one flat or two flats? I think it was one flat. There was an Italian girl who was the musician at church then. You were infatuated with her, you put her in the flat. Who was paying the rent I don't know but you told Molly that there was dividend coming from the shares that you use her money to buy. There wasn't and that is wrong. I told you never to do bad things to people. I've learnt in Africa that whatever you do bad, it will come and bite you in the backside one day."

After Melissa has advised Ray, he decides he will leave for Canada but Melissa, stern as she is, tells Ray to stay in England and rebuild his life.

He says: "Alright! I can't stay in England because they all know about me. Everybody talking about me." I says: "Did you hear that Melissa talk about you? I heard the things but I never had a bad word to say about you. I still love you. What are you goner do now?" He says: "Oh, I'm going to Canada—me and the family." I says: "You're not going to Canada man. You're going to stay in England. You're going to bite the bullet." He said: "But I can't. Everybody talking about me. I don't know what to do anyway. I don't know what to do." I says: "You know what to do. I'll tell you what you're goner do." He says: "You know I've got an application form—it's for a job as a youth probation officer." I said: "You're goner fill out the form, that's a start."

I think he took my advice—fill out the form. He got the job. He reckon he's got the gift of the gab. He talk his way through the interview. As I told you he's good with youth, so he would accompany them to court and he would do all kind of things. Then he got Abby—the white lady—to set up this after school club I tell you he started. So due to Cameron coming to visit and see how well it was going, they decided to give him funds. Then Boris Johnson came to visit here and visit the school as well.

They started giving Ray funding because the children were doing well—their grades were very good. Ray decided that instead of calling his after school club an after school club, he would call it an academy.

So Boris [Johnson] and him are talking and as I told you he's got the gift of the gab. Boris must have thought: 'This guy is smart, I can use him.' Boris started with Ray because he had ideas that

could be used. Ray became a Deputy Mayor to
Boris.

Melissa recalls the stories Ray told her about his childhood and
how she encouraged him to push past his struggles.

> When Ray was going to school, he told me one
> of his teachers, she use to tell him: "You'll never
> come to nothing! You'll never come to nothing!"
> He said: "My mother rather my brother than me.
> My mother never care about me." I said: "Stop it
> about all this bitterness. You are smart, use your
> smartness." This brought him into the Deputy.

Happy as she is that Ray, her 'son' is now Deputy Mayor of
London she notices that Ray seems to have forgotten about his
past.

> If you remember I told you that I use to tell Ray:
> "Don't do anything wrong to anyone because it
> would come back and bite you in the backside."
> Well Ray was swinging now because he is the
> Deputy Mayor of London. He's forgotten what
> he'd done earlier on. That's the biting in the
> backside!

Ray Lewis eventually gets publically exposed, with his wrong-
doings covered by television stations and newspapers. Melissa
never figures out who sold the story of Ray's past to the press
but she suspects it's a lady from their church.

I don't know who expose him because I never would. Even if the reporters are paying me and although I'm broke, I would never divulge certain things to them about Ray—I would never do that.

Well somebody, I think it was someone from church who spoke to the Newspaper about Ray when he became Deputy Mayor. I would never, never have done that. I haven't confronted the woman who I think did it—I'm only thinking, I'm not positive. But I think it's a lady who use to come to our church—she's a Barbadian lady. I think it was her who welch on him because she rang me the day and says: "Eh! Have you seen the news?" I said: "What is it?" She said: "Eh, eh—you see about Ray. You see about Ray?" I said: "What you talking about?" She say: "The newspaper people phone me and asking me. Have they phoned you?" I said: "No and even if they phone me I wouldn't say a Dickey Bird." Anyway, she was applauding the newspaper.

Melissa contacts the pensioner who Ray allegedly took money from, who at the time has cancer. Her name is Molly. Melissa promises Molly that she will have Ray pay her back.

I rang that woman who I told you about—the pensioner with the £30,000. The lady at that time had cancer. It was in remission but after all this, it starts up again. Before Ray became the Deputy Mayor, I said to the white woman: "Molly I'm

going to get Ray to pay you back your money."
She says: "How Melissa? How are you going to
get him to pay me back?" I said: "I'll get him to
pay you back."

He came round one day. I says: "Ray you're
going to pay back Molly her money." He says: "I
don't know how." I said: "You've started your after
school club and I hear a lot of the young ones in
church talking that you're really making money.
You're going to pay her back monthly out of it.
But you know something? I am telling Molly to
get the local Bishop involved." I think his name
was Ian. "You, Molly and Bishop Ian going to sit
down and arrange it. You are going to give the
Bishop a cheque every month and the Bishop will
pass it over to Molly." That was how Molly got
back her money.

One day I was in church after maybe about
two or three years. Molly came to me and whisper
in my ears: "Thank you Melissa." I said: "What
for?" She says: "He gave me all my money and he
even give me the interest on it." I said: "Thank
you God."

Melissa reveals what happened with Ray in the end.

I go a long way with all these things. Now Ray
still works for Boris, behind the scenes. He's a very
shrewd person because he got some funding for
this borough last year and there were two or three

Caribbean clubs and youth organisations that applied for it. They were refused. The University of East London got the money. There's a young guy, Irwin, that use to go to our church—he's Ray's friend—they're like brothers. Irwin has got a PhD—I can't remember in what. He use to work for the borough council, then he started working with Ray. All Ray's reports, Irwin does them. Ray will speak, tell him what he wants—Irwin will get it written up.

Though Ray no longer worked for the Mayor after 2008 he is still a mover and shaker in the local Black community.

So what is happening now? I've been to see Ray a few times because as I told you our church have a lot of youth and I use to say to Pastor P to get Ray to come and talk to the youths, not knowing that he's been there before I was there.

One day Pastor P said: "You know Ray?" I said: "Aaah! Good heavens—Ray is like you to me." He says: "I didn't know." There's a guy who's very active in church named Jake. Jake is Ray's wife first cousin, so they kind of know each other. I've been trying to get through to Ray so that he could tell us how to apply for some the funding which he controls.

What is happening now is that Ray move the after school club from where he was at the community centre and he got himself a school.

One day this year—I can't remember, I think it was March or April—I started driving up and down to find where his school was. Someone told me it was somewhere on a road name starting with 'Wus' something—the road has got a lot of garages. I wondered if it was this place where I use to go years ago to get my car fixed. They've got a lot of council garages round there. I started driving up and down but couldn't find the place. I saw this African man and I say: "Excuse me. Is there an after school club round here or an academy?" He says: "I think it's that building there." So I went and I rang the bell and someone answered the intercom. That voice sounded like Abby. I says: "Abby is that you?" She said: "I'd know that voice anywhere—it's Melissa." I says: "I'm outside." So she came down. We cuddled and said: "Hi, hi, hi." I says: "Look, is Ray here?" She says: "No, Ray has gone to a meeting." I said: "I need to see Ray, can you give me his number?" She says: "Alright, you take my number and I'll tell Ray when he comes that you called." Until now I haven't heard from Ray.

Interestingly, Ray never got in touch with Melissa, despite her passing the message along to Abby. A couple of weeks later, Melissa coincidentally meets the man who is the boyfriend of Ray's daughter. Melissa asks him to tell Ray to contact her.

Two weeks ago I was at church. We were having

Bible Study that evening on a Thursday. I saw this white guy with a can drink. I thought it was beer but it may have been a soft drink. He went into the church and he came back out. I was sat in my car because it didn't start until seven-thirty and seven o'clock I was outside sat in my car. He went back in again. So I got one of my friends—I think it was Jake—to help me in because of the steps. I usually sit at the back of the church—they put a chair there for me—I don't sit in the pews.

I sat there and this white guy came up to me and he says: "Excuse me, do you know where the toilet is?" I says: "The toilet is there. You have to go by the rostrum then over the back." So while I was sitting there I said: "Jake come here, watch that guy. You know Pastor P's office is at the back there and he's gone over there peeing. He looks to me as if he is kind of a drunkard." Jake looked at me and says: "Who you're talking about, that white guy?" I says: "Yeah." He says: "No! He comes here all the time." I says: "You mean he didn't know where the toilet is if he come here all the time?" He says: "You know Ray? He's Ray's daughter's boyfriend." I said: "What?"

Anyway when the guy came out of the toilet I says: "Hello, I have been told that you're Ray's daughter's boyfriend?" He said: "Yes." I said: "Good Heavens! Do you usually see Ray?" He said: "Yes, when I go to his house." I said: "If you go to the house and you see Ray, tell him that

Melissa—the fat lady—said to tell him that he's a fine one. Since I have been to his school and ask Abby to tell him to ring me, he hasn't. He hasn't phoned me."

One Sunday, Ray's daughter's boyfriend introduces Melissa to a woman, this woman is Ray's daughter.

So one Sunday I was at church and the white boy [Ray's daughter's boyfriend] came over and says meet so and so—I can't remember her name. I said: "Oh, it's you. I would never have recognised you because when you all left my Anglican church you were ten." She says: "Who are you again?" I says: "You remember Myrtle, Melissa and Pearla? Pearla's daughter use to come and sit with you when Ray and your mother want to go out." She says: "I can't remember." I says: "Ah well, there you are. When you go home tell your father that Melissa wants to see him. There are things he need to do and he is not helping as God put us on the face of this earth to help. He's only helping himself. He needs to come and tell us how to help these youngsters that are coming to church. It's not all of them that are working. There are some of them, they're street boys. The youngsters them go out and bring them in. We need to know how to provide support for them. Not only governmental handouts, we want to empower them so that they've got means and ways. Some of them don't even know how to go on interviews. We need to do all of that."

***

Melissa has not been happy with her employer for some time and in 2010 she decides to resign.

I left because my feet were so swollen and I was so ill that I just couldn't move anymore. I thought: 'That's it!' I did the Easter Bank Holiday weekend. On the Tuesday morning about seven o'clock I went in the office. I had about fifty pages of reports. I did all my notes and put on the computer what is to be actioned. We have what you call care managers in different boroughs and I put what is to be actioned on the care manager's desk.

There was a temp manager there from Rochester Care. She was a very cheeky woman— didn't like her, none of us liked her. I says to her: "You know I'm leaving." She said: "Oh, you have to give a month's notice." I says: "Let me tell you something now. I've been working here since 1998. When this company was bought out by the new directors, you lot didn't tell any of us that it was bought out. You just sent forms saying we have to re-apply for our jobs. We had to fill out new forms because you said you couldn't find some of them on the computer. I fill out the form.

What did you all do? Tell me what did you all do? We who was on contract, you started paying us hourly. If you pay me by the hour, I am entitled to give you one week's notice. That is exactly what I'm doing."

She started to protest. I says: "I couldn't care less. The company don't care about me so don't tell me about the company. I've done everything to keep this company afloat. Three, four, five o'clock in the morning when carers are phoning in sick, I'm the one who would be woken up by them. I have to find someone to cover those jobs. I don't want to hear anything."

Funnily enough I still have my letter of resignation—it's right there.

In 2010, Melissa has still not reconciled with her daughter, Jean, and while Cantrice is doing much better, Melissa has a few doubts.

My daughter looks as if she's walking in my footsteps. I would rather she didn't but it's looking that way. I've learnt something that I also wanted her to learn: Africa is Africa. Africans are Africans and West Indians are West Indians. We've been told we came from Africa but their mentality is a little different from ours.

She married a young Senegalese man last year in 2012—Mahmud—a very decent boy. I met his family because I went to Senegal to meet them last December—very decent. His grandmother—Bostabe—is still alive, a sweet old girl. She's eighty-six and when you look at her, she look just like me and she can walk about. She lives with her daughter, they're Muslim. The family has a hotel which the daughter manages. When I went there they were building an extension—a nursery—so that people who come there for day conferences can leave their children. They were also building a swimming pool. So they are doing well, very well.

If you're living in England and you're marry an African or a West Indian, it's beautiful. If you marry an African and you're going to live in Africa as a West Indian, it's a problem. When you don't speak their language, you have problems. This is why I'm praying to God that it won't happen to her. She is living here. Her husband will want her to go back to his country—I'm sure of that. She would have to learn his language to understand what they're saying.

My only hope now is my daughter, Cantrice—she's is pregnant now. Within the next three weeks she'll give birth. I want to see my grandchild; it's going to be a little girl. Her name is going to be Farah and I just want to see and love Farah. The rest of my time I'll just give to her and when I'm dead—I'm dead. I say: "Thank you God! At least you let me see my grandchild."

Melissa did get to see Farah her granddaughter before she died in August 2014. Extracts from the audio recording of these interviews were played at her funeral.

***

A Note From the Author

The original inspiration for *A Circle of Five* was Arabell Birdena Smith. She was born in Manchester, Jamaica in 1931 and came to England in 1961. To us she was Aunt Bell—a grandmother and anchor within our family. By 2010, Aunt Bell was already struggling with breast cancer when she asked me to type up several of her diaries intended as a legacy to her grandchildren. Until then no one knew Aunt Bell kept diaries.

In different ways these diaries were a revelation. I was astonished by how much I didn't know about life in the British West Indies in the 1930's and 40's, or about the early experience of immigration to Great Britain in the 1950's. Then came an understanding of the nature and value of her diaries. Days would go by with Aunt Bell logging when she got up, what she had for breakfast and the weather outside on her way to work. Then there would be an explosion of activity on what was happening to her, within her evolving family, at work, in the wider community and locality. In short, a wealth evidence—even testimony, over a protracted period.

It turned out that Aunt Bell was a prolific diarist and the five diaries she wanted transcribed was but a fraction of the number of diaries she kept. Her health deteriorated after 2010 and she died in 2016. I did not have permission to transcribe the rest of her diaries.

A Circle of Five came about through me finding another way of telling Aunt Bell's story. Though I could not use entries from her diaries, in spirit she is one of 'The Five'.

I am still amazed by the commitment, time, and effort 'The Five' invested in having their life histories recorded. Soon after interviews began, most said they told close family members to canvass opinions. They also consulted family members to check events and dates. In short, they all took the project very seriously. I do not know if any of them believed that their story would be published, nonetheless they completed the series of interviews.

Upon Jacaranda Books agreeing to publish *A Circle of Five* I telephoned the four remaining contributors. They were delighted.

Acknowledgements

Two people were instrumental in getting this work done and published. It was Chevorlette King who found and somehow persuaded each of 'The Five' to tell their life stories to a complete stranger.

Susan Beardmore advised on how the narrative could be structured from the beginning, she proofread manuscripts at different stages. It was Susan who found Jacaranda Books.

About the Author

As a member of the Social Science Council Research Unit on Ethnic Relations, Harris Joshua was the lead author of 'To Ride The Storm—The 1980 Bristol Riot and the State'—published by Heinemann Educational Books in 1983. He then joined Nottingham City Council starting as Equal Opportunities Officer and leaving as Assistant Chief Executive–Policy in 2001. He went on to become a Research Associate and Member of the Management Board at the Institute of Community Cohesion [ICoCo] based in Coventry University and led by Professor Ted Cantle—his former Chief Executive at Nottingham City Council. On retiring from ICoCo *A Circle of Five* is his first major project.

The image on the front cover, 'Stockwell Good Neighbours', is from *Windrush: Portrait of a Generation*, a photo-essay created by award-winning social documentary photographer, Jim Grover. It documented the lives and traditions of the 'Windrush Generation' in south London. The resulting launch exhibition, in the Oxo Gallery on London's Southbank, was enjoyed by some 13,000 visitors and was covered by national media. A 245-page book accompanied the exhibition.

www.windrushportraitofageneration.com

Stockwell Good Neighbours is a charity that was originally founded in 1974 to support the West Indian Community in Stockwell. The group, which still meets on a Monday, has around 80 members, mostly women, aged between 60 and 103. It's a lively, vibrant and fun-seeking group of elders who participate in a wide range of activities to help reduce isolation and loneliness and promote health and wellbeing. The group relies on donations, grants, and its own fund-raising.

www.stockwellgoodneighbours.org